AUTHORITY VESTED

AUTHORITY VESTED

A Story of Identity and Change in the
Lutheran Church–Missouri Synod

Mary Todd

WILLIAM B. EERDMANS PUBLISHING COMPANY
GRAND RAPIDS, MICHIGAN / CAMBRIDGE, U.K.

Library of Congress Cataloging-in-Publication Data

Todd, Mary.
Authority vested / Mary Todd.
p.   cm.
Includes bibliographical references (p.) and index.
ISBN 0-8028-4457-X (pbk.: alk. paper)
1. Lutheran Church — Missouri Synod — History.
2. Authority — Religious aspects — Lutheran Church —
Missouri Synod — History of doctrines. I. Title.
BX8061.M7 T63 2000
284.1'322 — dc21   99-051879

The author and publisher gratefully acknowledge permission to reprint material from
the following:

Walter O. Forster, *Zion on the Mississippi: The Settlement of the Saxon Lutherans in Missouri
1839-1841.* Copyright © 1953 by Concordia Publishing House. Reproduced with
permission under license number 99: 10-32.

Carl S. Meyer, ed., *Moving Frontiers: Readings in the History of the Lutheran Church–Missouri
Synod.* Copyright © 1964, 1986 by Concordia Publishing House. Reproduced with
permission under license number 99: 10-32.

C. F. W. Walther, *Church and Ministry (Kirche und Amt): Witnesses of the Evangelical Lutheran
Church on the Question of the Church and the Ministry.* Translated by J. T. Mueller.
Copyright © 1987 by Concordia Publishing House. Reproduced with permission
under license number 99: 10-32.

For my parents
the Reverend Daniel R. and Minette Baue Ludwig

†

He taught me how to live in — and still love — the church,
she taught me how to walk with God.

Contents

Foreword, by Martin E. Marty   ix

Acknowledgments   xiii

Abbreviations   xvi

1. Introduction   1

2. Defining Decade, 1831-1841: The Formative Years   17

3. Establishing an Identity: The Nineteenth Century   65

4. Identity Redefined: A Twentieth-Century Church?   97

5. The Issue of Authority: Woman Suffrage   143

6. "Not in God's Lifetime": The Significance
   of the Ordination of Women   203

7. The Problem of Authority   259

   Appendix   281

   Bibliography   295

   Index   331

Foreword

Two sets of forces, the one technological and the other political, preoc-
cupy and tear at the unity of most religious bodies, be they Muslim,
Jewish, Christian, or whatever.

The first, the technological, results from twentieth-century discoveries and inventions: "the pill," the means to perform *in vitro* fertil-
ization, the sophistication of abortion methods, the Human Genome
Project, the understanding of DNA. All these have made possible previously inconceivable variations on conceptions and acts that were
freighted with meanings for humans in all times and in all places. Since
these freightings were usually religious or close-to-religious, how the
various faith communities addressed them was a fateful question.

The second, the political: most of the changes result from what
passes under the banners of democracy and human rights. The pill "liberated" couples from restraints they had previously experienced in acts
of sexual intercourse. Women's rights movements and fiscal necessities
resulting from changes in the orientation of couples, families, and sin-
gles toward markets and consumption "liberated" women to add work
outside the home to their work inside the home. Among many kin
movements, homosexual rights forces were "liberated" from the shad-
ows and closets. Discoveries in medical procedures "liberated" medical
professionals and their patients from accepting fates — e.g., those that
were connected with infertility. None of the liberations has been complete; is liberation ever complete in a world that balances it with responsibility and tradition? But these revolutions moved enough to cre-

ate a sense of urgency, particularly in religious, especially in Christian communities, signallers of responsibility and bearers of tradition.

These issues come, however, paired with corresponding issues of Authority. From the most radical Amish communities to the one-billion-member Roman Catholic Church, from congregational through connectional to hierarchical bodies, the polities are all being challenged. Leadership has to be charismatic, bureaucratic, managerial, and ministerial at once if it is to be at all effective at rendering some kind of authority.

Authority takes many forms. It may be biblical. "The Bible says . . ." that homosexuals are sinning. That women should be submissive. That we should not take life at its beginnings or its ends. Many people of faith question the scriptures. Others engage in debates over interpretation. They become factions and rule out "the other."

Authority may be churchly, reliant on tradition and magisterial teaching. Claiming infallibility in faith and morals and near-infallibility in ruling even discussion of some gender issues — e.g., the ordination of women — does the Pope little good. He must tour the world, tirelessly invoking churchly authority and natural law to oppose abortion, birth control, the cohabitation of the unmarried, and the ordination of women to the priesthood. The Southern Baptist Convention in the United States, in polity on paper as far from hierarchical authority as a congregational-bureaucratic body can be, has been torn for thirty years by a crisis of authority. Its leadership style, say dissenters, is authoritarian. The generally liberal Episcopal Church has the same tensions, and its mixed polity involving bishops and laity does not help it.

Authority may be conciliar, conferential, conventional — as in church councils, conferences, and conventions — but it does not solve the questions about sex, gender, and generativity. So the bodies flounder and get distracted from other features of their work.

The times call for quick decisions. I often point out that it takes the church two or three centuries to deal with basic questions: in succession, on the Trinity, Christology, the "doctrine of man," the sacraments, councils, the Reformation, the Enlightenment, Modernity. And now, within two or three decades, the churches are supposed to untangle the strands that web the current controversies. It cannot be done.

We can, however, be informed by struggles, close up, of people who deal with the issues in particular church bodies, over periods of time. Here is where Mary Todd weighs in with *Authority Vested*. I had read a previous incarnation of her work in the form of a doctoral dissertation. At that time, as I recalled it when the galleys for this book were sent me, it had seemed to be a discourse about the Lutheran Church–Missouri Synod's refusal to ordain women, a discourse that "backed up" into the question of authority. Now it strikes me as a thesis about authority best illustrated by the issue of such ordination. Read either way, it invites and forces readers to deal with the connection between the two issues. One does not have to be a Missouri Synod Lutheran, a Lutheran at all, a Christian or a religious person at all, to become engaged by these pages. They deal with basic human themes.

Dr. Todd chooses to tackle this as a historian, a story-teller. Her story ought to hold attention. It has to do with some Saxon immigrants who gave fealty to a would-be tyrant bishop who got sent down the river for the usual — say critics of charismatic leaders in religion — mix of sexual and fiscal miscreancy. It continues with some rather poignant pages about an abandoned flock asking questions as to whether it was a church at all. One follows the story to find a post-immigrant church body moving into a time of prosperity, growth, and mission, only to be torn apart by questions of authority. And, all the while, refusing to ordain women at a time when most other Lutherans, many kinds of Christians, were making the change.

This is not the place to anticipate all the scriptural and social issues Mary Todd takes up. Let the reader enjoy the adventure. What will strike anyone who deals with them is the surprising character the controversy has taken. It would be easy to write off the Missourians — a national body despite the name — as being run by male chauvinists, patriarchs, authoritarians, traditionalists, who simply want to keep women in their place and use a few passages of St. Paul's writings in the New Testament to provide "literal" interpretations to keep them down.

While I grew up in the Missouri Synod and enjoyed participating in its evangelical and expansive mission just before the fall, I cannot claim sufficient familiarity to judge whether there are more chauvinists, patriarchs, authoritarians, or traditionalists than in other bodies that *do* ordain women. What surprises the reader, or at least this reader, is the evidence that the Missourians are especially tied up with the gender issue in ministry because of fissures, hair cracks, ambiguities, and unresolved agenda items that were present in the creation of the Synod. It cannot address the gender question because it cannot solve the authority issue.

While one thesis holds this all together, there are endlessly fascinating byways of plot. The history was familiar to me, but Mary Todd tells it from perspectives that throw new light on it. Members of church bodies that do ordain women can learn something about discontents that ensued upon such a liberating and evangelical act. Members of church bodies that do not ordain women can note some of the reasons about authority that complicate addresses to enduring and crucial themes.

Dr. Todd is a member of the church body in question, herself a partisan for ordination of women against all odds, someone who has reason to sound frustrated or angry, a person with, as they say, "an interest." I think most will be impressed by her fair-mindedness, her calm tone of voice, her patient story-telling, and her invitation to readers to find more angles than before on the sex-and-authority combination that will mark both resistant and bold church bodies and individuals alike.

MARTIN E. MARTY
Fairfax M. Cone Distinguished Service Professor Emeritus
at the University of Chicago

Acknowledgments

Academic writers often use this space to lament the loneliness of what Pooh's Eeyore called "this writing business," the process by which ideas and notes get turned into theses and dissertations, which then get turned into articles and books. True enough — no one sits at the computer but the author herself, and that's probably just as well. But in this case I've never felt left alone. Over my shoulder was a large balcony of supporters, without whom this project would never have come to pass. Absent their help and steady encouragement, I wonder at times how I might have fared the storms — emotional, intellectual, practical, and, yes, spiritual — that so often turned this ten-year journey into a fairly bumpy ride.

Above all, thanks are due my teachers and mentors. Gregg Roeber's careful reading and editing, and his persistent prodding to "do more," made for a better text and argument. Mutual respect allowed that, at the end of the day, neither of us had convinced the other of our differing positions. So be it. Other readers, including Martin Marty, Leo Schelbert, Steve Warner, and David Stein, provided insight and affirmation while offering valuable suggestions for both text and context. Peg Strobel did far more than read: she listened, asked hard questions, kept me on task and on track, and challenged me to write for a larger and more inclusive audience.

A historian needs a friend in the archives. I found a good one in Marvin Huggins, Associate Director of the Concordia Historical Institute in St. Louis. Additional help came from Elisabeth Wittman and Tom Rick at the ELCA Archives in Chicago and Roy Ledbetter at CHI.

ACKNOWLEDGMENTS

Lutheran librarians gave new meaning to the word "grace" — thanks are due Kris Flanders at the Klinck Memorial Library, Concordia University, River Forest, and Claire Buettner at the ELCA Resource Center in Chicago, and the staff at the reference desk of the Richard J. Daley Library at the University of Illinois at Chicago (UIC).

The Department of History at UIC provided support through the first award of the Robert V. Remini Dissertation Fellowship in American History and the Schelbert Award for the best dissertation in history. The Women's Studies Program at UIC offered me both community and opportunity as it encouraged me to explore the intersection of women and religion through stimulating feminist scholarship, teaching, and conversation.

This work depended heavily on the methodology of oral history, and special recognition as well as deep thanks are due the two dozen women and men who shared memories of their participation in various aspects of this history in taped interviews.

Charles Van Hof at Eerdmans gently combined challenge with cheerleading from the first time we talked about my work at a historical conference book exhibit.

Two communities surround me and sustain me on a regular basis: my colleagues and students at Concordia University, River Forest, Illinois, and the people of God at the Lutheran Church of the Holy Spirit.

Lest I leave someone out, I will simply thank the members of the balcony *en masse*. There are so many of you. Each knows the support you have given me; I hope you don't need to see your names in print to know how important that support was and continues to be. I am grateful to be so blessed with friendship.

Though my parents are not here to see the results of what they taught me, perhaps my children Jay and Whitney and granddaughters Dana and Rebecca will be among those for whom it will make a difference.

The newest member of the balcony, Del Klaustermeier, has brought companionship, joy, and the gift of distraction to the home stretch.

Finally, a word to the good number of both men and women of the cloth who model on a daily basis what I believe is public ministry at its finest. Growing up in a parsonage offers a child an interesting perspective on the ministry. That's where I learned that clergy are both human and holy. Thanks to you, I still believe it.

Acknowledgments

The original title of this work was a modification of the punch line of a joke which presumed a conversation between God and a church leader. The churchman asks God a number of questions about when certain changes might be expected in the church at large and, more specifically, within particular denominations. After hearing that the change will indeed come, but "not in your lifetime," the questioner puts to God one final query: "When will women be ordained in the Missouri Synod?" To this God replies, "Not in my lifetime." Over the years that this work has been in progress, "not in God's lifetime" has come to be a byword, a marker to measure the potential for change in the church. Like the joke, it always gets a laugh. Then again, with God all things are possible.

Abbreviations

AELC	Association of Evangelical Lutheran Churches
ALC	The American Lutheran Church
ArCL	Archives of Cooperative Lutheranism
CCM	Commission on Constitutional Matters
CHI	Concordia Historical Institute
CTCR	Commission on Theology and Church Relations
DTS	Division of Theological Studies
ELCA	The Evangelical Lutheran Church in America
ELiM	Evangelical Lutherans in Mission
ELS	Evangelical Lutheran Synod
ERA	Equal Rights Amendment
ILWML	International Lutheran Women's Missionary League
LCA	The Lutheran Church in America
LCMS	The Lutheran Church–Missouri Synod
LCUSA	Lutheran Council in the USA
LDA	Lutheran Deaconess Association
LLL	Lutheran Laymen's League
LWL	Lutheran Woman's League
LWML	Lutheran Women's Missionary League
NRSV	New Revised Standard Version
OHC	Oral History Collection
PCW	President's Commission on Women
SELK	Selbständige Evangelische Lutherische Kirche
WELS	Wisconsin Evangelical Lutheran Synod

1

Introduction

The Lutheran Church–Missouri Synod (LCMS), founded in 1847, celebrated its sesquicentennial in 1997. Like other major Protestant denominations in the United States, the 2.6-million-member church body struggles with issues of relevance and identity in a society where traditional labels no longer suffice to represent the position of a given group or claim the loyalty of its adherents. In times marked by significant membership losses, the blurring of denominational identities, and increasing calls for ecumenism, what remains as evidence of a church body's distinctiveness? What sets it apart? Since 1987, when the Evangelical Lutheran Church in America (ELCA) was formed by the merger of three previously separate church bodies, the Missouri Synod has stood in contrast to "the rest of the Lutherans."[1] There are obvious differences between the two — Missouri is half as large as ELCA and politically far more conservative on social issues. While ELCA struggles with its very limited history as a merged entity over against the long and differing histories of its predecessor church bodies, a hallmark of Missouri Synod identity politics is evocation of its seamless past.

---

1. Because 94 percent of the 8.3 million Lutherans in America are members of either ELCA or the LCMS, I use this distinction. Of the remainder, 413,000, or 5 percent of the total, belong to the Wisconsin Evangelical Lutheran Synod (WELS), the rest to one of eight smaller church bodies. *Yearbook of American and Canadian Churches 1998* (Nashville: Abingdon Press, 1998), pp. 306-16; also, *The Lutheran Annual 1999 of the Lutheran Church–Missouri Synod* (St. Louis: Concordia Publishing House, 1998), p. 416.

Beyond demographics, however, outside observers would immediately recognize the principal visible difference between these two main groups of Lutherans — the ELCA ordains women to the public ministry; the Missouri Synod does not. The synod's insistence on the exclusion of women from public ministry is today the most tangible and obvious element of its identity as distinct and separate from the main body of other Lutherans in ELCA. Yet this church body's position on women is not the primary differential, only the necessary evidence of what is — the synod's stance on the verbal inerrancy of scripture.[2]

In, with, and under any debate about what women may or may not do in the church is the question of authority. While the official position of the church frames its argument on authority in terms of a single passage of scripture in which women are forbidden to hold authority over men,[3] the root question is about another authority — the authority of scripture. What, if any, is the relationship between the question of the authority of scripture and authority in the church, that which women may not exercise over men? Adherence to verbal scriptural inerrancy guarantees that the pastoral office will remain filled by men alone, because the authoritative texts the church uses to support its position insist that women keep silent in the church and exercise no authority over men. Taking the words of scripture literally where the service of women is concerned provides the surest case for the synod's dogged but also relatively recent adherence to a doctrine of verbal scriptural inerrancy and infallibility, as set out in the "Brief Statement of the Doctrinal Position of the Missouri Synod," adopted by its 1932 convention:

> We teach that the Holy Scriptures differ from all other books in the world in that they are the Word of God. They are the Word of God because the holy men of God who wrote the Scriptures wrote only that which the Holy Ghost communicated to them by inspiration. We teach also that the verbal inspiration of the Scriptures is not a so-called "theological deduction," but that it is taught by direct state-

---

2. Verbal inerrancy implies an errorless scripture that is entirely trustworthy in *all* matters, whereas the notion of infallibility implies an errorlessness in matters of faith and salvation. See, e.g., Stephen T. Davis, *The Debate About the Bible: Inerrancy versus Infallibility* (Philadelphia: Westminster, 1977).

3. 1 Timothy 2:12 reads, "I permit no woman to teach or to have authority over a man; she is to keep silent" (NRSV, 1989, National Council of Churches of Christ).

ments of the Scriptures. Since the Holy Scriptures are the Word of God, it goes without saying that they contain no errors or contradictions, but that they are in all their parts and words the infallible truth, also in those parts which treat of historical, geographical, and other secular matters.[4]

More than any other, the synod's identification with the issue of verbal scriptural inerrancy marks its struggle for identity in this century and reflects the tension of reconciling orthodox Lutheranism with twentieth-century concerns.

This study follows a chronological narrative of the history of the Missouri Synod from its pre-emigration beginnings in Saxony through 1998, focusing on developments key to the several threads that combine to define this church body — its theology of ministry, its position on scripture, its understanding of women's place in the church — and to the links among them. To that end, it is a focused rather than a comprehensive history. By necessity, focus imposes limitations. To reduce the distinctiveness of the Missouri Synod to only its most obvious differences with other Lutherans would be to deny the complexity of this major American denomination. Fortunately, other studies have been written to help fill out the varied dimensions of the synod over its long history — its ethnicity,[5] its polity or form of governance,[6] its rhetoric,[7] its "triumphalism,"[8] its confessionalism,[9] its conservatism,[10] and its

4. *Brief Statement of the Doctrinal Position of the Missouri Synod* (St. Louis: Concordia Publishing House, 1932), p. 3.

5. Alan N. Graebner, "The Acculturation of an Immigrant Lutheran Church: The Lutheran Church–Missouri Synod, 1917-1929" (Ph.D. diss., Columbia University, 1965).

6. Carl S. Mundinger, "The Genesis of Decentralized Government in the Missouri Synod" (Ph.D. diss., University of Minnesota, 1942).

7. Laurie Ann Schultz Hayes, "The Rhetoric of Controversy in the Lutheran Church–Missouri Synod with Particular Emphasis on the Years 1967-1976" (Ph.D. diss., University of Wisconsin-Madison, 1980).

8. Jack T. Robinson, "The Spirit of Triumphalism in The Lutheran Church–Missouri Synod" (Ph.D. diss., Vanderbilt University, 1972).

9. Larry W. Neeb, "Historical and Theological Dimensions of a Confessing Movement within the Lutheran Church–Missouri Synod" (D.Min. diss., Eden Theological Seminary, 1975).

10. Jack Howard Greising, "The Status of Confessional Conservatism: Background and Issues in the Lutheran Church–Missouri Synod" (Ph.D. diss., St. Louis University, 1972).

uneasy association with fundamentalism[11] (interestingly, all written by sons and daughters of the synod).[12]

Central to all these aspects of the synod's identity is the notion of authority. In an effort to define its theology as unchanging amid the fast-moving forces of historical change, Missouri has had to continually redefine its understanding of authority — of scripture, of the ministry, of women, indeed, of the synod itself. In so doing, Missouri has redefined its own historic identity as a confessional Lutheran church body.

This account serves as a case study of the changes in self-understanding that became necessary as mainline denominations struggled to remain viable amid the growing pluralism of American religion in the twentieth century. The Missouri Synod is hardly the only church body to face internal division and controversy over the course of its history. Yet neither is its story so parochial that there are no lessons to be learned from this history.

Because the synod's identity as the twenty-first century turns is so often reduced by those outside the church to the question, "Are you the Lutherans who ordain women to the ministry or the ones who don't?", I find the question of women's service to the church primary to discovering how this church body understands itself. Why such resistance to a change that has taken place in every other major Protestant denomination since mid-century? Such mainline Protestant churches in the United States as Presbyterians and Methodists began ordaining women in the 1950s, largely due to sociocultural changes affecting the status of women, with the more liturgical churches (Lutherans and Episcopalians) joining the ranks in the 1970s. While its liturgical character might suggest a link between the Missouri Synod and the Roman Cath-

11. Milton L. Rudnick, "Fundamentalism and the Missouri Synod" (Th.D. diss., Concordia Seminary, St. Louis, 1963).

12. See also John C. Wohlrabe, Jr., "An Historical Analysis of the Doctrine of the Ministry in the Lutheran Church–Missouri Synod until 1962" (Th.D. diss., Concordia Seminary, St. Louis, 1987); Richard Donald Labore, "Traditions and Transitions: A Study of the Leadership of the Lutheran Church–Missouri Synod During a Decade of Theological Change, 1960-1969" (Ph.D. diss., St. Louis University, 1980); Leland Robert Stevens, "The Americanization of the Missouri Synod as Reflected within the *Lutheran Witness*" (Ph.D. diss., St. Louis University, 1986); and Mary Todd, "'Not in God's Lifetime': The Question of the Ordination of Women in the Lutheran Church–Missouri Synod" (Ph.D. diss., University of Illinois at Chicago, 1996).

olic Church in their shared refusal to admit women to the ordained ministry, synodical theologians are quick to point out that the synod does not support what they call the "orthodox"[13] or Roman Catholic position, which is based on the priest's representation of Christ, thereby requiring a male model. Instead, its justification for denying ordination to women links the Missouri Synod's widely acknowledged theological conservatism with the more fundamentalist segments of American Protestantism, who base their stance against women in ministry on a literal biblical understanding of gender roles, in particular one that requires male headship and female subordination. This singular reliance on a fixed reading of an "order of creation" defense for its every determination about the role of women in the church — by appeal to a verbally inerrant scriptural text — has been a relatively recent development in synodical history, without which the synod would have little support for its preclusion of women from ordained ministry.

Fundamental to an understanding of who can be a public minister of word and sacrament is agreement about what this ministry is. It is the contention of this study that ambivalence over definition and doctrine of ministry has required The Lutheran Church–Missouri Synod to adjust its theology each time it has been suggested that women might serve in quasi-public ministry opportunities — parochial school teaching, forming a women's auxiliary, voting or holding congregational or synodical office — previously closed to them. Observers will note that this pattern of adjustment has been the synod's usual response over the course of its history to any exception raised over definition of ministry. Because it does not have a clearly articulated understanding of the nature of public ministry, the synod has repeatedly had to redefine what it means by ministry, what it means by authority, and what that redefinition means for women in the church. In so doing the church has unavoidably redefined itself. A narrative of inconsistency records the struggle of this historically ethnic denomination to define itself over against the rapid social changes of the twentieth century, changes that have threatened both its intent and its attempt to remain in the world but not of the world.

13. Samuel Nafzger, telephone conversation with the author, May 17, 1991. Nafzger, executive director of the synod's Commission on Theology and Church Relations, used this term in reference to the Roman Catholic position on women and the priesthood, not in reference to the Eastern Orthodox Church.

Complicating the synod's efforts to retain either a consistency or internal cohesion is its polity, a unique form of congregationalism by which an advisory synod in convention declares policy and theology for the church at large while individual congregations are left to interpret those rulings locally. Yet, despite the stated principle of congregational autonomy, this is a church body in which clerical hegemony has been the rule. Its constitution, which in its statement of confession subscribes to the Book of Concord as "a true and unadulterated statement and exposition of the Word of God,"[14] requires that synodical officers, with the exception of the treasurer, be clergy. Missouri's tradition has been one of strong pastors (the German *Herr Pastor*) and clergy-dependent people.[15]

Finally, viewed through the lens of gender, what is remarkable and tragic about this history is the absence of women, both from the discussion forum and from any position of advocacy on their own behalf. Debate about women's participation and place in the church has been carried on among men, as has the decision-making process. In whatever stage of the synod's history, no matter what request was being made, women's roles have been marginal at best. Until the 1970s, no hearings were held, no opinions sought, no surveys taken, no women appointed to either commission or committee. The "woman question" was raised, studied, and answered by men. And when, beginning in the 1970s, women *were* appointed to task forces or commissions on women, they understood their assignment as limited and thereby limited themselves and their potential influence. Unlike most other church bodies, including the Roman Catholic, there is neither a professional female theological voice nor a visible feminist minority in the Missouri Synod. For these reasons the synod account parallels neither the Roman Catholic experience nor that of other mainline Protestant denominations, in which women took on varying degrees of agency as their church bodies struggled with the question of appropriate and acceptable levels of participation by gender.[16]

14. Constitution of The Lutheran Church–Missouri Synod, Article II.

15. For a current reflection on this tradition, see Walter Wangerin, Jr., "Preaching," in *Ragman and Other Cries of Faith* (San Francisco: HarperCollins, 1984), pp. 71-82, esp. p. 72.

16. See Barbara Brown Zikmund, "Winning Ordination for Women in Mainstream Protestant Churches," in *Women and Religion in America,* volume 3: *1900-1968,* ed. Rosemary Radford Ruether and Rosemary Skinner Keller (New York:

Those who hold "inadequate notions of God"[17] claim authority based on what they understand to be God's commands. Verbal scriptural inerrancy presumes constriction and limitation — of possibility, of imagination, of opportunity, of thought, indeed, of God. As long as the Missouri Synod understands the authority of scripture through an insistence on verbal scriptural inerrancy, it requires a ban on the ordination of women to support that posture. In what other instance is subscription to scriptural literalism so clear as in the command that "Women should be silent in the churches. For they are not permitted to speak, but should be subordinate"?[18] The two positions are inextricably entwined; one without the other would not stand. Thus the synod's identity depends on absolute adherence to the fusion of these two principles.

Definitions

Certain terms will be used in this narrative whose meaning may be taken for granted by some readers, but not readily by all. Nevertheless, these should be first introduced and defined apart from the context. By nature, brief (and thus necessarily general) definitions risk misinterpretation. Yet a preliminary sense of some of the terminology integral to Lutheran theology is an important foreground to the history of any particular Lutheran tradition.

The primary statement of the principles of Lutheran doctrine is the Augsburg Confession of 1530. After a series of disputes among theologians over interpretation of that confession, a larger collection of documents collectively known as the Book of Concord appeared in 1580. Missouri Synod Lutherans subscribe to this later collection of confessional

Harper & Row, 1986), pp. 339-48; Pamela W. Darling, *New Wine: The Story of Women Transforming Leadership and Power in the Episcopal Church* (Cambridge, Mass.: Cowley Publications, 1994); Frederick W. Schmidt, Jr., *A Still Small Voice: Women, Ordination, and the Church* (Syracuse, N.Y.: Syracuse University Press, 1996); Carl J. and Dorothy Schneider, *In Their Own Right: The History of American Clergywomen* (New York: Crossroad Publishing, 1997); and Mark Chaves, *Ordaining Women: Culture and Conflict in Religious Organizations* (Cambridge, Mass.: Harvard University Press, 1997).

17. Karen Armstrong used this term in a radio interview with Martin Marty on "The Nature of Fundamentalism," hosted by Milton Rosenberg, "Extension 720," WGN Radio, Chicago, September 7, 1994. For the classic text on notions of God, see J. B. Phillips, *Your God Is Too Small* (New York: Macmillan, 1961).

18. 1 Corinthians 14:34, NRSV.

statements, often referring to them as the Symbolical Books or Symbols. This expanded explication of the faith includes the three ecumenical creeds, the Unaltered Augsburg Confession and Apology, the Smalcald Articles (1537), the Treatise on the Power and the Primacy of the Pope (1537), Luther's large and small catechisms (1529), and the Formula of Concord (1577). If the Reformation (perhaps more accurately by original intention a restoration) was an effort to return the church to its formative character, then *confessionalism* can be understood as a movement to return Lutheranism to its formative character and period through subscription to the original documents of the faith.

Martin Luther's greatest contribution to Protestant theology was his teaching on justification by faith alone, apart from works. His teachings on the ministry, however, hold most significance for this study. Luther believed firmly in a set-apart office of the ministry, the pastoral office of Word and sacrament. The function of this ordained ministry was to represent the believers publicly, through preaching and teaching the Word and the administration of the sacraments of baptism and the eucharist.[19] It is this functional character of the ministry that differentiates the Lutheran understanding from the Roman Catholic, from which Luther broke. Luther rejected any notion of holy orders creating a clergy estate. At the same time he recovered the baptismal theology of the church by emphasizing the principle of the *priesthood of all believers.* By this Luther meant that every Christian, by virtue of the sacrament of baptism, is a priest of equal standing with and to every other Christian. There is no longer need for a mediator between God and humans since the mediation of Jesus Christ.[20] All Christians, said Luther, have a priesthood, but not all have a public priestly function.[21]

These two principles, or better, two ministries — whether described as one broad and one narrow or one common and one special[22] — are two

---

19. Martin Luther, "On the Councils and the Church, (1539)," in *Luther's Works,* American edition, ed. Jaroslav Pelikan and Helmut T. Lehman (St. Louis and Philadelphia: Concordia Publishing House and Fortress Press, 1955-1986), 41:154. Hereinafter cited as *Luther's Works.*

20. "To the Christian Nobility of the German Nation, (1520)," *Luther's Works,* 44:129.

21. *Luther's Works,* 29:16.

22. Eric W. Gritsch and Robert W. Jenson, *Lutheranism: The Theological Movement and Its Confessional Writings* (Philadelphia: Fortress Press, 1976), p. 111.

parts of a whole, the one ministry of the Word, and together they provide the proper Lutheran understanding of church and ministry, yet the relationship between the two has often been uneasy. The Lutheran confessions do not address the two principles in juxtaposition. Rather, the office of the ministry is most clearly explicated in the confessions, while there is only one direct reference to the priesthood of all believers in the symbolical books, and even that is in the context of the right of the church to choose and ordain ministers.[23] Luther's development of the universal priesthood comes, for the most part, early in his reforming career,[24] and was a significant part of his dispute with the Roman Catholic Church, which in reaction thought he was advocating the end of the priesthood itself. But as the Reformation progressed, emphasis on the priesthood of all believers dimmed.[25] It may be that the very lack of explication of the notion of a universal priesthood has contributed to the paradoxical status it holds in the church today, for the overarching emphasis of the church in writing and discussion has always focused on the office of public ministry. And the church admits it —

> No church has set forth the doctrine of the spiritual priesthood of all Christians more clearly and emphasized it more strongly than the Lutheran church, and especially the Lutheran church in America. And no church put this doctrine less into practice.[26]

Article V of the Augsburg Confession declares that "God instituted the office of the ministry, that is, provided the Gospel and the sacraments"; Article VII defines the church as the "assembly of all believers among whom the Gospel is preached in its purity and the holy sacra-

---

23. Treatise on the Power and Primacy of the Pope, *The Book of Concord,* trans. and ed. Theodore G. Tappert (Philadelphia: Fortress Press, 1959), p. 331. See Arthur Carl Piepkorn, "What the Symbols Have to Say about the Church," in *The Church: Selected Writings of Arthur Carl Piepkorn,* ed. Michael P. Plekon and William S. Wiecher (Delhi, N.Y.: ALPB Books, 1993), p. 41.

24. Eugene F. Klug, "Luther on the Ministry," *Concordia Theological Quarterly* 47 (1983): 293-95.

25. Arthur Carl Piepkorn, "The Sacred Ministry and Holy Ordination in the Symbolical Books of the Lutheran Church," *Concordia Theological Monthly* 40 (1969): 557.

26. August Pieper, "Are There Legal Restrictions in the New Testament?" *Theologische Quartalschrift* 13 (July 1916), trans. C. Lawrenz, *Wisconsin Lutheran Quarterly* 86 (Winter 1989): 49.

ments are administered according to the Gospel."[27] The confessors make clear that the public ministry is not derivative of the priesthood of believers, but is divinely established. Still, while both principles are essential to the church, as aspects of the Lutheran theology of ministry they exist in a not-always creative tension. Misunderstanding of each has at times in Missouri Synod history led to conflict between clergy and laity; misunderstanding of both over time has been a perpetual feature of congregational life. Indeed, a popular misconception of the notion of the universal priesthood, one that places it in competition with the set-apart office of public ministry, can lead to power struggles, elevation of the ordained ministry and devaluation of the ministry of the laity, and vice versa. Difficulty in retaining the balance or right relationship that Luther intended between these two complementary but different aspects of the ministry of the church has left Lutherans open to persistent charges of an inadequate theology of ministry, and of the church.[28]

Additionally, Lutheran understanding of the public ministry stresses the servant nature of the office. Lutherans have a *ministerium,* an office of service, as compared to the *magisterium,* or teaching authority, of the Roman Catholic Church. Accordingly, there is no higher office than the preaching office because there is only one ministry, the ministry of the Word. All who hold the office are equal.

The third principle which Luther is credited with introducing is the Lutheran concept of *sola scriptura* (scripture alone), the Bible as sole authority for faith, the only source and norm for teaching.[29] Luther's position was reiterated in the Formula of Concord: "The Word of God is and should remain the sole rule and norm of all doctrine."[30] Shared understanding of the *authority of the Bible* has been a source of difference and misunderstanding within the synod and with other Lutherans, as Lutherans debate what is meant by authority and the meaning of the

---

27. Augsburg Confession, V and VII, in Tappert, *The Book of Concord,* pp. 31-32.

28. See Roy A. Harrisville, *Ministry in Crisis: Changing Perspectives on Ordination and the Priesthood of All Believers* (Minneapolis: Augsburg Publishing House, 1987).

29. See F. E. Mayer, *The Religious Bodies of America,* 4th ed. (St. Louis: Concordia Publishing House, 1961), pp. 130-31, for a concise statement of Luther's view of scripture, which Mayer defines as "exclusively Christocentric. . . . Scripture alone is the Gospel alone."

30. Formula of Concord, Solid Declaration, Rule and Norm, in Tappert, *The Book of Concord,* p. 505.

term "Word of God." It is within this debate that the issue of interpretation, or hermeneutics, rests. The authority of scripture is implied but not directly addressed or further explained by the Reformers in the Lutheran confessions:

> We pledge ourselves to the prophetic and apostolic writings of the Old and New Testaments as the pure and clear fountain of Israel which is the only true norm according to which all teachers and teachings are to be judged and evaluated.[31]

The confessions go no further to outline a doctrine of scripture. It was, instead, orthodox Lutheran dogmaticians in the seventeenth century who first developed a doctrine that assigns divine inspiration and inerrancy to scripture, thus replacing Luther's material principle — the doctrine of justification by faith — with a formal principle — the words that convey that doctrine.[32] Where this developed doctrine of scripture differed from Luther's understanding was in its conflation of the theologians' use of the term "Word of God" with scripture, as Lutheran theologian Carl Braaten argues.[33] Verbal inspiration by the Holy Spirit became the authoritative measure, not the gospel message as Luther had claimed in applying the formula: *was Christum treibt* ("that which conveys Christ").[34] This narrowing of the application of the term stands in contrast not only to Luther's stress on "the authority of Christ against the authority of the Bible"[35] but to the three different meanings used interchangeably by Luther and Lutherans for "Word of God" — the incarnate Christ, the preached word (or proclamation), and the written word of scripture. Missouri Synod theologians contend that such a scripture/Word of God "disjunction" is "misguided"[36] and reject any accusation

---

31. Formula of Concord, Solid Declaration, Rule and Norm, in Tappert, *The Book of Concord,* pp. 503-4.

32. Arthur Carl Piepkorn, "What Does 'Inerrancy' Mean?" *Concordia Theological Monthly* 36 (1965): 577-93.

33. Carl E. Braaten, *Principles of Lutheran Theology* (Philadelphia: Fortress Press, 1983), p. 5. Also Kent S. Knutson, "The Community of Faith and the Word: An Inquiry into the Concept of the Church in Contemporary Lutheranism" (Ph.D. diss., Columbia University, 1961), esp. pp. 106-12.

34. *Luther's Works,* 35:396.

35. *Luther's Works,* 34:112.

36. Ralph A. Bohlmann, *Principles of Biblical Interpretation in the Lutheran Confessions,* rev. ed. (St. Louis: Concordia Publishing House, 1983), p. 132.

that the synodical position assigns scripture an enhanced authority. They particularly object to charges that the synod leans to a fundamentalist use of scripture.[37] Rather, they insist that they subscribe to nothing more than the principles of biblical authority in the Book of Concord, including Luther's principle that "Scripture interprets itself."[38]

Various controversies in the immediate post-Reformation period following Luther's death in 1546 led the reformers to debate the distinction between articles of the faith considered essential and those that could be deemed nonessential. The term most frequently used for the latter, indifferent things, is *adiaphora,* those matters of practice which are neither commanded nor forbidden by scripture but are left to the church to decide. The Adiaphoristic Controversy of 1548-1549 found Lutherans divided between those who held to Luther's teachings, led by the young and uncompromising theologian Matthias Flacius, and others who followed Philipp Melanchthon, lay theologian and primary author of the Augsburg Confession and its Apology.[39] The term *adiaphora* as applied to church usage is addressed in the Formula of Concord[40] and is set in a fairly restricted context of ceremonies of the church over against the emphasis of Roman Catholicism on required practices. Over the course of Lutheran history, use of the term has been enlarged to apply to other matters, but the general principle still applies to those practices for which there is neither definitive scriptural command nor prohibition, and the rule that follows permits local usage to vary as long as good order is maintained in the church and no offense is given.

Before it had even organized itself as a church body, the Lutheran leaders who would form the nucleus of The Lutheran Church–Missouri Synod were sardonically labeled "Missouri" by another Lutheran pastor in the United States with whom they were in theological dispute.[41] The

37. Horace D. Hummel, "Lutheranism and the Inerrancy of Scripture," *Concordia Journal* 14 (April 1988): 107.

38. Quoted by Paul Althaus, *The Theology of Martin Luther,* trans. Robert C. Schultz (Philadelphia: Fortress Press, 1966), p. 76.

39. Robert Kolb, *Confessing the Faith: Reformers Define the Church, 1530-1580* (St. Louis: Concordia Publishing House, 1991), pp. 63-81.

40. Formula of Concord, Epitome, 10, in Tappert, *The Book of Concord,* pp. 492-94; Formula of Concord, Solid Declaration 10, in Tappert, pp. 610-16.

41. See below, chapter 3, for the background of the dispute between the Missouri and Buffalo synods in which this reference originated.

pejorative was later turned around and adopted by the synod as a term by which it would fondly refer to itself. Its use in this study presumes the synod's use of the name "Missouri" as a self-referent.

Methodology and Perspective

It has been said that the Missouri Synod suffers from what Sidney Mead called "a kind of historylessness" or "antihistorical bias."[42] There is no scholarly, holistic history of the Missouri Synod. While its various chapters have been examined in dissertations and monographs, the church has followed a curious course in relating its history to its members. On each occasion of a significant anniversary of the synod's founding in 1847 — at seventy-five, one hundred, and 125 years — the synod has commissioned a history.[43] While each of these texts has varied in format, they share the celebratory, even triumphalist, tone a reader has come to expect in almost any commemorative history, whether of institution, organization, or nation.

Since the early decades of its existence, the synod has supported a publishing venture, Concordia Publishing House in St. Louis, Missouri. Almost exclusively, texts written about the Missouri Synod have been published by Concordia, whose editorial policy, in agreement with synodical bylaws,[44] requires that every manuscript be submitted to an

---

42. Sidney Mead, *The Lively Experiment: The Shaping of Christianity in America* (New York: Harper & Row, 1963), p. 108. Quoted in David W. Lotz, "The Sense of Church History in Representative Missouri Synod Theology," *Concordia Theological Monthly* 42 (1971): 597.

43. In 1922, W. H. T. Dau edited *Ebenezer: Reviews of the Work of the Missouri Synod During Three Quarters of a Century,* a series of essays written primarily by synodical professors and clergy covering the significant episodes and personalities of the founding and formative years of the church. In 1947, Walter A. Baepler wrote *A Century of Grace: A History of the Missouri Synod, 1847-1947,* and in 1973 Eldon Weisheit took what he called "a pastoral approach to history" in *The Zeal of His House: Five Generations of Lutheran Church–Missouri Synod History (1847-1972),* a somewhat whimsical survey "directed at church members who have little or no knowledge of church history." Each was published in St. Louis by Concordia Publishing House. No title was commissioned for the sesquicentennial; the anniversary committee instead authorized the production of a video, *Sent Forth by God's Blessing.*

44. Bylaws of the Lutheran Church–Missouri Synod, XI. Doctrinal Review, *Handbook of the Lutheran Church–Missouri Synod,* 1995 edition, pp. 135-37.

anonymous doctrinal review process to assure agreement with synodical positions.[45] There is something of a paradox embedded in this procedure, in which the synod can choose to publish only its own in-house approved version of its history, while discounting — if not outright dismissing — any text it does not itself publish. This becomes problematic for the researcher when she discovers the dearth of resources on synodical history published by any house other than Concordia. An interesting footnote is added upon learning that those scholars most interested in writing about Missouri Synod history have been primarily its own sons and daughters. One wonders if that is because, as Martin Marty suggests, "Lutherans are not exotic enough to inspire mere curiosity on the part of non-Lutherans."[46]

My own interest in this church body, its attitude toward women, its history, and its use of history, stems from my lifelong association with it. My father was a Missouri Synod clergyman for fifty years, my mother an advocate for women and an active churchwoman quite apart from her duties as a pastor's wife. Neither the home I grew up in nor the church in which I was baptized and confirmed raised barriers to women's development and agency. Instead, a combination of events within the synod, within Lutheranism, and within the nation at large in the 1970s led to my recognition of the significance of gender difference in the Missouri Synod.

It has been an awakening to know personally what Jonathan M. Butler has called the experience of "historian as heretic."[47] Because the preference since 1970 in the Missouri Synod has been to declare any

45. The requirement that any text published by church printing offices be in doctrinal agreement with the church had its roots in the guidelines drawn up in Saxony by the leaders of the original emigrant company. In their "Code for the Civil Community," provision was made for a Literary Board, to which "every item of printed matter" was to be submitted before distribution. Any item "directed against the existing constitutions of the church and the community, against the Old Lutheran confession of faith, and against genuinely Christian morals" was to be confiscated and "placed under the seal of the literary board." The Code is translated in Walter O. Forster, *Zion on the Mississippi: The Settlement of the Saxon Lutherans in Missouri, 1839-1841* (St. Louis: Concordia Publishing House, 1953), p. 582.

46. Martin E. Marty, *Health and Medicine in the Lutheran Tradition: Being Well* (New York: Crossroad, 1986), p. 8.

47. See his Introduction to Ronald L. Numbers, *Prophetess of Health: Ellen G. White and the Origins of Seventh-day Adventist Health Reform* (Knoxville: University of Tennessee Press, 1992), pp. xxv-lxvii.

discussion of women's ordained ministry closed, this research has challenged unwritten rules and established practice. The silence on the subject has been telling. In a church that has been fond of claiming and proclaiming internal unity in the face of heterodoxy on every side throughout its history, the self-critical voice has hardly been welcome, particularly when that voice has been a layperson's, and more so a laywoman's. I offer what historian George Marsden calls a "critical insider viewpoint,"[48] a standpoint that adds a perspective of self-consciousness to the process of what is already an "insider's enterprise," the writing of denominational history.[49] At the same time, scholarly critical distance demands an "outside-insider" approach — neither apologist nor hypercritic — to the enterprise of writing about one's own faith community.[50]

Using the synod's search for identity as an organizing principle, I suggest a periodization based on fifty-year time spans. The first two periods are each characterized by the overarching influence of a single theologian, the third by a struggle over whether the synod would define itself by the repristination of its earlier leaders' teachings, or by extending the confessional legacy of its first century into modern America. Because the developments regarding women's service in the church occur so late in the synod's history, primary emphasis is on the last of the three eras. The years since World War II have also been those in which the notion of authority has been most tested and contested in the synod. Today the question of identity — *what do we want this church to be?* — remains central but unanswered in the currently volatile character of the synod. A careful look at its history may offer some answers.

48. George Marsden, "Forum," *Religion and American Culture: A Journal of Interpretation* 3 (1993): 11. Quoted by Rosemary Skinner Keller, "Forum: Female Experience in American Religion," *Religion and American Culture: A Journal of Interpretation* 5 (1995): 3.

49. L. DeAne Lagerquist, "Who I Am and What I Do," *The Cresset* 56 (March 1993): 12-13.

50. Jan Shipps, "Remembering, Recovering, and Inventing What Being the People of God Means: Reflections on Method in the Scholarly Writing of Denominational History," in *Reimagining Denominationalism: Interpretive Essays,* ed. Robert Bruce Mullin and Russell E. Richey (New York: Oxford University Press, 1994), p. 193.

2

Defining Decade, 1831-1841:
The Formative Years

When he returned to his native Germany in 1854 to share his observations after ten years of teaching in America, church historian Philip Schaff remarked on "the multifarious differences of opinion and schools"[1] to be found among German Lutherans in the United States at mid-century. Despite this diversity, he observed three basic divisions. The terms he used to identify these groups are profoundly simple, yet they reveal much, for they reflect both the extent of each group's acculturation into American society and the level of its adherence to the fundamental principles of Luther. Schaff found New Lutherans, Old Lutherans, and Moderate Lutherans.

Of these three, the Old Lutherans were the newest Americans. And, though these immigrants from Saxony, Prussia, and Bavaria had arrived in America only fifteen years before Schaff recorded his observations, details of their various encounters in their new homeland had been widely reported. As Schaff described them:

> They are still entirely German, having not yet amalgamated at all with the English and American body; though they outwardly prosper very well, if we are to judge from the rapid increase of their ministers

1. Philip Schaff, *America: A Sketch of Its Political, Social, and Religious Character,* ed. Perry Miller (Cambridge, Mass.: The Belknap Press of Harvard University Press, 1961), p. 150.

and congregations. Their pastors are mostly well instructed, faithful, conscientious, and self-denying, though . . . very exclusive, and narrow-minded, and unable or unwilling to appreciate properly other churches and nationalities than their own. Luther is their highest human authority; and indeed, not the free, bold, world-shaking reformer, but the reactionary, scrupulous, intolerant Luther. . . . In their congregations they maintain a certain discipline and order, and are zealous for the parochial school. Over the experimenting New Lutherans they have the advantage of a fixed principle, a well-formed doctrinal basis, and a general logical consistency. They are, however, not harmonious. The office question, which has thrown even the strictly symbolical Lutherans of Germany into discord, in spite of all their boasted doctrinal compactness and unity, has arrayed them against each other in two parties, the Synod of Missouri and the Synod of Buffalo, which wage a newspaper war with a bitterness little creditable to Lutheranism and Christianity, and not at all fitted to inspire the Anglo-American, if he ever hears of it, with respect for this section of German Christendom. I refer to the controversy between the two views of the clerical office.[2]

That the earliest commentary of a church historian about Old Lutherans in America presents them engaged in a bitter controversy over the office of the ministry suggests that this has been an issue of vital significance to them from the outset. Indeed, debate about the ministry is a constant theme in the history of the Saxon branch of Old Lutherans, those Germans who would come to be known as The Lutheran Church–Missouri Synod. That debate is rooted in the formative event of the synod's history, the migration to America of more than six hundred Saxons in 1838 and 1839, an episode whose antecedents lay in the situation in which evangelical churches in the North German confederation found themselves during the post-Napoleonic period.

The Church in Germany
in the Early Nineteenth Century

The 150 years following the adoption of the Lutheran confessions as compiled in the Book of Concord in 1580 have been called the "age of

2. Schaff, *America*, pp. 150-51.

Lutheran orthodoxy."[3] Theologians wrote prolifically in exposition and clarification of the definitive doctrinal position of the Lutheran Church as contained in its confessions, scripture, and Luther's works. The writings of these scholastics served not only to develop the principles of Lutheran doctrine, but to defend them against the positions argued by others, whether Catholics, Calvinists, or "enthusiast" Quakers. Their defensive stance over time, however, earned orthodox theologians — also called dogmaticians — a reputation as rigid and intolerant interpreters of doctrine, even as it provided them a basis for unity in their confessional posture. Their insistence on a strict adherence to the Lutheran confessions *(Verkonfessionalisierung)* resulted in

> an unprecedented hardening of Lutheran doctrine. Not only did the guardians of orthodoxy endeavor to keep pure the teaching of their communion but the truth had to be stated in accepted phrases. Any deviation in phraseology was immediately viewed with great suspicion. . . .
>
> Lutheran orthodoxy did not only succeed in theologizing the Christian faith but in so doing it often distorted it. . . . While it paid lip service, for instance, to the authority of the Bible, the real authority was now lodged in the orthodox perspective upon the Bible. Deviation from that perspective and its accepted forms of expression was considered deviation from Scripture and hence heresy.[4]

But by the early eighteenth century, as Jaroslav Pelikan notes, "The people had grown weary of the endless and useless theological disputes in which their pastors and professors engaged . . . while true and vital Christianity was too often neglected."[5] Now orthodoxy was being challenged by two very different modes of thought: pietism and rationalism. While pietism appealed to a more personal and less formal expression of faith than orthodoxy, rationalism appealed to reason, and as the Enlightenment spread over the European continent, reli-

3. Robert D. Preus, *The Theology of Post-Reformation Lutheranism,* vol. 1: *A Study of Theological Prolegomena* (St. Louis: Concordia Publishing House, 1970), p. 45.

4. F. Ernest Stoeffler, *The Rise of Evangelical Pietism* (Leiden: E. J. Brill, 1965), p. 183.

5. Jaroslav Pelikan, *From Luther to Kierkegaard: A Study in the History of Theology* (St. Louis: Concordia Publishing House, 1950), pp. 77-78.

gious traditions based on revelation and faith alone felt the influence of these parallel movements. One theological and one secular, one based on experience and one on reason, each introduced an emphasis on individualism that would have a profound impact on both religious and political events of the eighteenth century.

The turn of the nineteenth century saw the first signs of a religious renewal from what pietists in particular had called the age of "dead" orthodoxy.[6] A rising movement of confessionalism, based on a desire to return to the orthodoxy of the sixteenth and seventeenth centuries, grew in reaction to the prevalence of rationalism being preached from Lutheran pulpits. These confessionalists mixed their neo-orthodoxy with a renewed spirit of pietism. Emerging in Germany in the 1670s, pietism stressed the need for individual regeneration or conversion, and as such, favored a style of preaching that would affirm that message.[7] Confessionalists who complained about rationalist sermons that addressed the practical issues of daily living, but not the spiritual condition of the people, found appealing pietist messages that confronted people with the reality of sin in their lives. By focusing on an individual's sinfulness and need for regeneration, pietism challenged socioeconomic status and thereby introduced a leveling tendency among traditionally disparate groups.[8] Rationalists emphasized thought and reason, and thus valued a learned public ministry who would interpret scripture for the people. Pietists, by contrast, stressed a personal heart religion and, while not denying the need for a clerical office, worked to restore Luther's notion of the priesthood of all believers. In addition, pietists introduced the practice of small group gatherings *(collegia pietatis)* among the people, so they could study the Bible for themselves. The challenge to existing authorities and attention to individualism that pietism contributed to the German *Erweckungsbewegung,* or Awakening, was simultaneously spreading through the young United States as a result of its own Second Great Awakening.

6. Dale W. Brown, *Understanding Pietism* (Grand Rapids: Wm. B. Eerdmans Publishing Co., 1978), p. 23.

7. Mary Fulbrook, *Piety and Politics: Religion and the Rise of Absolutism in England, Württemberg and Prussia* (Cambridge: Cambridge University Press, 1983), p. 32.

8. Fulbrook, *Piety and Politics,* p. 95. For the socioeconomic influence of pietism, see also A. G. Roeber, *Palatines, Liberty, and Property: German Lutherans in Colonial British America* (Baltimore: The Johns Hopkins University Press, 1993), pp. 63-66.

More than anything else, it was the action of the political rulers of several German states that mobilized the confessional movement. In 1817, to celebrate the three hundredth anniversary of the Reformation, King Frederick William III of Prussia outlined a plan of union to combine the Lutheran and Reformed Protestants into one "rejuvenated, evangelical, Christian church,"[9] with a goal of ending religious conflict and thereby strengthening the state. The means by which this union was to be formalized was a joint Reformation celebration of the eucharist in Berlin and subsequently, through the introduction of a new liturgy, or Agenda.[10]

The Congress of Vienna in 1815, following the Wars of Liberation, had left the former states of the defunct Holy Roman Empire a loose confederation of thirty-nine states, so the action of the Prussian king had no direct impact on Protestants in other states. But Prussia's position as a leader among the northern German states meant that smaller states would likely consider similar action, and indeed several did.[11] To orthodox Lutherans, the Prussian Union realized their fear of a unionistic tendency that they believed threatened the very purity of their Lutheran heritage. In their minds, union was evidence of the extent to which rationalism had permeated and polluted the faith. But because of the commingling of church and state, there was outwardly little the confessionalists could do to protest. One visible act of resistance was the posting of ninety-five theses on Reformation Day 1817 by Klaus Harms, a Lutheran pastor at Kiel.[12] Harms's action, three hundred years after Luther's, warned against the rationalism and unionism of the church and gave hope to other orthodox Lutherans who saw a dangerous trend in the move away from their historic faith.

In Saxony, despite the fact that rationalism there was not only less strident but seemed to be fading in influence, there were small pockets of strident antirationalist Lutherans. Many belonged to Bible

---

9. Walter H. Conser, Jr., *Church and Confession: Conservative Theologians in Germany, England, and America, 1815-1866* (Macon, Ga.: Mercer University Press, 1984), p. 18.

10. Conser, *Church and Confession*, p. 21.

11. Conser, *Church and Confession*, p. 18.

12. Kenneth Scott Latourette, *The Nineteenth Century in Europe: The Protestant and Eastern Churches*, vol. 2, *Christianity in a Revolutionary Age* (New York: Harper & Brothers, 1959), pp. 20-21.

and missionary societies in a popular voluntary associationism that paralleled the activity in antebellum America.[13] Paradoxically, though they supported these agencies as a new means of advancing their orthodoxy, the primary target of the antirationalists was any trend that hinted at liberalism or modernism, which they gathered under the term *Neologie*.[14] These feared "new doctrines" included a variety of alarming tendencies ranging from what they understood as moral laxness to a retreat from scriptural authority. Coupled with the threat of unionism and the impositions on clergy by the state church, neology provided the antirationalists visible evidence of the distance between the state of the church and the letter and the spirit of the Lutheran confessions.

"God's Elder Brother"[15]

One of the key antirationalist figures in Dresden, the capital city of Saxony, and the individual most directly responsible for the emigration of Saxon Lutherans to America, was the pastor of St. John's Church, Martin Stephan. Stephan, born in 1777 in Moravia to Catholic parents who converted to Lutheranism, was orphaned early and took up a trade as a journeyman weaver. As a young man in Breslau he was befriended by local pietists by whose help he was able to continue his education, first at the *Gymnasium* and then at the Universities of Halle and Leipzig. In 1809 he dropped out of Leipzig and became pastor of a congregation in Bohemia, and the following year took the call to St. John's, Dresden. St. John's parish was a so-called Bohemian congregation, chartered in 1650 as an exile church for refugees from Bohemia who had fled to

13. Carl S. Mundinger, *Government in the Missouri Synod: The Genesis of Decentralized Government in the Missouri Synod* (St. Louis: Concordia Publishing House, 1947), pp. 21-22.

14. Walter O. Forster, *Zion on the Mississippi: The Settlement of the Saxon Lutherans in Missouri 1839-1841* (St. Louis: Concordia Publishing House, 1953), p. 22.

15. This curious term is Carl Mundinger's. See *Government in the Missouri Synod*, pp. 67-68. Mundinger ventures into psychohistory to argue that Stephan suffered from a maladjusted personality. This reference, however, is to the clergyman's followers, who Mundinger suggests were so taken by Stephan's charisma that they lost sight of his humanity and so blurred the distinction between the man and his office. Stephan happily let them do so.

Dresden during the Thirty Years' War. Because its charter granted the congregation exemption from state church rule, St. John's was able to call its own pastor,[16] and so called Stephan despite his not having completed his theological education.

After a few years of relative anonymity in Dresden, Stephan soon became known as a leader in the Saxon Bible and the Dresden Mission societies[17] as well as the local branch of the German Society for the Promotion of Pure Doctrine and Holy Life.[18] Congregations are not always pleased when their pastors become too involved in activities outside the parish, and St. John's, as early as 1814, complained that Stephan was neglecting his pastoral duties, and that he was attracting new followers as a result of his charismatic leadership.[19]

If anything describes the nature of Martin Stephan, it would be the manner in which he attracted people. His personal magnetism stemmed not, apparently, from a dynamic preaching style. Contemporaries, in fact, disagreed about Stephan the preacher as much as they did about his personal character.[20] Called by some dry, by others capti-

16. Ludwig Fischer, *Das falsche Märtyrerthum oder die Wahrheit in der Sache der Stephanier. Nebst etlichen authentischen Beilagen* (Leipzig: Wilh. Alex. Kuenzel, 1839), pp. 9-10. Translated as *The False Martyrdom or the Truth in the Matter of the "Stephanier" in addition to a Number of Authentic Appendices*, trans. Fred Kramer, 1985, unpublished ms., Concordia Historical Institute, St. Louis, Missouri. Other exceptions to the practice of the Saxon state church that St. John's was allowed included the use of the Bohemian language and congregational oversight by means of a "spiritual council" that consisted of both male and female elders.

17. Marvin A. Huggins, "Martin Stephan: First Lutheran Bishop in America," *Concordia Historical Institute Quarterly* 44 (1971): 141.

18. Mundinger, *Government in the Missouri Synod*, p. 22.

19. Forster, *Zion on the Mississippi*, p. 32.

20. The subject of Martin Stephan has been the source of considerable dispute over the course of the synod's history. His descendants decry what they call "the party line," the portrayal in Missouri Synod histories of Stephan's character and behavior that has in their opinion demonized the bishop and not only denied him any credit for leadership of the Saxon emigration, but made him the scapegoat for the Saxons' subsequent troubles. The family denies, among other charges, any financial malfeasance on Stephan's part (Naomi Stephan, great-great-great granddaughter of Martin Stephan, in a telephone conversation with the author, December 17, 1994). See also a handwritten essay by Theo. M. Stephan, great-grandson of Martin, which accuses synod historians of perpetuating a myth regarding the Perry County "drama" by misrepresentation of facts and their reliance on "the grotesque theory that since 'tradition' has it so and so, it must be true." Theo. M. Stephan,

vating, he was described by Dr. Benjamin Kurtz of the General Synod, who in 1827 had traveled to Germany on behalf of the new Gettysburg Seminary, and who was invited to hear Stephan preach:

> Mr. Stephan was then about fifty years old, and his countenance and the contour of his head reminded us very forcibly of Dr. Dwight, the late President of Yale College. His sermon was plain, vigorous, and evangelic, and well calculated to enlighten the mind and affect the heart. . . . Fancy a very plain, matter-of-fact man, rather tall, somewhat inclined to austerity, with a slight tinge of melancholy in his features.[21]

Stephan was married and the father of eight children, seven girls (three of whom were deaf-mute) and a boy, also named Martin. Of his wife Julia history has recorded little, since the only source of information was Stephan himself, who claimed his unhappy marriage was not a result of anything he had done, but was instead "another of the crosses he was called upon to bear as a champion of Christ."[22]

Stephan's presence and behavior were forceful and eccentric enough to produce one of two reactions — people either became totally devoted to him or seriously questioned his character. In 1821 he was attacked in a Dresden newspaper as

> a heretical false prophet and fanatic, with dangerous teachings destructive to civil government, who was trying to found a sect, calling themselves "Stephanier." This congregation . . . was a mob of very ignorant boneheads, crazy fanatics, whose meetings led to lunacy and murder.[23]

"The Truth About the So-Called 'Treasure Chest,'" unpublished ms., William Koepchen Papers, CHI.

Stephan's apologists remain unpublished, though an exhaustive manuscript was written in 1935 by William Koepchen, a Missouri Synod pastor in New York City, to present an alternative or revisionist version of the story of the Saxon emigration and "prepare the reader for an intelligent celebration" of its approaching centennial. See Koepchen, "Pastor Martin Stephan and the Saxon Emigration of 1838," unpublished ms., Koepchen Papers, CHI.

21. *Lutheran Observer,* 6 (March 8, 1839): 2. Quoted in Carl S. Meyer, *Moving Frontiers: Readings in the History of the Lutheran Church–Missouri Synod* (St. Louis: Concordia Publishing House, 1964), pp. 132-33.

22. Forster, *Zion on the Mississippi,* p. 69. Julia's family were architects to the king of Poland. See note 20.

23. Koepchen, *Pastor Martin Stephan,* p. 19.

In denying these accusations, Stephan wrote to the paper, insisting

> I am neither the founder of a sect nor the leader of a sect. I belong
> neither to an old or to a new sect. I hate all sectarianism and fanati-
> cism. . . . I am an evangelical Lutheran minister. . . . I have no peculiar
> religious opinions.[24]

Stephan had been attracted to pietism and its various compo-
nents — its personal appeal, its emotionalism and devotionalism. His
congregation had a long tradition of gathering for midweek devotion
and study. In the 1820s, largely due to Stephan's affecting manner,
these meetings attracted numerous followers, at the same time attracting the attention of suspicious local government officials. Because it was a violation of the civil code to hold private gatherings,
known as conventicles, even under the guise of worship, Stephan was
frequently suspected of breaking the law. Though he repeatedly denied he was holding conventicles — the separatism of which suggested sectarianism — he never discontinued the small group gatherings. In his mind it was "not a separate meeting place [that]
constitutes a sect, but false doctrine. . . . Not the place but the preaching makes a sect."[25]

As the decade of the 1820s lengthened, Martin Stephan's personal
following grew, as did his influence over them. Before long this "ordained spellbinder"[26] — like his American contemporaries of the same
decade, Robert Matthews and Joseph Smith — had founded a movement.[27]

---

24. Koepchen, *Pastor Martin Stephan*, p. 19.

25. Koepchen, *Pastor Martin Stephan*, p. 19.

26. Heinrich H. Maurer, "Studies in the Sociology of Religion: IV. The Problems of Group-Consensus; Founding the Missouri Synod," *American Journal of Sociology* 30 (1924): 674.

27. Antebellum America had its share of self-styled religious leaders whose
stories are reminiscent of Stephan's, the difference being Stephan's position as an
ordained clergyman. Robert Matthews had a vision in 1830 that he claimed revealed his true identity as the Prophet Matthias. He subsequently established a personal kingdom in Sing Sing, New York, over which he ruled absolutely. See Paul E.
Johnson and Sean Wilentz, *The Kingdom of Matthias: A Story of Sex and Salvation in
19th-Century America* (New York: Oxford University Press, 1994). For Joseph Smith,
founder of the Mormons, see Jan Shipps, *Mormonism: The Story of a New Religious Tradition* (Urbana: University of Illinois Press, 1985).

Stephanism

The movement that eventually came to be known as Stephanism took hold in Saxony in the early 1830s, when a group of theology students at the University of Leipzig fell under Stephan's influence. The students, calling themselves The Awakened, "loathed the rationalism and cynicism of their professors of renown as much as the riotous and frivolous student life."[28] Seven young men had been meeting regularly for prayer and the study of a rather intense form of pietism with an older candidate of theology by the name of Kuehn.[29] As their study progressed, Kuehn's insistence on the necessity of personal spiritual struggle grew, to the point that some of his young followers suffered physical and emotional collapse.

This Leipzig group — later to become the nucleus of the clergy who founded the Missouri Synod — included Ernst Gerhard Wilhelm Keyl, Ernst Moritz Buerger, Theodor Julius Brohm, Ottomar Fuerbringer, Johann Friedrich Buenger, and two brothers, Otto Herman and Carl Ferdinand Wilhelm Walther. As C. F. W. Walther described their "holy club":

> These believers, who had withdrawn from the world, had to bear much scorn and contempt. They were called mystics, pietists, sanctimonious fellows, obscurantists, bigots, and other names less flattering. Hated by some as contemptible hypocrites or pitied as unfortunate, deluded religious enthusiasts, they were cast out by the unbelieving world and to some extent also by their own kinfolk. They, however, were filled with an inner joy in their God and Savior.[30]

When this group of men, all still in their twenties, became acquainted with Martin Stephan in the early 1830s, they eagerly sought the senior pastor's counsel, particularly in matters of conscience over the condition of the state church. Stephan's pietism reinforced his anti-

28. Theodore Buenger, "The Saxon Immigrants of 1839," in *Ebenezer: Reviews of the Work of the Missouri Synod During Three Quarters of a Century*, ed. W. H. T. Dau (St. Louis: Concordia Publishing House, 1922), p. 4.

29. There is no extant record of Kuehn's first name, despite extensive archival searches in Germany by August Suelflow, director emeritus of Concordia Historical Institute, St. Louis.

30. W. G. Polack, *The Story of C. F. W. Walther* (St. Louis: Concordia Publishing House, 1947), p. 14.

rationalist defense of biblical truth,[31] both of which must have appealed to the younger men who were so caught up with both ideas, and his influence steadily grew into dominance over the young pastors and candidates. He advised them on calls and career; they in turn were attracted to his strong personality and his obvious dedication to orthodox Lutheranism. He became their mentor; they became his inner circle.[32] Their devotion was often intensely personal. C. F. W. Walther was convinced that Stephan rescued his very soul during an especially dark time, when he wrote Stephan of his agony and received a reply from the Dresden pastor assuring Walther that he was indeed forgiven in Christ.[33]

If the young pastors needed Stephan for spiritual leadership, Stephan also needed the Leipzig brotherhood as followers. Beginning in 1831 and 1832, his reputation for eccentricity had become more marked. Long noted for his habit of taking late night walks, he began to invite some of his followers, both men and women, to accompany him to a vineyard lodge that had been provided to him by friends. On occasion his gatherings lasted all night and drew the attention of the local officials in Dresden, always suspicious that Stephan might be holding the illegal conventicles they feared as subversive.

But to his little band of disciples, Stephan could do no wrong, and they were quick to strike out at anyone who dared attack their leader. Stephan, of course, did nothing to discourage the attention of the young men, who would brook no criticism of him. Rather, the Stephanites, as they came to be called, saw any opposition as persecution of their beloved leader, who they held to be "the champion of orthodoxy, the defender of the faith."[34] After all, one later claimed, Stephan told them that the real target was not he but the church.[35] Meanwhile the older pastor himself seemed to thrive on the adulation

---

31. Karl Hennig, "Die Auswanderung Martin Stephans," *Zeitschrift für Kirchengeschichte*, 38 (Stuttgart, 1939): 147.

32. Ernest Theodore Bachmann, "The Rise of Missouri Lutheranism" (Ph.D. diss., University of Chicago, 1946), pp. 81-84.

33. Polack, *The Story of C. F. W. Walther*, p. 18.

34. Forster, *Zion on the Mississippi*, p. 63.

35. G. H. Loeber, *History of the Saxon Lutheran Immigration to East Perry County, Missouri in 1839*, trans. Vernon Meyr (Cape Girardeau, Mo.: Center for Regional History and Cultural Heritage, 1984), p. 3.

he received; it likely served to bolster his boldness, a posture that only added to the mounting irritation of his opponents. It could be argued that Stephanism was nothing more than a cult of personality in which impressionable young people devoted themselves to an older and seemingly wiser role model — the dynamic personalities of the early pietist founders had attracted similar followings. Yet as Stephanism spread beyond Dresden over the course of the 1830s, it drew charges of sectarianism and exclusiveness, legalism and literalism, and an intentional elevation of the office of the ministry, as evidenced by the group's emphasis on priestly functions and increasing difficulty in gaining audience with Stephan himself.[36]

As the young Stephanites completed their theological training and passed their examinations, they became eligible for pastorates, but their declared orthodoxy worked against their placement in a congregation. In the German states a pastor represented both church and state, and a cleric with a decided antagonism to the authority of the consistory was deemed a potential troublemaker. A provision at the time, however, allowed a member of the nobility, as patron of his territory, to appoint clergy to the congregations on his estate. So it happened that a nobleman sympathetic to Stephanism, Count Detlev von Einsiedel, appointed two of Stephan's protégés to churches in his territory.

In Saxony, the clergy were members of the second estate, a privileged class in society *(Standesperson)*. Yet advantages of social standing and secured income were not enough to outweigh the dangers the orthodox clergymen associated with the liberalism they saw spreading through both church and government. Stephan had for some time contemplated the idea of leaving Germany[37] — he had, in fact, mentioned it

36. Fischer, *Das falsche Märtyrerthum*, p. 62.
37. The first public hint that Stephan viewed emigration as an option is found in an 1824 sermon: "They plead for justice and protection. If they are not heeded, if their request is not granted, then they are not revolutionaries but must forsake a country which no longer wants to tolerate them and must seek one where they might find the desired freedom." Paul H. Burgdorf, "Pastor Martin Stephan's Published Sermons on *The Christian Faith*," *Concordia Historical Institute Quarterly* 63 (1990): 94. Dr. C. E. Vehse, a prominent lay leader of the emigration, claimed that Stephan had talked of emigrating to Australia as early as 1811. Carl Eduard Vehse, *The Stephanite Emigration to America* (1840), trans. Rudolph Fiehler (Tucson, Ariz.: Marion R. Winkler, 1975), p. 2.

to Benjamin Kurtz during the American's visit to St. John's church in Dresden in 1827, which Kurtz described twelve years later:

> He complained of the difficulties attending the faithful discharge of ministerial duty in Dresden, of the awful progress that neology and infidelity and looseness of morals had made among the clergy in Germany; of the restrictions imposed by the police on him and his flock in carrying on their religious exercises; the opposition and even persecution suffered in consequence of his adherence to the antiquated orthodoxy of the bible; and especially of the fact that ministers of the gospel were compelled in a sense to be officers of government and to prostrate themselves and the church to political subserviency, &c. And then the good man sighed for a land of perfect religious freedom, for a peaceful and retired home for himself and his congregation, where they might worship God according to the convictions of their own judgment without being subject to arbitrary restraints, vexatious requirements, &c., on the part of the Government. He finally remarked that he at times had serious thoughts of emigrating to the United States and his congregation were anxious to accompany him, with no other view than to enjoy liberty. . . . We encouraged him in this idea.[38]

In 1833, as Stephanism was gaining both notoriety and opposition, Stephan wrote to Kurtz, then editor of the *Lutheran Observer,* asking his counsel regarding emigration. He had already spoken of it to his followers in 1830, when political changes in Saxony forecast the advent of liberal tendencies in the kingdom.[39] A series of developments beginning with a revised constitution, reorganization of government departments to include a new Ministry of Worship and Public Instruction, the resignation of his protector, the conservative von Einsiedel, from the cabinet, and increased freedom of the press all boded poorly for Stephan. From this point on, the idea of emigration became more compelling as Stephan's troubles with the state intensified.

The degree to which Stephan was being harassed is debatable, though he certainly believed it and so convinced his congregation. In 1833 St. John's published a pamphlet to defend its pastor against the

---

38. *Lutheran Observer* 6 (March 8, 1839): 2. Quoted in Meyer, *Moving Frontiers,* p. 133.

39. Forster, *Zion on the Mississippi,* p. 85.

"fairy tales" and "silly stories" being spread about him, in particular the charge made by the city physician, Dr. Roeber, that six people had "lost their minds" after attending some of Stephan's meetings.[40] This defense against the hostility their pastor engendered was coupled with the congregation's statement of faith (*Glaubensbekentnisse*), in which they declared that, "We alone have the correct, pure doctrine through Stephan and we alone constitute a proper, pure Lutheran church under Stephan."[41] With this statement, the people of St. John's only enflamed an atmosphere already hostile to Stephan's arrogance and elevated their pastor and, with him, themselves, to new heights of pretense.

As long as Stephan refused to discontinue his nightly walks and his social gatherings, he had been kept under surveillance by Dresden police at the request of a nervous Department of Church Supervision.[42] Early in February 1836 he was arrested for the first time after police raided a home where he was visiting, and charged with disturbing the peace. The subsequent investigation resulted in an injunction that barred Stephan from "any further participation in nocturnal meetings of this nature, within the city or outside it, which give offense already because of the unseemly time chosen."[43] Stephan, not content to accept this ruling, appealed through his attorney, claiming that he required the evening walks for his health: "I am in need of exercise in the evening air and the aroma of the pines."[44] His shallow self-defense convinced neither the authorities nor the community that his questionable behavior was justified.

The relatively minor charge leveled against Stephan in this episode had an impact that reached far beyond community disapproval. Within weeks of his arrest, Stephan called a meeting of his closest followers, the pastoral candidates and teachers, at which he raised the

---

40. Koepchen, *Pastor Martin Stephan*, p. 30. The doctor's 1820 report is cited in full in Rudolph Zaunick, "Der Dresdner Stadtphysikus Friedrich August Röber (1765-1827) ein sächsischer Gesundheitswissenshaftler in der Nachfolge Johann Peter Franks," *Acta Historica Leopoldina* 4 (1966): 60-62. Roeber's opinion on the state of mind of his patient Eckhardt found the man's degeneration into madness a result of his "tendency to religious enthusiasm," due in large part to his attendance at conventicles held by the "fanatical Bohemian pastor Stephan."

41. Fischer, *Das falsche Märtyrerthum*, p. 30.

42. Koepchen, *Pastor Martin Stephan*, p. 41.

43. Forster, *Zion on the Mississippi*, p. 91.

44. Koepchen, *Pastor Martin Stephan*, p. 44.

question of emigration, not as an imminent necessity, but as a serious possibility. On May 3rd, another meeting was held, this one attended by prominent Stephanite laymen as well as clergy. Stephan's message indicates he had decided on emigration:

> There has never been a time in the history of the Church like the present. A Luther would be thrown in the Elbe, if he returned. . . . Pray that God leads His people out of this Sodom and delivers them, and takes His Church to another land, where it can serve His name undisturbed.[45]

This meeting established substantial ground rules for the emigration, even though no definitive timeline had been set. The meeting notes reveal that the nineteen men in attendance made several decisions: at some point in the future they would leave Germany, and when they did, they would travel to America, to the state of Missouri. Their choice of destination had been based on Stephan's reading of a popular piece of booster literature written by Gottfried Duden, who had emigrated to Missouri in 1824 and praised the productivity of the "first-quality land" of the Missouri River valley and the "second-rate land" of its hills. Duden's emigration handbook cautioned readers to make thoughtful preparations, including adequate "capital, good leadership and medical protection for the first two years, and the presence of friendly families from the fatherland."[46] Finally the men accepted a document, a "Constitution for the Lutheran Church after It has Safely Landed," that outlined the structure of the emigration community, one which definitively established the clergy as the ruling class. Then they waited for a sign as to when they should leave.[47]

Official interest in Martin Stephan's nighttime wanderings seemed to wane following his arrest and the injunction, for a period of quietude followed until November 9, 1837. Late that evening Dresden police raided a gathering at the vineyard lodge that Stephan fre-

---

45. Forster, *Zion on the Mississippi*, p. 97.

46. Gottfried Duden, *Bericht über eine Reise nach den westlichen Staaten Nordamerikas und einen mehrjährigen Aufenthalt am Missouri (in den Jahren 1824, 25, 26, und 1827), in Bezug auf Auswanderung und Übervölkerung, oder: Das Leben im Innern der Vereinigten Staaten und dessen Bedeutung für die häusliche und politische Lage der Europäer, etc.* (St. Gallen, 1932), pp. 53, 54, 221-23. Quoted in Meyer, *Moving Frontiers*, pp. 87-89. Duden's report was first published in Germany in 1829.

47. Forster, *Zion on the Mississippi*, pp. 98-99.

quented, and when he arrived ordered him to appear at a hearing, after which the Ministry of Worship suspended Stephan from office. Dresden officials again introduced the charge of holding conventicles, and further accused him of immoral conduct. In the end, the pastor was placed under house arrest.[48]

The November sequence of events was the sign that prompted the Stephanites to move toward emigration. Stephan had made himself thoroughly unwelcome in Saxony as a result of his arrogant and persistent disregard for the civil law. Stripped of his right to perform the duties of his office, he had little choice but to leave, if he were allowed. It should be noted that despite the general opposition to Stephanism, Stephan himself was the only one who was obviously in trouble. The rest of the Stephanite clergy continued on as before, defending orthodoxy and defending Stephan as their persecuted leader. Publicly they did nothing to challenge the state church whose condition they decried and despised.

Emigration or Exodus?

Like the Puritans who emigrated two hundred years earlier to Massachusetts Bay, the Stephanites saw emigration as the only hope for the preservation of the true faith. In their minds, the situation in the fatherland had become hopeless. But that was likely true only in their minds. Aside from Stephan's own personal sense that he was being hounded by the authorities, there was no cease and desist order insisting that the Stephanite pastors mend their ways. Ludwig Fischer, catechist and lay preacher at St. Peter's church in Leipzig, wrote critically about the Stephanites several months after they had left Germany:

> Toward the end of last year seven hundred otherwise quiet, contented, peaceful citizens left also our fatherland. They will build a paradise on the still inhospitable banks of the turbulent Missouri River into which the devil cannot enter. One with the spade, another in the shop, one teaching, the other growing food, a few probably also in warding off the red Indians, they will as members of their own free "apostolic-Lutheran church," practice their religious

48. Forster, *Zion on the Mississippi,* pp. 101-3.

confession, which, according to them, is despised, ridiculed, subjugated, even all but annihilated among us. Before their departure they declared that the Evangelical church is in a state of siege, not only in Saxony, but in all of Germany, and have bombarded this part of the Christian world from Luther's mighty fortress; however, in the course of this partial bombardment of the world, they fell out of their own fortress, for they were really seeking nothing else but to shatter the sublime and glorious edifice of their Christian church into tiny splinters.[49]

Fischer wrote to defend the state church of Saxony against the charges leveled against it by Stephan and his followers, whom he called "sour and arrogant saints."[50] Whether conditions in the homeland made it necessary for the Saxons to leave was not a question asked only by Fischer and other contemporaries in the wake of the emigration. The emigrants would be asking themselves the same question before long.

Nevertheless, within weeks of Stephan's house arrest and suspension, three laymen met to begin the development of the plan to emigrate to America. These three — Franz Adolph Marbach, attorney and director of the project, H. F. Fischer, a local merchant, and Gustav Jaeckel, a cashier who served as secretary — stipulated the details of the emigration according to Stephan's wishes. Jaeckel's notes indicate that at their first meeting, on December 6, 1837, the three agreed that the religious structure of the proposed community would be a ministerium consisting of one bishop and nine deacons, that the bishop was to be distinguished from the other clergy by "sacerdotal attire," including a lace-trimmed alb and distinctive headgear, and that no heretics or persons refusing to submit to church discipline be included among the emigrants.[51] That three laymen would agree to an episcopal church polity without comment is not unusual in light of the consistorial church structure in Saxony. It is better explained by the dominant role the authoritative and authoritarian Stephan played in their minds and in their plans. The laymen attached their very welfare and that of the church to the person of Stephan, claiming "the reverend archbishop"

49. Fischer, *Das falsche Märtyrerthum*, pp. iii-iv. Fischer's was not the only polemic against the Stephanites. See also Gottlob von Polenz, *Die öffentliche Meinung und der Pastor Stephan. Ein Fragment* (Dresden and Leipzig, 1840).

50. von Polenz, *Die öffentliche Meinung*.

51. Mundinger, *Government in the Missouri Synod*, pp. 61-62.

to be "the most important object of our concern."[52] In addition, they determined both the destination — St. Louis — and the route — through the port of New Orleans and up the Mississippi River — and that the community would function from a common treasury.

Once these primary decisions had been made, Stephan appointed an Advisory Committee to be headed by Marbach. He also included Fischer and Jaeckel, two theological candidates, and two additional laymen. There is no question that Stephan, despite his absence from most meetings, remained the director of this committee, though the members carried out the specifics of his plans. They were entirely devoted to their leader.

On February 15, 1838, another attorney, Dresden archivist Dr. Carl Eduard Vehse, age thirty-five, joined the Advisory Committee, and was assigned the task of negotiating with government officials an arrangement regarding Stephan. The committee authorized its envoy Vehse to secure for Stephan: (1) safe passage out of Germany, (2) a pension including benefits for his wife and children, as they would not be joining him in America, and (3) a quashing of all legal proceedings against him.[53] Despite his repeated run-ins with the authorities, Stephan continued to insist on special treatment out of respect for his office, and his loyal followers continued to defend his right to demand it. Vehse recalled Stephan's explanation of his difficulties: "God may yet have great purpose for me, wherefore I have here had to undergo shame and humiliation. Whom God would make great he first humbles. . . ."[54]

The most essential matter for the committee's attention was the financial arrangement earlier agreed to. The Credit Fund was to serve as the source for all expenses, for purchase of land once the emigrants had arrived in America, and for church and school buildings to be erected on that land. To be gathered from voluntary contributions from community members, the treasury was intended to cover the travel costs even of those who could not pay in full, though whether the emigration was business or charity was a frequently debated issue. At its height, Credit Fund deposits totaled $80,604.81.[55]

---

52. Mundinger, *Government in the Missouri Synod,* pp. 61-62.
53. Forster, *Zion on the Mississippi,* pp. 122-23.
54. Vehse, *The Stephanite Emigration to America,* p. 4.
55. Forster, *Zion on the Mississippi,* p. 164.

The committee drew up several documents beginning with the Emigration Code, adopted on May 18, 1838, which began with a statement of faith and then went on to the purpose of the emigration:

> After the calmest and most mature reflection they find themselves confronted with the impossibility, humanly speaking, of retaining this faith pure and unadulterated in their present homeland, of confessing it, and of transmitting it to their descendants. They are, therefore, constrained by their conscience to emigrate and to seek a land where this faith is not endangered and where they consequently can serve God undisturbed in the manner which He has graciously revealed and established, and enjoy undisturbed the unabridged and pure means of grace (which God has instituted for the salvation of all men), and preserve them thus unabridged and pure for themselves and their descendants.
>
> To these means of grace belong primarily: *the office* of reconciliation in its entire scope and with unrestricted freedom, pure and free *divine worship*, unabridged and pure *preaching* of God's Word, unabridged and pure *Sacraments, pastoral ministration* and the *care of souls* without let or hindrance.
>
> A land such as they seek is the United States of North America, where complete religious and civil liberty prevails and energetic and effective protection is given against foreign countries as nowhere else in the world. These States they therefore have chosen as the goal, and, indeed, the only goal, of their emigration, and consequently as their new home.[56]

In addition, the Emigration Code established the ecclesiastical and civil code as authority for the community and the Credit Fund as its financial base, called for adherence to church discipline and mutual aid, and stated the itinerary. Subsequent documents included a Code for the Credit Fund, traveling regulations for those emigrating (including the reverence to be granted "the primate" Stephan, supervision of women and children, care of the sick and support of the indigent), regulations for settlement, which included a detailed plan of the city and the economic activity needed to sustain the settlers, and a code for the civil community, outlining the governmental and justice structure to be fol-

56. "Brief Outline of the Emigration Code," in Forster, *Zion on the Mississippi*, pp. 566-68. Emphasis in the original. See the Appendix for the complete text of the Articles of Emigration as translated in Forster.

lowed. The detail of these documents is extensive, including stipulations that hired help were to work on a fixed but fair scale of wages for no more than eight hours a day (a radical claim, since not even the early labor movements organizing in New England at the time were calling for less than a ten-hour day), and that women were forbidden to wear "corsets and their equivalents, such as dresses stiffened in the upper part with whalebone."[57]

Vehse became the primary agent for arranging the actual travel for the community, and during the summer of 1838 began negotiations for its transit. Originally he arranged for two vessels, but as the company grew, additional ships were added until five had been contracted. Through these business dealings word of the Saxon venture became public, and criticism in the press of the Stephanites was renewed. Stephan and company seemed to serve as magnets for public comment, as immigration historian Marcus Lee Hansen notes: "Few bands of emigrants have ever received the publicity that contemporary observers bestowed upon the Stephanists."[58] In response to news of the impending emigration, a variety of people completely unassociated with the Stephanites tried to join the company. But by and large the emigration was made up of people who wished to follow Stephan, thereby seeming to confirm that this was a religiously motivated migration, unlike most in the nineteenth century which were undertaken for economic reasons.[59]

Families packed belongings and memories and individuals began to ready themselves for the journey. Some wondered whether it was wise to leave at all. Agnes Buenger was not sure she wanted to give up her position in Saxony and asked her brother, theological candidate (not yet ordained) J. F. Buenger, whether she had to leave. His answer

57. "Regulations for Settlement of the Lutheran *Gesellschaft* Emigrating with Herr Pastor Stephan to the United States of North America," in Forster, *Zion on the Mississippi,* pp. 576-79.

58. Marcus Lee Hansen, *The Atlantic Migration, 1607-1860: A History of the Continuing Settlement of the United States* (Cambridge, Mass.: Harvard University Press, 1940), p. 136.

59. However, it must be noted that from the earliest migrations to America, "Emigration was often the result of a bundle of motives. . . . Religion often provided the language and the frame of reference to explain decisions that involved family, financial and incidental matters as well as the service of God." David Cressey, *Coming Over: Migration and Communication between England and New England in the Seventeenth Century* (New York: Cambridge University Press, 1987), p. 74.

reflected the brash boldness by which the leaders of the company understood their decision: "If you wish to go to hell, stay here; if you wish to be saved, go with us to America."[60] In other cases, families split as some members chose to stay and others chose to leave. C. F. W. Walther wanted to include his orphaned niece and nephew on the journey, but did not have the approval of their legal guardian, so he spirited the children away to the safe keeping of his friend Buenger's mother just prior to sailing. Mrs. Buenger was arrested and jailed for five weeks for abducting the "stolen" Schubert children, which delayed her departure until December. Meanwhile, the real kidnapper, Walther, was already at sea when a warrant for his arrest was issued.

The polarization of voices over Stephanism only increased as the emigrants' departure neared. Vocal opposition did not prevent the government from granting the emigrants passports, even to Stephan, who bided his time still under house arrest with guards inside his home. His troubles with the law had worsened, to the degree that the Advisory Committee decided they should hire an outside attorney to represent Stephan, even though no charges against him had ever been proven. During the summer charges of sexual misconduct were leveled. Finally even St. John's parish filed a complaint against its pastor on the grounds of "indecent and unchaste manner of life," frequent neglect of pastoral duties, and embezzlement.[61] The only way he was allowed to leave Germany at all was to plead for mercy from the king, which he received,[62] and to put up bail, which his loyal followers collected from among those waiting in port to depart for America.[63]

No one among the Stephanites looked askance at any of these last-minute arrangements. But then, the Stephanites had never questioned their leader's behavior, instead rushing to his defense whenever they felt he was being unfairly maligned. C. F. W. Walther, when challenged by theologian A. G. Rudelbach's concern over the young pastor's "deification" of Stephan, replied: "Shall I desert the man who by the grace of God has saved my soul?"[64] Those who were intent to follow

---

60. As related by Agnes Buenger's son to Carl Mundinger in Mundinger, *Government in the Missouri Synod*, p. 42 n. 6.

61. Fischer, *Das falsche Märtyrerthum*, p. 53.

62. Koepchen, *Pastor Martin Stephan*, pp. 91-92.

63. Forster, *Zion on the Mississippi*, p. 183.

64. Polack, *The Story of C. F. W. Walther*, p. 32.

Stephan thought they were following God; those who watched them go believed the company was following Satan.

In the early weeks of November 1838 five ships carrying 665 Saxons left Bremen harbor bound for New Orleans. Only four ships arrived. Heavy storms in and around the English Channel likely caused the loss of the *Amalia*, its fifty-six passengers and crew, and most of the company's goods. During the long journey the Saxon pilgrims maintained their religious practice through worship and instruction of the 160 children in the company.[65] The average age of the emigrants was only twenty-five, due in part to a large contingent of unmarried adults. The ratio of women to men was four to five. Most of the men were craftsmen, though the leadership was dominated by men from the professional class, most obviously the clergy.[66]

On board one of the ships an event took place that was to have a dramatic impact on the community as a whole. One pastor had been assigned as leader to each of the vessels, while Stephan and the rest of the clergy were aboard the *Olbers*. As Stephan later wrote:

> Our ecclesiastical polity was to be modeled after the Swedish Lutheran Church, having its government vested in a bishop. That was the general wish of all members of the congregation. When our ship was in the Gulf of Mexico, I was, without any foreknowledge or doing on my part, elected bishop by the clergy and with the full and voluntary approval of the congregation.[67]

Stephan was referring to the action taken on January 14, 1839, when a document drawn by Stephan's pastor and spiritual advisor, O. H. Walther, was signed by the representatives of all those on board the *Olbers* elevating Stephan to the position of bishop. While the Stephanites had already in Saxony begun to refer to Stephan as bishop, there is no evidence that any action to officially confer the title on him had been planned. Various accounts dispute what shipboard developments might have made this action necessary before the company's arrival in America. Did Stephan suddenly realize the many changes that arrival in America would introduce?

65. Walter A. Baepler, *A Century of Grace: A History of the Missouri Synod 1847-1947* (St. Louis: Concordia Publishing House, 1947), p. 25.

66. Forster, *Zion on the Mississippi*, pp. 234-35.

67. Letter from Martin Stephan to the United States consul in Leipzig, October 12, 1841. Quoted in Koepchen, *Pastor Martin Stephan*, p. 162.

He said as much to Vehse that evening: "It must be that I reach American soil as Bishop. You know that I have no other intention; I shall not mince words. All would go lamely if I did not do so!"[68] Or were there some on board who began to weary of or question the authority Stephan had assumed unto himself? Those aboard the *Olbers* were the core leadership of the community, and therefore those whose acknowledgment of Stephan's ultimate authority was most essential. The document they signed that day — Stephan's Investiture[69] — has as its primary feature the establishment of an episcopal polity for the emigrant community:

> You have already for a long time occupied the position of a bishop and performed episcopal functions among us. However, this has become even more apparent since the plan, considered according to God's Word, of transplanting the Lutheran Church from Germany to the United States has been put into execution. You have been recognized by all individual congregations and congregation members as the father of all, as highest shepherd of souls, and as leader; without the name of a bishop you have exercised the office of bishop with paternal kindness, firmness, justice, care, and wisdom. Now that you are about to step on the soil of America, it becomes urgently necessary that this inner, tacit choice receive external and public expression. We have been instructed by you in many things, and from this instruction an abiding conviction has resulted in us that an episcopal form of polity, in accord with the Word of God, with the Old Apostolic Church, and with our Symbolical Writings, is indispensable. Such a form of polity, in which a greater or smaller number of clergymen are subordinated to a bishop in the government of the Church and form a council with him and under his leadership, is therefore our joint, fervent, and earnest desire. . . .
>
> In consequence of all this, therefore, we approach you with the reverent, urgent plea: Accept, Reverend Father, also for the future the office of bishop among us, bestowed upon you by God, and grant that we may now already express with this name our unqualified confidence in your fatherly love and pastoral faithfulness toward us, and the assurance of our sincere, complete, and childlike obedience toward you.

68. Vehse, *The Stephanite Emigration to America*, p. 7.
69. See the appendix for the text as translated by Forster. Original is in the Saxon Immigration Collection, CHI.

The Investiture was signed on board only by the clergy traveling with Stephan. The names of those who had preceded the *Olbers* to New Orleans and St. Louis were added later. It was important that all agreed to Stephan's terms, for he was not a man who courted a loyal opposition. One was either with him or against him. Still, Stephan must have breathed a sigh of relief that all this was achieved so easily. He remarked to Vehse: "Now everything will go actively and bravely forward. It is only to be asked that there be no uneasiness because of recalcitrance or stupidity on part of the people which might make this holy office more difficult."[70] The episcopacy was officially in place.

Once the ships reached New Orleans, people and goods needed to be transferred to steamboats that would take the emigrants up the Mississippi to St. Louis, their intended destination. This task was accomplished in short order except for Stephan's retinue, which delayed its departure from New Orleans for ten days before leaving on board the *Selma*. During the wait supplies were purchased for Stephan by Louise Guenther, specifically assigned to provide "especially for the needs of the Herr Bishop."[71] Once they got underway, what should have been a trip of less than a week lasted three weeks due to low water. During the river journey, Stephan became convinced that the Saxons' devotion to his leadership had been less than unconditional. He sensed opposition, and therefore required a renewal of their loyalty. To that end, on February 16, 1839, another document was drafted, a Pledge of Subjection to Stephan. It reads, in part:

> The lamentable spiritual state of a large part of the congregation which emigrated with us — which state has become manifest during our whole journey and has grown ever more pronounced — has filled us with deep sorrow. The sins which hold sway among us and which especially cause us distress are: great indifference to God's Word and despising of the holy office of the ministry, in particular a damnable spirit of mistrust and dissatisfaction toward our Right Reverend Bishop, which has frequently found expression in shocking insolence, utter lack of all Christian love of one's fellow man; on the other hand, a morbid tendency toward slandering, vengefulness, envy and ill will, hypocrisy and disobedience to the orders given by His Reverence, heathenish unbelief and worldly-mindedness, and all in all

70. Vehse, *The Stephanite Emigration to America*, p. 8.
71. Forster, *Zion on the Mississippi*, p. 216.

such behavior as brings shame and discredit upon the Christian name. . . .

Above all, we affirm and testify before the countenance of the omniscient God, in agreement with the truth, that we have complete and firm confidence in the wisdom, experience, faithfulness, and well-meaning fatherly love of our Very Reverend Bishop; and we abhor all distrustful, suspicious statements and thoughts, in which he is accused of injustice, harshness, aggrandizement, selfishness, carelessness in the administration of our temporal goods, etc.

We reaffirm with sincere heart that we are determined to adhere steadfastly and firmly to God's Word and the pure old-Lutheran confession of faith. We further declare that we are determined to hold fast with heart and soul, to keep most faithfully, and to live, suffer, and die under the episcopal method of church polity.[72]

The text of the Pledge insists that it was being made "voluntarily, without persuasion and haste, after mature consideration,"[73] yet its very necessity raises questions about the company's trust of and enthusiasm for their leader. What egregious charges had been made against him were they renouncing? And why was the episcopacy so vital to their governance as a community?

One member of the group refused to sign this Pledge — H. F. Fischer, one of the trio who had initially laid out Stephan's emigration scheme in Saxony. Stephan was so outraged by Fischer's desertion that he "invoked the gross secular ban" on him, which forbade him from ever living in the Stephanite settlement.[74] For the time being, Fischer remained alone in his stance. Once the *Selma* reached St. Louis, it took O. H. Walther only a week to secure the ratification of Stephan's position as bishop by the clergy who had arrived earlier. Yet another document, a Confirmation of Stephan's Investiture, was signed by four clergy, three candidates, and twelve "deputies" elected by majority vote of the congregations that had sailed on the other three ships.[75] Even an absence of more than three months from Stephan's autocratic presence

---

72. Forster, *Zion on the Mississippi*, pp. 293-94. The document goes on for several pages, repeating much of what the company had already agreed to, and concludes with three paragraphs of personal contrition and deference to Stephan's authority.

73. Forster, *Zion on the Mississippi*, p. 295.

74. Vehse, *The Stephanite Emigration to America*, p. 18.

75. Forster, *Zion on the Mississippi*, pp. 298-301.

gave no pause to these men, whose prompt assent to such a dramatic pronouncement hints at prior awareness and even consent to Stephan's intentions. After all, the establishment of his episcopacy secured the place of the clergy in the hierarchical scheme of the emigration.

The documents signed by the emigrant company assigning Martin Stephan mastery over all aspects of their affairs may appear to be coerced loyalty oaths, but it must be remembered that this community had agreed to an episcopal form of governance while still in Saxony. Their deference to Stephan's "supreme authority" is clearly stated in the traveling regulations that outlined in detail the various dimensions of the *Gesellschaft*, the community. The emigrants had cast their lot with an absolutist leader, and to him they entrusted their fortunes and their future. The various pledges were not part of a reciprocal covenant or compact, however. Stephan was required to pledge nothing in return. If the bishop began to have questions about the solidarity of the company and felt a visible demonstration of his authority would serve as a reminder of the intentions with which they had left Germany, there is no hint that anyone in the company other than Fischer had begun to doubt his leadership. Indeed, the Saxons expressed their devotion to their leader's vision by their willing obedience, as historian E. Theodore Bachmann notes:

> Seldom has any band of immigrants landed on these American shores under such stern marching orders. It seemed . . . they found solace in surrendering their independence. . . . The Stephanists had exchanged the bondage of the past for a new separatism.[76]

In good faith the emigrants agreed to renew their loyalty to the bishop in exchange for the promise he had made of a new Zion. They did not know he would lead them into a spiritual wilderness instead.

On American Soil

An immigration of more than six hundred people was a newsworthy event in St. Louis, the city that served as gateway to the American West in 1839. The Saxons were publicly welcomed in both German and En-

76. Bachmann, "The Rise of Missouri Lutheranism," p. 105.

glish language newspapers, with accompanying advice as was the habit of the press. *Der Anzeiger des Westens,* the first German newspaper west of the Mississippi River and notoriously anticlerical in its editorial stance, reported the Stephanites' arrival by noting that "the intellectual and secular affairs of the community rest almost without any control in the hands of the clergy, who enjoy unqualified authority and obedience in their sect."[77] The *Daily Evening Gazette* advised the Saxons to buy out the departing Mormons, as "we cannot suppose that any sect could make themselves so obnoxious as the Mormonites."[78] The press had become an instrument of considerable influence in this period; opinion was not limited to the editorial page. Religious groups were frequent targets of criticism, especially those who exhibited unfamiliar peculiarities. Newspapers also offered a place to carry on protracted battles between various warring groups. As the central means of mass communication to immigrant communities in the mid-nineteenth century, foreign-language newspapers in particular provided an unparalleled service.

Missouri had been admitted to the Union as a slave state in 1821 under the terms of the Missouri Compromise a year earlier. Until 1803 it had been French, and briefly Spanish, territory, so its primary religious tradition was Roman Catholic, Protestants having been forbidden to settle there prior to 1795.[79] In the wake of Thomas Jefferson's purchase of the Louisiana Territory from the French, migration opened

77. *Anzeiger des Westens,* January 26, 1839. Quoted in Gotthold Guenther, *Die Schicksale und Abentueur der aus Sachsen ausgewanderten Stephanier. Ihre Reise nach St. Louis, ihr Aufenthalt daselbst und Zustand ihrer Colonie in Perry-County* (Dresden: Verlag von C. Heinrich, 1839), pp. 38-39. Guenther was a layman in the emigrant company.

78. *Daily Evening Gazette,* January 22, 1839. Mormons had begun settling in several counties in the northwest corner of Missouri in the mid-1830s after Joseph Smith announced that God had revealed Missouri to him as the site of the new Zion. But local residents, less than pleased with the Mormon influx, objected to the Saints' different beliefs and practice, their separatism, their sense of chosenness, and their unswerving loyalty. By 1838 violence and vigilantism had broken out in full force. The so-called Mormon War ended in the governor's order of expulsion from the state. During the spring of 1839, as the Saxons were arriving in Missouri, the Mormons were relocating across the Mississippi River to Nauvoo, Illinois. See Stephen C. LeSueur, *The 1838 Mormon War in Missouri* (Columbia, Mo.: University of Missouri Press, 1987).

79. Russel L. Gerlach, *Immigrants in the Ozarks: A Study in Ethnic Geography* (Columbia, Mo.: University of Missouri Press, 1976), p. 111.

the territories west of the Mississippi to American settlers, who introduced various forms of Protestantism — Baptist, Presbyterian, Episcopal, and Methodist — into Missouri.[80] Foreign settlers who preceded the Saxons included both German and Irish Catholics. The arrival of the Stephanite Lutherans introduced a new element not only to Missouri but also to Philip Schaff's "motley sampler of all church history."[81]

The Saxons' stay in St. Louis was intended to be temporary, a transitional phase in the emigration, as their plan had always been to purchase a parcel of land where they could live permanently and "separately." The Traveling Regulations spelled out a plan in which groups of men would make "excursions into the surrounding territory" with the goal of purchasing land for the settlement. Other members of the community were instructed to support themselves "by the practice of their trade" in the city. In the meantime, the Credit Fund would provide for those who could not provide for themselves. Upon purchase of the land, all men who could work were to go immediately to the site of settlement to begin construction of the buildings and prepare the land for farming, and once this preliminary work had been done, the remainder of the emigrant community was to follow.[82]

Stephan had his own agenda for this phase of the settlement. He used his two months in St. Louis to enhance the office to which he had been elevated on board ship. Contrary to the Code of the Credit Fund, he continued his control over its management, which he insisted remain in his hands until the land purchase was final. His plans for a set of exquisite clerical vestments, including a mitre, staff, cross and chain, were set into motion despite the loss of the *Amalia,* on which most of the goods of the company had been shipped. A number of women in the company were put to work making these garments and the other items were ordered. In addition, Stephan sent his deputies to attend a Roman Catholic outdoor service in order that they might observe how things were done in that tradition. Stephan busied himself drawing up plans for his residence in the permanent settlement and introduced the

80. R. W. Heintze, "Religious Organization in Missouri Before 1839," *Concordia Historical Institute Quarterly* 1 (1929): 93.

81. Schaff, *America,* p. 80.

82. "Traveling Regulations for the Lutheran *Gesellschaft* Emigrating with Herr Pastor Stephan to the United States of North America," in Forster, *Zion on the Mississippi,* Appendix b, The Codes, pp. 572-76.

practice of having guests who attended events at his home kiss the bishop's hand.[83] That he resumed his habit of nightly walks came as no surprise.

In the meantime, those entrusted with selecting the site of the settlement had found 4,475 acres of riverfront property about one hundred miles south of St. Louis in Perry County. Both accessible government land and a site offered to the immigrants only fifteen miles from the city had been vetoed by Stephan,[84] whose "mind was fixed on the wilderness."[85] Supposedly the land in Perry County, whose hills rise up sharply from the Mississippi River, reminded the purchasing committee of the geography of their Saxon homeland. The sale was finalized in April and May 1839 for $9,234.25, or a bit more than two dollars an acre.[86] An additional one thousand dollars purchased a landing on the river. Promptly on April 26th, Stephan left St. Louis for the site of his new kingdom, taking some, but by no means all, of the Saxon settlers with him.

"News of a Deplorable Character"

The day after Stephan's departure, the Saxon pastors who remained in St. Louis felt it important to place a notice in *Anzeiger des Westens* to defend their bishop against "mendacious inventions of malicious spitefulness."[87] In response to another anticlerical attack the following day, they again declared that there was no hierarchy in their company, and that they were but "a congregation of exiles."[88] The pastors' vigorous defense of their leader was to become for them a regrettable and premature action.

Martin Stephan's grand plan to transplant his Saxon congregants onto American soil, where he could rule over them by their own authority, began to unravel while he was still in St. Louis. His departure for Perry County provided a window of opportunity for some of the increasingly disgruntled Saxons to express their concerns about his leadership.

83. Forster, *Zion on the Mississippi,* pp. 353-54.
84. Gerlach, *Immigrants in the Ozarks,* p. 41.
85. Vehse in Forster, *Zion on the Mississippi,* p. 376.
86. Forster, *Zion on the Mississippi,* pp. 378-79.
87. Koepchen, *Pastor Martin Stephan,* p. 144.
88. Koepchen, *Pastor Martin Stephan,* p. 149.

Some members of the Saxon community, who had earlier been told that "the Church depends on two eyes, the eyes of Bishop Stephan,"[89] opened their own eyes and began to take notice of Stephan's expenditures on himself while in St. Louis, including the purchase of a new carriage, fine wines, the house he was renting, and his personal retinue of live-in seamstresses and a tailor. Vehse, one of the first to suspect Stephan of malfeasance, objected to the appearance the bishop's behavior gave the local population: "Highly proper Americans, who are particularly sensitive about relations with the womenfolk, were mightily offended because of the Bishop's 'house' into which gradually more and more young maids were introduced."[90] Questions began to be raised even among the clergy once Stephan insisted on previewing their sermons. Still they went along with him wordlessly when he banished one of their number, Ernst Buerger, to a woodchoppers' camp outside the city after accusing him of false doctrine and forbidding him any contact even with his own wife.[91] It must be remembered that the position of the clergy in the scheme of the community was entirely dependent on retention of episcopal governance, of which Stephan was the head.

Despite the bishop's behavior, of gravest concern at this point was the Credit Fund. No one knew its status or balance as long as it remained in Stephan's control, and his freewheeling spending signaled his own lack of concern. Knowing that the bulk of the remaining funds were needed for the anticipated land purchase, nevertheless in March Stephan ordered salaries paid to himself and the pastors and candidates and teachers.[92] During the St. Louis interlude, a few of the emigrants had opted out of the community and asked that the money they had invested in the Credit Fund be returned. Some even sued for recovery and won.[93] And still no one knew that there was no money left.

The final thread in Stephan's undoing came from what might be considered his greatest weakness — women. In St. Louis on the first

---

89. Vehse, *The Stephanite Emigration to America,* p. 10.

90. Vehse, *The Stephanite Emigration to America,* p. 11.

91. *Memoirs of Ernst Moritz Buerger,* trans. E. J. Buerger (Lincoln, Mass.: Martin Julian Buerger, 1953), p. 46. Quoted in Meyer, *Moving Frontiers,* p. 136.

92. Forster, *Zion on the Mississippi,* p. 367. Stephan paid himself $500, each pastor $100, each candidate $30, and each teacher $25. No one questioned whether the Credit Fund could support these payments.

93. Koepchen, *Pastor Martin Stephan,* p. 113.

Sunday of May, Pastor Loeber preached a sermon (the text for which is not recorded) which must have spoken directly to several of the women in the pews. Later that day, two women went to Loeber independently to confess sexual liaisons with Stephan, with more women coming forward in the days following. Loeber took this information to C. F. W. Walther, and together they told Pastors Keyl and Buerger, now back from his exile to the woodchoppers' camp. After a week the clergymen told laymen Vehse and Jaeckel. Before long there were only a few in the Saxon community who didn't know. Martin Stephan was one of those.

The St. Louis leadership was unsure of how to proceed with this information. One thing is sure. Whereas in Saxony they had loudly defended their bishop whenever accusations or suggestions of impropriety were raised against him, in America they offered no defense. More than their location had changed; for the first time they were willing to entertain the possibility that the old charges, first made in Dresden, were true. The only issue about which they disagreed was what to do about it. Vehse and some of the laymen wanted to press civil charges against Stephan, but were later advised by "prominent residents" of St. Louis that such an action might result in Stephan's lynching.[94] Walther and the clergy were less sure how to proceed, but they were agreed that they, the clergy, would handle this situation themselves. No laymen were invited to participate in the deliberations.

C. F. W. Walther ("little Walther"), the youngest of the clergy at twenty-seven, was chosen to go to Perry County to spread the news of the charges against Stephan among the settlers there. He arrived on May 15th with a concocted story that the St. Louis Saxons did not want to wait any longer before joining the others in Perry County.[95] Stephan, who had been biding his time in Perry County planning his bishop's palace on a bluff still known as Stephansberg overlooking the Brazeau Creek, was none too pleased to see Walther, especially as he had given orders that no one was to come into the settlement without the bishop's permission. Walther's presence was an annoyance that Stephan tried to avoid for most of a week. He began to speak of a conspiracy against him. He was not wrong.

After a week in Perry County, Walther returned to St. Louis, where he and the other clergy alone made two decisions: one, they needed to

---

94. Vehse, *The Stephanite Emigration to America,* p. 13.
95. Vehse, *The Stephanite Emigration to America,* p. 13.

proceed with somehow removing Stephan from the community, and two, the primary charge against him would be financial mismanagement. For a time they had considered simply suspending him from office, but they later decided that he needed to be both deposed and excommunicated. All of these actions they claimed were within their realm of authority as clergy. Though Vehse continued to raise what he saw as a pressing issue, that of separating the business or secular affairs of the community from the spiritual, the pastors told him it was not an appropriate time to discuss that. The clergy would handle the situation.

On May 29th, the rest of the Saxon emigrants left St. Louis on two riverboats for Perry County. There they would join not only those from the company who had previously traveled south with Stephan, but an additional 108 Saxons who had just arrived by way of New York with J. F. Buenger, who had delayed sailing until December (when his mother was released from jail on the "stolen children" charge). Before they left St. Louis, the clergy arranged for a notice to appear in the June 1st issue of *Der Anzeiger des Westens,* which said in part that they had been "victims of a disgraceful deception by this man" and that they had "defended him in ignorance and loyal affection."[96] And they recanted their statement of just a month earlier in which they had insisted on upholding his honor.

The question of how to proceed against Stephan still remained unsettled even after both boatloads of Saxons arrived. Pastors Keyl and Loeber, wearing clerical robes and bands, went to Stephan's home to read him the charges and tell him of a council meeting to be held the next morning. Stephan twice refused to attend, claiming no council had any authority over him and that he "was not aware of having committed anything wrong."[97] So the council of clergy and laymen met without Stephan, at which time they excommunicated him from the congregation and pronounced a sentence of deposition upon him, which they read to the assembled people and then to Stephan himself. The sentence claimed he had "committed sins of fornication and adultery, as well as of profligate malfeasance with alien properties," and that he was guilty of false teaching.[98]

96. Koepchen, *Pastor Martin Stephan,* p. 155.
97. Stephan's letter to the U.S. consul in Leipzig. Quoted in Koepchen, *Pastor Martin Stephan,* p. 165.
98. Vehse, *The Stephanite Emigration to America,* pp. 124-25.

Even after hearing the sentence pronounced, Stephan refused to leave his home. At that point the people began to agitate. Some took it upon themselves to search his house, where they found no small amount of money. The crowd's actions frightened Stephan, who asked Vehse to protect him from "the rabble outside."[99] Suddenly the once magisterial bishop was a dethroned old man of sixty-two in danger of destitution, convinced he was too old to work to support himself. But there was little sympathy left among a people who had committed their future and their fortunes to this "spiritual deceiver."[100] The leadership drew up one further document in which Stephan was required to renounce any claim on the community. He was allowed to keep a few items of clothing and furniture, books, and one hundred dollars. Finally he was given a choice: return to Germany, face trial in America, or be ferried across the river to Illinois. Stephan chose exile. Since it was by this time late in the day, the company agreed to let their former leader stay the night, but not in his house, so he spent the night with his Bible in a tent near the river. The next morning, on the last day of May 1839, Martin Stephan was rowed across the Mississippi River by Teacher Mueller and Henry Bimpage, the company's land agent. The deposed bishop was set ashore at a rock formation called Devil's Bakeoven with a spade and an ax and instructions not to attempt to return to the Perry County settlement.

One thing Stephan did not lose as a result of this episode was his hubris. He violated the ban against returning to Missouri on several occasions, and even sued the Saxons in 1841 in an attempt to recover damages from them. After repeated continuances, the Perry County Circuit Court, in its June 1842 term, found the defendants — the clergy and lay leaders still in Perry County — guilty on two counts, one of trespass and one of unlawful appropriation of property. Stephan had sued for damages of five thousand dollars, the "great value" he placed on a lengthy inventory of personal property he claimed had been kept from him. His petition on the charge of trespass charged the defendants had "with force and arms made an assault on said Plaintiff, and beat, wounded, and ill-treated him so that his life was despaired of," then "imprisoned him," and broke into his home to seize his property before putting him over the river. He again assessed his damages at five thou-

99. Vehse, *The Stephanite Emigration to America,* p. 16.
100. Vehse, *The Stephanite Emigration to America,* p. 2.

sand dollars. In each case the court awarded him damages in the sum of one cent and court costs.[101]

Attorney Vehse records a slightly different story about the final resolution of Stephan's removal: Vehse himself walked with the rather pitiful-looking Stephan to the "ferry," or rowboat, with Stephan all the while complaining about the injustice of the treatment accorded him. A room had already been rented for him on the Illinois side of the river, and the cane he carried with him was reported to be hollow, in order that Stephan might smuggle additional money stolen from the Credit Fund. Funds were later found to be missing. Still Vehse remained unconvinced that buying Stephan out was an appropriate action for a Christian congregation. "It was basically wrong," he wrote.[102]

Once Stephan had been removed, the clergy decided it wanted to question his housekeeper, the ever-loyal Louise Guenther. The woman admitted to having a sexual relationship with Stephan, and implicated without accusing seven other women.[103] Within days of this questioning Guenther herself was missing, having followed Stephan to Horse Prairie, Illinois, where she lived with him until his death seven years later in 1846.

When word of the events in Perry County reached St. Louis, a local newspaper noted in its edition of June 15th: "News of a deplorable character is reaching us from the 'Old Lutheran' settlement in Perry County."[104] Little did anyone reading that notice know the paradox embedded in that observation.

101. *Martin Stephan v. Frederick Wm. Barthel, Henry C. Bimpage, Gustav Jaeckel, Ernst G. W. Keyl, and Francis Marbach,* Trover and Conversion, Circuit Court of Perry County, Missouri, no. 600; *Martin Stephan v. Gotthold H. Loeber, Ernest W. Keyl, Ernest M. Buenger, Henry C. Bimpage, Frederick W. Barthel, Francis A. Marbach, John G. Palisch, and Gustavus Jaeckel,* Trespass Vi et Armis, Circuit Court of Perry County, Missouri, no. 601; 1841-1842. Petitions, affidavits, and court orders are in the Saxon Immigration Collection, CHI.

102. Vehse, *The Stephanite Emigration to America,* p. 17. Bachmann cites a rare confession allegedly attributed to Stephan in which he admitted to "unnecessary expenditures." The entire issue of the accounting of the company's finances remains unresolved.

103. Forster, *Zion on the Mississippi,* pp. 426-27.

104. Polack, *The Story of C. F. W. Walther,* p. 46.

"What Are We?"[105]

Before the Saxons had even had time to consider what it meant to be transplanted into a new homeland, their identity as an ecclesial community had been shaken to its core as a result of the Stephan episode. Having migrated for primarily religious motivations, they had to wonder whether there was reason any longer to stay in Missouri.

The Saxons' problems were unlike those besetting other Lutherans in the United States. While the "New Lutherans" and the "Moderate Lutherans" were also debating issues of ecclesial identity, those groups had begun a process of Americanization, most obviously by adopting English as their language of worship. In contrast, the Saxons were confronted with a question fundamental to the very nature of their transatlantic transplanting. They had organized themselves as a church, traveled together as a church, pledged themselves as congregants to their pastor. Now, without the bishop, were they still a church?

What exactly was left? The settlers would be haunted by questions over the two years following Stephan's exile, a period of grief and loss that was compounded by the strangeness of their new surroundings. They retained what remnants of identity were left in Stephan's wake through the solidarity of shared language and experience and as a result were frequently criticized by neighbors for their exclusiveness.

Having experienced dramatic change during its first few months in America, for the time being the structure of the Saxon community continued as outlined by the regulations Stephan had drawn up for the settlement. The most immediate impact came once the Credit Fund was audited and was found to be almost totally depleted. The effect of that news was profound, as the settlers learned that there would no longer be provisions made for their food or shelter. From this point on, each was responsible for the survival of one's self and family unit.

The day after Stephan's exile, on June 1st, though they considered themselves still the ruling segment of the colony, the clergy took action to legitimate their status. When they left Germany each had resigned his call to the congregation he served there. In the interim they had no calls. What, then, were they, especially now that they had no bishop to confirm their ministry? Quickly they subdivided the Perry County acre-

---

105. Pastor Buerger's question, in his memoirs, p. 49. Quoted in Meyer, *Moving Frontiers*, p. 137.

age into five sections, distributing the land among those who had paid into the Credit Fund. Each section was named after a town in Germany which the settlers had left and each pastor joined those who had been in his congregation there[106] — Loeber went to Altenburg; Keyl's people settled Frohna; C. F. W. Walther took Dresden; and Buerger founded Seelitz. The fifth section was Wittenberg, "the city" to be built at the landing on the Brazeau River. For the time being, no pastor was assigned there. This plan, designed to authenticate the pastors' place in the post-Stephan emigration scheme, for the first time (other than when they were at sea) broke the community into separate congregations.

Since the disclosures about Stephan had first been made public, Vehse had never stopped raising the issue of a division of power between the secular and spiritual dimensions of the community. Now he demanded to know, who was going to be in charge? There was no singular presence in Stephan's absence, no charismatic figure who could fill his void. For good or ill, the reality of Stephan's now-vanished absolutism revealed no heir apparent. The bishop had far outdistanced his lieutenants in both age and experience. What was left after his downfall was a handful of very young clergymen whose average age was thirty-four. While Vehse was hardly older than that himself, he remained uncomfortable enough with the leadership potential of the clergy that he continued to bring up the question of dividing the administrative authority, and the clergy continued to insist that they were serving as the stipulated "ministerium" and that was as it should be according to the intention of the emigration and settlement codes.[107]

Vehse did not waver from his objection, claiming that the changed circumstances offered a perfect opportunity for "a thorough review" of the Stephan episode. At first the clergy agreed, but as Vehse recalls,

> When lay members of the congregation, voluntarily coming forward, actually took part in discussion, desiring to participate in the general conduct of affairs, the clergy became of another mind and opposition developed. They explained: "Not everything about Stephan was wrong; in many matters he acted rightly; it is regrettable that the clerical office is so slightly honored, a misfortune that there is no one

106. Meyer, *Moving Frontiers,* p. 137.
107. Forster, *Zion on the Mississippi,* p. 438.

who has such authority as Stephan had — a second Stephan is needed."[108]

The clergy may have lost their leader but they had not lost their understanding of the ministerial office, nor their intention that the colony be maintained under clergy rule. Their primary dilemma in the wake of Stephan's deposition was how they would replace him, and with whom. Why the laymen felt it was suddenly appropriate to reconsider totally the construct on which the emigration had been built must have seemed like folly to the devastated pastors. But nothing was more serious in Vehse's mind. The clergy's resistance left the laymen little choice, so Vehse and his friends Fischer and Jaeckel resigned from the Administrative Board on which they had served. Their frustration stemmed from the clergy's refusal to consider a plan for division of the land, still held in the whole by the community, to the clergy's failure to see the need for financial restructuring when only two thousand dollars remained in the Credit Fund, to the general lack of resolution of issues within the community, to a lack of clarity over authority and management.[109] The laymen's resignations left the clergy right where they thought they wanted to be — in charge — though almost totally incapable of knowing how to proceed.

Vehse and friends, while no longer involved in administration of the settlement, continued to agitate by keeping their central question before the clergy. Before long they added an additional challenge by questioning the clergy's accountability in the emigration scheme at large.[110] On September 19th the three laymen issued a "Protestation," the purpose of which, according to Vehse, was

> to represent the relationship of the clergy to their congregations according to divine ordinance, as they are set forth in the Bible and in the confessional writings of our church. . . . It defines the bounds within which the three estates of the preaching office, the government, and the congregation are to move. And in this respect it is a contribution to Protestant church polity. Most particularly, this writing is concerned with the rights of congregations.[111]

108. Vehse, *The Stephanite Emigration to America,* pp. 18-19.
109. Vehse, *The Stephanite Emigration to America,* p. 126.
110. Forster, *Zion on the Mississippi,* p. 442.
111. Vehse, *The Stephanite Emigration to America,* p. 21.

This Protest, based on an exaggerated understanding of the fundamental Lutheran doctrine of the priesthood of all believers, outlined in painful detail the misuse of the ministry by "the false Stephanite system" in order to elevate the status of the clergy. In three chapters, Vehse addressed (1) the rights of a congregation, (2) Stephanism's disregard of the rights of a congregation, and (3) the legitimacy of the Saxon emigration, which he considered "of the devil, a matter of lies and deceit."[112] The document went on at length to elaborate each of these points, buttressed by supporting citations from scripture, the symbolic writings, Luther, and frequent quotes from pietist theologian Phillip Jacob Spener.

The Protest served as a letter of indictment against the pastors. The laymen believed that the clergymen knew already in Germany what Stephan was about, but chose to follow him anyway, drawn by his posture on the elevated status of the ministry, as it served to enhance their own stature:

> The teaching of the office of the ministry was by Stephan torn altogether from its context, and represented by the clergy as exercising rights without the same having duties over against the congregation, therefore as having an independent office ordained of God, to whom alone they were accountable. He said nothing of the office of the spiritual priesthood, which is in exact and necessary relation to the office of the ministry. Thus he made the office of the ministry a bugbear, such as is used to frighten children.[113]

On November 9th, having had no answer to the Protestation from the clergy, the three laymen added a Supplement to the Protest. Five days later they issued a Closing Statement claiming that the manner in which the clergy handled Stephan's deposition was the root of their dispute. Here, finally, was the primary complaint and key issue — the clergy had refused to allow the laymen any participation in the ultimate disposition of Stephan. Insisting that it was an ecclesiastical decision that was theirs alone ignored the part the laymen had played in the organization and implementation of the emigration, and of their partnership in the management of the civil affairs of the community. The

112. Vehse, "A Summary of the Protestation," in *The Stephanite Emigration to America,* p. 40.
113. Vehse, "A Summary of the Protestation," p. 102.

entire enterprise had been located in and depended on the person of the bishop. No structure or provision had been made for life without him. For six months now those who had cast their lot with Stephan had been cast adrift regarding governance of the community in his absence.

It was November 20th when the clergy finally responded to any of this correspondence. They answered by means of a brief letter written in what the laymen called "a distant tone," admitting that they had "unknowingly allowed themselves to be used as tools to further hierarchical Stephanistic designs" and that they now "wholeheartedly renounce and detest such ungodly priestly domination and tyranny over souls, now that its true nature has increasingly been brought to light." And then they declared that *for the sake of peace* they would also renounce any form of episcopal polity, even though it was permitted in scripture and practiced in prior times.[114] This is key — the clergy never changed their fundamental notion of the ministerial office, but merely adjusted their stance on church governance. They continued to cast the blame on Stephan and claimed their ignorance of his intentions, but they never renounced the episcopal system under which the emigration had been organized. Other than a repetition of their renunciation of Stephan the man, they conceded little, and they never addressed the itemized charges leveled against them in the Protest.

They may not have known how to answer. The reticence of the clergy may have been due in part to having their position challenged by persons holding a fundamentally different understanding of ministry than their own. Vehse's Protest placed the authority of ministry squarely in the universal priesthood of all believers by virtue of baptism, but this is not the basis for the office of ministry according to Luther or the Lutheran confessions, which regard the ministry of the Word to be a particular ministry to which some are permanently called out and set apart by ordination. The Saxon clergy understood the confessional basis of ministry far better than did the laymen, which is why they subscribed to the position on episcopal polity they did. Nevertheless, the positions of laymen and clergy were directly at odds.

The months of silence on the part of the pastors hinted that this would be a protracted debate. Vehse decided to return to Germany, and he wrote his account of the emigration, *Die Stephan'sche Auswanderung*, as he sailed home in the winter of 1840. Obviously dispirited by the to-

---

114. Vehse, "A Summary of the Protestation," pp. 114-16. Emphasis added.

tality of events over the past year, he admitted to "having in the Stephanite emigration lost so much in the way of 'Christian community.'"[115] Yet he did not write simply to make public the whole sordid story, but because he felt compelled to leave a record of his analysis for those who stayed in Perry County. Vehse believed the publication of his account was essential for the community he left behind:

> It is urgently necessary that the members of the congregation themselves quietly and thoroughly evaluate the situation in which they find themselves and come to precise understanding of the hierarchical schemes that were in store for them and which our writing now exposes. Such is only then possible if the account is printed and circulates among them in numerous copies instead of being found only in a single handwritten copy. Reading or hearing only once affects little; each individual must for himself deliberately consider this unparalleled deception from all sides.[116]

Critics, both contemporary and current, have accused Vehse of being both anticlerical and meanspirited, yet his account of the emigration remains the most honest assessment written by a participant.

The actions of the Vehse trio were the spark that ignited a genuine war of words within the Saxon settlement that lasted for almost two years, for the laymen's challenge went to the heart of the Stephanite migration — where was the authority in the church? Did it rest with the people or with the pastors? On what ultimate authority does the governing authority rest? The very nature of the challenge polarized the community into two factions, those who supported the protesting laymen and those who stood with the clergy. The struggle that ensued is a reflection of the difficulty with which the ministry is defined in the Lutheran tradition. The crisis that followed Stephan's deposition was far more serious than Stephan's betrayal of his followers' trust, which helped inaugurate it. Dispute over definition of church and ministry, viewed by the disillusioned emigrants through the lens of their own recent experience, led to an anomie that lingered in the colony for almost two years and became the capstone of the defining decade in Missouri Synod history.

Pastor Buerger raised the fundamental questions in his account

115. Vehse, "A Summary of the Protestation," p. 136.
116. Vehse, "A Summary of the Protestation," p. 19.

of the "spiritual distress" in which the colonists found themselves in the summer of 1839:

> Doubt began to be expressed concerning the legitimacy of our emigration. The question arose: What are we? Did our pastors rightfully resign their office in Germany? Do they here have a proper call? Are they not seducers, who have enticed us to this man, and helped toward tearing asunder family ties, so that children forsook their parents and spouses their mates? Are we to be designated a Lutheran congregation, and is the Lutheran Church in our midst, the Lutheran ministry, the rightful administration of the Sacraments, etc.? . . . The confidence had been shaken.[117]

Profound questions about the very identity of the church in America pervaded the Perry County settlement, even though there had been some positive changes. In August the communal land had finally been divided and deeded to individual members of the emigration; in September a log cabin college was built by the candidates, and the coveted school was opened in December. They had survived the heat of a Missouri summer and its dreaded mosquitoes, and they had not yet seen the things they feared most: Indians, wild beasts, and Mexican soldiers.[118] A variety of fevers cost them some souls, and the depletion of the Credit Fund threw them back on their own resources. These things they could deal with — issues of survival. But as news of Vehse's departure and the laymen's quarrel with the clergy spread through the colony, a dark mood settled in with the winter.

The clergy called a Day of Penance for the Perry County congregations on November 29, 1839, at which they again repeated their regret over their blind allegiance to Stephan. But by its limitation, their repentance sounded hollow, for there was no agreement among them about the extent of their error. Walter Forster, historian of the Saxon migration, describes the problem:

> The fact was, the pastors were uncertain individually and in disagreement among themselves and with their people as to just what was wrong, wherein they had erred and still did err, what they ought to

117. Buerger, trans., *Memoirs of Ernst Moritz Buerger,* p. 49. Quoted in Meyer, *Moving Frontiers,* p. 137.

118. Loeber in a letter to relatives in Germany. Quoted in Baepler, *A Century of Grace,* p. 17.

admit and what not. This uncertainty and lack of consensus among the pastors reacted unfavorably upon the people, who neither knew nor could explain exactly what they thought about themselves or the pastors, or what they expected of the latter. But while there was no unanimity among the people, the scruples, vacillation, and uncertainty of the clergy naturally tended to lower respect for them and to prompt the people to become more extreme in their views and more exacting in their demands. Partial confessions from the pastors fanned the growing flames of resentment at those who had deceived, misled, and — some said — defrauded them.[119]

And so the people proceeded to press the issue. They wanted to know what the pastors had to say about the emigration. Had it been a good thing or evil? All they had in writing was the statement of the three laymen. The congregation in St. Louis, where O. H. Walther was pastor, sent for a copy of Vehse's Protest. Teacher J. F. F. Winter wrote that many of the people desired that the pastors, in answer to the lay theses, write something "on the whole Stephanistic tendency," which "was not at once clearly recognized by us."[120] Calls and actions on the part of the laity prompted "a regular epidemic of confessions,"[121] letters of apology, and position papers on the nature of the emigration from clergy, candidates, and teachers. The candidates refused to preach. Buerger was so tormented that he seesawed between resigning his call and apologizing to his congregation. C. F. W. Walther lapsed into a period of depression and could not even serve his parish, writing in despair to his brother in St. Louis: "My conscience . . . calls me a kidnapper, a robber . . . , a murderer . . . , a member of a mob, a mercenary, an idolator. . . ."[122] Loeber wrote a Renunciation of Stephanism in which he acknowledged his own guilt.[123] But not even the pastors' self-disclosure of grief or regret seemed to lighten the deep sense of despair that held the Saxon community in its grip.

119. Forster, *Zion on the Mississippi,* pp. 508-9.

120. J. F. F. Winter, "Mr. J. Frederick Ferdinand Winter's Account of the Stephanite Emigration," trans. Paul H. Burgdorf, *Concordia Historical Institute Quarterly* 12 (1940): 123-24. Winter wrote his recollections of the entire episode beginning with the emigration in a letter to relatives in Germany dated April 1841.

121. Mundinger, *Government in the Missouri Synod,* p. 102.

122. Forster, *Zion on the Mississippi,* p. 515.

123. Buerger, trans., *Memoirs of Ernst Moritz Buerger,* p. 50. Quoted in Meyer, *Moving Frontiers,* 140.

It is likely that many would have packed up and returned to Germany if they had held the resources to do so. But there was nothing left in the Fund that had brought them to Missouri. Without resolution to this crisis the community would surely dissolve. In the absence of Vehse, the chief protester, Marbach, assumed leadership of the laymen's position. He was joined by Pastor Buerger and by F. W. Barthel, treasurer of the community.

In January 1841 O. H. Walther died suddenly in St. Louis. His grieving congregation voted to call his brother C. F. W. to be their pastor. But the younger Walther felt he could not respond to the call as long as he was embroiled in the standoff in Perry County. He had, after considerable study of Luther's writings, come to reconsider Vehse's arguments, and he proposed a modified version of Vehse's theses as listed in the Protest as an alternative to dissolving the community.

Early in March Marbach delivered a manifesto charging that the entire Saxon enterprise had been wrong, that they were not a church at all, and their only recourse was to admit their corporate sin and return to Germany.[124] As a result of this direct challenge to the Saxons' continued existence as a community, a public debate was called for April in the little log cabin college. In the absence of leadership from the other clergy, Walther offered to present his new vision for the community. Attorney Marbach took the opposing side. The task of this disputation was to settle the prevailing question, "Are we a Church of God or only a rabble?"[125] Marbach argued that by separating itself from the church in Germany through emigration, the Saxons were no better than a sect, and might as well return home in repentance. Walther held that they were in fact a church despite all they had suffered and set out eight theses to support his position. His redefinition of the church, as the totality of all believers, brought relief, assurance, and legitimacy to the community. They had not sold their souls to Stephan after all. Walther's affirmation of the Saxons' existence as the visible church, through adherence to word and sacrament and common confessions, allowed them the opportunity to begin again. His adoption of a modified version of Vehse's insistence on the rights of the congregation appeased the laity in their position that they were indeed the church. But the perpetual question of which came first, pastor or people, though seem-

124. Mundinger, *Government in the Missouri Synod,* p. 110.
125. Polack, *The Story of C. F. W. Walther,* p. 47.

ingly settled by Walther's ceding to Vehse's argument, and reiterated in his many subsequent writings on church and ministry, remained the residue of the Stephan decade. Walther started with the question that needed to be answered first, and his Altenburg theses did not settle any question other than whether the Saxons now in Missouri could call themselves a church. While not outlining a doctrine of the ministry, Walther did present a straightforward doctrine of the church. For the time being, that was enough.

By the codes under which they had organized themselves, and by reiteration of those terms in shipboard pledges, the Saxon emigrants had mistakenly conflated the identity of their community with the identity of one individual, their bishop Martin Stephan. When that individual was removed from their midst, what remained to define the community? In addressing the question, "what are we?" Walther never attempted to defend or even explain the end of the episcopacy, but developed his case on completely different terms. Nowhere in his Altenburg theses does he identify the church with an individual, but everywhere with the community. Yes, they were church.

The Altenburg Debates, held on April 15th and 21st, 1841 — according to one contemporary "the Easter Day of our sorely tried congregation,"[126] — brought to a close the bitter divisiveness of the post-Stephan period and marked the end of the formative decade in the Saxon church's history. Within days, Walther left for St. Louis, where he led his brother's church to prominence as the mother church of the Missouri Synod, and he, at age twenty-nine, accepted the mantle of leadership of both Saxon congregations and clergy.

Conclusion

The decade of events described under the term *Stephanism* is not a well-known story among Missouri Synod Lutherans. But this foundational episode in the synod's history was formative to its character and deserves close scrutiny. Within six years of the Altenburg Debates, a church body was born whose organization and doctrine were definitively shaped by key players and lessons from the Stephan decade. If

126. George A. Schieferdecker, Missouri Synod, Western District, *Proceedings*, 1856, p. 7.

Stephan's story had turned out differently and he had not been deposed in disgrace, then certainly this history would not only be better known, it would qualify as myth, the founding tale. But because it does not cast a favorable light on the founders, because it raises hard questions about the intentions of the Saxon emigration, and because it shook the founding community to its very core, it has instead been dispatched in the official accounts as an anomaly.

In-house histories of The Lutheran Church–Missouri Synod treat the Saxon emigration episode in a consistently curious manner. The whole story of the emigration from Saxony is held up as a noble venture led by true men of God, even though its principal leader proved himself unworthy shortly after their arrival in the United States.[127] To simply dismiss Stephan as a womanizer or embezzler without looking more deeply at the men who followed him and how they received that information is no more accurate. It was popular in the days and months immediately following Stephan's deposition to blame him for every trouble the emigrants encountered. But the clergy's claim of being duped did not absolve them from their own culpability and complicity in the community's distress.

From where does the later genius of Walther come if not out of the lessons he and his brother clergy learned from their blind devotion to Stephan? There is no evidence to suggest that their convictions about the elevation of human authority in the ministerial office left them when Stephan did. The resistance of the clergy to Vehse's Protest and their dogged refusal to make a wholesale confession of their collaboration in advancing the Stephanite episcopacy through emigration allies them with the hierarchical model of ministry Stephan established and intended. The ease with which they cast the blame on Stephan for the deceit he practiced on them relieved the pastors of their own collu-

---

127. In 1938, to commemorate the centennial of the Saxon emigration, the Missouri Synod produced a full-length film, "Call of the Cross." It was widely distributed to congregations throughout the synod, hand-carried in some cases by seminary graduates who had not yet been ordained because there were so few congregational calls during the Depression. The film was made with local actors on the grounds of Concordia Seminary, St. Louis, and depicts Stephan as the original leader of the emigration. However, after a dramatic scene in which he drops to his knees in prayer as the emigrant company reaches the Perry County site, Stephan simply disappears from the film without comment, at which point Walther assumes leadership — both of the people and of the rest of the story.

sion in his grand scheme to establish a clerical autocracy in the Missouri wilderness. As students these men had become completely enchanted with and devoted to Stephan, their father confessor. His sway over their most formative years, their young adulthood, had lasting impact. They remained in his company and carried out his wishes with little hint that they ever questioned anything Stephan said or did. G. H. Loeber described their error as "consent by silence."[128] Perhaps most interesting, after examining the length and depth of their loyalty in Saxony and through the emigration itself, is how quickly they turned on Stephan when the same accusations that had been made against him repeatedly in Germany were heard in America.

The clergy's inability to even respond to the charges of the laymen's Protest for a matter of months indicates not only their resistance to any model of church organization other than the episcopacy, but also how incapable they were of functioning apart from Stephan's dynamic leadership. The pastors could neither agree among themselves nor exercise authoritative leadership within the community. Because their only experience of church structure had been either the consistorial system in Saxony or the episcopal system under Stephan, his deposition left a leadership vacuum that threatened the future of the entire emigration enterprise. Stephan had commanded tremendous authority through his pastoral office, but the people were unwilling to invest any clergy with that kind of authority ever again. In turn, the pastors remained unwilling to assume the leadership called for either by their office or the situation itself. It should be no surprise that the colony floundered until the primary question of its identity had been resolved. Once they had been assured, by means of Walther's Altenburg theses, that despite the desperate circumstances of their early months in America, the Saxon remnant was indeed a church, then identity for both pastors and people was clarified. A church was necessary to call a pastor. The next step would involve redefining the terms of the relationship between pastor and people.

The Perry County dilemma, however, revealed the tension between the two aspects of Lutheran understanding of ministry, since the case made by the laymen in the Protest was not based on ideas totally unfamiliar to the clergy. Stress on the universal priesthood of believers that minimized but did not deny the distinction between clergy and la-

128. Loeber, *History of the Saxon Lutheran Immigration*, p. 4.

ity was a remnant of the pietism which had been so much a part of their practice in Saxony. The pastors eventually acknowledged the contribution of the laymen in introducing clarity in the midst of crisis through the careful explication of issues as laid out in the Protest.[129]

The paradox of the Stephan decade lies in its resolution. The Saxons left Germany claiming they could not there practice a true confessional Lutheranism, but the eventual shape of their church in America was very different from what either the Lutheran confessions or its founder Stephan had envisioned a church to be. Planting their church on American soil allowed the Saxons opportunity to redefine through compromise what had been taken for granted in Germany regarding church structure.

Still, the resolution of the Stephanite crisis resulted in the clergy agreeing in principle with a modified congregationalism as their stated church polity, but with a profound ambivalence with regard to their status as pastors. They had left Germany as *Standespersonen,* members of one of the highest and most respected classes in society, and came to America, land of the separation of church and state and above all — where religion was concerned — of voluntarism. Their entire concept of authority in terms of the office of ministry had been upended. Walther may have staved off crisis by redefining the church at Altenburg, but the experience of the defining decade would leave the ministry itself in a perpetual state of redefinition.

129. A. C. Stellhorn, "The Saxon Centennial and the Schools, IV. Rescue from Doctrinal Uncertainty," *Lutheran School Journal* 74 (1939): 393.

3

Establishing an Identity:
The Nineteenth Century

Within days following the Altenburg debates, C. F. W. Walther had traveled to St. Louis to tell the members of his brother's congregation in person that he would accept the call to be their pastor. The colonists in Perry County, meanwhile, continued the business of adjusting to their new homeland, but with one essential difference. The question over the legitimacy of their enterprise had been settled with Walther's presentation of his theses on the church. They could carry on in good conscience.

Those Saxons who had chosen to stay in St. Louis from the time of the original landing had organized a congregation under Pastor Otto Herman Walther. They had been given permission by Christ Episcopal Church to use either its sanctuary or its basement for worship on Sunday afternoons, and they continued to do so for three years. And while they did not seem to suffer in the same way the post-Stephan identity crisis of their Perry County coreligionists, still the St. Louis Saxons retained a vested interest in the questions that were being raised and in the welfare of their fellow emigrants. They had, after all, been a part of the joint venture, as had their pastor. Following publication of Vehse's Protest in November 1839, O. H. Walther's congregation officially rebuked their pastor for his loyalty to Stephan,[1] then sent for a copy of the Protest in order to study the issues.

1. Walter O. Forster, *Zion on the Mississippi: The Settlement of the Saxon Lutherans in Missouri 1839-1841* (St. Louis: Concordia Publishing House, 1953), p. 469.

This St. Louis congregation was eventually to become both mother church and model for other churches of the Saxon Lutherans, but when C. F. W. Walther began his ministry there it had neither a building of its own nor a name. As the Saxons believed in the concurrent establishment of preaching and teaching stations (church and school), the one thing it did have was a parochial school, which had been started shortly after the immigrants' arrival in St. Louis. The first teacher, Carl Ludwig Geyer,[2] had been succeeded by Walther's longtime friend, J. F. Buenger. The congregation soon purchased a lot on Lombard Street between Third and Fourth, and construction of a church building began.[3] Affirming the primacy of the laity in the management of the temporal affairs of the congregation — the lesson he learned from Vehse and friends — while accepting his own pastoral responsibility to guide in doctrine and worship, Walther did not suggest a name himself, but instead offered guidelines by which the members themselves might select a name for their parish. Following their pastor's belief that a church should not be named for a man, but should proclaim by its name a confession, Walther's parishioners named their church Trinity.[4]

Based on his newfound commitment to an autonomous congregational polity, Walther then suggested the parish develop a constitution as an instrument for its governance, local structure being especially necessary in his mind in the absence of state authority such as the German consistory. The process by which the Trinity constitution came into being was purposefully deliberate, for the governing model would reflect the lessons learned from the Stephanite episode. Among the laity there was strong suspicion of and vocal opposition to any form of hierarchical structure, to the degree that the pastor was not allowed to attend congregational voters' meetings. Yet the congregation recognized its need for pastoral leadership and especially depended on him to provide the appropriate citations from "Father Luther" that were so important to its decision-making process.[5] So Walther himself

2. A. C. Stellhorn, "The Saxon Centennial and the Schools: III. Settlement in Missouri," *Lutheran School Journal* 74 (1939): 343.

3. W. G. Polack, *The Story of C. F. W. Walther* (St. Louis: Concordia Publishing House, 1947), p. 61.

4. Polack, *The Story of C. F. W. Walther*, p. 61.

5. Ernest Theodore Bachmann, "The Rise of Missouri Lutheranism" (Ph.D. diss., University of Chicago, 1946), p. 142.

drafted a constitution and proposed it to his people. The document was based on scripture, the Lutheran confessions, and the principle of congregational autonomy developed from Walther's Altenburg compromise. It outlined in twenty-one paragraphs the rights and responsibilities of the membership.[6] By spring of 1843 the constitution was ready for adoption, but only by male members of the 325-member parish.[7] The question of women's participation had been raised during the study process, but as was the case in antebellum American civil society, the women of Trinity would not have the right to vote, only the right to "declare that they belong to the congregation."[8]

The issue in Perry County in 1841 had been whether the gathered emigrants could legitimately consider themselves a church. By his articulation of theses on the church at Altenburg, Walther had resolved that issue. Now in St. Louis, as pastor of a growing congregation, the more pressing issue was the ministry. Vehse and the laymen had challenged the clergy with their Protest's heavy emphasis on the universal priesthood. The relationship between the two elements of the ministry required clarification, especially among people so previously reliant on the person of a charismatic clergyman.

In 1842 Walther articulated the basis of his doctrine of ministry in a sermon preached on the twelfth Sunday after Trinity. He outlined the rights and duties of the "spiritual priesthood" that belonged to every Christian, with an oblique reference to the Saxons' recent history:

> If Christian congregations do not want to come again under a human yoke, an ungodly human domination, they must hold fast to the precious right of the spiritual priesthood, which all Christians possess. This priesthood is their right to present offerings, to pray, to search the Scriptures, to examine and judge all teachings, to teach one another, and to exhort, admonish, and comfort one another. . . .
>
> Through holy baptism, every Christian has been consecrated, ordained, and installed into the ministry. . . .

6. Constitution of Trinity Lutheran Church, St. Louis, Missouri, 1843, in Carl S. Meyer, *Moving Frontiers: Readings in the History of the Lutheran Church–Missouri Synod* (St. Louis: Concordia Publishing House, 1964), pp. 167-69.

7. Polack, *The Story of C. F. W. Walther,* p. 62.

8. Carl S. Mundinger, *Government in the Missouri Synod: The Genesis of Decentralized Government in the Missouri Synod* (St. Louis: Concordia Publishing House, 1947), p. 146.

> Women as well as men, young as well as old — all Christians are
> spiritual priests and teachers of the word. . . .
> Every Christian . . . is a teacher of the Gospel.[9]

Following the development of his theme that every Christian was "by
the call of Christian love" a *Seelsorger,* a caretaker of the souls of others,
Walther went on to differentiate the spiritual priesthood from the pastoral office:

> God has also instituted, for the sake of order, the special office of
> pastor [*Predigtamt,* literally "the preaching office"] to teach the Gos-
> pel publicly, administer the sacraments, and handle the keys of the
> kingdom of heaven. Of this, there is certainly no doubt among us.
> Pastors are the called public servants of Christ.[10]

Walther presented the classic articulation of the ministry as Luther had
outlined it three hundred years earlier. The distinction between lay and
clergy roles as delineated by Walther in this sermon was the foundation
upon which pastor and people at Trinity would function. Yet as the
church grew beyond one congregation in St. Louis and new circumstances arose, the practical application of this doctrine would become
more complicated.

Reaching Out

Despite the stabilization and then growth of Trinity congregation under
his leadership, Walther longed for a gathering of like-minded congregations beyond the Saxon parishes in Perry County and St. Louis. In 1844
he convinced the people of Trinity to subsidize the printing and distribution of their own biweekly church paper as a publication that might serve
as both announcement and invitation to other Lutherans. The first issue
of *Der Lutheraner* was published on the seventh of September 1844, and
introduced itself by identifying the need for such a publication:

9. C. F. W. Walther, "Bringing Souls to Christ: Every Christian's Desire and
Duty," sermon for the 12th Sunday after Trinity, 1842, in *Gnadenjahr: Predigten über
die Evangelien des Kirchenjahrs* (St. Louis: Concordia Publishing House, 1891), pp.
439-45; trans. Bruce Cameron in *Missio Apostolica: Journal of the Lutheran Society for
Missiology* 6 (1998): 6-16.
10. Walther, "Bringing Souls to Christ," pp. 439-45.

The German population of America's West is growing manifestly every day. With it the number of those is growing who confess the faith of Luther, which was at one time preached to the Germans. But of no other group are the members so orphaned here as the evangelical Lutheran. . . . The German Lutherans are therefore in great temptation to leave the faith of their fathers. . . . Our dear brethren in the faith in this part of our new fatherland therefore need to be encouraged to remain loyal to their faith; they need to be warned against the dangers of apostasy which here threaten so many; they need weapons to defend themselves against those who challenge the truthfulness of the faith which they have learned from their youth in the catechism; they need the comfort that the church to which they profess adherence has not yet disappeared, and that they therefore have no reason at all to seek refuge in another communion.[11]

The masthead of *Der Lutheraner* bore the motto, "God's Word and Luther's doctrine pure shall now and forevermore endure *(Gottes Wort und Luthers Lehr' vergehet nun und nimmermehr)*."[12] Its mission, according to editor Walther, was fourfold:

> to make readers familiar with the doctrines, the treasures and the history of the Lutheran Church; furnish proof that the Lutheran Church is indeed the ancient true Church of Christ on earth, not merely one of the Christian sects; to be of service to its readers by teaching them how a true Lutheran, though a sinner, may be a firm believer, live a truly Christian life, bravely bear up under the cross, and, departing this life, enter the glories of heaven; to expose false doctrines and ungodly practices, paying particular attention to those Lutherans, wrongly so called, who in the guise and garb of Lutheran teacher preach and disseminate error, unbelief, and sectarianism, to the prejudice and shame of pure and Scriptural Lutheranism.[13]

Here, then, was both agenda and challenge, as Walther did not hesitate to put other Lutherans in America on notice that the Old Lutherans in

11. *Der Lutheraner* 1 (Sept. 7, 1844): 1.
12. Polack, *The Story of C. F. W. Walther*, p. 74. A more literal translation would read: "God's Word and Luther's teaching will vanish neither now and nevermore."
13. H. Birkner, *"Der Lutheraner* from 1844 to 1847," in *Ebenezer: Reviews of the Work of the Missouri Synod During Three Quarters of a Century*, ed. W. H. T. Dau (St. Louis: Concordia Publishing House, 1922), pp. 43-44.

Missouri understood themselves to be the guardians of confessional-ism in their new homeland, ready to hold all other Lutherans account-able. And they did. As Walther learned of developments in the east among the various groups that made up "American Lutherans," he challenged their drift from a solid confessional posture, accusing them of compromise and "pseudo-Lutheranism."[14]

Walther's confessionalism, championed in *Der Lutheraner,* de-pended heavily on the words of the reformer himself. As the laymen at Trinity Church looked to their pastor to provide proof-texts from Luther to settle congregational disputes and order congregational discipline, so Walther looked first to Luther for evidence of the theological position he advocated through the pages of his journal. He believed that "there is no other possible way to find the *Lutheran* doctrine in its purest, brightest, most complete, and most original form (after Scripture) than in *Lu-ther.*"[15] Walther was well respected for his knowledge of both Luther and the confessions, but he almost always turned to Luther first. Later, as a professor, his annotations to a seventeenth-century theology text dem-onstrated his heavy dependence, after Luther, on both the symbolical books and the writings of the orthodox theologians.[16] But his preference in writing and speaking was always to quote Luther. Walther rarely re-ferred to the confessions in his sermons.[17]

Responses to *Der Lutheraner* were mixed. Those who often felt its sting were likely to read it as polemical, as editorial comment from the General Synod's *Lutheran Observer* shows: "[T]he same narrow and big-oted spirit which prevails among this school in Prussia seems to rule with undiminished force in the West. Thank God, this unholy spirit can never enter our English churches."[18] Walther was accused of put-ting the confessions before scripture,

14. Carl Mauelshagen, "American Lutheranism Surrenders to Forces of Con-servatism" (Ph.D. diss., University of Minnesota, 1936), p. 94.

15. Letter from C. F. W. Walther to the Rev. F. W. T. Steimle, January 25, 1861, in *Walther Speaks to the Church: Selected Letters of C. F. W. Walther,* ed. Carl S. Meyer (St. Louis: Concordia Publishing House, 1973), p. 37. Walther's emphasis.

16. Johann Wilhelm Baier, *Compendium Theologiae Positivae, Adjectis Notis Amplioribus,* ed. C. F. W. Walther (St. Louis: Concordia Publishing House, 1879).

17. Arthur Carl Piepkorn, "Walther and the Lutheran Symbols," *Concordia Theological Monthly* 32 (1961): 616.

18. Mauelshagen, "American Lutheranism Surrenders to Forces of Conserva-tism," p. 93.

charged with idolizing the fathers of the Church, with promoting dead orthodoxy, with doing nothing but rehashing the antiquated opinions of men long dead and gone, with endeavoring to graft a withered branch of the church of Germany on the flourishing tree of American Lutheranism.[19]

But to one man in Indiana, *Der Lutheraner* was evidence that he was not alone: "Thank God there are yet more Lutherans in America!" said Friedrich Conrad Dietrich Wyneken, upon reading the first issue.[20] Wyneken, who had been serving congregations in Indiana since 1838, and who would later be known as the Missouri Synod's "Father of Home Missions," had just written his own appeal to Lutherans in his German homeland for whatever help they could send to address "the spiritual misery of the brethren who have emigrated to America."[21] Walther's little four-page newspaper had quickly become the agent of outreach its editor had hoped it would. Whether intentional or not, it could not help but become an agent of alienation as well to those Lutherans who did not share similar theological opinions with the Saxons.

Other Lutherans in Other Places

All the while the Saxons were coping with their various struggles, other German Lutherans were settling in America. Men like Wyneken had preceded them to do mission work among the new arrivals, but the reality of the American frontier often appalled the missioners. Not only were conditions primitive, but the new homeland introduced new dangers to German migrants — all manner of vice and indecency, but perhaps worst of all, in Wyneken's words, was "the stream of greed, which in America has reached its utmost depth and most sweeping force."[22] The need for spiritual leaders to minister to these Germans was made more compelling by Wyneken's report that people were willing to accept just about anyone who represented himself as a preacher. In one city a cooper who turned

19. Julius A. Friedrich, "Dr. C. F. W. Walther," in *Ebenezer*, p. 30.
20. Friedrich, "Dr. C. F. W. Walther," in *Ebenezer*, p. 30.
21. "The Distress of the German Lutherans in North America," published in 1844 in Pittsburgh; quoted in Meyer, *Moving Frontiers*, pp. 91-97.
22. "The Distress of the German Lutherans in North America," pp. 91-97.

out to be a wife and child abuser (but not a clergyman) had just been run out of town, and Wyneken wondered how the Germans could have hired this man in the first place: "When I reproved the people for accepting everyone who came to them as a preacher without asking for credentials, they rejoined: 'He had a tremendous gift of gab, we had to have a preacher, and he was cheap, too.'"[23]

Stories like this one drove Wyneken back to Germany in 1841 to appeal in person for more clergy. There he met Wilhelm Loehe, a confessional Lutheran pastor at Neuendettelsau in Bavaria.[24] Loehe was moved by the need Wyneken described and began immediately to raise both recruits and funds for the missionary endeavor to the "German heathen" in North America. Loehe's *Sendlinge* (missionaries) and *Nothhelfer* (emergency helpers) were not trained clergy, but Loehe saw to it that these men would become trained. In 1846 a theological seminary was opened in Fort Wayne, Indiana, made possible by contributions raised by Loehe and other donors. Loehe himself never came to America, so the oversight of the new seminary was assigned to Wilhelm Sihler, one of Wyneken's early missioners to Ohio, who became both president and professor at the Fort Wayne school.[25]

"Loehe men" were sent to develop mission outreach in the states of Ohio, Indiana, and Michigan, but their efforts, while primarily to minister to German immigrants, were not limited to those who were already Lutheran. Loehe had taken a special interest in Indian missions, and sent several of his missioners to work among the Chippewa in the Saginaw Valley in Michigan while establishing German settlements there, most notably at Frankenmuth.[26] Despite Loehe's philanthropy in endowing mission work in America, the number of pastors, trained or not, was completely inadequate to the far greater numbers of Germans migrating to America. This single factor would prove crucial to the future of German Lutheranism in the United States, for, even in these early years of settlement, the question of *who* could minister was not easily answered.

23. "The Distress of the German Lutherans in North America," pp. 91-97.

24. For background on Loehe and the confessional movement in Germany after the Saxon emigration, see Walter H. Conser, Jr., *Church and Confession: Conservative Theologians in Germany, England, and America, 1815-1866* (Macon, Ga.: Mercer University Press, 1984), ch. 3. Conser terms Loehe a neo-Lutheran.

25. Meyer, *Moving Frontiers,* p. 195.

26. Meyer, *Moving Frontiers,* p. 118.

Several months after the Saxons arrived in Missouri, another group of Lutherans reached America. Most settled in Buffalo, New York, but some continued on to Milwaukee, Wisconsin. Sharing an Old Lutheran conservatism with the Saxons, this group of Prussian Lutherans had similarly followed the lead of a charismatic pastor, Johannes Andreas Augustus Grabau. Unlike Stephan, who had been frequently accused but never found guilty of charges in Germany, Grabau had first been suspended from office and then arrested and imprisoned for his refusal to use the Prussian Union Agenda.[27] As his strong opposition to the state-enforced union of Lutherans and Reformed seemed certain to continue upon his release, his request to emigrate was granted, and he gathered a company of nearly one thousand to travel to America with him. Five shiploads of Prussians arrived in New York City in September 1839. Most of the company traveled west as far as Buffalo, New York, but a group of Silesians continued on to Milwaukee.[28]

Had Martin Stephan retained control over his own emigration company, the Grabau Lutherans might have found in the Saxons a potentially compatible group with whom to affiliate. It seemed Grabau thought so, even after learning of Stephan's removal. In 1840 he sent a copy of a pastoral letter *(Hirtenbrief)* to the pastors in Perry County suggesting the two groups consider establishing a joint seminary and asking their theological opinion of his handling of a matter within his own company. The Silesian portion of Grabau's followers who had settled in Freistadt, near Milwaukee, were temporarily without their pastor, L. F. E. Krause, and wrote Grabau to ask whether a layman could serve in Krause's absence. Because Grabau held a high view of the office of ordained ministry, which he based on Article XIV of the Augsburg Confession and the German church orders *(Kirchenordnungen)*, the conclusion of his lengthy pastoral letter was simply no.[29]

27. Alfred H. Ewald, "From a German Jail: Who Has Authority in the Church?" in *Church Roots: Stories of Nine Immigrant Groups That Became The American Lutheran Church,* ed. Charles P. Lutz (Minneapolis: Augsburg Publishing House, 1985), pp. 41-59.

28. August R. Suelflow and E. Clifford Nelson, "Following the Frontier," in *The Lutherans in North America,* rev. ed., ed. E. Clifford Nelson (Philadelphia: Fortress Press, 1980), pp. 154-55.

29. William M. Cwirla, "Grabau and the Saxon Pastors: The Doctrine of the Holy Ministry, 1840-1845," *Concordia Historical Institute Quarterly* 68 (1995): 87-88.

The Saxons were far too caught up in their own crisis over church and ministry to respond to Grabau's letter promptly, let alone to affirm his episcopal position that the ordained ministry was a divinely instituted estate *(Stand)*. When Loeber, on behalf of the Saxon clergy, finally did reply in 1843, he wrote Grabau that they could not agree with his elevation of the ordained ministry. Their experience, Loeber said, comparing themselves to "children who have been burned,"[30] had informed their belief, having so recently learned firsthand of the dangers of an elevated clergy class. The Saxons believed that by being unclear on "the unessential and the essential, the divine and the human order," Grabau had "unnecessarily restricted the priesthood of all believers."[31] The ministry, they said, was not an elite estate, but an office *(Amt)*. This response outraged the Prussian pastor, who disputed their interpretation of Luther, labeled the Saxons "Missourians," and accused them of "a lax, unchurchly spirit"[32] and "disregard for the office of the ministry."[33] Further, he insisted that if they "did not recant their error, he could not recognize them as true Lutherans," and "if they did not repent, he would have to excommunicate them from the Church."[34] Grabau and the Saxon pastors were arguing past each other, with the Saxons claiming they took no issue with church order, only with absolutism where orders were concerned. They instead preferred that congregations exercise their Christian liberty, as they considered church orders and ordination middle matters, or *adiaphora*.[35] But Grabau's insistence on the way things had been done in Germany allowed no room for variance in practice in America.

In 1845 Grabau formally organized his congregations into the

---

30. G. H. Loeber, *Der Hirtenbrief des Herrn Pastor Grabaus zu Buffalo vom Jahre 1840. Nebst den zwischen ihm und mehreren lutherischen Pastoren von Missouri gewechselten Schriften. Der Oeffentlichkeit übergeben als ein Protestation gegen Geltendmachung hierarchischer Grundsätze innerhalb der lutherischen Kirche* (New York: H. Ludwig & Co., 1849), p. 75. Hereinafter cited as *Hirtenbrief.*

31. Loeber, *Hirtenbrief,* pp. 20-37.

32. D. H. Steffens, "The Doctrine of the Church and the Ministry," in *Ebenezer,* p. 149.

33. John C. Wohlrabe, Jr., "An Historical Analysis of the Doctrine of the Ministry in the Lutheran Church–Missouri Synod until 1962" (Th.D. diss., Concordia Seminary, St. Louis, 1987), p. 35.

34. Arthur Both, "The Missouri Synod and the Buffalo Synod," in *Ebenezer,* p. 125.

35. Loeber, *Hirtenbrief,* p. 25.

Synod of the Lutheran Church Which Emigrated from Prussia, which would more commonly be known as the Buffalo Synod. The battle over church governance and ministry was joined early between the two divisions of Old Lutherans, and proved irresolvable. The irony is that the basis of their agreement in Germany — the Lutheran confessions — had become the basis for their disagreement in America.[36]

Walking Together: An Emerging Synod

As Trinity in St. Louis set a pattern for like-minded German Lutheran congregations to follow, so its pastor set a pattern of leadership that would not only prevail during his lifetime, but would be upheld forever after by the church body he helped organize. The legacy of C. F. W. Walther's preeminence as a — if not *the* — father of the church must be considered more carefully than it has been to date by both his biographers[37] and church historians. The combination of Walther's "rescue" of the floundering Saxon colonists at Altenburg and his forty-year tenure as pastor of the mother church, synodical president, and primary professor and president of the St. Louis seminary has cast a long shadow. His dominance has not only eclipsed the contributions of others who pioneered Lutheran frontiers with him, but created a larger-than-life figure. Walther's words are thus the synod's words.[38]

Walther's words in *Der Lutheraner* provided the link he sought with other confessional Lutherans in America. Correspondence began in 1845 between the three men who would together build a gathering of German Lutheran churches — Walther, Wyneken, and Sihler. One of Loehe's men who was a member of the Ohio Synod had written to Walther about the possibility of forming a synod — an assembly of

36. Conrad Bergendoff, *The Doctrine of the Church in American Lutheranism* (Philadelphia: Board of Publication of the United Lutheran Church in America, 1956), p. 12.

37. Polack, *The Story of C. F. W. Walther;* Lewis W. Spitz, Sr., *The Life of Dr. C. F. W. Walther* (St. Louis: Concordia Publishing House, 1961); Arthur H. Drevlow, John M. Drickamer, and Glenn E. Reichwald, *C. F. W. Walther: The American Luther* (Mankato, Minn.: Walther Press, 1987); and a planned volume by August R. Suelflow.

38. For a discussion of the future implications of this position for the synod, see Jack T. Robinson, "The Spirit of Triumphalism in The Lutheran Church–Missouri Synod," *Currents in Theology and Mission* 1 (1974): 13-20.

churches (the word means "walking together") — with the Saxons. Walther agreed, in a letter that carefully outlined his intentions. The proposed synod should be an advisory body (not judicial), thereby upholding the autonomy of the individual congregation, and its chief function should "be directed toward the maintenance and furtherance and guarding of the unity and purity of Lutheran doctrine."[39] He also believed that lay delegates of member congregations should have equal representation with clergy, though he felt a pastor should be the chair of the assembly. True to the model he had established at Trinity, Walther seemed committed to lay involvement in the polity of the proposed synod, but his advocacy was not without ambivalence. In a letter to Sihler he admitted that he had "a kind of horror of a real representative constitution. I do not find it in Holy Scripture."[40] Despite Walther's conflicted feelings, his compromise in Perry County bound him to the more democratic structure. He went on to defend his concept of an advisory synod in terms of a positive gathering of individual congregations by saying that he did not view the synodical structure as "a concentration of ecclesiastical power."[41]

Several of the Loehe men who had severed their relationship with the Ohio Synod over, among other issues, Ohio's use of the English language, met in Cleveland in late 1845 to begin discussion of a new synod. A meeting with the Saxons was then arranged for May 1846 in St. Louis. Over the course of a week together, the Saxon pastors and the "Loehe men" drafted a constitution for the new synod and arranged to meet again in Fort Wayne in July, at which time it was agreed that the synod they envisioned would hold its founding meeting in Chicago the following spring. The proposed constitution was to be printed in *Der Lutheraner* for congregations to study in preparation for the convention. Members of Walther's own Trinity congregation had already met ten times to study the document before authorizing their pastor's attendance at the Fort Wayne meeting. They finally approved the draft constitution if it was amended to ensure that the synod was to be an advisory body only, "the resolutions of which are to become effective

39. C. F. W. Walther to A. Ernst, August 21, 1845. Quoted in Meyer, *Moving Frontiers,* p. 143.

40. August R. Suelflow cites Walther's letter as "quoted from *Theological Monthly* 2 (1922): 129" in "Walther and Church Polity," *Concordia Theological Monthly* 32 (1961): 634.

41. Suelflow, "Walther and Church Polity," p. 634.

only after their approval by the congregations composing the body."[42] Still fearful of clergy dominance, or "priest rule," the Trinity laity insisted that the integrity and the autonomy of the local congregation be assured.[43]

The first convention of *Die Deutsche Evangelische Lutherische Synode von Missouri, Ohio, und andern Staaten* (The German Evangelical Lutheran Synod of Missouri, Ohio, and other States) assembled at First St. Paul's Lutheran Church in Chicago on April 25, 1847. Present, along with the Saxons, were representatives of the Loehe men who had previously been affiliated with the Ohio and Michigan Synods. Twelve pastors and sixteen congregations signed the constitution as charter members, ten pastors and a parochial school teacher became advisory (non-voting) members. C. F. W. Walther was elected president.

The organization of the new synod was outlined in its constitution. The "bottom-up" structure based on the autonomy of the local congregation and the advisory nature of the synod made it very different from previously established synods in American Lutheranism. Here was a church body whose organizing principles were minimal and straightforward — "Matters of doctrine and of conscience shall be decided only by the Word of God; all other decisions shall be by majority vote."[44] What to the founders seemed so self-evident thereby received no further explication. The synod established no commissions or boards of theological review, but assumed consensus would be obvious. If anyone thought to ask how these "matters of doctrine and conscience" would be decided or by whom, or even what exactly was meant by "Word of God," by which such matters were to be decided, there is no record.

One is tempted to assign the origin of the Missouri Synod to the prevailing phenomenon known as the democratization of American Christianity, which Nathan Hatch has characterized as pervasive in the first half of the nineteenth century: "Increasingly assertive common

---

42. H. Kowert, "The Organization of the Missouri Synod in 1847," in *Ebenezer*, pp. 94-110, and Steffens, "The Doctrine of the Church and the Ministry," p. 148.

43. Trinity's amendment (Article VII of the present synodical constitution) was accepted by the founding convention but was not added to the constitution until 1853 due to a stipulation that amendments were to have unanimous approval of member congregations. Suelflow, "Walther and Church Polity," p. 636.

44. Constitution of the German Evangelical Lutheran Synod of Missouri, Ohio, and other States, 1847, article III.

people wanted their leaders unpretentious, their doctrines self-evident and down-to-earth, their music lively and singable, and their churches in local hands."[45] But the men who laid the foundation of this synod were brand-new Americans, not natives heady with the process of extending the rights of the common man. Most spoke only German (indeed insisted on it) and believed that their language was the means of preserving their German culture, heritage, and faith.

In addition, the polity of the new synod, while both congregational and democratic, affirmed the position of clergy in leadership. Of all synodical offices, only the treasurer might be a layman. The pastoral office was also guaranteed in the sense that there were to be no contractual arrangements, such as term of service, attached to the divine call to office conveyed by a congregation to a clergyman. It was clergy who drafted this organizational outline, and clergy who secured their own place within it.

Where authority was definitively established was in the office of synodical president, who was to serve as overseer of all pastors and congregations in the new synod. Despite the advisory nature of the synod, this supervision, requiring the president to regularly visit every parish, translated under the "matters of doctrine and conscience" provision as control over doctrine and practice.

For its part, the Saxon laity as a whole was neither anticlericalist nor populist, though certainly some individuals were outspoken in their antipathy toward the clergy. Instead, the laity's guardedness about authority in their congregations should be viewed as a reaction to the severe disillusionment they had experienced over the Stephan episode. People who in good faith had invested their resources into a common treasury in trust that they would be provided for now had no foundation for trust left except in whatever authority they could secure for themselves. Congregational autonomy was about self-protection from the excesses of hierarchicalism in light of betrayed trust; synodical clerical equity based on congregational autonomy assured the clergy of independent leadership over one's own parish at the same time that it was a safeguard against the ambition of another Stephan. Memory of the acute crisis of authority the company had faced in Perry County left both people and pastors on guard. The only means by

45. Nathan O. Hatch, *The Democratization of American Christianity* (New Haven: Yale University Press, 1989), p. 9.

which they could continue in relationship with one another was within a system of checks and balances that offered each some sense of security as well as control over the other. The people called the pastor and determined his salary; the pastor held the respect of the people by virtue of his divine call and his education.

When he learned of the constitution adopted at the founding of the Missouri Synod, Wilhelm Loehe was not pleased. He disliked Walther's congregationalist emphasis, which he felt "lacked an ordering of ecclesiastical powers."[46] He feared the German clergy had fallen easy prey to American democratic political ideas, which Loehe in his distrust of lay people saw as "mob rule."[47] His own men had welcomed alliance with the Saxons due to a shared emphasis on confessionalism and retention of the German language. In sending them to America Loehe had warned them against the "new measures" being employed by revivalists as well as the unionism of Lutherans wishing to speak English.[48] He had not warned them against union with those holding differing views on church polity and the ministry. (Before long Loehe would be confronted with similar democratic impulses at home, as the revolution of 1848 introduced reform measures into the state church, including lay representation at church conferences.)[49]

But more than congregational polity, the central issue over which Loehe disagreed with the governing structure set in place by the Missouri Synod constitution had to do with the office of the ministry. Like Grabau, Loehe believed in a strong clergy whose leadership over the congregation was indisputable. The ministry to Loehe was an elevated office, divinely instituted by God and responsible only to God.[50] His high church understanding led him to reject completely Walther's congregational basis of the call, believing that giving the laity control over their own congregations meant abdication of what was rightly clerical privilege. Loehe worried that

46. Conser, *Church and Confession,* p. 263.

47. Mundinger, *Government in the Missouri Synod,* p. 189.

48. Wilhelm Loehe, "General Instructions for Our Friends in America," quoted in Meyer, *Moving Frontiers,* pp. 98-101. As they left for America, Loehe gave to each of his men a handwritten copy of the detailed terms under which they were being sent.

49. Conser, *Church and Confession,* p. 65.

50. Kent S. Knutson, "The Community of Faith and the Word: An Inquiry into the Concept of the Church in Contemporary Lutheranism" (Ph.D. diss., Columbia University, 1961), p. 119.

his men would be "in danger of forgetting the high divine honor of their office and becoming slaves to their congregations."[51] Even the clergy's retention of virtually every position of leadership in the new synod was not a satisfactory resolution to Loehe's displeasure.

Walking Separately: Disagreement and Discord

The debate over the doctrine of the ministry persisted through the early years of Missouri Synod history. Indeed, Theodore Tappert argues that it was the central issue of mid-nineteenth-century Lutheran confessionalism. Tappert uses the observation of German historian Emanuel Hirsch to describe what he calls both a "preoccupation" and "a peculiar and unprecedented thing"[52] — that the church would "suppose that it can best serve God and Christ by talking about itself, its majesty, and its power, by edifying itself (in every sense of the word), and by thanking and praising God for itself."[53] Yet that is exactly what was going on as each little pocket of German Lutherans — whether represented by Walther, Grabau, or Loehe — held to its own truth. And, as long as that was the case, there was little hope for a larger gathering to develop. Rather, the various camps would only retreat further into their own positions.

Because the synod believed that frequent discussion of doctrinal issues was important in staying alert to "dangerous trends,"[54] time was allotted at conventions and space in publications for study of currently contested questions. To that end, the 1850 convention of the Missouri Synod determined that the synod's position should be in writing, and asked its president, C. F. W. Walther, to author a book outlining the doctrines of church and ministry. *Die Stimme Unserer Kirche in der Frage von Kirche und Amt* (The Position of Our Church on the Question of the

51. Letter from Wilhelm Loehe to L. A. Petri, December 16, 1847, in James L. Schaaf, "Wilhelm Loehe and the Missouri Synod," *Concordia Historical Institute Quarterly* 45 (1972): 60.

52. Theodore G. Tappert, ed., *Lutheran Confessional Theology in America, 1840-1880* (New York: Oxford University Press, 1972), p. 229.

53. Emanuel Hirsch, *Geschichte der neuern evangelischen Theologie*, 5 vols. (Gutersloh, 1949-1954), vol. 5, p. 145. Quoted in Tappert, *Lutheran Confessional Theology*, p. 229.

54. Mauelshagen, "American Lutheranism Surrenders to Forces of Conservatism," p. 130.

Church and the Ministry)[55] was published in 1852, in which Walther developed nine theses on the doctrine of the church and ten theses on the ministry. He used three forms of evidence to support his argument — scripture, the Lutheran confessions, and the writings of Lutheran theologians. In the preface, Walther acknowledged that the subject matter had "divided present-day Lutherans into two camps" before defending Missouri's position against the "slander" Grabau had inflicted on the young church body. While Loehe is not mentioned by name, the sting of his criticisms is evident in Walther's defensive repudiation of "the charge made against us" that the Saxons were overly influenced by American principles: "We did not pattern the doctrine of the church after the conditions prevailing here, but we established the church according to the doctrine of our church."[56]

What Walther was attempting to do was keep Loehe and shed Grabau. The controversy with the Buffalo Synod had early on reached a low level of name-calling and diatribe, with Grabau calling the Saxons "heretics and false prophets preaching to mobs" and "a synod of abomination and a Temple of Babel."[57] The Saxons answered back by accusing Grabau and his company of being "papists and tyrants."[58] Perhaps worst of all was Walther's charge that Grabau was "a second, unrevised edition of Stephan."[59] Whatever shared heritage and emigrant experi-

55. C. F. W. Walther, *Church and Ministry (Kirche und Amt): Witnesses of the Evangelical Lutheran Church on the Question of the Church and the Ministry,* trans. J. T. Mueller (St. Louis: Concordia Publishing House, 1987). The original edition was published in 1852 with subsequent editions in 1865 and 1875. These later editions were largely to correct "errata" in earlier printings, with some additional citations. The book is most commonly known by its shorter title, *Kirche und Amt.* The theses are included in the Appendix.

56. Walther, *Church and Ministry,* Preface to the First Edition, pp. 7-10. Loehe had written to Walther to express his fear that "the fundamental strong mixing of democratic, independent, congregational principles in your constitution will cause greater damage than the mixing of the princes and secular authorities have brought to the church in our homeland." Letter from Wilhelm Loehe to C. F. W. Walther, September 8, 1847, in Schaaf, "Wilhelm Loehe and the Missouri Synod," p. 60.

57. Mauelshagen, "American Lutheranism Surrenders to Forces of Conservatism," p. 152.

58. Mauelshagen, "American Lutheranism Surrenders to Forces of Conservatism," p. 152.

59. L. Fuerbringer, ed., *Briefe von C. F. W. Walther,* 2 vols. (St. Louis: Concordia Publishing House, 1915-16), vol. 1, p. 88, as cited in Tappert, *Lutheran Confessional Theology,* p. 231.

ence these Lutherans who had left Germany in parallel quests for religious liberty might have enjoyed seemed a remote memory in the midst of this contentious debate.

Was the ministry an office of service, as Walther claimed, or a special class, as Grabau insisted? Was the Office of the Keys — ecclesiastical authority — given to the congregation or to the pastor? By whom is the call to ministry conveyed, by God directly or from God through the congregation? Was ordination a divine or a human institution? These questions, and the corresponding interpretations used in support of the differing views, reveal a profound theological division that would persist throughout the first decades of Missouri Synod history.

In his 1851 theses on the ministry, Walther declared that the public ministry (1) is "distinct from the priesthood of all believers," (2) was divinely instituted, (3) is not more holy or special "to that of ordinary Christians . . . but is a ministry of service," (4) is conferred by God through a congregation's call, and (5) is the highest office in the church, from which all other offices derived. Additionally, he maintained that ordination was in itself not a divine institution but "merely an ecclesiastical rite" that publicly confirmed one's call.[60] Walther thereby reaffirmed the principles he had outlined in 1842. The ministry was necessary even in light of the Lutheran concept of the priesthood of all believers, because not everyone by means of their "general calling as Christians" can perform the public functions of the office.[61] To that end, a congregation of believers transfers *(übertragen)* the office and its authority to a pastor through a divine call. The ministry, therefore, cannot exist apart from a congregation. What had been hammered out in the agony of the crisis years in Perry County and finally settled by the Altenburg theses — that there is first church, and then ministry — remained the fundamental core of Walther's position.

Walther's understanding of the ministry was firmly held to by the synod, but it was not long before exceptions developed and had to be addressed. The question was raised already in the 1850s in the case of itinerants, or traveling preachers *(Reiseprediger)* along the American frontier. Itinerants were laymen who serviced the spiritual needs of German immigrants in outlying areas as "home missionaries." Could these men *sans* congregations perform pastoral acts, including adminis-

60. Walther, *Church and Ministry,* pp. 21-22.
61. Walther, *Church and Ministry,* p. 161.

82

tering the Lutheran sacraments of baptism and communion? After considerable discussion the synod determined that *Reiseprediger* could baptize but, as the celebration of the eucharist "presupposes the existence of a Christian congregation," they could commune only in cases of "unusual spiritual trials."[62] The synod based its decision on what is called the "law of love." The 1865 convention of the Western District adopted twenty-eight theses in response to the *Reiseprediger* question, of which three are particularly significant in explaining the exception:

> Love is the queen of all laws, more so than all regulations [*Ordnungen*]. . . . There are cases of necessity in which also the regulation of the public office of the ministry cannot and should not be observed. . . . A case of necessity occurs when, by legalistic observance of the regulation, souls would be lost instead of saved and love would be therefore violated.[63]

The itinerant exception was simply the first in a series of exceptions that would arise over time, including teachers in parochial schools as well as professors in seminaries and synodical colleges, foreign missionaries, military chaplains, and administrators within the church and its agencies. Every succeeding exception would require the synod to review and then adjust its understanding of the doctrine of the ministry, and every exception would be the subject of considerable debate. The synod still prided itself on its "unmoving theology,"[64] by which it meant that doctrine was complete as outlined in the confessions; it could not develop beyond that. Indeed, there could be no development for Walther, who considered doctrine "a heavenly building long completed."[65] To that end, there was in Missouri's mind no such thing as an "open question" where doctrine was concerned. This became another significant point of disagreement with Loehe, who, unlike Walther, believed that the Reformation was a developing movement.[66] Because there were matters on which neither scripture nor the confessions spoke clearly,

62. Missouri Synod, Western District, *Proceedings,* 1865, pp. 57-62.

63. Missouri Synod, Western District, *Proceedings,* 1865, pp. 57-62.

64. Meyer, *Moving Frontiers,* p. 366.

65. C. F. W. Walther, *Lehre und Wehre* 5 (1859): 1-12, in *Editorials from Lehre und Wehre,* trans. Herbert J. A. Bouman (St. Louis: Concordia Publishing House, 1981), p. 50.

66. Mauelshagen, "American Lutheranism Surrenders to Forces of Conservatism," pp. 156-57.

disagreement between Lutherans on open questions was acceptable. Walther, on the other hand, regarded every matter as settled and therefore "every *new* so-called truth as an *old* or also new — error. . . . Nothing will ever induce us to abandon the ark of our beloved church and plunge into the pounding waves of changing current opinions."[67] The issue of open questions would continue to haunt any dialogue between Missouri and other Lutheran church bodies well into the twentieth century.[68]

Missouri repeatedly asked the Buffalo Synod to discuss the differences between the two groups, which Grabau refused to do. Each side appealed to Loehe, whose support had been essential to Missouri's founding. Loehe thought he could mediate the dispute between the two factions of Old Lutherans, believing as he did that different positions, as long as they were based on the confessions, were possible. Missouri, not wishing to alienate its benefactor, invited Loehe to come to its 1851 convention. When Loehe was unable to attend,[69] Walther and Wyneken, now president of the synod, went to Germany to meet with him in the fall of 1851 to present their side of the debate. Whatever hope the Missouri leaders might have had for reconciliation was short-lived, as Loehe's next visitor was Grabau. In 1854 Loehe lent his support to the formation of a new Iowa Synod — which had as a central principle the existence of open questions — and sent a black-bordered letter to one of his missioners in Michigan, in which he declared their relationship irrevocably broken:

> Much more than in the doctrine of the church and the ministry, regarding which we would tolerate you and besides even allow you to make your opinions as binding as possible, do we differ with you in the truly papistic territorialism which you have boldly set up on the basis of your independent theories. . . . You demand free mission territory as though you were the masters and can tolerate no one as your

67. Mauelshagen, "American Lutheranism Surrenders to Forces of Conservatism," p. 61.

68. See, e.g., Theodor Hanssen, *The Historical Open Questions Among American Lutherans* (Burlington, Iowa: The Lutheran Literary Board, 1936).

69. Why Loehe was unable to travel to America is not recorded, but since the events of 1848 he had been increasingly relentless in his challenges to the authority of the state church, which finally suspended him from office in December of that year. He spent much of 1852 in suspension before being reinstated to his parish in Neuendettelsau in September. Conser, *Church and Confession*, pp. 57-72.

neighbor who does not share your doctrine of the ministry, even though he agrees with you in essentials.

. . . You have set your course, your system, and are finished — and done it is and resolved that Grabau and we and our sort are at best erring Lutherans and brethren. You, on the other hand, are great and highly elated, full of the joy of truth and victory! . . .

. . . You are taking our people who have emigrated from us, our students whom we have sent, the expenses they have incurred, all, everything you are taking, and we can go elsewhere; because the truth is involved and the proof in this instance is an easy one, that you can forsake everything if only you can preserve your theological speculation.

It is not because we fear your talk of schism, your territorialism and neo-papacy, your bad conclusions from propositions which do not fit your circumstances, and your theories. . . .

. . . [O]ur mission efforts among you are at an end. . . . Lutheran doctrine, intolerant and motivated by a blind zeal, turns even against its parents.

. . . The tent must be removed when one wishes to proceed elsewhere.[70]

Loehe saw in the Missouri Synod's insistence on the rightness of its position an almost adolescent rebellion against the confessionalism he believed they had all once shared in Germany. He wrote about Missouri:

People are striving to reach a level of unity that is not attainable except by continual fragmentation and dissolution of the church. The Lutheran theology of the 16th and in part the 17th century is the standard of judgment for exegesis. There is an end of peace and at least of that love which tends to prompt people to walk together wherever their doctrinal standard is rejected.[71]

70. Loehe to G. E. C. F. Sievers, August 4, 1853. Quoted in Meyer, *Moving Frontiers,* pp. 122-25. Despite his use of the second person in this personal correspondence, Loehe appears to direct his criticism past Sievers to the leaders of the Missouri Synod, with whom the Michigan pastor had affiliated. The writer's frequent references to his fondness for his missionary are sprinkled throughout a broadside citing his anger and sorrow over irreconcilable differences with the church body he had a significant part in founding.

71. Wilhelm Loehe, *Kirchliche Mitteilungen aus und über Nord-Amerika* (1859), reprinted in *Lehre und Wehre* 6 (1860): 1-13, trans. Jacob Heckert, "Fidelity to the Written Word: The Burden of the Missouri Synod," *Concordia Journal* 1 (1975): 70.

The factor that he did not, perhaps could not, understand was what the Saxons had been through since leaving Germany. The immigrants who had traveled together as a community had also suffered together as a community. For the almost two years that the Saxons in Perry County and St. Louis languished in despair over their situation, they nevertheless remained together. Only a few individuals chose to return to Germany, the most prominent among them Vehse. The resolution of their identity crisis left the community intact and in agreement over their purpose in emigrating. That experience must have served as powerful evidence to Walther in his own sense of the validity of his interpretation of church and ministry. And when he stated his convictions firmly upon the Loehe men's inquiry about possibly forming a synod together, they deferred to Walther's position. They, after all, had traveled to America as individuals and had no comparable experience from which to argue a different position on church polity. Loehe, still in Germany, knew no structure other than that in place under the consistory and state church. In the end, it was not only time and distance by which the Saxons were removed from Germany, but lived experience. There was another, less positive, side to what they had gone through together. The Saxon remnant would remain a community, but one in isolation.

Walther and Wyneken never issued a statement of regret over the loss of Loehe's support and alliance, or over the theological quarrel that had precipitated it, but addressed themselves instead to an expanding church body that already had outgrown its original constitution. Since its founding the synod had increased in congregations and clergy tenfold, its growth primarily due to the steady influx of German immigrants at mid-century.[72] In 1854 it became necessary for the synod to divide itself into four districts geographically, each with a president who would serve as overseer of the churches in his area as the 1847 constitution had intended the synodical president to do. It was important that internal unity be assured and not assumed. The means by which that could be carried out was through the oversight of a "visitor" who could observe a pastor's preaching, teaching, and caregiving on a somewhat regular basis. District presidents were to assume that duty.[73]

72. LaVern J. Rippley, *The German-Americans* (Lanham, Md.: University Press of America, 1984), p. 73.

73. Constitution of the German Evangelical Lutheran Synod of Missouri, Ohio, and other States, 1854, in Meyer, *Moving Frontiers,* pp. 149-61.

Despite its inability to come to terms with those Lutherans with whom it shared common roots, the synod continued to search out potential partners among other Lutherans. But even with the obvious advantages of a unified body of geographically distant Lutheran congregations, there were limits to unity. From its founding until the troubles that plagued the synod in the 1970s, there was perhaps no issue that served to identify Missouri better than its restrictive position on fellowship with other Lutherans. The widespread fear of "unionism" that still prevails has led outside observers to cast a knowing and disparaging sneer at the mention of "Missourians."

Yet the synod's seeming rigidity on the terms by which fellowship was possible did not preclude *any* possibility of union. In 1856 synod leaders extended an invitation to a free conference to be held in Columbus, Ohio, in October. Missouri's interest in meeting with other confessional Lutherans was in large part a reaction to events ongoing among other American Lutherans, in particular the publication in 1855 of the Definite Platform in the General Synod, an attempt by Samuel Schmucker, Benjamin Kurtz, and Samuel Sprecher to introduce an American Recension to the Unaltered Augsburg Confession of 1530.[74] The Definite Platform wished to qualify American Lutheran adherence to the Confession by removing five errors which the authors claimed were unscriptural and which they claimed had been acknowledged as such for some time. To its supporters, adoption of the Definite Platform would not only reduce the number of "Lutheran particularities" that might stand in the way of union but serve to remind the church that scripture alone was the rule and norm of faith and practice. In the end, there were very few in the General Synod who supported the Platform, but its appearance and the controversy surrounding it had raised serious concern further west.

Even though some in Missouri had long considered the General Synod to be "pseudo-Lutheran,"[75] to confessionalists like Walther any effort to diminish the emphasis on the Augsburg Confession was of grave concern. He felt it important to do something, thus his call for a free conference, at which he encouraged all subscribers to the Augsburg

---

74. See David A. Gustafson, *Lutherans in Crisis: The Question of Identity in the American Republic* (Minneapolis: Fortress Press, 1993), ch. 7.

75. Wilhelm Sihler, "Synodalrede," Missouri Synod, Central District, *Proceedings*, 1855, p. 10. Quoted in Meyer, *Moving Frontiers*, p. 254.

Confession to gather annually for in-depth discussion of the Confession. Conferences were held each year between 1856 and 1859. Their nature as "free" conferences kept them from becoming occasions for talk of church union, though that may have eventually been the case had the Civil War not intervened. No further conferences were held after 1859.

The Synodical Conference

The resistance of the Missouri Synod to extend itself in fellowship to other Lutherans without full doctrinal agreement — as the synod denied the possibility that there were any debatable or "open questions" on doctrine — was met with derision by observers within American Lutheranism. Charges of sectarianism were added to accusations of Missouri's "Pharisaic exclusiveness" and the "bigotry" of these "Jesuits in disguise" in various General Synod publications.[76]

In the years immediately following the Civil War the profile of American Lutheranism shifted. Theodore Tappert observes that in twenty years more than thirty synods appeared, giving the "impression of disunity if not total confusion."[77] Splintering among Lutherans became as common in the postwar period as it had been among other American Protestants before the war. The dispute over the Definite Platform had prompted an emerging confessionalism among some in the General Synod who could not tolerate the direction the American Lutherans who controlled that synod wanted to follow. Differences between the two positions intensified over a number of issues and finally reached an impasse in 1866, which led to the organization of the more conservative General Council in 1867. The split had come over the question of identity: Would these Lutherans be Americans first or Lutherans first?[78] The parties divided over questions of compromise and integrity, questions not unlike those confronted earlier by the infant Missouri Synod.

The new General Council was eager to explore fellowship with the Missouri Synod, which it believed held a compatible confessional

76. Th. Engelder, "Why Missouri Stood Alone," in *Ebenezer*, pp. 110-13.
77. Tappert, *Lutheran Confessional Theology*, p. 26.
78. See Gustafson for a history of these developments.

stance. But Missouri was not interested in being courted except on its own terms and would agree only to free conferences, which the synod thought "the most fitting and proper way to a true doctrinal and synodical unity."[79] Instead, the synod pursued the development of the Synodical Conference, a federation of synods organized in 1872 only after it was agreed that all participants were in doctrinal agreement. Charter members included, besides the Missouri Synod, the Ohio Synod, the Norwegian Synod, the Minnesota Synod, and the Wisconsin Synod.

The primary purpose of the Synodical Conference was the promotion of mission work. Matthias Loy, president of the Ohio Synod, had pressed for a cooperative union so resources could be shared. Of primary importance to Loy was the question of language. Ohio had a long history of mission work in English, and even Walther had conceded by this time that the church could hardly afford to ignore English if it was to reach the children of its members. As the German synods had only German-speaking seminaries, affiliation with likeminded synods that used English was desirable. Ironically, it was over the use of English that William Sihler and other Loehe men had left the Ohio Synod and made the initial inquiries to Walther that led to the formation of the Missouri Synod.[80]

Following the Missouri Synod's own model of confederation, the Synodical Conference was determined to be advisory only. The gathered synods acknowledged Missouri's leadership by electing C. F. W. Walther their first president.

The Predestination Controversy

Over the course of time, as the synod weathered the storms of its early decades, its consistent responses to persistent challenges helped to solidify its identity as a church body, both for itself and to those outside its parameters. Grabau had assigned the label "Missouri" as a pejorative even before the synod had incorporated the word into its name, but the

79. Missouri Synod, Western District, *Proceedings,* 1867, pp. 45-48. Quoted in Meyer, *Moving Frontiers,* p. 256.

80. Carl S. Meyer, "Ohio's Accord with Missouri, 1868-1880," in *The Maturing of American Lutheranism,* ed. Herbert T. Neve and Benjamin A. Johnson (Minneapolis: Augsburg, 1968), p. 193.

shorthand reference stuck, and came to mean very different things, depending on one's location within or without the synod.

It is at times easier to define oneself by what one is *not* than to know how to say who or what one is. There are a few things Lutherans know they are not. One is Roman Catholics, another is Calvinists. So when Walther, father of Missouri Synod Lutheranism, was accused in the 1870s and 1880s of being a "Crypto-Calvinist," a controversy was sure to follow.

Walther's early nemesis in what came to be known as the Predestination, or Election, Controversy[81] *(Gnadenwahlstreit)* was Professor Gottfried Fritschel of the Iowa Synod. Predestination was not a teaching to which Lutherans subscribed but was central in Calvinist theology. Fritschel's accusation that Walther's teaching on election was Calvinist led to a request that the doctrine be reviewed at a subsequent synodical convention. In 1877 Walther presented an essay to the Western District in which he stated clearly and forcefully his position by his favorite means of response, theses. He outlined the principal difference between the Lutheran understanding of election as God's doing alone and the Calvinist claim that human actions add a second element, which Calvinists considered a "double predestination" — to salvation and damnation, or election and rejection.

The controversy flared again the following year, fueled by a disappointed office-seeker. Friedrich A. Schmidt, a professor of the Norwegian Synod, took issue with Walther on the issue of predestination following the election of Francis Pieper to be professor at Concordia Seminary by the 1878 synodical convention.[82] Because Schmidt reportedly had wanted the faculty position, the incident became impetus for his attack on Walther.[83] Schmidt published his charges in his journal, *Altes und Neues* (Old and New), in which he also declared his own position, based on the principle of *intuitu fidei,* that God chose or elected individuals in view of the faith they would later profess.

---

81. Also referred to as the Predestinarian Controversy.

82. John M. Drickamer, "The Election Controversy," in *C. F. W. Walther: The American Luther: Essays in Commemoration of the 100th Anniversary of Carl Walther's Death,* ed. Arthur H. Drevlow, John M. Drickamer, and Glenn E. Reichwald (Mankato, Minn.: Walther Press, 1987), p. 163.

83. Christian Hochstetter, *Die Geschichte der Evangelisch-lutheranischen Missouri-Synode in Nord-Amerika, und ihrer Lehrkämpfe von der sächsichen Auswanderung im Jahre 1838 an bis zum Jahre 1884* (Dresden: Heinrich J. Naumann, 1885), p. 355.

Walther responded in writing in 1881 in a publication whose very title minced no words about what was at the root of the dispute: *The Controversy Concerning Predestination, That Is, A plain, trustworthy advice for pious Christians that would like to know whose doctrine in the present controversy concerning predestination is Lutheran, and whose is not.*[84] Walther — arguing that God alone is responsible for salvation — read Schmidt's charges as a challenge to his core identity as a Lutheran. Since his youthful struggles in Leipzig, Walther had been shaping and reshaping his theological location. But it had always been solidly within a confessional Lutheran tradition. Now late in life to be accused of not being Lutheran, but a masked Calvinist, brought a swift and sure response:

> Whoever . . . tries to make you believe that we teach that horrible Calvinistic doctrine of predestination, grossly transgresses the eighth commandment, in bearing false witness against his neighbor and slandering us; and God will judge it hereafter; for with heart and soul we condemn Calvin's doctrine of predestination, so help us God! — [85]

It is important to recognize that this controversy took place entirely within the recently organized Synodical Conference, which was founded on and grounded in full doctrinal agreement among member synods. Both sides used scripture and the confessions to argue their positions. The "burning question" of predestination pitted Walther and his synod against many in the Ohio Synod, in particular Matthias Loy, its president, and like Walther, a seminary professor.[86] The debate became so bitter and rancorous, with charges and countercharges going both ways, that the only resolution was division. Unable to accept Walther's Thirteen Theses on election as the Missouri Synod had at its 1881 convention, the Ohio Synod and the Norwegian Synod left the Synodical Conference that fall. Individual pastors left each synod, some by choice and others in the wake of Missouri's declaration that there could be no disagreement on this question. Unity meant unity in all things. Missouri meant what it said, declaring in convention that

---

84. Translated by Aug. Crull (St. Louis: Concordia Publishing House, 1881). Quoted in Meyer, *Moving Frontiers,* pp. 269-71.

85. Meyer, *Moving Frontiers,* p. 271.

86. The term is Loy's in "The Burning Question," *Columbus Theological Magazine* 1 (1881): 1-28. Quoted in Eugene L. Fevold, "Coming of Age, 1875-1900," in Nelson, *The Lutherans in North America,* pp. 313-25.

anyone who disagreed with the synod on this issue would not even be allowed to pray with them.[87] The belligerence was not new. From the first, Missouri had struck out in print at those who dared to disagree. A polemical tone marks far too much of the synod's literature, in which bitter invectives of intolerance declared tightly drawn boundaries.[88]

The intensity of the long struggle over predestination helped to further define the Missouri Synod both for itself and for other Lutherans, but not without cost. Walther's intransigence over *reine Lehre* — a pure doctrine, whether of the ministry or of election — had narrowed the field of potential allies. At the same time, the contentiousness and strident language of the debate had distanced the synod still further from those with whom it disagreed. By the time it was over, Missouri's position in American Lutheranism was more insular than ever.

Shall We Become an English-Speaking Church?

Lost to the Missouri Synod in the Predestination Controversy were those congregations using the English language rather than German. The first English-speaking congregation had been organized in 1856 in Baltimore by a Missouri-trained pastor and was later served by clergy from the Ohio Synod seminary. But the split between the Ohio and the Missouri Synods over predestination meant the English mission parishes were among those that left Missouri. Earlier, in August 1872, Walther had attended a free conference in Gravelton, Missouri, to discuss mission work among English-speaking Lutherans. The few congregations and clergy represented were a legacy of Tennessee Synod mission work in southeastern Missouri at least ten years before the Saxons ever arrived in Perry County. Now they hoped to affiliate with the German Lutherans of the Missouri Synod.

Those assembled at the free conference found they were in complete doctrinal agreement, but the Germans were reluctant to intro-

87. John H. Tietjen, *Which Way to Lutheran Unity? A History of the Efforts to Unite the Lutherans of America* (St. Louis: Concordia Publishing House, 1966), p. 76.

88. See Laurie Ann Schultz Hayes's insightful analysis of the persistence and nature of controversy over the course of Missouri Synod history, "The Rhetoric of Controversy in The Lutheran Church–Missouri Synod with Particular Emphasis on the Years 1969-1976" (Ph.D. diss., University of Wisconsin-Madison, 1980).

duce English into their churches, despite Walther's earlier statements of resignation that English would be the language spoken by the immigrants' children.[89] Their use of German had served to retain not only the culture of the fatherland but the language of the Reformers, of the church itself. As such, they believed, the teachings of the church were best conveyed in their original language. It was yet another means by which the synod could define itself. Already in 1843 Walther had included in the constitution of Trinity congregation a provision that only German was to be preached by the called pastor.[90] And the synod's own constitution required exclusive use of German in synodical conventions.[91] So the little English-speaking parishes in southern Missouri were encouraged instead to form their own conference, which they did, calling themselves the General English Evangelical Lutheran Conference of Missouri and other States.[92]

In 1887, still small but growing, the English conference again petitioned the Missouri Synod, this time to join as the English Mission District. Again it was encouraged to form its own synod, suggesting "the time is not yet ripe" to "harmonize the establishment of an English District within its midst."[93] In 1890 the English Evangelical Lutheran Synod of Missouri, Ohio, and Other States was organized. Within a year the new synod had eleven congregations in eleven states. Its remote membership stayed connected through its English-language publication, the *Lutheran Witness,* and two colleges, one in North Carolina and one in Kansas. Despite its steady growth, the English Synod still wished to be a part of the Missouri Synod, and thus persisted in putting the question before Missouri. By 1909 Missouri was finally prepared to respond favorably.

The entry of the English District into the Missouri Synod in 1911

---

89. *Lehre und Wehre* 16 (1870): 58, 59.

90. Constitution of Trinity Lutheran Church, St. Louis, Missouri, 1843, in Meyer, *Moving Frontiers,* pp. 167-70.

91. Constitution of the German Evangelical Lutheran Synod of Missouri, Ohio, and other States (1854), in Meyer, *Moving Frontiers,* pp. 149-61.

92. See P. E. Kretzmann, "The Beginnings of Permanent English Lutheran Work in Missouri," *Concordia Historical Institute Quarterly* 3 (1931): 100-5; H. B. Hemmeter, "Early English Mission Efforts in the Missouri Synod," *Concordia Historical Institute Quarterly* 11 (1938): 67-74; and John H. Baumgaertner, ed., *A Tree Grows in Missouri* (Milwaukee: Agape Publishers, 1975).

93. Missouri Synod, *Proceedings,* 1887, pp. 69-70.

did not mean the synod was ready to be an English-speaking church. Rather, it was adding an English-speaking arm by accepting the English Synod's offer of the *Lutheran Witness* and allowing its members to speak English at synodical conventions. The official language of the synod would remain German, but only for a short time. The synod had no idea in 1911 of the events that would challenge a singular feature of its identity before the end of the decade.

Conclusion

The death of C. F. W. Walther in 1887 brought to a close the formative years of the Missouri Synod. Walther felt he was leaving his church body in good hands, as he passed the mantle of theological leadership to his protégé, Francis (Franz) Pieper. In the first fifty years of its history, the Missouri Synod had established itself as a key player in American Lutheranism. Its most obvious achievement was the steady growth in congregations and members. More significantly, the synod was engaged in an intentional effort to define itself over against other gatherings of Lutherans. Because it had so early in its history faced an internal challenge that struck at the very roots of its being — the crisis following Stephan's exile — the young church body was able to be clear in representing who it was and what it stood for, whether entertaining overtures of fellowship or fending off accusations and critique. To that end, this period of its history can be seen as a time of self-authorizing, in which the young synod established itself vis-à-vis other Lutherans in America.

The synod had a singular advantage in accomplishing that task in that it looked totally to one man for leadership and direction. C. F. W. Walther, from the time of the Altenburg debates in 1841 until his death in 1887, was the preeminent figure of the Missouri Synod, which still today considers him the foremost Lutheran of the nineteenth century. Other influential leaders of the synod in its formative period, in particular Wyneken and Sihler, assume a subordinate role to Walther.[94] Church historians who view the period with a wider lens

---

94. Bachmann discounts Walther as sole "guiding genius of the synod," and argues that the developments of the synod's early years were possible largely due to a consensus among several key leaders — Walther, Wyneken, and Sihler — and the laymen at Trinity, St. Louis (p. 199).

agree that Walther was one of perhaps four most influential Lutheran leaders of the nineteenth century, along with Samuel Schmucker, Charles Porterfield Krauth, and Benjamin Kurtz. Nevertheless, it was Walther to whom Missouri looked for leadership; it elected him the first president of the synod, later returned him to that office, named him professor of theology when the seminary moved to St. Louis in 1849, and president of the seminary in 1854. In addition, he served as first president of the Synodical Conference and continued as editor of both the lay publication *Der Lutheraner* and the professional journal *Lehre und Wehre* throughout his tenure in these various offices. But Walther was first a called pastor, and he remained pastor of Trinity congregation until his death. According to the synod's understanding of ministry, as developed by Walther himself, a call was extended by a congregation alone. Any other position Walther or any other pastor held was secondary.

Because the primary leadership positions of the synod — president of the church body and, as president of the seminary, chief theologian — had all been collapsed into this one man, the identity of the synod over this period was what Walther said it was. Throughout his career he kept before his church the rallying cry he had first trumpeted in 1848: "Back, you Lutherans, back to Luther, to his Reformation church and doctrine!"[95] Whatever else Walther did he did in light of this clarion call. He restored to Lutherans the heritage of their origin and found within that heritage the essence of his theology. Yet his theology of scripture "tended toward biblicism," for he was "not an exegete" but a systematic theologian.[96] And to the extent that he relied on the words of the Reformers and the orthodox theologians who succeeded them, he was often called "a *Zitatentheologe,* a 'quotation theologian.'"[97] He not infrequently faced accusations of merely repristinating the theology of the confessions, due to his dependence on the dogmaticians of the seventeenth century. Critics often found his writings to be riddled with rigidity and invective, as he set definitive boundaries around his church.

Yet in the very longevity and consistency of his leadership,

95. *Der Lutheraner* 5 (September 12, 1848): 1.
96. Carl S. Meyer, "Walther's Theology of the Word," *Concordia Theological Monthly* 43 (1972): 262, 275.
97. Tappert, *Lutheran Confessional Theology,* p. 33.

Walther's legacy was remarkable. He shaped his synod's identity and became its authority. However, his singular dominance and the formidable model he set left the church insufficiently equipped to cope with the sociocultural changes of the coming century.

At the end of the nineteenth century, the Missouri Synod remained as it had begun in Saxony — an ethnic enclave that looked to one leader for direction and course. The leader was different, but the confessional base was the same. Transplanting the church to America had presented new challenges and required adaptation in its understanding of church and ministry. The severe crisis of identity and authority the emigrant company faced shortly after its arrival in Missouri was resolved only by compromise over definitions of church and ministry. But once that crisis was past, there would be no more compromise on those issues. The church's identity would depend on it.

4

Identity Redefined:
A Twentieth-Century Church?

B y the end of the nineteenth century, the Missouri Synod had established itself as a theologically conservative, German-speaking church body located predominantly in the rural heartland of the American midwest. In 1900 the synod could boast of 1,135 congregations with a total baptized membership of 728,240.[1] The first fifty years of its history had been marked by the church's struggle for identity over against other conservative Lutherans rather than in relation to American society at large. Convinced that retention of the German language in worship and official actions was necessary to the preservation of the faith, the synod began the new century secure in the relative isolation of its ethnic and theological identity.

Over the next fifty years the synod would be challenged by forces both beyond and within itself. Those developments tested the synod's ability to retain the identity it so cherished while reluctantly adapting to sociocultural and theological changes that swept through it and past it. Armed with its old but trusted tools of scripture and the Lutheran confessions, Missouri coped most often by trying to declare it-

---

1. *Statistisches Jahrbuch der deutschen evangelisch-lutherischen Synode von Missouri, Ohio und Anderen Staaten für das Jahr 1900* (St. Louis: Concordia Publishing House, 1901). The synod continued to publish a Statistical Yearbook through 1994, when its discontinuation was announced, and after which data was to be stored electronically.

self removed from whatever controversy was swirling around it. In the end, reliance on its nineteenth-century posture proved inadequate to the forces of the twentieth century. Eventually, the synod was forced to redefine itself.

Some of the issues that would engage the synod's attention during the first half of the twentieth century were ideological questions imposed on all elements of American Protestantism by the modernist/fundamentalist controversy and a rising spirit of ecumenism. Others were questions faced by America itself during World War I and the campaign for woman suffrage. Still others were particular to developments within the synod. Each in its own right challenged Missouri's notions of authority; each in its own right required the synod to expand its understanding of itself.

In the wake of the Civil War, the triple forces of industrialization, urbanization, and immigration forged a much different nation from that of the antebellum era. The closing decades of the nineteenth century brought a new complexity to American life, and to its churches. Questions about language, loyalty, interfaith cooperation, social responsibility, biblical scholarship, and — for the first time seriously — gender, generated discussion and debate from local pulpits to national conferences. In this climate, the Missouri Synod's intentional efforts to remain aloof from the events of society at large would not stand as the country in which the church had planted itself changed dramatically, and as America's changes came to be reflected in its churches.

But, as the nineteenth century closed, the synod seemed determined to continue in the tradition of the sainted Walther and gave deliberate notice of that intention. The leaders to whom the church looked for judgment and guidance were the seminary faculty, which numbered six in 1895.[2] In 1899 the two top theological posts in synod were again collapsed into one clergyman as they had so often been under Walther. Franz Pieper, elected president of the seminary in 1887, was in 1899 elected president of the synod, and served in that position until 1911, when the synod mandated a full-time presidency. For those twelve years, the synod would again, as it had with Walther, look to one clergyman for leadership and direction. But the direction

2. Carl S. Meyer, *Log Cabin to Luther Tower: Concordia Seminary During One Hundred and Twenty-five Years Toward a More Excellent Ministry 1839-1964* (St. Louis: Concordia Publishing House, 1965), p. 297.

Francis Pieper wanted to take his church was backward. If any theme runs through the teaching, preaching, and writing of Missouri's theologians of the Pieper era, synod historian Carl Meyer suggests it was "the conservation of the heritage and the theology of the past."[3] That position had already come to be sorely tested before the century turned.

The Modernist/Fundamentalist Controversy: Which Are We?

Already in the late nineteenth century, the seeds of the primary religious controversy of the new century were taking root. Religious thought since the 1870s had been influenced by modernism — also called liberalism — a response that advocated a modification or reshaping of theological posture as a means of adapting to cultural change. Modernism reflected the growing importance of natural science as applied to prior claims of truth and a progressive and optimistic attitude toward change. Theological modernism stressed the immanence of God and the possibilities inherent in humanity and human progress, offering a future far more optimistic than one burdened by humanity's original sin.[4] Some modernists also advocated a Social Gospel, a particularly Protestant Christian element of the broader progressive-era reform that encouraged social activism, especially in the cities, where the worst abuses of modern society were everywhere apparent. All of this optimism was more than many traditional Protestants could handle; the most vocal reaction to modernism came from conservative theologians who by 1920 came to be known as fundamentalists.

The very root of the modernist/fundamentalist conflict lay in one's understanding of the Bible. Adherence to a doctrine of biblical inerrancy was the one essential on the various lists of "fundamentals" to which believers subscribed. The rest of the list followed from and depended on a verbally inerrant scripture. Fundamentalists accused modernists of denying the authority of the Bible through their emphasis on

3. Meyer, *Log Cabin to Luther Tower,* p. 99.

4. On modernism and its influence, see William R. Hutchinson, *The Modernist Impulse in American Protestantism* (Durham, N.C.: Duke University Press, 1992); and Martin E. Marty, *Modern American Religion,* vol. 1, *The Irony of It All, 1893-1919* (Chicago: University of Chicago Press, 1986).

a higher critical approach to the scriptures. Higher criticism, brought to America from German graduate schools, applied a historical-critical lens to the Bible, which "came to be seen as a human as well as a divine document."[5] Modernists borrowed the new language of evolution to argue that advances in biblical scholarship offered opportunity for the development of Christianity. To fundamentalists, who believed higher criticism threatened the very authority of scripture and that no development of a timeless faith was necessary, the obvious defense was an insistence on biblical inerrancy and the verbal inspiration of the original texts.

The theologians of the Missouri Synod declared themselves on neither side of this running battle, though the synod's position on scriptural authority certainly found it leaning toward the fundamentalist side. A *Lutheran Witness* editorial took strong issue with the "New Theology," which co-editor Theodore Graebner called "simply the old rationalism which rejects the authority of the Bible and substitutes for it the authority of reason."[6] Graebner's use of the term "rationalism" was sure to put his readers on notice regarding a dangerous trend. Rationalism stood for all the ills from which the Missouri Synod church fathers had fled in Saxony and against which they continued to preach. W. H. T. Dau minced no words in warning of the modernist threat:

> The views which modern critical theologians hold of the origin of the Scriptures practically destroy both the causative and the normative authority of the Bible, and render it useless . . . for doctrine, for reproof, for correction, for instruction in righteousness.[7]

Dau's dire assessment called for the church to guard itself against the higher critics' "war against Protestantism that is to crush the Protestant Scripture-principle."[8] Friedrich Bente, writing in 1904 in *Lehre und Wehre,* affirmed that principle *(Schriftprinzip),* by declaring: "She

5. Grant Wacker, "The Demise of Biblical Civilization," in *The Bible in America: Essays in Cultural History,* ed. Nathan O. Hatch and Mark A. Noll (New York: Oxford University Press, 1982), p. 124.

6. [Theodore] G[raebner], "New Theology and Higher Criticism," *Lutheran Witness* 41 (September 12, 1922): 295.

7. [W. H. T.] D[au], "Scripture Proof in the View of the Modernists," *Theological Quarterly* 19 (1915): 65.

8. Dau, "Scripture Proof in the View of the Modernists," p. 66.

[the church] confesses the verbal inspiration and infallibility of the entire Holy Scripture."[9] Perhaps most significantly, foremost synodical theologian Franz Pieper wrote in the preface to the final volume of his *Christian Dogmatics:* "Modern Protestant theology has abandoned the objective divine authority of Scripture and put in its place 'Christian experience.'"[10] Pieper devoted an extensive portion of the third volume to the qualities and authority of a verbally inspired and "perfectly inerrant" scripture.[11]

Given the centrality of scriptural authority to Missouri Synod theological identity, one wonders why the synod did not simply weigh in on the side of the fundamentalists, rather than continue to snipe from the sidelines. But Missouri was adamant about its sympathies and its constituency:

> There are no liberals, there are no rationalists, and there are no modernists and there are no unionists. God has graciously preserved the Missouri Synod from being overrun with these parasites who sap the life-blood of a number of church bodies.[12]

Synodical authors on occasion cheered on the fundamentalist cause while keeping their distance from it. Different lists of principles identified as "Fundamentals" appeared at various stages of the controversy, which lasted through the 1920s, but always heading any list was an inerrant Bible. Missouri's theologians praised this emphasis on scripture at the same time they criticized fundamentalists' "wrong attitude"

9. F. B[ente], "Vorwort," *Lehre und Wehre* 50 (1904): 6. Carl Meyer, citing the original German, finds Bente's the first use of the term "verbal inspiration and infallibility." See Meyer, "The Historical Background of 'A Brief Statement,'" *Concordia Theological Monthly* 32 (1961): 422 n. 53.

10. Franz Pieper, *Christian Dogmatics,* vol. 1 (St. Louis: Concordia Publishing House, 1950), p. ix. The German volumes of *Christliche Dogmatik* were published in 1917 (vol. 2), 1920 (vol. 3), and 1924 (vol. 1). Publication of the first volume, on Luther's primary teachings on justification and Christology, was to coincide with the four-hundredth anniversary of the Reformation in 1917. Pieper found it natural to follow the first with a second volume on "the results and consequences of justification." Volume 1 was written last and addresses the nature of theology, God, creation, and anthropology, in addition to the major section on scripture.

11. Pieper, *Christian Dogmatics,* vol. 1, pp. 193-367. On verbal inspiration and inerrancy see pp. 217-28.

12. [Martin S.] S[ommer], "The Differences of Opinion in the Missouri Synod," *Lutheran Witness* 42 (April 10, 1923): 119.

toward the scripture.[13] Yet it was not only on the scripture issue that Missouri agreed with the basic doctrinal claims of fundamentalism. When the International Prophetic Conference in 1914 adopted a "Confession of Faith," the *Lutheran Witness,* declaring it agreed with all but one of the confession's ten points, rejoiced "to find so much Lutheranism in men of non-Lutheran denominations."[14] The single point over which co-editor Martin Sommer disagreed with the fundamentalists had to do with their premillennialism, the belief that the end of the world will be preceded by a literal thousand-year reign of Christ. In its steadfast rejection of "chiliasm," as Missouri called premillennialism, the synod declared itself to be amillennialist, denying the literal depiction of the end times rendered by millennialists.

The very obvious reason Missouri kept its official distance from any identification with fundamentalists was its fear of the dreaded unionism, the pejorative the synod applied to any fellowship, or unity, between churches without full doctrinal agreement.[15] Fundamentalism may have taken on a different face in each denomination it influenced, but the movement also transcended denominational boundaries. Missouri's persistent fear that its doctrinal purity would be tainted by affiliation with anyone whose teachings did not agree in full with its own orthodoxy clearly precluded alliance with any of the Reformed church bodies within which the fundamentalist/modernist conflict was raging.[16] Nevertheless, Missouri Synod theologians kept a close watch on developments within those denominations, all the while presuming their own church body to be removed from the influence of the controversy.[17]

13. John H. C. Fritz, "Will the Fundamentalists Win Out in Their Fight Against the Modern Liberalists?" *Theological Monthly* 4 (1924): 239.

14. [Martin] S[ommer], "A Confession of Faith," *Lutheran Witness* 33 (April 9, 1914): 58.

15. Milton L. Rudnick, *Fundamentalism and the Missouri Synod: A Historical Study of Their Interaction and Mutual Influence* (St. Louis: Concordia Publishing House, 1966), pp. 84-86.

16. For a cogent argument on the reticence of Lutherans in general to embrace either side of the fundamentalist/modernist controversy, see Mark Granquist, "Lutherans in the United States, 1930-1960: Searching for the 'Center,'" in *Reforming the Center: American Protestantism, 1900 to the Present,* ed. Douglas Jacobsen and William Vance Trollinger, Jr. (Grand Rapids: Wm. B. Eerdmans Publishing Co., 1998), pp. 234-51.

17. The clippings and files of several prominent Missouri Synod theologians from this era contain numerous articles and editorials from the Baptist *Watchman-*

Despite the official declarations that the synod had remained above the fray, fundamentalism had an unquestionable impact on Missouri's pastors. Seminary professor Herbert Bouman reflected on the introduction of fundamentalist thinking among Missouri clergy:

> Most of our Lutheran theology was in German, or Latin, for that matter. There was often very little available in English, or accessible, solid Lutheran theology. There was some, of course, from the Eastern Lutherans. And so, our pastors were looking for English theological literature, and that was right about the time of the great liberal/fundamentalist controversy . . . the early part of this century. And naturally, the sympathies of our people were with the people who believed in the deity of Christ and all those things. And so they bought conservative, Reformed theological books in English, and they bought Spurgeon's sermons and others, and unconsciously absorbed Reformed kind of thinking, and thought in all honesty, "That's Lutheran."
>
> And this goes on for generations. It can finally have a rather significant effect. Nobody's to blame for that, except maybe the theological teachers. But that's the way it happened. . . . I used to watch the pastors' libraries that would be sent to the seminary for book auction, and aside of the old German standards . . . or a few volumes of Luther in German, or a few volumes of sermons by some of our old homeleticians, the rest was Reformed theology.[18]

Its fear of unionism provided the synod an unequivocal excuse, if it needed an excuse, for remaining neutral in the fundamentalist/modernist controversy. While that debate dominated the early decades of the twentieth century, its reach did not extend into every denomination or church body. To Missouri, fundamentalism and modernism represented two extreme and highly unattractive alternatives, so the synod chose neither. Theological neutrality, however, is not only an oxymoron, but an impossible posture to maintain. More important to the synod was its intentional desire to preserve its own confessional Lutheran identity. Missouri simply did not wish to be compared theologi-

---

Examiner and *The Presbyterian*. Papers of Theodore Graebner, Walter A. Maier, William Frederick Arndt, Concordia Historical Institute, St. Louis.

18. Herbert J. A. Bouman, interview transcript (1976), Archives of Cooperative Lutheranism ALC-AELC-LCA Oral History Collection, ELCA Archives, Chicago, pp. 25-26.

cally to anyone, not to other Protestants and certainly not to Roman Catholics. The exclusiveness such a posture exhibited only perpetuated the synod's already insular reputation.

How American the Church Is!

A reader of Missouri Synod periodicals published in the early twentieth century might judge that this was a church body with a great deal to say about many different issues. Indeed, the synod had a lot to say, but very little of it had to do with the sociocultural changes taking place in America. The *Lutheran Witness,* for example, the synod's English-language periodical, varied in its attention to social issues depending on the current editor, but for the most part, paid little attention to them.[19] Missouri repeatedly argued about theological matters, often in critique of other Lutherans. Its lack of attention to the wider society changed quickly when the "ethnic ghetto"[20] that was the church was challenged at the core of its identity, its German heritage.

America tried valiantly to stay out of the Great War in Europe, and did succeed in remaining at least officially neutral while the warring parties waged a three-year standoff on the continent between 1914 and 1917. To the Missouri Synod, a German church body that was still speaking its native tongue even after seventy-five years in a new homeland, American neutrality was an appropriate position. The thoroughly German church body hardly advanced a pro-German argument, as historian Frederick Luebke recounts:

> In few German-American churches was the identification with the German government so weak and the retention of German language and culture so strong as in the Lutheran Church–Missouri Synod. . . . From the outset it adopted a remarkably neutral stance on the war issue in its official publications. Their most frequent ob-

19. Leland Robert Stevens, "The Americanization of the Missouri Synod as Reflected within the *Lutheran Witness*" (Ph.D. diss., St. Louis University, 1986), p. 123.

20. Alan N. Graebner, "The Acculturation of an Immigrant Lutheran Church: The Lutheran Church–Missouri Synod, 1917-1929" (Ph.D. diss., Columbia University, 1965), pp. 43-44.

servation was that the war was the hand of God chastening a sinful world.[21]

As the war dragged on, the synod began, justifiably, to be worried about the possibility of American involvement. Despite the government's efforts to maintain a neutral stance, reports of alleged German atrocities and the 1915 sinking of the *Lusitania* with American passengers aboard pushed American public opinion away from the Central Powers and in favor of the Allies. Once war had been declared in April 1917, the nation rallied to the war effort, and the all-or-nothing patriotism Americans expected during wartime both removed any possibility of neutrality and called for repudiation of all things German. Now the synod's worst fears were realized. Its primary badge of identity, worn proudly for seventy-five years, was the German language — treasured, however, more as a legacy of the Lutheran faith than of its homeland. Americans didn't care, however, why the Lutherans spoke German, only that they did. Pressure to speak English was increasingly felt in German communities, congregations, and schools.

Missouri was prevented from making a wholesale change in language use by its own polity. Because the synod was by nature and constitution advisory only, change would have to be effected at the congregational or district levels. A number of districts had begun initiatives to introduce English in worship and instruction prior to the war.[22] The most evident change the synod could make was to drop the word German from its name at the 1917 convention, at which the church body became the Evangelical Lutheran Synod of Missouri, Ohio, and Other States.[23] At the congregational level the change was swift, as the number of parishes holding an English-language service went from one-sixth of all congregations to three-fourths of all congregations in the three years between 1917 and 1920.[24]

21. Frederick C. Luebke, *Bonds of Loyalty: German Americans and World War I* (DeKalb, Ill.: Northern Illinois University Press, 1974), p. 102.
22. Paul T. Dietz, "The Transition from German to English in the Missouri Synod from 1910 to 1917," *Concordia Historical Institute Quarterly* 22 (1949): 97-127.
23. Missouri Synod, *Proceedings,* 1917, pp. 43-50. In 1917 a new constitution was adopted which incorporated the name change. It was ratified by the congregations in 1918. *Der Lutheraner* 74 (July 30, 1918): 263.
24. Kathleen Neils Conzen, "The Germans," in *Harvard Encyclopedia of American Ethnic Groups,* ed. Stephen Thernstrom et al. (Cambridge, Mass.: Harvard University Press, 1980), pp. 405-25.

German Americans had felt an intense pressure during the war to assure their fellow citizens they were Americans first. The nativist episodes chronicled in local church histories — pastors being run out of town, church buildings or even a pastor's beard being painted with yellow stripes — represented the worst of the home-front hostility toward the German enemy.[25] In the face of a campaign of antagonism, Missouri Synod Lutherans were quick to prove their loyalty to the United States, especially in Nebraska, where the state Council of Defense targeted certain Lutheran pastors for refusing to support the war effort.[26] Support of Liberty Bond or war stamp sales were important token gestures, but the switch to the English language was real evidence of the synod's sincerity about its assimilation into American society. Though *Lutheran Witness* co-editor Theodore Graebner announced in 1921 that "the language question in our own body is settled,"[27] it took the decade of the 1920s for the transition to be generally implemented. By 1927, the vast majority of synodical parochial schools were using English only.[28]

The end of the Great War left Americans ready to retreat from further international responsibility. But the defeat of Germany also left the country without a defined enemy, and the nation began to turn on itself. Nativist feelings were transferred from German Americans to Communists, anarchists, African Americans, and Jews, and a longstanding anti-immigrant sentiment that had begun in the 1880s succeeded in 1924 in closing the door on the great wave of immigrants that had been peopling American cities. With the decline and virtual end of immigration, the primary source for Missouri Synod mission work disappeared. From its beginning, the church had directed most of its activity into home mission, seeking out German immigrants to

25. Frederick Nohl, "The Lutheran Church–Missouri Synod Reacts to United States Anti-Germanism During World War I," *Concordia Historical Institute Quarterly* 35 (1962): 57. Alan Graebner presents perhaps the most thorough accounting of nativist behavior in his dissertation, "The Acculturation of an Immigrant Lutheran Church."

26. Robert N. Manley, "Language, Loyalty and Liberty: The Nebraska State Council of Defense and the Lutheran Churches, 1917-1918," *Concordia Historical Institute Quarterly* 37 (1964): 1-15. See also Neil M. Johnson, "The Patriotism and Anti-Prussianism of the Lutheran Church–Missouri Synod 1914-1918," *Concordia Historical Institute Quarterly* 39 (1966): 99-118.

27. Stevens, "The Americanization of the Missouri Synod," p. 157.

28. *Lutheran Witness* 48 (April 16, 1929): 140.

gather into congregations. Not only had the church given up the German language, but it now also had to ask if it would have to give up a membership composed primarily of German Americans.[29]

Changing Roles for Women in Missouri

Significant among the reform movements of the progressive era was the first wave of American feminism, primarily a single-issue crusade focused on winning the vote for women. The synod might easily have retained its usual posture of not commenting on social change except for the concomitant issue of woman suffrage in the church, addressed in the next chapter. But the women's rights movement was in reality about far more than suffrage alone — changes in society reflected the movement of women into the workforce, calls for maternal and child health, including birth control, and increased activism by women's organizations. Missouri would not be exempt from the impact of these sociocultural changes.

From the first, and wherever possible, congregations of the Missouri Synod endeavored to open a parochial school as soon as the congregation itself had been established. The school — to Walther "the gem" of the church and the key to its future[30] — was the means by which the children of the congregation were to be grounded in the Lutheran faith. The model was set in Perry County as well as by members of the Saxon remnant who stayed in St. Louis. The founding constitution of the synod required that member congregations provide Christian education for their children,[31] and congregational constitutions often required parents to send their children to parochial school in order to be members.[32] This declared need for both church and school was far more easily agreed to

29. F. Dean Lueking, *Mission in the Making: The Missionary Enterprise Among Missouri Synod Lutherans, 1846-1963* (St. Louis: Concordia Publishing House, 1964), p. 263.

30. Frederick C. Luebke, "The Immigrant Condition as a Factor Contributing to the Conservatism of the Lutheran Church–Missouri Synod," in *Germans in the New World: Essays in the History of Immigration* (Urbana: University of Illinois Press, 1990), p. 7.

31. Constitution of the German Evangelical Lutheran Synod of Missouri, Ohio, and other States, 1847, article II.

32. Constitution of Trinity Lutheran Church, St. Louis, Missouri, 1843, in Carl S. Meyer, *Moving Frontiers: Readings in the History of the Lutheran Church–Missouri Synod* (St. Louis: Concordia Publishing House, 1964), p. 169.

than was the relationship between the two public representatives of those institutions — pastor and teacher. That relationship had become mired in the larger debate about what constitutes "ministry."

A persistent question in Missouri Synod history has been where the parochial school teacher fits in a synodical model that demarcates only two categories — clergy and lay. Is the teacher a pastor or a layman? The answer to that question requires another look at the doctrine of the pastoral office. The distribution of voting power in the synod as it was organized in 1847 required that the number of clergy and lay representatives to synod be equal. Where did that put the teacher? Like the pastor without a parish, again according to the founding constitution, the teacher was considered not a voting member of synod, but an advisory member.[33] When teachers later inquired whether they could serve as lay delegates, the synod ruled that they could not.[34]

Stephen Schmidt, chronicler of parochial educators in the Missouri Synod, maintains that the offices of pastor and teacher were often collapsed into the person of the pastor from the earliest years of the synod.[35] Most often this need resulted simply from a shortage of teachers, so the pastor had to perform both roles. But there was also a sense in which the laity looked to the pastor as authority in all things. Indeed, Lutheran emphasis on the preached Word implies a teaching function through the pastor's sermon. And, in the scriptural description of the office, the roles of pastor and teacher are joined.[36] Some pastors assumed the teaching responsibility out of necessity, and some assumed it through the status given their office. When a congregation also had a called teacher, the latter situation only inflamed the already status-anxious teacher. A competition between the two offices, both congregationally and synodically, has been a persistent element of the synod's history.

33. Constitution of the German Evangelical Lutheran Synod of Missouri, Ohio, and other States, 1847, article III.

34. Missouri Synod, *Proceedings,* 1874, 79.

35. Stephen A. Schmidt, *Powerless Pedagogues: An Interpretive Essay on the History of the Lutheran Teacher in the Missouri Synod* (River Forest, Ill.: Lutheran Education Association, 1972), p. 23.

36. Ephesians 4:11 reads: "The gifts he gave were that some would be prophets, some evangelists, some pastors *and* teachers . . ." (NRSV). Emphasis added. While most English translations of the Bible use the conjunctive reference above, some commentators suggest that the proper sense of the original Greek is more accurately translated as pastor-teacher, or even teaching shepherd.

The combination of a shortage of teachers and the authority inherent in the preaching office lent support to those who argued, as Walther did, that there was only one office in the church, that of pastor, and that all other offices were derivative from that single office. Walther carried on something of a running debate with J. C. W. Lindemann, director of the Teachers' Seminary in Addison, Illinois, over the definition of office.[37] Lindemann — like many teachers in succeeding generations — understood the teaching office to be distinct in and of itself, a two-part office that was both spiritual and secular, having a responsibility to the civic community as well as to the faith community. And while he agreed with the need for pastoral supervision of the teaching office, he disagreed with Walther's interpretation of the pastoral office as the highest office in the church, with other offices as auxiliary to it (in Thesis VIII of Walther's theses Concerning the Holy Ministry or Pastoral Office).[38] One can understand the confusion. Teachers were neither pastors nor laymen in a church body that granted representation to only those two categories. The debate over where teachers belonged in this schema continued well into the next century, and continues still.

Who could be a teacher? This question centered on gender. By the last third of the nineteenth century, the teaching profession in American common schools had become feminized, thanks in good measure to Catherine Beecher's advocacy of the appropriateness of women — by nature nurturers — as teachers.[39] The synod recognized women teachers as both necessary and appropriate, noting that from the sixteenth century in Germany, church and school orders allowed for women teachers as long as they were trained.[40] J. C. W. Lindemann was not at

37. Letters from C. F. W. Walther to J. C. W. Lindemann, June 4, 1864 and September 27, 1866, in Carl S. Meyer, ed., *Walther Speaks to the Church: Selected Letters by C. F. W. Walther* (St. Louis: Concordia Publishing House, 1973), pp. 56-57.

38. C. F. W. Walther, *Church and Ministry: Witnesses of the Evangelical Lutheran Church on the Question of the Church and the Ministry,* trans. J. T. Mueller (St. Louis: Concordia Publishing House, 1987), p. 22. Interestingly, Lindemann later left teaching for the ordained ministry. Schmidt suggests that he was "never a strong advocate of the teacher" though he did persist in arguing the difference between the two ministries. See Schmidt, *Powerless Pedagogues,* pp. 60-61.

39. Kathryn Kish Sklar, *Catherine Beecher: A Study in American Domesticity* (New York: W. W. Norton, 1973), esp. ch. 12.

40. K. Bormann, "Über die Wirksamkeit der Lehrerinnen," *Evangelisch-Lutherisches Schulblatt* 3 (1867): 72-75; E. A. W. K[rauss], "Was sagen die alten

all averse to women teachers in parochial schools, as long as the church not follow the model of Roman Catholics and have too many women teaching. While he felt that women could certainly be used in lower grades and in all-girls' schools, he limited the extent to which women could serve in Missouri Synod classrooms: "We can never entrust our more mature male youth to 'schoolmistresses.'"[41]

By 1897, as the number of women teaching in the synod's parochial schools grew to more than a hundred,[42] the seminary faculty was asked for its opinion on this trend. In response, Professor George Stoeckhardt aligned himself with Lindemann's position from twenty-five years earlier — women might teach as long as their teaching was limited to small children. That role for women was not only appropriate, said the professor, but biblical: "These offices are to be filled according to the gifts God gives his people and many women have the gift to teach children." Stoeckhardt added a caution that a woman should not consider teaching her "life goal," which, according to the synod, ought to be marriage and raising a family.[43] Stoeckhardt's acknowledgment of the presence of women in Missouri's day schools was noted that same year by the synodical convention. Without taking action, the synod recognized that if the number of women teaching continued to increase, some provision would have to be made for their training.[44] Some in Missouri disagreed with Stoeckhardt, as evidenced by an article in the *Schulblatt*, which cautioned congregations about appointing women teachers. The writer did not forbid women teaching but strongly felt they were not to teach religion, particularly to older boys.[45]

Missouri had long held that woman's role was precisely defined by the quaint German expression *Kinder, Küche, und Kirche* (children, kitchen, and church). The reference to church in that triad, however, was

---

lutherischen Kirchen- und Schulordnungen des 16. Jahrhunderts über Anstellung von Lehrerinnen?" *Schulblatt* 31 (1896): 328-32.

41. [J. C. W. Lindemann], "Die Lehrthätigkeit der Frauen innerhalb der Christenheit," *Evangelische-Lutherisches Schulblatt* 7 (1872): 77, 78.

42. A. C. Stellhorn, *Schools of the Lutheran Church–Missouri Synod* (St. Louis: Concordia Publishing House, 1963), p. 232; Schmidt, *Powerless Pedagogues,* p. 97.

43. Georg Stoeckhardt, "Von dem Beruf der Lehrerinnen an christlichen Gemeindeschulen," *Lehre und Wehre* 43 (1897): 65-74.

44. Missouri Synod, *Proceedings,* 1897, p. 124.

45. Herman Speckhard, "Thesen, den Beruf der Gemeindeschullehrer unserer Synode und die Anstellung von Lehrerinnen innerhalb derselben betreffend," *Evangelische-Lutherisches Schulblatt* 32 (1897): 326-33.

meant to imply woman's attendance at worship, where, throughout the nineteenth century at least, she was to be seated with other women and the children, and would wait to commune until the men had returned to their seats.[46] Paul's letters provided the scripture passages used to define woman's role: women are enjoined to be silent in the churches and to hold no authority over men (1 Corinthians 14:34-36 and 1 Timothy 2:8-15). Women's limitation on teaching only prepubescent boys was understood in light of 1 Timothy 2:12. A boy child was not yet a man.

Strangely enough, no vocal opposition surfaced, either in the nineteenth century or in the early twentieth, as women sought admission to the teacher training program at Concordia College, Seward, Nebraska. Far more contentiousness surrounded the question of woman suffrage in the churches, though the same scriptural proscriptions were recited to define woman's role, no matter what activity women were interested in pursuing.[47]

In 1919 five women enrolled at the Seward college. This development prompted the 1920 synodical convention to refer to a committee the question of establishing a "ladies' seminary," which was "to give young ladies opportunity to secure a higher education at a synodical institution as well as to train them up for teachers in our schools and assistants in our heathen missions."[48] The church had long felt it should train its own workers, so it is puzzling that the next convention declined to pursue a separate women's college while making no alternative recommendation about the training of women teachers.[49] And despite synod's inaction, at least one male teacher, worried about the possibility of more women teachers, wrote of his concern about the "feminization of the teaching profession."[50] While supporting women

46. Graebner, "The Acculturation of an Immigrant Lutheran Church," pp. 17-18. See also James W. Albers, "Perspectives on the History of Women in the Lutheran Church–Missouri Synod during the Nineteenth Century," in *Essays and Reports* 9, 1980 (St. Louis: The Lutheran Historical Conference, 1982): 137-83.

47. See chapter 5 on the woman suffrage issue.

48. Missouri Synod, *Proceedings*, 1920, p. 29. In 1873 the synod considered purchasing property in Springfield, Illinois, for a proposed "ladies' seminary" to train young women as parochial school teachers. The plan was abandoned when funding became unavailable. *Der Lutheraner* 29 (November 1, 1873): 212; *Der Lutheraner* 30 (April 1, 1874): 55.

49. Missouri Synod, *Proceedings*, 1923, p. 11.

50. John Eiselmeier, "The Feminization of the Teaching Profession," *Lutheran School Journal* 60 (1925): 17-20.

teachers in principle, teacher John Eiselmeier blamed low teacher pay on the fact that there were fewer men in the profession. However, his main interest was that male students have male role models in their classrooms:

> To put the education of boys in the years in which their manhood is developing essentially in the hands of women cannot be without danger to the best interests of the community. . . . It is one of the essential duties of the American school to win back the male teacher.[51]

Eiselmeier's concern went unanswered as the synod in 1926 approved women teachers' education at Seward, though limiting female enrollment to 20 percent of the total enrollment. It gave the same approval to the Canadian synodical college at Edmonton.[52] As the number of women in parochial school classrooms continued to increase, the church body in 1929 reluctantly agreed that "the employment of woman teachers in our parish schools cannot be avoided altogether, nor should it be discountenanced under all circumstances."[53] This hardly enthusiastic admission was embedded in a declaration of the synod's obvious preference, that calling male teachers should "by all means remain the rule and order."[54] Still no definitive action was taken to improve teacher training for women. Indeed, the synod seemed to go out of its way to be sure the women who pursued such training never forgot their subordinate status, as placement of male candidates remained practice and preference in the synod through 1936.[55] But the number of women teaching steadily increased; more than five hundred taught in synod day schools in 1926.[56] The numbers grew, but the synod continued its pattern of supporting a principle while ignoring the practice. Finally a Seward faculty member wrote in 1931 that the synod really had only two alternatives — either no longer employ these women or start training them.[57] Slowly the church agreed, and in 1938 Concordia Teachers College in River Forest, Illinois, became the second

---

51. Eiselmeier, "The Feminization of the Teaching Profession," p. 20.
52. Missouri Synod, *Proceedings*, 1926, p. 77.
53. Missouri Synod, *Proceedings*, 1929, p. 74.
54. Missouri Synod, *Proceedings*, 1929, p. 74.
55. Schmidt, *Powerless Pedagogues*, p. 100.
56. Missouri Synod, *Proceedings*, 1926, p. 79.
57. L. G. Bickel, "Woman Teachers," *Lutheran School Journal* 66 (1931): 408-9.

synodical institution to admit women to its teacher-training curriculum, though women were to equal no more than 30 percent of the college's male enrollment.[58]

Stephen Schmidt believes the opposition to women teachers increased after this period as male teachers struggled with their perennial lack of identity vis-à-vis the public ministry, and to that end, the admission — even through the synod's reluctant encouragement — of women as trained synodical teachers only made the status of the male teacher more ambivalent.[59] To male teachers, who always considered themselves more clergy than lay, the presence of women teachers defied the men's understanding of their own status and role. Teachers shared the anxiety over status that shadowed all professionals in the rising middle class.[60] While synodical literature in the 1930s repeatedly affirmed that parochial school teachers and pastors each held a divine call to a public ministry of the Word,[61] how were male teachers to understand women in their profession? Did women teachers carry a different status, and if so, would that help clarify or further muddy the confusion over definition of the teaching office?

Once women were admitted to the teacher training programs of the synod, the question of the status of teachers became a semi-permanent feature of synodical conventions. A report to the 1941 synodical convention reviewed the doctrine of ministry and agreed that, yes, a woman teacher served in an auxiliary office of the one ministry of the pastoral office, but she should be reminded that "in relation *to men in general* God places women into a subordinate position" and that "God has excluded women from *the ministry proper.*"[62] By this disclaimer the synod was able to define the woman teacher within its prescribed teachings on women and ministry. There would also be a visible reminder of

58. Missouri Synod, *Proceedings,* 1938, p. 61.

59. Schmidt, *Powerless Pedagogues,* p. 100.

60. Burton J. Bledstein, *The Culture of Professionalism: The Middle Class and the Development of Higher Education in America* (New York: W. W. Norton & Company, 1978), p. 23.

61. Wm. C. Kohn, "Eine herzliche Bitte an die Lehrer zum Wohl unserer Gemeindeschulen," *Lutheran School Journal* 66 (1930): 1-8; L. August Heerboth, "Beruf und Amt eines Gemeindeschullehrers," *Lutheran School Journal* 67 (1931): 49-65; F. Pfotenhauer, "Die Herrlichkeit des Lehrerberufs," *Lutheran School Journal* 70 (1935): 241-44; H. Strasen, "Die Lehre vom Beruf unter gegenwärtigen Verhältnissen," *Concordia Theological Monthly* 7 (1936): 93-106.

62. Missouri Synod, *Proceedings,* 1941, 157-58. Italics in the original.

her subordinate status. She would not have the advisory status of the male teacher. Gender would continue to define her — certification requirements were lower for women, as was compensation; women's calls, though considered divine, were restricted; women teachers were subordinate to male teachers.[63] Even their documents of office were different. While a male teacher held a "Diploma of Vocation," a female teacher held a "Solemn Agreement."[64] A church that found it difficult to deny that women were part of the public ministry of the church found it difficult to explain how such a role could be reconciled to other prohibitions it held on women's service. Indeed, Stoeckhardt had declared that "a teacher in the Christian school, in so far as she teaches religion, exercises a part of the *publica doctrina* (public teaching of God's Word)."[65] Thus, rather than doctrinal consistency, the synod settled for practical limitations on her service.

Male teachers threatened by the military draft during World War II had appealed their status, claiming to be "ministers of religion." The Selective Service accepted the synod's request for exemption and assigned male teachers to the same category as pastors.[66] After the war, continuing need for clarification regarding teachers' status before the federal government, particularly concerning their standing before the Internal Revenue Service,[67] led the synodical convention in 1953 to declare that its teachers should properly be called "ministers of the Word,"[68] but the question of the status of the teacher, male or female, remained unresolved, a particular disappointment to educators on the synod's Board for Parish Education

63. Schmidt, *Powerless Pedagogues*, p. 106.

64. Stellhorn, *Schools of the Lutheran Church–Missouri Synod*, pp. 351-53, 426-27.

65. Stoeckhardt, "Von dem Beruf der Lehrerinnen," 71. See also the difficulty in explaining the difference gender makes in A. C. Mueller, "Women Teachers," *Lutheran Education* 89 (1953): 65-68.

66. Stellhorn, *Schools of the Lutheran Church–Missouri Synod*, p. 464.

67. The Internal Revenue Service (IRS) in 1949 challenged the income tax return of Eldor Eggen, an LCMS teacher in Michigan, who had claimed "minister of the Gospel" status in exempting his rental housing allowance from his declared income. (Pastors' housing allowances or parsonages are tax-exempt.) Extended legal proceedings and appeals followed until the IRS in 1950 ruled that "teaching in a Lutheran parochial school is a function of the public ministry in the Lutheran Church, and that a Lutheran teacher has the status of a minister of the Gospel within the Lutheran Church." Stellhorn, *Schools of the Lutheran Church–Missouri Synod*, pp. 467-71.

68. Missouri Synod, *Proceedings*, 1953, p. 327.

who had proposed to the convention that it recognize regularly called teachers as clergy.[69]

Would that step have been more easily taken by the synod were women not professional workers in the teaching ministry of the church? Or would the synod have continued its insistence on a teaching office separate and distinct from and auxiliary to the pastoral ministry? The postwar accommodations made by Missouri in its redefinition of the teaching office were concessions to governmental demands for clarification of teacher status and were not due to any reassessment of its doctrine of ministry. This seems a very weak means of addressing the fundamental questions the teachers had long been asking: Who are we and where do we fit in the scheme of the church? But the synod would respond in like manner less than ten years later when it again adjusted its understanding of the office of pastoral ministry for what appeared to be no more than utilitarian reasons.[70]

By 1965, distinctions between male and female teachers' status became even more unclear when the synod declared that women teachers carried the same status as male teachers at the same time it entertained the question of whether male teachers should be ordained.[71] Difference in male and female teacher status was to be explained "in keeping with Scriptural principles and our synodical stand in relation to the position of woman in the church."[72] Since 1954 the number of women teaching in the parochial schools of the Missouri Synod has ex-

69. Missouri Synod, *Proceedings,* 1953, pp. 323-24.

70. See below for this 1962 change.

71. Commission on Theology and Church Relations, minutes, November 1, 1965, unprocessed files, CHI. The question of ordaining male teachers was referred to the CTCR by the 1965 synodical convention. The matter was referred to a subcommittee for study, and was subsequently addressed by the CTCR in its 1973 report, "The Ministry in Its Relation to the Christian Church." The CTCR found "no biblical or theological reasons why teachers could not be ordained to perform that function of the Ministry to which they are called." The Commission included both male and female teachers in its analysis and concluded that ordination *to the office of teaching the Word* was something the synod could approve, noting that "this is a vastly different question from the question of the ordination of women to the pastoral office." The synod never acted on the CTCR's recommendation. See Samuel F. Nafzger, "The CTCR Report on 'The Ministry,'" *Concordia Theological Quarterly* 47 (1983): 98-99.

72. Missouri Synod, *Proceedings,* 1965, p. 99.

ceeded the number of men.[73] Yet the synod's doctrine of ministry continued to be inadequate to define either men's or women's various roles in a congregation or within the synod at large. Missouri's limited understanding of the pastoral office in the nineteenth century forced the synod to continually readjust its doctrine of ministry in the twentieth century as teachers and other auxiliary offices pressed for clarification of their status relative to the pastoral office. Rather than address itself to the primary question of the nature of ministry, the synod has responded by repeatedly redesigning and redefining its categories of ministry, most often to comply with federal government regulations.[74]

One of those categories of ministry was Missouri's twentieth-century adaptation of a practice dating to the first century. In 1911 Pastor Friedrich Herzberger of St. Louis presented a paper to the annual meeting of the Associated Lutheran Charities in which he proposed that the Synodical Conference reclaim the first-century model of the deaconess as a new ministry opportunity for women.[75] In the early church, deaconess (from the Greek *diakonia*) ministry was a ministry of service to women by unmarried — though not necessarily never married — women. Considerable controversy surrounds role definition and status of both deacons and deaconesses in the early church. The office of deaconess was an ordained office during the fourth and fifth centuries, but at no time did deaconesses hold clergy status.[76] Much of the confu-

---

73. *Statistical Yearbook of the Lutheran Church–Missouri Synod for the Year 1954* (St. Louis: Concordia Publishing House, 1955), p. 248.

74. Missouri Synod, *Proceedings,* 1983, pp. 178-81, by which the synod defined three categories of professional church workers: Category I included ordained pastors, Category II included commissioned teachers and Directors of Christian Education, and Category III included consecrated Certified Professional Church Workers-Lay (deaconesses, lay ministers, and parish workers). *Proceedings,* 1989, pp. 116-17, agreed that deaconesses could be advisory members of synod. In 1992 the IRS granted women teachers and deaconesses the same tax status as male teachers. LCMS *Reporter* 19 (March 9, 1992): 2. At the 1992 convention the categories of professional church workers were reduced to two: Ministers of Religion-Ordained and Ministers of Religion-Commissioned. *Proceedings,* 1992, p. 155.

75. Frederick S. Weiser, *Love's Response: A Story of Lutheran Deaconesses in America* (Philadelphia: The Board of Publication of the United Lutheran Church in America, 1962), p. 69.

76. The Apostolic Constitutions (c. 380) provided for the ordination of deaconesses "with the laying on of hands and the invocation of the Holy Spirit," and the Council of Chaldecon in 451 stipulated that a deaconess was to have reached the age of forty before her ordination. Jeannine E. Olson, *One Ministry, Many Roles:*

sion lies in the contemporary understanding of ordination, which reserves the rite to those in the pastoral office of word and sacrament, whereas the early church ordained men and women *to* specific offices, one of which was deaconess. Like deacons, deaconesses performed a variety of duties, both pastoral and liturgical, including assisting at baptisms, teaching catechumens, taking the eucharist to the sick, and providing charity within the community. A primary duty lay in the maintenance of decorum, the deaconess serving as liaison between women in the congregation and the priest.[77]

When deaconess ministry was revived in Europe in the 1840s, there was no conception of its being an ordained ministry, but it was definitely a gendered ministry. The deaconess was a single woman held in high regard for her extraordinary self-sacrifice in her service to those in need. In the 1850s a deaconess program was begun in Neuendettelsau, Bavaria, at the initiative of Pastor Wilhelm Loehe. Loehe's piety and social concern had led him to establish numerous social welfare and assistance programs, and his training program for deaconesses attracted Lutheran women from the European continent and Scandinavia. Through the establishment of hospitals and other institutions of mercy, "Loehe women" — deaconesses trained at Neuendettelsau — made an important, though scarcely recorded, contribution to American Lutheranism, just as had the "Loehe men" who were instrumental in the founding of the Missouri Synod. Lutheran deaconesses in the General Synod began serving in America in the mid-nineteenth century, and were soon followed by deaconesses of the ethnic synods. While not exclusively nurses, most deaconesses received nurse's training and served in that capacity. The deaconess movement for the rest of American Lutherans peaked in the 1930s, and since that time the number of women involved in deaconess work has continued to decline.[78]

Herzberger's suggestion was not acted on until 1919, when the Lutheran Deaconess Association (LDA) of the Synodical Conference was

---

Deacons and Deaconesses through the Centuries (St. Louis: Concordia Publishing House, 1992), p. 59.

77. Olson, *One Ministry, Many Roles*, pp. 50-60; Gillian Cloke, *'This Female Man of God': Women and Spiritual Power in the Patristic Age,* AD *350-450* (New York: Routledge, 1995), pp. 205-11; Ross Shepard Kraemer, *Her Share of the Blessings: Women's Religions Among Pagans, Jews, and Christians in the Greco-Roman World* (New York: Oxford University Press, 1992), pp. 181-83.

78. Weiser, *Love's Response,* p. 70.

founded with the encouragement of Pastor Philip Wambsganss, who had read Herzberger's book on women's work in the church and whose mother had been a deaconess prior to her marriage. The men who organized the LDA were determined that their deaconesses would be different from those in the other Lutheran synods, whose dark garb and title "Sister" too closely resembled Roman Catholic nuns.[79] The program started slowly but several early changes quickly refined the nature of deaconess ministry. The first deaconess students attended nursing school at the Lutheran Hospital in Fort Wayne, Indiana, where in 1922 a motherhouse was established on the hospital grounds.[80] In 1935 deaconess training was approved as a separate program from nursing, and from that time admitted only women who had already received professional training in social work, teaching, or nursing. In 1943 the program was relocated from Fort Wayne to Valparaiso University, also in Indiana. Within five years, from 1941 to 1946, the deaconess curriculum expanded from a two-year course to a four-year degree with a major in theology,[81] and deaconess assignments began to include placement in congregations. In 1957 the LDA built Deaconess Hall on the Valparaiso campus as both dormitory and center of student life.[82]

The deaconess ministry began in the Missouri Synod just as the New Woman was becoming a topic of concern for conservative observers, both religious and secular. The usual voices who worried in synodical periodicals about "feministic women" made surprisingly little comment about this new ministry opportunity for women in the Synodical Conference. In 1920, the year the Lutheran Deaconess movement was officially incorporated, the *Lutheran Witness* praised the Synodical Conference for joining the ranks of other churches that already offered this good work.[83] The lack of extensive comment on

79. J. Jeffrey Zetto, "Aspects of Theology in the Liturgical Movement in the Lutheran Church–Missouri Synod, 1930-1960" (Th.D. diss., Christ Seminary-Seminex, 1982), pp. 432-43.

80. F. Dean Lueking, *A Century of Caring: The Welfare Ministry Among Missouri Synod Lutherans, 1868-1968* (St. Louis: LCMS Board for Social Ministry, 1968), p. 17.

81. Lueking, *A Century of Caring,* p. 17.

82. Olson, *One Ministry, Many Roles,* p. 302.

83. J. R. Graebner, "Deaconesses," *Lutheran Witness* 39 (July 20, 1920): 227-28. See also [Theodore] G[raebner], "Our Deaconess Work," *Lutheran Witness* 40 (August 2, 1921): 245-46, and Philip Wambsganss, "Our Deaconess Work," *Lutheran Witness* 41 (April 25, 1922): 140.

this new development was the synod's silent nod that as long as women were doing women's work — ministry that was appropriate for women — there need be no question about the possible usurpation of male authority. The women who pursued deaconess training and eventually were placed in synodical parishes were "mercy people" whose primary interest was in service, and the work they did was well within the church's understanding of the proper role for women. No debate about this new auxiliary office was necessary. It wasn't public ministry. Or was it? Historian of the American deaconess movement Frederick Weiser believes that

> The genius of the diaconate then is also the very frustration of church bureaucrats who have never known quite what to do with it. . . . Its focus is people in need, in need of God's Word and in need of other, less "religious" forms of healing.[84]

Here, like teachers, a category of professional church workers had evolved in the Missouri Synod whose status was neither clearly clergy nor lay. No clarification was immediately required, however, because everyone in this category was a woman.

Herzberger, in proposing the reintroduction of the deaconess, had anticipated that there would be concern about this new-for-Missouri ministry, and admitted that on some occasions "the female diaconate has assumed an unbiblical form." He then reassured his audience that, because "the pure Word of God reigns supreme in our Synodical Conference, we need not fear that the female diaconate in our midst will be conducted on any other than Biblical lines."[85] From the first, Lutheran deaconesses have been consecrated, not ordained, to a ministry of Word and service, though officially they have been classified since 1992 as "commissioned ministers of religion."[86] The deaconess program never generated the same fears surrounding male teachers' status anxiety as more and more women entered parochial school teaching in the 1940s. During a decade in which American women won the right to vote, cut their hair and their hems, and went to work in greater numbers than ever before, some of the most conservative Lu-

---

84. Frederick Weiser, "The Lutheran Deaconess Movement," *Lutheran Forum* 28 (1994): 24.

85. Weiser, *Love's Response*, 70.

86. See note 74.

therans in America allowed women access to two ministry opportunities and said hardly a word about either.[87]

The second period of the synod's history served to bridge the nineteenth and twentieth centuries. The sociocultural changes of American society confronted its churches with one change after another, each requiring adaptation and often adjustment of previous attitudes. The synod had responded with reserved approval to the entrance of women into ministries of parochial school teaching and deaconess work. Would it also look favorably on laywomen's request to serve the church in another way?

Despite the congregational polity established by the synod in the nineteenth century, Missouri was slow to recognize the need for any associations for its lay people. The synod's slowness was not due solely to clergy reticence about the influence voluntary groups might exert on their members.[88] This had, after all, been a clergy-dominated church from its beginnings in Saxony. Deference to and dependence on clergy had long been a mark of the synod's layfolk. Alan Graebner attributes much of that behavior to the immigrant nature of the synod, combining German respect for authority and obedience with a "pastoral paternalism" based on the clergyman's greater education and status within church and community.[89] In the nineteenth century the principal activity in which lay men participated was the voters' assembly, because, as had been the case at Trinity, St. Louis, whose constitution provided the model for the synod, women were welcome as members but not as voters in the synod's congregations.

The first lay organization reluctantly agreed to by the synod was the Walther League, begun in 1893 after young people in the Synodical Conference pressed their church bodies to approve a national organiza-

87. Developments in the LCMS in the 1970s (see chapter 6) led some women in the LDA program to ask the synod to establish a deaconess training program at one of its synodical colleges. Because the LDA had become inter-Lutheran in 1969, the new opportunity for women to be ordained to pastoral ministry in other Lutheran church bodies became an issue with which some students were uneasy. In 1980, the Concordia Deaconess Program was established at Concordia College, River Forest, Illinois. See Olson, *One Ministry, Many Roles*, p. 306.

88. For the history of Missouri Synod laity, see Alan Graebner, *Uncertain Saints: The Laity in the Lutheran Church–Missouri Synod* (Westport, Conn.: Greenwood Press, 1975).

89. Graebner, *Uncertain Saints*, pp. 8-15.

tion.[90] Torn between a fear of allowing youth a group of their own within a congregation, and realization that it might be better for young people to associate together under the auspices of the church than of society at large, pastors admitted the potential value of a Lutheran youth organization. From the first, women as well as men participated in Walther League meetings and events, which led quickly to the question of women's status as members, including their right to vote and hold office. Because the League seemed unable to resolve the question on its own, in 1899 it pursued standard synodical (and German) practice on controverted issues by asking the faculty at Concordia Seminary, St. Louis, to render an opinion on "the ladies question," which had been unresolved for three years.[91] The faculty, in what League historian Jon Pahl considers a "subtle threat" not to sanction the League (which, indeed, the synod did not until 1920), cited the "law of silence for females" as applicable to all public gatherings in the church. The faculty opinion went on to add that, "All women in general are subordinate to men."[92] Then they finally answered the question they had been asked about woman suffrage:

> Whoever votes tries to establish his or her opinion or will over and against another. And when women vote about the same issue about which men vote and decide, it does not follow the "subordinate state" upon which women through the law are dependent.[93]

There was the crux of it: the professors considered voting an exercise of authority. Here was the position they would hold consistently as the question of woman suffrage arose in succeeding decades, first in civil society and then within synodical congregations. Yet the Walther League chose to ignore the judgment of the seminary faculty, and at its 1900 convention, allowed women to be voting members, though not national officers, of the new organization.[94]

In 1917 the Lutheran Laymen's League (LLL) had been organized,

---

90. This history is engagingly told by Jon Pahl in *Hopes and Dreams of All: The International Walther League and Lutheran Youth in American Culture, 1893-1993* (Chicago: Wheat Ridge Ministries, 1993).

91. Pahl, *Hopes and Dreams of All*, p. 47.

92. Pahl, *Hopes and Dreams of All*, p. 50.

93. Pahl, *Hopes and Dreams of All*, p. 51.

94. Pahl, *Hopes and Dreams of All*, p. 53.

largely to assist the synod in reducing the massive debt it had accumulated.[95] Prosperous businessmen met to pledge their personal funds as well as to develop fund-raising programs for the church. The synod could hardly object to the laymen's generosity and interest in putting the clergy's fiscal house in order.

In contrast to the synod's after-the-fact approval making the Walther League its official youth organization in 1920, and its gratitude over the laymen's initiative, the church's response when asked about the formation of a women's auxiliary ten years later was far less ambivalent. One clergyman, likely not a lone voice, was heard to say, "My God, don't let them do it!"[96]

Nevertheless, sporadic small groups known as Ladies' Aids *(Frauenverein)* had formed in the latter half of the nineteenth century, often as sewing circles and usually to assist hospitals or orphanages or mission houses. As a natural extension of the home, organization of a Ladies' Aid was frequently encouraged by the pastor of a congregation.[97] These local groups were later supplanted by larger auxiliaries officially attached to such institutions. The difference lay in both size and scope, as auxiliaries generally did considerable fund-raising, such as the Ladies' Auxiliary Dime Savers Program which substantially reduced the indebtedness of the Chicago old folks' home, the *Altenheim.*[98]

For at least ten years prior to the 1938 synodical convention, women's groups beyond local societies had been organizing in some districts of the Missouri Synod, and the enthusiasm with which they were received encouraged the women who had initiated these groups to investigate the possibility of forming a national organization. When compared to other Protestant church bodies, this development took place very late in the synod's history. Missionary societies and women's auxiliaries affiliated with national denominations had been part of the

95. Graebner's perceptive *Uncertain Saints* is a history of the Lutheran Laymen's League from its founding through 1970.

96. Minette Ludwig, personal statement to author, n.d.

97. An example is the founding of the Trinity Lutheran Ladies Aid of Block, Kansas, in 1912. See Carol K. Coburn, *Life at Four Corners: Religion, Gender, and Education in a German-Lutheran Community, 1868-1945* (Lawrence, Kans.: University Press of Kansas, 1992), pp. 50-55.

98. A. G. Roeber, *Good and Faithful Servants: The Centennial History of the Lutheran Home and Services to the Aged Ministry in Arlington Heights, Illinois 1892-1992* (Arlington Heights, Ill.: Lutheran Home for the Aged, 1991), pp. 19-20.

widespread growth of women's organizations in the post–Civil War years.[99] Other Lutheran churches had supported in particular the formation of mission societies to raise both consciences and funds about the new field of foreign mission work, which often included women missionaries.[100]

Impetus for a women's organization that extended beyond congregational boundaries began with the Lutheran Woman's League (LWL) of Oklahoma, which organized in 1928 to do mission work for local home mission needs. Almost simultaneously the Central District Missionary Endeavor in Indiana began at the urging of the Reverend Philip Wambsganss,[101] who had earlier been instrumental in the founding of the Lutheran Deaconess Association. Shortly thereafter, in 1929, a struggling Lutheran Laymen's League began to seriously consider establishing a woman's auxiliary, and invited sixteen women to a meeting in St. Louis to discuss the possibility.

In the course of two extended meetings, the women and men debated the virtues of women of the church organizing as an auxiliary to the LLL or as an independent organization. Inspired by the success of both the Walther League and the LLL, the women developed the outline of a constitution for their proposed Lutheran Women's League and its primary goal, mission support. Despite the tentative encouragement of the synod's Board of Directors for such an organization, the officers of the LLL, in deference to the clergy, felt a matter of this importance should be reviewed by the district presidents before further planning occurred.

When the question of a national women's organization was sub-

99. See Barbara Brown Zikmund, "Women's Organizations: Centers of Denominational Loyalty and Expressions of Christian Unity," in *Beyond Establishment: Protestant Identity in a Post-Protestant Age,* ed. Jackson W. Carroll and Wade Clark Roof (Louisville: Westminster/John Knox Press, 1993), pp. 116-38; and Rima Lunin Schultz, "Women's Work and Women's Calling in the Episcopal Church: Chicago, 1880-1989," in *Episcopal Women: Gender, Spirituality, and Commitment in an American Mainline Denomination,* ed. Catherine M. Prelinger (New York: Oxford University Press, 1992), pp. 19-71.

100. See, e.g., L. DeAne Lagerquist, *From Our Mothers' Arms: A History of Women in the American Lutheran Church* (Minneapolis: Augsburg Publishing House, 1987).

101. Ruth Fritz Meyer, *Women on a Mission: The Role of Women in the Church from Bible Times up to and including a History of the Lutheran Women's Missionary League during Its First Twenty-Five Years* (St. Louis: Concordia Publishing House, 1967), pp. 65-68.

mitted to the College of Presidents, the church leaders cautioned against it, for three disparate reasons: first, the women of the church already had "ample opportunity for service"; second, "a great deal of adverse opinion" on the subject had been heard in pastoral conferences; and finally, pastors were already "overburdened" with organizations and another one would simply mean more work for the synod's clergy.[102] The reaction of the presidents should hardly have come as a surprise, as a significant article in the premier edition of the *Concordia Theological Monthly* had warned:

> God has placed the business of the Church in the hands of men, and therefore any and every attempt of a woman publicly to influence these affairs is a usurpation of rights which cannot be squared with God's plain command and prohibition.[103]

The author, P. E. Kretzmann, went on to suggest that ladies' aids "conducted under the auspices of the congregations," altar guilds, or sewing-circles, all "may certainly prove a great blessing to the Church," as long as they were "rightfully managed and conducted," but "to go beyond this sphere . . . is precarious."[104] The College of Presidents would later that year reiterate Kretzmann's caution regarding the autonomy of the congregation:

> Large organizations or federations of women's clubs within the Church in danger of becoming busybodies in other men's matters, since their enthusiasm for the cause in which they believe is apt to lead them to a propaganda that may interfere with the work of the individual congregation.[105]

The question of women's service to the church through a national organization raised concern not only about the proper place of women, but about the proper understanding of the polity. Determined to preserve the congregation supreme, the College of Presidents' response looked beyond the immediate appeal of the women to organize, to a danger that

---

102. *LLL Bulletin* 2 (October 22, 1930): 44. Quoted in Meyer, *Women on a Mission,* p. 85.

103. P. E. Kretzmann, "The Position of the Christian Woman, Especially as Worker in the Church," *Concordia Theological Monthly* 1 (1930): 356.

104. Kretzmann, "The Position of the Christian Woman," p. 59.

105. Kretzmann, "The Position of the Christian Woman," p. 360.

the church might lose its sense of self through the synod's own growing bureaucracy of agencies and organizations. Its conservative judgment required the women to regroup and decide whether to pursue their dream or to respect the judgment of the district presidents.

Throughout the 1930s the women of Missouri continued to organize locally and on the district level to devote time and what funds they could raise in already difficult Depression years for missions variously defined (often through spare change gathered in what the women called "mite-boxes"). As the church reaped the benefits of the women's efforts in mission work it could otherwise not afford, the financial value of the women's work became evident. By 1938 several of the larger women's groups were again ready to propose the formation of a national women's organization, and this time the synod was ready to reconsider its earlier objections. After having so recently approved the training of women as professional church workers, how was Missouri going to explain its objection to women organizing as volunteers? Two lengthy and detailed overtures or proposals were sent to the synodical convention, one from the Central District and one from the women who earlier in the decade had done considerable spadework at the initiative of the LLL. The resolutions were adopted and the question of a synod-wide women's group was referred to a Synodical Survey Committee, which was to report to the 1941 convention.[106]

The committee, composed of five men, reported its conclusions by using some of the very words in the 1938 resolutions:

> the women of the Church offer a potential but heretofore oft-neglected power in the Church. We feel that this dormant power can be enlisted for the benefit of Synod without sacrificing any of the Scriptural principles governing woman's position in the Church.[107]

The convention accepted the report of the committee, which had included a plan of organization, but agreed that the women themselves should determine the details of their organization. However, pastoral oversight would be assured through the appointment of pastoral counselors at each level of the organization, and the synodical president was to appoint a committee of pastors to arrange the first meeting.[108]

106. Missouri Synod, *Proceedings,* 1938, pp. 342-45.
107. Missouri Synod, *Proceedings,* 1941, p. 393.
108. Missouri Synod, *Proceedings,* 1941, p. 405.

The founding convention of the Lutheran Women's Missionary League (LWML), official auxiliary of the synod, was held in Chicago in July 1942. Fifteen districts sent delegates and over one hundred other women attended the two-day event. Perhaps the most pressing question was what name the new organization would carry. Various combinations of Lutheran, women and federation, union or league were offered — even under consideration was "The Behnken League," named for the incumbent synodical president,[109] evidence of the elevated esteem in which the Missouri laity held its principal officer. The women chose in the end to include the word *missionary* to reflect their primary emphasis and purpose of mission work.

By the 1944 synodical convention, the pastoral oversight committee reported to the synod on the organization of the LWML, whose objectives were "To develop and maintain a greater mission consciousness among the women of Synod: Missionary Education — Missionary Inspiration — Missionary Service; [and] to gather funds for mission projects."[110] A publication, the *Lutheran Woman's Quarterly,* had been authorized, and the startup funds loaned to the organization by synod had already been repaid.

In the course of a decade, the synod had moved from a cautionary fear of yet another organization of laypeople, as well as an unexpressed but implied concern over an organization of women, to granting its hearty approval to the Lutheran Women's Missionary League. The women would be doing "women's work," which was understood to be nonthreatening according to the synod's separate gender spheres mentality. The relationship between synod and its official women's auxiliary has remained courteous, and the women consider themselves ancillary partners to their church body. The primary basis of their relationship is financial, as the church has readily seen the advantage of receiving funds it otherwise would not have had. The women are happy to oblige generously and appear to thrive on the synod's gratitude. But it is at the same time a curious relationship, in which the women are safely off doing volunteer mission work while failing to recognize the obvious opportunity their auxiliary status grants them to be advocates

109. Marlys Taege, *WINGS, Women IN God's Service: The 50th Anniversary History of the Lutheran Women's Missionary League of the Lutheran Church–Missouri Synod* (St. Louis: Lutheran Women's Missionary League, 1991), p. 40.

110. Missouri Synod, *Proceedings,* 1944, pp. 192-95.

for the women of the church. Immensely loyal to their church, the women of the LWML, like the synod itself, have drawn boundaries around themselves as to their perception of their mission.

Clarifying Itself Doctrinally

The various adaptations by which the synod met the challenges of the early twentieth century through the language change and the admission of women to new ministry opportunities should not be understood as having compromised its basic theological position. Missouri intended to be doctrinally unchangeable. The one topic that seemed to dominate the activity of American Lutherans in the first decades of the century was increased fellowship. Smaller Lutheran synods approached one another, held conferences, wrote theses of agreement, and merged into new synods, all at what seems a dizzying pace to the historian trying to keep score of the various synodical negotiations.[111] Some of these unions were based on a common ethnic heritage, others on shared doctrinal positions. Joint Lutheran efforts during the war led to the formation of a pan-Lutheran organization, the National Lutheran Council, in 1918.[112] Still, the Missouri Synod, smarting from severed ties with several synods due to the Predestination Controversy of the early 1880s, engaged in discussions of unity only very tentatively until the mid-1920s, and refused to join the National Lutheran Council. Never did it waver from its insistence that there could be "no union without unity."

In 1897 Franz Pieper had written "A Brief Statement on the Doctrinal Position of the Missouri Synod" to reaffirm the synod's scriptural basis and confessionalism in its jubilee year.[113] The title is some-

111. See John H. Tietjen, *Which Way to Lutheran Unity? A History of the Efforts to Unite the Lutherans of America* (St. Louis: Concordia Publishing House, 1966), and Theodore Graebner, *The Problem of Lutheran Union and Other Essays* (St. Louis: Concordia Publishing House, 1935).

112. Fred W. Meuser, "Facing the Twentieth Century, 1900-1930," in *The Lutherans in North America,* rev. ed., ed. E. Clifford Nelson (Philadelphia: Fortress Press, 1980), p. 404.

113. Francis Pieper, *A Brief Statement of the Doctrinal Position of the Missouri Synod, in the Year of Jubilee, 1897,* trans. W. H. T. Dau (St. Louis: Concordia Publishing House, 1897).

what misleading, as Pieper's Statement did not address the whole of Missouri Synod doctrine, but instead primarily addressed controverted questions between the various German-language synods. The document was in large part a restatement of the synod's position on election, so recently the center of inter-Lutheran dispute and division.

For the first time in 1917, the Missouri Synod appointed a union committee to begin exploratory discussions with others in the Synodical Conference, meaning those synods with which Missouri was most closely aligned on doctrine.[114] Initially the discussion at the meetings of the Intersynodical Committee, composed of representatives from five synods (Missouri, Wisconsin, Ohio, Iowa, and Buffalo), focused on the doctrines of conversion and election. Because these issues had created such contentiousness during the Predestination Controversy, the Committee agreed to base its discussion on the Lutheran confessions alone, and to that end restricted the use of citations to only those theologians who had lived prior to the completion of the Book of Concord in 1580.[115] This innovative tactic was employed to prevent reliance on later sources — in Missouri's case, the seventeenth-century dogmaticians. The tactic must have worked, since the Intersynodical Committee eventually reached agreement on a significant number of doctrines, from election to fellowship, church and ministry, and even a primary problem in the nineteenth century, "open questions,"[116] theological problems not readily solved by scripture. The Intersynodical Theses, or "Chicago Theses Concerning Conversion, Predestination, and Other Doctrines," were approved by the representatives of the five synods in 1928.[117]

But by the 1929 synodical convention in River Forest, anti-union sentiments again prevailed in Missouri. Concern had been raised over the Ohio Synod's fellowship with the Norwegian synods, nearly all of whom had merged in 1917. Missouri had substantial doctrinal differences with the Norwegians. More significant, however, was the influence of chief synodical theologian Franz Pieper, who was expressly interested only in "what is truly Lutheran doctrine."[118] His contention

114. Carl S. Meyer, "The Historical Background of 'A Brief Statement,'" *Concordia Theological Monthly* 32 (1961): 532.
115. Meuser, "Facing the Twentieth Century," p. 445.
116. Meuser, "Facing the Twentieth Century," p. 445.
117. Meyer, "Historical Background," p. 536.
118. Meyer, *Log Cabin to Luther Tower,* p. 241.

that the Chicago Theses were inadequate expressions of doctrine was influential enough to cause the convention to reject the Theses and instead recommend that the president of synod appoint a committee to respond to the Theses by presenting "the doctrine of the Scriptures and the Lutheran Confessions in the shortest, most simple manner."[119]

The convention got what it asked for, as the committee prepared "A Brief Statement on the Doctrinal Position of the Missouri Synod." Authored primarily by Pieper, the Brief Statement of 1932 is essentially the same as his 1897 Brief Statement. It was intended only to address the points of disputation with the Chicago Theses, and not, according to Pieper himself, a basis for future fellowship negotiations.[120] The document consists of nineteen sections, each outlining Missouri's position on one of the controverted issues. The first paragraphs address scripture; the longest section is on the doctrine of the church. The Brief Statement was adopted by the 1932 synodical convention as "a brief Scriptural statement on the doctrinal position of the Missouri Synod,"[121] an action that served as tribute to its author, Franz Pieper, who had died in 1931. Convention proceedings do not indicate that the Brief Statement generated any extended floor debate aside from the concern of one district which "expressed surprise that these theses do not cover all doctrines."[122] And one seminary professor commented on the response of the convention and subsequently of the synod:

> [T]here was not a big deal. There was not to be a confession of faith, anything like this. Merely a set of theses, which our theologians might use in their discussions with the new ALC. . . . And after it had been adopted, there was no great jubilation, no "Now Thank We All Our God" singing or anything like that. . . . No great fanfare that we finally had accomplished this great task. The thing was never discussed in seminary faculty meetings. Congregations were never asked to vote on it or anything. It was sent out to all the pastors. . . . It took the Brief Statement from '32 to '47 to get into the synodical *Proceedings*.[123]

119. Missouri Synod, *Proceedings*, 1929, pp. 112-13.
120. Theodore Graebner, "'The Cloak of the Cleric,'" unpublished ms., April 20, 1950. Published in *Concordia Historical Institute Quarterly* 44 (1971): 5.
121. Missouri Synod, *Proceedings*, 1932, pp. 154-55.
122. Missouri Synod, *Proceedings*, 1932, pp. 154-55.
123. E. J. Friedrich, interview transcript (1977), Archives of Cooperative Lutheranism ALC-AELC-LCA Oral History Collection, ELCA Archives, Chicago, pp. 17-18.

To the degree that the Brief Statement and the Lutheran Confessions can be compared as documents, an important similarity exists beyond the very obvious stylistic likeness (we teach this . . . ; we condemn, reject, warn about that . . .). Each was a product of the contemporary religious scene, and each was written in response to the controverted issues of that time. The confessions, compiled late in the sixteenth century, addressed the primary disputed issues between the Reformers and the Roman Catholic Church, one of the most critical being the abuses of the powers exercised by the papacy and the bishops of the church. The Reformers did not include a doctrine of scripture, likely because the authority of scripture in itself was not a contested issue at the time, though of primary dispute was the locus of authority of interpretation. Likewise, in the middle period of the Missouri Synod's history, the doctrine of the ministry — at the core of nineteenth-century disputes — was not at issue; but questions about the authority of scripture were central, especially in light of the long fundamentalist/modernist controversy in which one's position on other matters depended on what authority one was prepared to give scripture. The Brief Statement's position on church or ministry is not as significant here as is its opening paragraphs on scripture. *That* the Brief Statement was written was enough for the time. It was a document of clarification. But it was also a document that fundamentally altered the confessional base of the synod. The authority assigned to that narrowing by succeeding generations extended the influence of the Brief Statement far beyond its original intention.

Discussions on fellowship resumed after 1932 and continued through the 1930s. Despite Pieper's claim that the Brief Statement was not intended as a basis for fellowship negotiations,[124] the 1938 synodical convention accepted the document as "the doctrinal basis for *future church-fellowship* between the Missouri Synod and the American Lutheran Church,"[125] which had been formed in 1930 through the merger of the Iowa, Ohio, and Buffalo Synods. The 1947 convention, marking the synod's centennial, affirmed that the Brief Statement "correctly expresses its doctrinal position."[126] By 1956, the Brief Statement apparently had been elevated to the status of the confessions themselves, as the

---

124. See note 120.
125. Missouri Synod, *Proceedings*, 1938, p. 231. Italics in the original.
126. Missouri Synod, *Proceedings*, 1947, p. 476.

synod resolved "that we reject any and every interpretation of documents approved by the Synod which would be in disagreement with the Holy Scriptures, the Lutheran Confessions, and the Brief Statement."[127] As the authority granted the Brief Statement by the synod increased over time, so did the concern of a number of clergy about what they perceived to be a dangerous innovation in the church's confessional position.

A Statement in Response

The most serious internal struggle Missouri faced in its second fifty years, and one that directly challenged several dimensions of the synod's understanding of authority, came as the result of the failed fellowship efforts in the 1920s and 1930s, actions which, to the more progressive clergy in the synod, signaled the church's persistent retreat into insularity.[128] In early September 1945, forty-four Missouri Synod clergymen responded to an invitation from E. J. Friedrich, president of the Colorado District of the synod, to meet at the Stevens Hotel in Chicago to discuss "a pernicious spirit" that had

> lifted its ugly head in more than one area of our beloved Synod. This spirit has its origin in a wrong approach to the Holy Scriptures and in a tragic misconception of the very essence of the Gospel and the nature, functions and mission of the Church. It is characterized by barren, negative attitudes, unevangelical techniques in dealing with the problems of the individual and the Church, unsympathetic legalistic practices, a self-complacent and separatistic narrowness, and an utter disregard for the fundamental law of Christian love.[129]

The initiative for this gathering — "the most significant, memorable, Spirit-filled meeting I have ever attended," recalled one participant[130] —

127. Missouri Synod, *Proceedings*, 1956, p. 546.
128. This episode is discussed in detail in Jack T. Robinson, "The Spirit of Triumphalism in The Lutheran Church–Missouri Synod: The Role of 'A Statement' of 1945 in the Missouri Synod" (Ph.D. diss., Vanderbilt University, 1972).
129. Letter from The Committee to Friend and Brother, September 20, 1945. Theology and Church Relations Collection, CHI.
130. Herbert Lindemann, "Personal Reflections on the Twenty-Fifth Anniversary of the Publication of 'A Statement,'" *Concordia Historical Institute Quarterly* 43 (1970): 166.

was the direction in which the synod appeared to be turning since its 1938 convention. The dialogue about fellowship that began in the 1920s and led to agreement on the Intersynodical Theses in 1928 had been resumed since the 1930 formation of the new American Lutheran Church from the Iowa, Ohio, and Buffalo Synods. Pieper's Brief Statement had become the basis for Missouri's participation in the negotiations and in 1938 was accepted along with the *Declaration of the Representatives of the American Lutheran Church* as the doctrinal basis for future altar-and-pulpit fellowship between the two church bodies.[131] However, following the synod's approval, anti-union forces within the church began to agitate against this action[132] and by the 1944 convention had achieved considerable strength to oppose the proposed fellowship.

It was the tone of that 1944 convention in Saginaw — a meeting that had "manifested a spirit of separatism, of isolationism, and of un-Lutheran 'fundamentalism'" and was the "'low water mark' in the theology and polity of the Synod up to that time"[133] — that prompted the group of more moderate clergy to gather in Chicago at Friedrich's invitation. In particular, the "horrible theological climate" of "fault-finding [and] innuendo" was blamed on a publication called the "unofficial, partisan, polemic periodical,"[134] the *Confessional Lutheran*, introduced in 1940, and ideas fostered by a group of pastors in the Chicago area known as the Chicago Study Club.[135]

The meeting at the Stevens Hotel was a virtual "who's who" of the synod. Present were district presidents, seminary professors, a university president, church executives, and prominent clergy. Costs of the almost exclusively clergy-attended meeting were underwritten

131. Missouri Synod, *Proceedings*, 1938, pp. 231-33.

132. Bernard H. Hemmeter, "Reflections on the Missouri Synod," *Concordia Historical Institute Quarterly* 43 (1970): 176.

133. Thomas Coates, "'A Statement' — Some Reminiscences," *Concordia Historical Institute Quarterly* 43 (1970): 159.

134. Laurie Ann Schultz Hayes, "The Rhetoric of Controversy in The Lutheran Church–Missouri Synod with Particular Emphasis on the Years 1969-1976" (Ph.D. diss., The University of Wisconsin-Madison, 1980), pp. 142-43.

135. Richard R. Caemmerer, interview transcript (1978), Archives of Cooperative Lutheranism ALC-AELC-LCA Oral History Collection, ELCA Archives, Chicago, p. 47; A. R. Kretzmann, interview transcript (1978), Archives of Cooperative Lutheranism ALC-AELC-LCA Oral History Collection, ELCA Archives, Chicago, p. 50.

by interested laymen.[136] Following the presentation of several position papers, nine members of the group drew up twelve theses affirming the "evangelical heritage of historic Lutheranism"[137] and condemning the abuses they perceived as "trends and tendencies"[138] within the synod. The document was called simply *A Statement*. The central issue was identified as the doctrine of the church, which had been addressed in one of the position papers, "Organization and Church," by O. P. Kretzmann, president of Valparaiso University, who said of the synod:

> In late years there has been a marked shift of emphasis from the Scriptural and historically Lutheran position. . . . [The synod] has moved into the center of thought and life to such an extent that the very purposes for which it was organized are endangered. The original emphasis on the priesthood of all believers and congregational freedom and responsibility has been supplanted by a demand for a rigid organizational loyalty which must result in either a dead uniformity rooted in fear or in a reaction to the opposite and equally undesirable extreme of irresponsibility and revolt.[139]

"The heart of it was the meaning of the church. . . . We didn't realize at the time how simple it was," recalled Richard Caemmerer of the seminary faculty.[140] Their principal concern over the doctrine of the church had to do with the synod's position on fellowship, which had been moderating in the 1920s and 1930s and then began to narrow as the prospects of fellowship with the ALC loomed. But equally troubling was the loveless legalism the signers believed was inherent in the substitution of "human judgements, synodical resolutions, or

136. E. J. Friedrich, interview transcript (1977), Archives of Cooperative Lutheranism ALC-AELC-LCA Oral History Collection, ELCA Archives, Chicago, pp. 24-25. One layman whose contribution made the meeting possible, according to Friedrich, was Ernest J. Gallmeyer, a member of synod's Board of Directors. Others included W. C. Dickmeyer, chair of the Valparaiso University Board of Trustees and the only layman to attend the meeting, and Congressman John William Boehne (D-Indiana).

137. *Speaking the Truth in Love — Essays Related to A Statement. Chicago, Nineteen Forty-Five* (Chicago: Willow Press, n.d.), pp. 7-9. See the Appendix for the text.

138. E. J. Friedrich, "Forward," *Concordia Historical Institute Quarterly* 43 (1970): 154.

139. Mimeographed copy, Statement of the Forty-Four Collection, CHI.

140. Caemmerer, interview transcript, p. 50.

other sources of authority for the supreme authority of the Scripture."[141]

The forty-four signers agreed that *A Statement*, with a cover letter explaining its origin, should be mailed to every pastor in the synod. Another participant recalled that "Time was of the essence since the time and purpose of the meeting were known and false rumors were already in motion, accusing the group of trying to disrupt and corrupt the Synod."[142] Indeed, President John Behnken had been previously alerted that "a meeting of a revolutionary group in the synod" was planned for the week after Labor Day.[143]

Within a church body rampant with suspicion over infection of its pure doctrine through fellowship with other Lutherans, the "Forty-four"[144] or the "Statementarians," as they came to be known, were immediately attacked for their meeting, their method, their theses, and their arrogance. Conservatives who considered the action of the "Forty-four" a "fellowship controversy"[145] on par with the earlier Predestination Controversy demanded both the immediate retraction of *A Statement* and the swift expulsion of its signers. The signers' strategy of distributing *A Statement* to the entire clergy roster meant that this debate would not be limited to a few principals, but that every one of the synod's 3,627 parish pastors at the time[146] would learn of the signers' concern. As a result, several hundred wrote to ask to have their names added to the document.[147]

The leadership of the synod responded less favorably and called for a meeting between the "Forty-four" and the College of Presidents and synod praesidium (president and vice presidents) in February 1946. Papers were to be presented and discussion advanced as to the content of *A Statement*. In what one of the participants called "one of the most dismal

141. *Speaking the Truth in Love*, p. 7.
142. Harold H. Engelbrecht, "Concerning 'A Statement,'" *Concordia Historical Institute Quarterly* 43 (1970): 169.
143. Robinson, "The Spirit of Triumphalism," pp. 216-17.
144. Coates claims there were actually only forty-two signers. See Coates, "'A Statement' — Some Reminiscences," p. 160.
145. A. T. Kretzmann, "The Statement of the 44, 1945-1979," *Concordia Historical Institute Quarterly* 55 (1982): 69.
146. *Statistical Yearbook of the Evangelical Lutheran Synod of Missouri, Ohio, and Other States for the Year 1945* (St. Louis: Concordia Publishing House, 1946), p. 140.
147. Engelbrecht, "Concerning 'A Statement,'" p. 170; mimeographed list of 214 subsequent signers, Statement of the Forty-Four Collection, CHI.

episodes in Synodical history," the meeting only set the stage for further debate when the "Forty-four" were asked to withdraw their statement and refused.[148] Later it was agreed that ten of the signers of *A Statement* and ten men appointed by President Behnken would meet to discuss the document. The "Ten and Ten" held three meetings that extended over eleven days.[149] One of Behnken's appointees recalls an important breakthrough when the two sides were able early on to agree on "the principles of *Sola Scriptura*," in particular two statements:

> The "Scriptural Principle" means that each statement of the canonical Scriptures, whether it deals with questions of salvation, of Christian conduct, of history, of science, or of any other matter, was verbally inspired by the Holy Ghost in order to be believed. . . .
>
> When dealing with two Scripture passages or truths that seem to be in conflict, it is not the function or prerogative of human reason to eliminate or to modify one passage or truth. Each passage or truth must be allowed to stand and must be accepted as binding, since each is divinely inspired.[150]

However, despite the Ten and Ten agreement in principle, A. T. Kretzmann noted in regret that "these basic principles of Bible interpretation unfortunately were not transferred to the controverted teachings and texts, with the result that no agreement was reached in further meetings."[151] A primary point of contention emanated from the position of the "Forty-four" that there could be more than one correct interpretation for a passage of scripture, a complaint focused in this case on a single text — Romans 16:17[152] — which opponents of fellowship cited in support of their extreme position on union.[153] The scriptural principles to which the two sides had agreed were obviously understood very differently by each.

148. A. T. Kretzmann, "The Statement of the 44, 1945-1979," p. 72.
149. A. T. Kretzmann, "The Statement of the 44, 1945-1979," p. 73.
150. A. T. Kretzmann, "The Statement of the 44, 1945-1979," p. 74.
151. A. T. Kretzmann, "The Statement of the 44, 1945-1979," pp. 74-75.
152. "I urge you, brothers and sisters, to keep an eye on those who cause dissensions and offenses, in opposition to the teaching that you have learned; avoid them" (NRSV).
153. Larry W. Neeb, "Historical and Theological Dimensions of a Confessing Movement within the Lutheran Church–Missouri Synod" (D.Min. thesis., Eden Theological Seminary, 1975), pp. 79-80.

Even while these discussions were proceeding, agitation was growing among some in the synod that several of those who had signed *A Statement* were members of the faculty at the St. Louis seminary. A request to investigate the five professors was rejected by the chair of the Board of Electors on procedural grounds.[154] Additionally, calls for the removal of Theodore Graebner as co-editor of the *Lutheran Witness* persisted, accusing Graebner of "propaganda for unscriptural doctrine."[155] Some in the Northern Illinois District even attempted to ban the *Witness* from circulation in that district.[156] And a Chicago attorney dropped his membership in the Concordia Historical Institute based on his objection to the Statementarians — whom he accused of promoting a "New Deal religion" — and their control of the Institute and its journal.[157]

It is not clear whether any more meetings would have brought the two groups closer to reconciliation of their differences. That became a moot point when John Behnken signed an agreement with the "Forty-four" that effectively brought the entire episode to a truncated conclusion. In January 1947 the original signers of *A Statement* agreed, "in the interest of peace and harmony in our midst and for the furtherance of the Kingdom of God at large," to withdraw their document, but not recant it.[158] They simply agreed no longer to promote *A Statement* or to continue as a group. Behnken's end-run around the Ten and Ten was a political move to resolve this contentious episode before the summer convention that would mark the synod's centennial. His attempt at resolution satisfied neither side. One of the signers believed the "Forty-four" made "a strategic mistake" in offering to withdraw *A Statement* as "a basis for discussion," which led many in the synod to assume the signers had retracted the document.[159] In fact, Graebner felt it necessary to continually remind Behnken in correspondence both that *A Statement* had never been repudiated by the synod and that the signers

154. Typewritten notes, Theodore Graebner papers, box 109, CHI.

155. Typewritten notes, Theodore Graebner papers, box 109, CHI.

156. Robinson, "The Spirit of Triumphalism," p. 262.

157. John C. Eich, letters to W. G. Polack, March 21 and April 15, 1948. Theodore Graebner papers, box 109, CHI. Graebner found Eich's correspondence with Polack to be "dripping with venom."

158. J. W. Behnken, "Dear Brother," to the clergy of the Missouri Synod, Oak Park, Illinois, January 18, 1947. Statement of the Forty-Four Collection, CHI.

159. Coates, "'A Statement' — Some Reminiscences," p. 163.

had never been censured.[160] One of Behnken's Ten accused the president of backing off from his intention to take disciplinary action against the "Forty-four" if they did not "renounce their unscriptural position. . . . Instead the praesidium cosigned an Agreement with those whom they had from the very first accused of false doctrine."[161]

The story of *A Statement* is one of the more curious chapters in the history of The Lutheran Church–Missouri Synod. Fear of controversy has regularly led Missouri to compromise, as happened in Perry County after Stephan's deposition. As contentious as the argument became over *A Statement,* with lines drawn and sides taken, Behnken simply put the issue to rest. But the issues that document addressed and the behaviors that had originally moved the "Forty-four" to address their concerns in writing did not disappear. A century after Walther thought he had settled the question "what is the church?" this very issue had come back to haunt the synod. The twentieth-century debate differed from that of the nineteenth century in one important way. This argument over the doctrine of the church was carried on exclusively among the clergy, where the Perry County debate not only included, but was initiated by, the laity. By not including the laity in the discussion, the clergy had not only mistakenly collapsed church and ministry into one but had also forgotten its responsibility to the people of God.

The word "turning point" appears frequently in the recollections of the "Forty-four."[162] After the Chicago meeting, *Lutheran Witness* co-editor Theodore Graebner — one of the *Statement* signers — reported on the meeting under the headline, "Discussion Group in Chicago Adopts Statement," and he commented that the group had gathered over concerns about "the harm which might come to orthodoxy through an arrogant self-sufficiency."[163] Five years later Graebner, shortly before his death, would write less cryptically about the meeting and its ensuing statement, which called for

---

160. Correspondence between Theodore Graebner and John W. Behnken, Graebner papers, box 109, CHI.

161. A. T. Kretzmann, "The Statement of the 44, 1945-1979," pp. 78-79.

162. The November 1970 issue of the *Concordia Historical Institute Quarterly* was devoted to the twenty-fifth anniversary of A Statement and gathered the memories of most of the twenty still living signers.

163. *Lutheran Witness* 64 (September 25, 1945): 323.

the discussion of Missouri Synod attitudes sometimes inexactly characterized as "traditionalism." Traditionalism was placing human authority above that of the Word of God; made fellowship dependent on acceptance of every terminological detail in ecclesiastical dogma; treated the New Testament body of saving doctrine as a code of law; paid lip service to the Sola Scriptura but actually operating with synodical resolutions.[164]

A turning point implies a change, or a "before and after" watershed. *A Statement* might have been a turning point for the synod if the discussion it tried to initiate had been allowed to continue. The agreement reached to withdraw the document as a basis for discussion was unfortunately taken by most of the synod to mean that there would be no discussion. Behnken's Agreement was yet another unsatisfactory compromise. As another of the "Forty-four" recalled:

> At a time when the Synod was getting ready to celebrate its first centennial, the Forty-Four restated some basic Lutheran principles in relation to a rapidly changing church in a rapidly changing world, and it was their avowed hope to help pave the way into a very uncertain and hazardous future.[165]

Despite the changes the fifty years between 1897 and 1947 had brought, Missouri declined a rare and significant opportunity for the church to reflect on its past and consider its future.

The signers of *A Statement* directly challenged the Missouri Synod's understanding of its own authority on several counts. What O. P. Kretzmann had identified as the problem — the synod's increasing claim to authority over against that of the congregations — resulted in Missouri's violating the central principle of its *raison d'être*. Additionally, the Forty-Four questioned the synod's elevation of synodical resolutions over the authority of scripture, while at the same time declaring there to be but one exegesis for a scriptural reference. Finally, they argued that the synod's reliance on its historic position against unionism had resulted in granting new authority to tradition itself. In response there was no response, officially at least.

164. Theodore Graebner, "The Cloak of the Cleric," p. 3.
165. Walter E. Bauer, "To Recall As Well As I Can," *Concordia Historical Institute Quarterly* 43 (1970): 173.

Conclusion

The second fifty years of Missouri Synod history served as a time of transition for the church body. Confronted with a barrage of new challenges, the decisions Missouri would be required to make were critical to its self-identity and its accommodation to the larger society. The children and grandchildren of the immigrants who had founded the synod were now caught up in the massive changes that were helping to reshape their adopted homeland, and thereby their church itself.

Implicit in every challenge was the synod's perception of a threat to its doctrinal purity and its claim to be the true church. More than any other change, the wartime shift from German, the language of the faith, to English required the church to adjust its view of what constituted purity in doctrine. Always before, the synod had rejected a language change, convinced that the true faith could be conveyed only in the original tongue of the Reformers.

Was the change in language alone enough to bring the church into the twentieth century? In 1926, several years after the synod had hurried to prove its loyalty by discarding German, an editorial in the *Christian Century* described the Missouri Synod as "almost as rigid and unbending as Rome, and it consciously isolates itself from the other portions of American Protestantism."[166] Missouri's insularity had long been a target for caustic commentary. The synod's self-imposed quarantine served both as its defense and its preservation. Having given up a vital aspect of its identity seemed not to have changed the church body's reputation as provincial and aloof.

Considerable overlap connects the issues that confronted the synod in this middle period of its history. As Missouri had hoped America would stay neutral over the war in Europe, so the synod tried to present a neutral posture amid the fundamentalist/modernist controversy. It was easy to distance itself from the neo-rationalist modernists, but it was far more difficult for the synod to declare itself nonaligned to the fundamentalist cause, especially due to the primacy of the scripture issue in the controversy. The Scopes trial in 1925 did not end the teaching of creationism in America's schools; it only brought to a close the very public debate between fundamentalists and

166. Editorial, "What Is Disturbing the Lutherans?" *Christian Century* 43 (July 22, 1926): 910.

modernists.[167] The fundamentalist mentality that had locked onto the conservative element of many denominations remained strong. In 1932, the Missouri Synod adopted as its official doctrinal position a document that declared the inerrancy and infallibility of the Bible just as forcefully as the fundamentalists had.

The death of Franz Pieper in 1931 marked the end of the long era in which one individual had spoken for the synod. Changes in the synod's structure in the 1920s, when a Board of Directors was instituted to manage fiscal affairs of the church, meant that the synodical president elected in 1935 would be an administrator, not the primary theologian of the synod as Walther and Pieper had been. Still Pieper's shadow loomed large and extended well past his death. His methodology of citing proof-texts — whether from scripture or from Luther, Walther, or the seventeenth-century dogmaticians — set a standard that remains synodical practice.[168] Pieper's almost solitary reliance on those sources earned him a reputation as a "repristination theologian," a title of either pride or scorn, depending on one's theological perspective. Repristination theologians situate the essence of true Lutheranism in a dogmatic application of the Lutheran confessions coupled with an inerrant scripture. Pieper himself never completely rejected the title, claiming instead that, in the good sense of the term, his synod was "committed to repristination theology."[169] His Brief Statement, about which little was said at the time of its 1932 adoption, became a flash point decades later in a controversy that forewarned of future controversies. His narrowing of the confessional base of the synod through his absolute insistence on a verbally inerrant Bible set the stage for dramatic confrontation and conflict, as it significantly altered confessional Lutheran understanding of the normative authority of scripture. And Pieper's demand for total conformity before fellowship could be agreed upon narrowed as well the terms of intrasynodical fellowship, as ultraconservative forces within the synod began to demand not only unity, but uniformity, in doctrine and practice. One scholar, who considers Pieper to have been the "most influential conservative systematic

167. See e.g., Edward J. Larson, *Trial and Error: The American Controversy Over Creation and Evolution* (New York: Oxford University Press, 1985).

168. Leigh D. Jordahl, "The Theology of Franz Pieper: A Resource for Fundamentalistic Thought Modes Among American Lutherans," *Lutheran Quarterly* 23 (1971): 130.

169. Pieper, *Christian Dogmatics,* vol. 1, p. ix.

theologian on American soil,"[170] judges his legacy as one of "static abstractionism and stifling traditionalism . . . Orthodoxy at its narrow worst."[171]

Despite the narrowing of focus along some theological dimensions, the Americanization of the synod had brought with it a general sense of acceptance about certain changes taking place in society. The Intersynodical Theses serve as further evidence of the synod's moderation in the 1920s, and despite Franz Pieper's cautions about "no union without unity," fellowship discussions with the American Lutheran Church continued and held promise in 1938. On social issues such as birth control, Missouri relaxed its guard no less carefully. Yet an observable pattern now emerged in the synod's response. Decreased polemic was followed by resigned assent.[172]

As much as the synod would have preferred to remain immune from the changes that were reshaping American society at the end of the nineteenth and beginning of the twentieth century, these changes nevertheless impacted the synod in significant ways. By 1947, the centennial of its founding, broader social changes had pulled Missouri into the twentieth century. The synod announced its own accommodation by again changing its name, now to The Lutheran Church–Missouri Synod.[173] The first half of the twentieth century had presented the church body with an assortment of challenges to its identity, and the synod had met those challenges, not always happily, through struggle and adaptation.

The most serious challenges to Missouri's identity, however, came from within, and were revealed in the division in the synod resulting from the publication of *A Statement.* The signers, worried over the direction they saw their synod headed since the late 1930s, reacted by issuing a public call to debate in the form of twelve theses. A century earlier, the lay party in Perry County had issued a similar call with Marbach's manifesto that asked publicly, "Are we a church?" The "Forty-four"

170. Jordahl, "The Theology of Franz Pieper," p. 123.

171. Leigh D. Jordahl, "Schmucker and Walter: A Study of Christian Response to American Culture," in *The Future of the American Church,* ed. Philip J. Hefner (Philadelphia: Fortress Press, 1968), p. 85.

172. See Alan Graebner, "Birth Control and the Lutherans: The Missouri Synod as a Case Study," in *Women in American Religion,* ed. Janet Wilson James (Philadelphia: University of Pennsylvania Press, 1978), pp. 229-52.

173. Missouri Synod, *Proceedings,* 1947, pp. 446-47.

were asking what kind of a church the synod had become. John Behnken's desire to avoid conflict foreclosed the possibility of discussion — perhaps even another Altenburg Debate — that the signers believed was essential to the future of the church. Because the issues raised by *A Statement* remained undiscussed and therefore unresolved, the subtle lines that divided the very conservative from the moderately conservative began to grow deeper and wider. After a hundred years of walking together, the road ahead was not assured. Further changes in church and society would present Missouri with additional challenges — some of them new, some of them simply new versions of old issues.

A new issue for the synod in its middle period was the gender issue, which emerged almost simultaneously on a number of different fronts, each indirectly challenging the synod's understanding of ministry — women wished to be trained as parochial school teachers and deaconesses beginning in the 1920s and to serve in an official auxiliary of the church body in the 1930s. Missouri met each of those challenges by first adjusting its understanding of the parameters of women's service, then extending new opportunities to its women for service, all the while restating the biblical proscriptions limiting that service. A fourth challenge involving gender was introduced in this period, and would prove more formidable as the synod raised mighty objection, but finally came to accept: woman suffrage in its congregations. As part of the "woman question" — what may women do in the church? — suffrage mobilized far more comment and generated far more fear than had any of the activities women began entering in the 1920s and 1930s. The difference between the synod's response to suffrage and its reluctant acceptance of the other ministry opportunities centered on the issue of authority and would require of the church yet another adjustment in its doctrine of ministry.

5

The Issue of Authority:
Woman Suffrage

The passage of the Nineteenth Amendment to the United States Constitution in August 1920 received little attention from the Missouri Synod. Because it considered itself removed from the political sphere, the church body had neither lobbied in favor of woman's right to vote nor come out strongly against it since 1887, when Francis Pieper railed against the United States Senate for having brought the proposed Sixteenth Amendment to the Senate floor for a vote for the first time. Pieper's editorial called woman suffrage "a proposal that stands all natural order on its head."[1] Herein lay the principal argument that directed the synod's response on the woman question one hundred years ago, and remains today: the "line drawn, not by man's hand, but by God's, over which woman may not step without upsetting the order of God."[2] Synod's theologians used this line as the benchmark by which gender roles were to be defined. Their position held that the roles were timeless, which gave them a handy measure by which to judge any changes in

1. *Lehre und Wehre* 33 (1887): 56. Pieper's outrage was directed not only at the one-third of the senators who voted for the amendment, but at the *Lutheran Observer,* periodical of the General Synod, which he accused of "a reprehensible misuse of the Word of God" in citing Acts 5:38 to suggest that woman suffrage would fail if it was a human action, but could not be suppressed if it was from God.
2. [W. H. T.] D[au], "Scripture on the Woman Question," *Lutheran Witness* 16 (February 7, 1898): 132.

American society that challenged gender roles. The synod's response, then, to the renewed activity of the suffragist movement in the 1890s brought an occasional reference to the folly of the "fanatical" woman who pressed for the "pernicious mischief" of suffrage: she was "a repulsive caricature, a woman without femininity that will not be what it should and cannot be what it wants to be."[3] Even after antisuffragist activity had peaked in the 1910s, *Der Lutheraner* quoted a leader of the "antis" in support of the argument that suffrage would be a violation of the separate spheres of women and men:

> women would exercise a good influence on the country and its politics soonest if they would turn their time and their interests more and more to the care of the sick, the aged, the children and the insane instead of taking part in the wild struggle for political office; for only then have they filled the place in which God has put them. . . . For women to take part in politics is against the created order, which has assigned to the woman her place for all time.[4]

But by 1919, such a bold and outright dismissal no longer seemed an adequate response. The challenges the German-speaking synod had faced during the recent war with Germany had required rapid accommodation and assimilation to American ways and had raised important questions about the synod's loyalty. It is not, therefore, surprising that the synod grudgingly accepted two new constitutional amendments that it really did not favor, one granting woman suffrage, the other sanctioning the prohibition of alcohol.

Without editorial comment or indication of the author or source, the synod's English-language periodical, the *Lutheran Witness,* printed in its "Hearth and Home" section in 1915 a poem entitled "Women's Rights." In answer to the question, "The rights of women, what are they?" the poet provided a long list of the many opportunities for "silent influence" found in woman's domestic sphere. Sounding an argument often used by antisuffragists, woman had "The right to labor, love and pray" and need not ask for more, since "Thou hast enough to answer for."[5] Yet by mid-1919, after both houses of Congress had

3. A[ugust] G[raebner], "Frauenrechte," *Der Lutheraner* 50 (April 24, 1894): 71-72.

4. [Theodore] G[raebner], *Der Lutheraner* 71 (June 8, 1915): 226.

5. *Lutheran Witness* 34 (June 1, 1915): 174.

passed the suffrage amendment and sent it to the states for ratification, the *Witness* took a very different approach to the subject. In the first of a three-part series called "Attitude Lutherans Should Take Towards Woman's Suffrage," author Louis J. Sieck provided an explanation for the earlier absence of comment:

> Many of us have been accustomed to regard Woman Suffrage as too insignificant and too absurd to deserve serious attention. Most of us felt . . . that we could never be induced to discuss this question earnestly. We actually avoided it, hoping secretly that it would die a natural death. Instead of favoring us with an early and natural death, the Woman Suffrage movement has grown to such proportions that the time has come when it cannot be disregarded by the Church. . . . Equal rights, or suffrage, constitutes one of the profoundest questions which can arise in human government.[6]

Sieck, a pastor who would later become president of Concordia Seminary, St. Louis, had prepared his essays for colleagues in the St. Louis area Pastors' and Teachers' Conference, who resolved that they should be printed in the *Witness*. Using as a model "the three great institutions of God on earth," he addressed woman's place in home, church, and state, by arguing that God established not only gender difference at creation but assigned the genders "their respective spheres and mode of life." To threaten this difference, then, was to "unsex" both women and men. The home was woman's sphere, and both church and state depended on her staying there.

While Sieck allowed that woman holds "an equal position with man in the Church in the offers of God's grace in the Gospel, equal privilege of service, the right to meet with the Church, the right quietly and unostentatiously to express her opinion," she is barred from voting, leadership, and public ministry according to "apostolic practice."[7] Sieck here argued for a limitation of woman's role based on tradition, not scripture. On the question of civil suffrage, he declared that "whatever aims to take woman out of her proper sphere and place her on the same level with a man is a blow at the home upon which the welfare of Church and State rests." Still, because the Bible provides neither defini-

6. Louis J. Sieck, "Attitude Lutherans Should Take Towards Woman Suffrage," *Lutheran Witness* 38 (May 13, 1919): 149-50.
7. Sieck, *Lutheran Witness* 38 (May 27, 1919): 162.

tive prohibition nor permission, Christian liberty allows a woman her choice whether to vote or not to vote. Sieck's caution continued as he worried that the woman voter might spend so much time studying political questions that she would neglect her home, "robbing it of its natural right, a mother's care." He concluded by warning against the "evils" of modern feminism, "one of the most serious menaces to the home, Church, and State which the devil has put to work in our country," and with a prayer for more women who are "content to furnish, educate, and train men — the queens of the world in their own sphere."[8] Sieck finally found a way around the lack of biblical evidence on the issue of voting by resorting to dependence on tradition — the way things were, and therefore, always should be. However, his argument equated a restriction on women's activities based on the nineteenth-century notion of separate gender spheres with "apostolic practice," which implies historical continuity. Such reliance on a vision of the recapture and restoration of a glorified past is a means by which fundamentalists not only cope with the stresses of change, but upon which they base their opposition to change. Though the synod during these years was doing its best to distance itself from either label in the fundamentalist/modernist controversy, its behavior and speech betrayed a strong fundamentalist leaning. Missouri's position on verbal biblical inerrancy was not the only point of comparison with a fundamentalist posture, as Sieck's appeal to tradition indicates.

The ratification of the Nineteenth Amendment in 1920 did not put an end to the synod's fear of the enfranchised woman. Theodore Graebner, seminary professor and editor of the *Lutheran Witness,* in his regular column in the *Homiletic Magazine* called "Letters to a Young Preacher," advised a young pastor who asked for an opinion on woman suffrage that woman "may vote, shall vote" as long as she stayed out of the political sphere. He continued:

> All politics, in the last analysis, is concerned with taxes. In this women have an immediate interest, even if they are not themselves in business or own property.
>
> There are many sins against which we must warn. Let us not make more sins than there are. Above all, let us not leave the consciences in doubt unless it is a matter in which we are ready to excommunicate

8. Sieck, *Lutheran Witness* 38 (June 19, 1919): 179-80.

those who act according to a conviction which we possibly cannot share. Either institute proceedings of church discipline or leave the matter alone. And I certainly would not say "Thou shall not" unless I can quote Scripture. . . . In the articles printed in the *Lutheran Witness* the movement for woman's suffrage was properly characterized, and where its sponsors have spoken wildly and wickedly, the article quotes Scripture against them, stating that no Christian can associate himself with such company as the Feminists are, but will vigorously oppose them. But when the right to vote is granted, the unrighteous means and purposes involved in the Feminist movement no longer enter into the equation. Even if we know that in the end woman will not be benefited, but harmed, by the right of suffrage, we need not forbid our women to vote. The thing is done, women now have the right. . . . Now let them vote.[9]

Graebner's point on not making "more sins than there are" would become a primary theme of many of his later writings, in which he consistently warned against an abundance of "Thou shall nots. . . ."[10] Graebner became increasingly concerned about what he called the synod's legalism, especially during the so-called Fellowship Controversy of the 1930s and 1940s, and was a signer of *A Statement*. Perhaps the most articulate critic of his own church body in the first half of the twentieth century, Graebner did not hesitate to reveal the development of his thinking in his prolific writings.

9. Theodore Graebner, *Pastor and People: Letters to a Young Preacher* (St. Louis: Concordia Publishing House, 1932), pp. 126-27. Graebner's columns, "chips from an editorial workshop" dating from 1920 to 1930, were gathered for publication a decade later, as Graebner explained in his foreword, because "the conditions under which we do our work as a Church suffer continuous change, and new problems arise." He said of his replies, "Doctrinally, they represent the stand of the Lutheran Confessions. In their practical application of Scripture they do not claim to offer anything startlingly novel. Where they touch on matters undecided in the Scriptures, the opinions in these letters, and the advice given, reflect the evangelical stand of the fathers of our Synod" (pp. iii, iv).

10. See Theodore Graebner, *The Borderland of Right and Wrong*, 4th enl. ed. (St. Louis: Concordia Publishing House, 1938); a 1946 paper read to the New York Pastoral Conference, "For a Penitent Jubilee," *Concordia Historical Institute Quarterly* 45 (1972): 3-28; and two essays unpublished until more than fifteen years after his death, "The Burden of Infallibility: A Study in the History of Dogma," *Concordia Historical Institute Quarterly* 38 (1965): 88-94, and "'The Cloak of the Cleric,'" *Concordia Historical Institute Quarterly* 44 (1971): 3-12.

Woman Suffrage in the Church

The synod's reluctant position endorsing woman suffrage in the United States did not imply an equivalent endorsement for such a right in the church. In this case, the Lutheran doctrine of the Two Kingdoms assured that women's roles in the realms of church and state would remain distant and unconnected.

The first father of the Missouri Synod, C. F. W. Walther, had offered his opinion on woman's place in the church on only two occasions during his long tenure over the church in the nineteenth century. In congregational meetings, Walther believed all adult males were entitled to participate by "speaking, deliberating, voting, and resolving. But women and the young are excluded."[11] He repeated his position in his textbook on pastoral theology, published in 1872.[12] Walther added no commentary but on each occasion merely cited 1 Corinthians 14:34-35 ("women are to be silent in the churches. For they are not permitted to speak, but should be subordinate."). Walther's successor, Franz Pieper, in his massive text *Christian Dogmatics,* never directly addressed the matter of woman suffrage, but did cite two statements of Luther's that women were to be excluded from church government.[13] Pieper claimed that Luther was consistent in arguing that God's creation of men and women as different sexes required they have each have a different "sphere of activity."[14] Contending that the scriptural position makes home the woman's sphere, any public speaking or teaching by women is therefore strictly forbidden according to the "universal permanent order."[15] In a 1913 paper read at a

---

11. C. F. W. Walther, *Die rechte Gestalt einer vom Staate unabhängigen Evangelisch Lutherischen Ortsgemeinde,* 2nd ed. (St. Louis: Aug. Wiebusch & Son, 1864), p. 50.

12. C. F. W. Walther, *Amerikanisch-Lutherische Pastoraltheologie* (St. Louis: Druckerei der Synode von Missouri, Ohio, u. a. Staaten, 1872), p. 371.

13. Franz Pieper, *Christian Dogmatics,* vol. 1 (St. Louis: Concordia Publishing House, 1950), p. 524. In the American edition of *Luther's Works* the citations read slightly differently from those which Pieper cites: "[The character and industry of women] has not been destined by God for government of the state or church," *Luther's Works,* American edition, ed. Jaroslav Pelikan and Helmut T. Lehmann (St. Louis and Philadelphia: Concordia Publishing House and Fortress Press, 1955-1986), 6:60; and "[W]omen (much less children and fools) cannot and shall not occupy positions of sovereignty," 41:155.

14. Pieper, *Christian Dogmatics,* vol. 1, p. 525, where he cites Luther: "Everyone functions most efficiently in that for which he was created," 15:131.

15. Pieper, *Christian Dogmatics,* vol. 1, p. 526.

district convention, Pieper maintained that this "prohibition is to be in force in all places and at all times until Judgment Day."[16] Pieper's position on the woman question was both insistent and constant, as he reminded his audience that "God Himself most certainly may grant exceptions to the rules which He has laid down for us; but it is not for us to do so. . . . We are bound to the order which God has instituted."[17]

The synod had not had to deal with the issue of woman suffrage in the church until the renewed civil suffrage movement brought questions from some of its congregations. A 1908 editorial in *Der Lutheraner* dismissed the action of the Finnish Lutheran Suomi Synod in granting woman suffrage in the church as an "unbiblical and un-Lutheran innovation."[18] It had long been German custom that a seminary or university faculty, both individually and corporately, be asked to issue expert opinions *(Gutachten)* when questions arose in congregations.[19] In line with custom, Missouri Synod pastors wrote former professors, and laypeople wrote editors and synodical officials. The suffrage question was finally addressed by W. H. T. Dau on behalf of the faculty of Concordia Seminary in 1916.

A pastor and two laymen had written the seminary faculty in the winter of 1916 on the question of woman suffrage in the church.[20] When, in 1923, Concordia Publishing House issued Dau's response in the form of a tract,[21] identifying features in the correspondence had been deleted. The case apparently involved a congregation in which at least two laymen argued that women should have the right to vote in church voters' meetings, which they held were separate from and not prohibited by the scriptural proscriptions on women speaking in church. But the pastor held that voting by women violated the scrip-

16. Pieper, "The Laymen's Movement in the Light of God's Word," a paper read at the Southern Illinois District convention, 1913, in *What Is Christianity? and Other Essays,* trans. J. T. Mueller (St. Louis: Concordia Publishing House, 1933), p. 155.

17. Pieper, "The Laymen's Movement," pp. 156, 157.

18. [Ludwig] F[uerbringer], *Der Lutheraner* 64 (Sept. 8, 1908): 287.

19. See A. G. Roeber, *Palatines, Liberty, and Property: German Lutherans in Colonial British America* (Baltimore: The Johns Hopkins University Press, 1993), p. 130.

20. It is clear from Dau's reply that the original query had come in two parts, the first as letter from a "Rev. M.," and a second letter a week later from "Mr. J." and "Mr. R." Although the question had to do with women voting, all the inquiries, of course, had been made by men.

21. W. H. T. Dau, "Woman Suffrage in the Church," Concordia Publishing House, 1923.

tural injunction that they be "subject to men in all things."[22] Dau's exhaustive reply rested on the principle that the act of voting is "an act of sovereignty," not merely the expression of one's wish but the intention to see that wish carried out. By that definition, the act of voting was to be considered an exercise of authority and, as such, was clearly contrary to woman's subjection in all things.

In addressing point-by-point the letters the faculty had received, Dau inserted a corrective to the laymen's understanding of what role a woman was allowed to play when a congregation was calling a pastor. In the Missouri Synod, any confirmed member of a congregation, without regard to age or gender, has a right of veto over a pastoral candidate, as Dau explained:

> Even though the woman cannot speak or vote in the congregation at the election of a pastor, she has nevertheless the right of veto: she can make known to the congregation that she will not accept a certain person as her pastor, and the congregation is compelled to heed her protest.[23]

This right of protest or veto dates back to the original 1843 constitution of Trinity congregation in St. Louis, which provided the model for congregational constitutions when the synod was founded four years later. It followed from Article XIV of the Augsburg Confession regarding the necessity of a regular call and is a fundamental principle in the synod's understanding of the congregation as source of the external call to ministry:

> The right to call, elect, and accept the minister or ministers, the schoolteacher or schoolteachers, and all other officials of the congregation shall always remain with the entire congregation and shall never be delegated either to an individual or to a smaller body in the congregation.[24]

But, as Dau was careful to clarify, a veto is not a vote, and this right does not translate to other congregational decisions. This extraordi-

22. Ephesians 5:24.
23. Dau, "Woman Suffrage in the Church," p. 12.
24. Constitution of Trinity Lutheran Church, St. Louis, Missouri, 1843, in Carl S. Meyer, *Moving Frontiers: Readings in the History of the Lutheran Church–Missouri Synod* (St. Louis: Concordia Publishing House, 1964), p. 168.

nary exception stands in peculiar juxtaposition to the synod's firm prohibition on woman suffrage.

In his Prefatory Note to the reprint of the original opinion, Dau cautioned his readers against the "feministic movement," which "thoughtful men are dreading . . . principally for the women's sake," and which he predicted would eventually prove not to have "elevated or liberated woman, but lowered and shackled her." Like Louis Sieck's argument against civil suffrage, Dau's primary focus was the "domain and relationships which the Creator designed for her as wife, mother, daughter, sister."[25] Any movement or action, then, which threatened the separation of spheres sanctioned in creation was deemed by these clergymen to pose grave danger to church order. On this principle the synod's position on women rested. So the *Lutheran Witness* declaration in 1898 that women were to be excluded from congregational meetings "because they are women, not because they are always and necessarily inferior to men in mental capacity,"[26] was reaffirmed by the seminary faculty opinion. Clergy were reminded in pastoral conferences that "the stand of absolute silence of the woman, not only in the divine service, but also in all the business relations of the Church" was a settled question, based on "the unalterable decrees of God."[27] Besides, a 1920 conference essayist went on, "we tremble to think of a voters' meeting in which both sexes are represented."[28] As long as the synod understood the right to vote as "the right to rule or govern,"[29] women would be prohibited from doing so.

25. Dau, "Woman Suffrage in the Church," p. 2.
26. George Luecke, *Lutheran Witness* 16 (March 7, 1898): 150.
27. Paul Lindemann, "The Woman in the Church," *Theological Quarterly* 24 (1920): 30, 35. Lindemann, complaining that "this troublesome paper . . . was imposed upon us by a heartless and thoughtless conference," claimed he was inclined, for the sake of argument, to take a radical stand in favor of women's rights in the church, but, "much as we love the ladies and are naturally inclined to give them everything they want," he could not when he examined the scriptural references in light of the Bible's "unchangeable authority in this and all other matters." He admitted his relief, therefore, "that the women in the Lutheran Church have not yet been permeated to any great extent with the general modern spirit of female restlessness" (pp. 30-48, 103-21 *passim*).
28. Lindemann, "The Woman in the Church," p. 121.
29. J. H. C. Fritz, "Shall Women Vote in the Churches?" *Lutheran Witness* 51 (April 26, 1932): 161.

Times Change, the Church Doesn't

The issue of woman suffrage in the church was not officially raised at a synodical convention until 1938, the same convention that authorized the formation of a woman's auxiliary to the synod. The convention essayist, J. T. Mueller, had affirmed in his presentation the synodical prohibition against woman suffrage, but a delegate objected to Mueller's remark, and the question was referred — in what would become the synod's standard practice on this issue — to a committee of three, who met and reported back to the convention. Their brief report acknowledged that, despite the assertion of "our dogmatician Dr. F. Pieper" and "the accepted position and practice of Synod that woman shall not be granted voting membership in the Christian congregation," there were some in the synod who felt that the prohibition was not scripturally required. The convention approved a resolution to have woman suffrage restudied in congregations, pastoral conferences, and district conventions.[30] In fact, however, no study committee was ever appointed. Did the contrast between the synod's enthusiasm for a women's auxiliary and its reluctance to pursue study of woman suffrage reflect Missouri's awareness of the potential suffrage held for bringing women closer to the governing structure of the church, while an auxiliary kept them safely at a distance?

The matter was not addressed in convention again until fifteen years had passed, by which time Resolution 27 at the 1953 synodical convention in Houston stated that, regarding the synodical position on suffrage based on two New Testament texts, "there is a sincere difference of opinion among clergy and laity concerning the full and correct application of these texts to the question of woman suffrage in the church."[31] There existed already in the early 1950s a very few scattered congregations who had approved of and were practicing woman suffrage, and whose constitutions had been accepted by their districts. These included Grace Lutheran Church in Evanston, Illinois, and at least one congregation in Maryland.[32] The resolution recommended that the president of synod appoint a committee of five to prepare a

---

30. Missouri Synod, *Proceedings,* 1938, p. 346.

31. Missouri Synod, *Proceedings,* 1953, p. 484.

32. Richard P. Jungkuntz, telephone conversation with author, February 4, 1995; letter from Walter Stuenkel to Mrs. Bob Hisel, April 10, 1962. Walter Stuenkel papers, in Stuenkel's possession. Used by permission.

thorough study of all texts related to suffrage, and that this committee report to the next convention, to be held in St. Paul in 1956. By a rising vote (generally employed in parliamentary procedure as an expression of appreciation) that "expressed its esteem for the women of the Church and their work," the synod in convention adopted the resolution.[33]

In November of that year, an article appeared in the *Lutheran Witness,* written by a pastor who cautioned the church against woman suffrage *and* against allowing women to omit the word "obey" from their marriage vows. Citing Dau's earlier tract and the usual Pauline texts, Henry George Hartner argued that men had been given sovereignty over women, but that authority

> also gives them a tremendous responsibility toward the women of the church. If we do not want the spectacle of a wife standing up in some future voters' meeting . . . and at the top of her shrill voice giving her husband a good dressing down in public assembly, . . . then let's correct the neglects which have brought about woman suffrage in other churches. . . . The more the men of our church enlist the interest and co-operation of the women in every permitted area of church work and service, the less desire there will be among women or anybody else for invading the area where God is asking all men to work harder to build His kingdom.[34]

This article attracted at least one angry response from a layman in Alabama who wrote to synodical president John Behnken to take issue with the tone of Hartner's argument:

> Men who are unwilling to grant women the right to speak in an open assembly of the church are men who are afraid. And men who are afraid must seek to maintain their position by basing their stand on Biblical verses which hinder rather than advance the work of the church.[35]

33. Missouri Synod, *Proceedings,* 1953, p. 484.
34. Henry George Hartner, "Woman Suffrage in the Church," *Lutheran Witness* 72 (November 10, 1953): 5.
35. Letter from Franz Schenk to John W. Behnken, November 12, 1953. John W. Behnken papers, Box 24, Concordia Historical Institute, St. Louis, Missouri.

There is no record that Behnken ever responded to the writer's insightful observations. Following usual synodical practice, the matter had been assigned to a committee. The church would wait to take its cues from the committee's recommendations and report.

The Office of Woman in the Church

In 1950 a book was published in Austria by Fritz Zerbst, a Lutheran clergyman concerned about the wartime critical-shortage-of-men decisions of most European churches to allow theologically trained women *(Theologinnen)* into the practice of public ministry. Zerbst's study, a dissertation entitled *The Office of Woman in the Church: A Study in Practical Theology,*[36] attracted little attention in Europe or elsewhere until Albert G. Merkens, a professor at Concordia Seminary, St. Louis, "stumbled onto it" while traveling in Germany in the early 1950s. Merkens, who found Zerbst's argument "foundational," arranged with the Synod's General Literature Board for Concordia Publishing House (the Missouri Synod publisher) to publish the book once he finished translating it into English.[37] A pastor in Austria when he wrote his dissertation, Zerbst later served as superintendent of his diocese and as assistant president of the Synod of the Evangelical Church of the Augsburg Confession before becoming Professor for Practical Theology at the University in Vienna in 1955.[38] The 1950 publication of Zerbst's book in Europe served as a conservative re-

---

36. Fritz Zerbst, *The Office of Woman in the Church: A Study in Practical Theology,* trans. Albert G. Merkens (St. Louis: Concordia Publishing House, 1955). Originally published in German as *Das Amt der Frau in der Kirche: Eine praktisch-theologische Untersuchung* (Vienna: Evangelical Press Association in Austria, 1950). Zerbst's dissertation was written in 1944.

37. General Literature Board, LCMS, minutes, February 12, 1954, CHI, and the recollections of Merkens's son, the Rev. Guido Merkens, in a telephone conversation with the author on January 27, 1995. Albert Merkens's papers, which are in the possession of his son, do not include any reference to the Zerbst book. In the preface to his translation, Albert Merkens called the text "a refreshing find," whose scriptural exegesis is "sane and solid, constituting the main body of content and enunciating the basic principles which should govern the relations between men and women," and is offered in solution to "a vexing problem."

38. *Evangelisches Kirchenlexion,* Register, Göttingen, 1961.

sponse to the 1948 report of the World Council of Churches on the Life and Work of Women in the Church, which examined the wartime situation he deplored.[39] The uncritical and unconditional acceptance of Zerbst's thesis by the Missouri Synod is curious not only in light of Missouri's tendency to rely solely on its own fathers and their orthodox predecessors for guidance, but also in the fact that the question of the ordination of women had never been raised in the synod and was certainly not an issue in the 1950s.

Zerbst's thesis challenges the ordination of women on historical grounds — by tradition, women have been excluded from the ministry for centuries — and argues that the implications of women's ordination for practical theology are dire. Nearly half his book is given over to a discussion of three New Testament passages that have been widely cited as scriptural evidence prohibiting women from the office of public ministry.[40] Zerbst then addresses the question of office and women in the history of the church, from the first century through the Reformation and to women in foreign missionary work. Conceding that the Lutheran confessions do not address the issue of women in ministry, he agrees that there is nothing in the nature of the pastoral office that excludes women from serving in that office. Still, he concludes that women must be prohibited from the office of the ministry on the basis of his reading of the philosophical argument from the "order of creation." The order of creation, for Zerbst, is understood to be a fixed order intended by God to define the relationships between created beings. Based on the creation account in Genesis 2, woman was created as man's subordinate. This order predates and was neither altered by human sin in the Fall (Genesis 3), nor is it alterable by human action. It is entirely the intention of the

39. *Revised Interim Report of a Study on the Life and Work of Women in the Church* (Geneva: World Council of Churches, 1948). See also John E. Lynch, "The Ordination of Women: Protestant Experience in Ecumenical Perspective," *Journal of Ecumenical Studies* 12 (1975): 173-97. In 1948 the Church of Denmark granted authorization for women to receive the holy orders. The first ordination of a woman in Europe took place in 1947. Margaret Lamberts Bendroth suggests that order of creation arguments (such as Zerbst used) to limit women's service became popular in the postwar period, when the concept of order became an important element of neo-evangelical theology. Bendroth, *Fundamentalism and Gender, 1875 to the Present* (New Haven: Yale University Press, 1993), p. 112.

40. 1 Corinthians 11:2-16; 1 Corinthians 14:34-36; 1 Timothy 2:11-15.

Creator. The order of creation infers a hierarchy based on created differences.[41]

41. The "order of creation" is an old but ill-defined concept with roots in natural law reasoning that has been variously used to justify slavery, social class, and gender relations, among other human relationships. It is most often understood as a top-down hierarchical arrangement (picture a triangle) with God at the top, followed by those who have been given authority over others by God (fathers, men, rulers, masters), with those who are dependent on that authority (children, women, subjects, slaves) at the bottom.

There is more emphasis on the order of creation as it applies to gender relationships in Reformed theology than in Lutheran. (Zerbst cites the work of John Calvin liberally.) Karl Barth, in *Christian Dogmatics*, III/1, *The Doctrine of Creation* (Edinburgh: T. & T. Clark, 1958), used the expression "the unequal duality of male and female," to describe the genders, suggesting that "to be created good man needs a being like him yet different from him," 288-90. Barth later developed this point in contending that an order which implies superordination and subordination follows from the duality. *Christian Dogmatics*, III/4, 169. George H. Tavard believes that Barth "unwittingly re-introduced a myth of over and above, before and after, and justifies it by saying it is God's command." Tavard, *Woman in Christian Tradition* (Notre Dame: University of Notre Dame Press, 1973), p. 181. JoAnn Ford Watson argues that Barth's "fallacious use of analogy . . . inappropriately correlates the divine-human relation of Jesus Christ to the human male-female relationship," which then becomes for Barth a divinely ordered relational sequence resulting in a functional inequality and sexual hierarchy. Watson, *A Study of Karl Barth's Doctrine of Man and Woman* (New York: Vantage Press, 1995), pp. v, 46. Emil Brunner disagreed with what he calls Barth's natural law construct, claiming that women are simply different from men, and that no hierarchy should be implied in that difference. Brunner, *The Divine Imperative,* trans. Olive Wyon (Philadelphia: Westminster Press, 1947), pp. 375-80.

The Lutheran understanding begins not with Luther, who never directly used the term, but with Adolph von Harless in the nineteenth century, in his reference to orders of the Creator in *Christliche Ethik,* 6th ed. (Stuttgart, 1864), p. 477. Following Harless, Werner Elert also rejected an implied hierarchy or fixed arrangement, emphasizing instead Luther's malleable understanding of orders or stations as the context into which the individual Christian is placed in life. Elert, *Morphologie des Luthertums,* vol. 2, 2nd ed. (Munich: C. H. Beck'sche Verlagbuchhandlung, 1952), pp. 37-79. A primary problem with a theology of orders is the static nature of such. Can one subscribe to the concepts of order and orders amid historical change and development? Pieper in particular rejects the possibility, declaring with Barth that the orders are for all time. *Christian Dogmatics*, vol. 1, pp. 523-26. Lutheran theologian Carl Braaten argues that the use of orders can still be applicable in the church, if understood in a radically different way, as a basis for Christian social ethics. Braaten, "God in Public Life: Rehabilitating the 'Orders of Creation,'" *First Things* 8 (1990): 32-38.

For a critique of the Missouri's Synod's use of the order of creation, see Ed-

As evidence for the validity of his argument, Zerbst locates the order of creation in the institution of monogamy in marriage:

> . . . Monogamy presumes a definite ordering of the relations between man and woman. . . . The NT consistently requires for monogamy that woman be in subjection. If such ordering of relations between the sexes were not co-established in monogamy, then marriage would in individual cases be turned into a battle for leadership and supremacy. It would become a breeding ground for sin.[42]

Zerbst understands his exegesis, or textual analysis, of the scripture to show not only a close correlation between the position of woman in monogamy and her position in the church, but to gender relations in general.[43] Fundamental to his argument against women in ministry, then, is the preservation of marriage and of gender difference. Indeed, Zerbst's entire case is centered on gender difference and that which he considers its required concomitant, a hierarchy based on the order of creation. While he does not dismiss the possibility that a woman may be gifted for ministry, she must still be precluded from the office:

> The charisms which women receive and the newly created situation in Christ do not disannul this ordinance of God. Therefore, the office of teaching, or the office of church government, is not to be conferred upon woman, though she may have received the necessary charism. The practice of the church in the formation of its offices must not be in conflict with its teachings. The church has adopted the divine order of creation with respect to this matter.[44]

---

ward H. Schroeder, "The Orders of Creation — Some Reflections on the History and Place of the Term in Systematic Theology," *Concordia Theological Monthly* 43 (1972): 165-78.

Feminist theologians largely reject the notion of the order of creation as a divine mandate, arguing instead that the order of creation, on which the subordination of women depends, has been overthrown by the order of redemption since the death and resurrection of Christ. See Kathryn Tanner, *The Politics of God: Christian Theologies and Social Justice* (Minneapolis: Fortress Press, 1992). For a more positive reading of Calvin's notions of order, see Jane Dempsey Douglass, *Women, Freedom, and Calvin* (Philadelphia: The Westminster Press, 1985).

42. Zerbst, *The Office of Woman in the Church*, p. 110.
43. Zerbst, *The Office of Woman in the Church*, pp. 61, 111.
44. Zerbst, *The Office of Woman in the Church*, p. 116.

Because the church has accepted this understanding of the order of creation, therefore, it must — in Zerbst's thinking — be upheld for all time. The preservation of marriage depends on the preservation of the order of creation that is reinforced within the institution of monogamous marriage. Zerbst's primary fear was that denying the order of creation allows the blurring of gender difference and thus threatens the principle of subordination. He also believed there were dangers inherent in the destruction of that principle:

> Paul detected in the teaching office of woman a desire "to usurp authority" over the man, an annulment of woman's subordination, and a peril to the marriage institution. . . . The Holy Spirit rules through human agencies, the witnessing office-bearers. Therefore Paul strives to set forth clearly that wherever the authority to rule the congregation is conferred upon woman, there the subordination of woman is nullified. The order of creation, however, cannot be nullified in one area of church practice without consequences for the proclamation of its whole message and for the life of the congregation. The fear is not unfounded, therefore, that there is something hidden behind the demands for the ordination of woman into the office. . . . The opening of the full ministry to women is to express the nullification of differences between the sexes; it is to indicate that the order of creation has been annulled already in this world — if not generally, at least in the ecclesiastical domain. . . . Whether or not the ordination of woman into the office actually or in the long run serves to edify the church cannot be determined. . . . This question must not be placed at the center of reflection. If that were done, then one could also with equal justification regard as normative the assertion that the ordination of woman into the office would cause the men of the congregation to withdraw from public service and would result in the development of a "woman's church."[45]

Unless the principle of woman's subordination is upheld — and this can only be done by adherence to the concept of the order of creation, according to Zerbst — there is no basis for the prohibition of women from the office of the ministry.[46] For the church to violate this

45. Zerbst, *The Office of Woman in the Church*, pp. 120-21.
46. Zerbst, *The Office of Woman in the Church*, p. 116.

timeless order would be to deny God's intention at creation and thus threaten the foundations of familial, political, and social order.

The ordination of women was not an issue in the Missouri Synod in the early 1950s, while Albert Merkens was translating Zerbst's work, but the question of woman suffrage in the church was. The 1953 synodical convention had asked President John Behnken to appoint a committee to study the question, and Albert Merkens had been appointed to that committee. Merkens would prove to be the link by which Fritz Zerbst's reliance on an immutable order of creation argument became essential to the synod's understanding of, and justification for, women's place in the church.

Making It Official

In 1972 Edward Schroeder, then a professor of systematic theology at Concordia Seminary, St. Louis, corresponded with some of the members of the 1953 suffrage committee in an attempt to learn about the process they had followed in preparing their report to the convention. Schroeder was particularly interested in the influence of the Zerbst book on the committee report. By this time Albert Merkens had died, but Schroeder did hear from Professors Fred Kramer and Victor Bartling, who related that Merkens had introduced to his colleagues the book he had translated, and which was published in English by Concordia Publishing House in 1955.[47]

The heavy reliance on Zerbst and his emphasis on the order of creation distinguishes the report this committee eventually made to the 1956 convention. The committee began by saying that its assignment had not been "an easy one" due to the wide variance among biblical scholars in their interpretation of the key passages and their "present-day applicability." But "at the time we took up our work, there came into our hands what we regard as the most generally satisfactory study of the problem of Woman in the Church that has appeared up till now"[48] — the Zerbst book. While admitting that "Zerbst is not wholly

47. Schroeder, "The Orders of Creation," p. 169 n. 5. Other members of the committee included Theodore Nickel and Martin Zschoche. There are no extant records from the committee in the Concordia Historical Institute or elsewhere, only its final report as printed in the convention *Proceedings*, 1956, pp. 553-71.

48. Missouri Synod, *Proceedings*, 1956, p. 554.

adequate in all respects," that his primary issue is the ordination of women to ministry, and implying that his European perspective "does not give direct answer to all the questions on the status of women which arise in our American church life," the committee nevertheless recommended the book to the convention delegates, declaring his treatment of the concept of subordination to be "classical." Its report follows closely Zerbst's own outline.[49]

The committee began with a definition of the terms "order of creation" and "order of redemption" — a restoration to wholeness made possible through the death and resurrection of Jesus Christ — and then proceeded to address the primary scripture passages that are central to any debate over women's role in the church. Galatians 3:26-29 is cited as the "grand text on the Order of Redemption," which in verse 28 reads: "There is neither Jew nor Greek, there is neither slave nor free, there is neither male nor female; for you are all one in Christ Jesus." But the committee, arguing that this text had been "frequently absolutized" with regard to women in the church, declared its insistence that

> the Gospel of Redemption does not cancel, however much it may modify, as it works in the world, national and social distinctions and transfigure the relations between the sexes. Far from cancelling the mundane orders, this passage expressly confirms them with respect to our existence in the present world.[50]

49. Missouri Synod, *Proceedings,* 1956, pp. 555, 565. After the committee acknowledged its reliance on Zerbst, its report went on to state that it had received and considered "the letters of quite a number of pastors and laymen dealing with our problem." Because no records from this committee exist, the content and concerns of that correspondence remain unknown.

50. Missouri Synod, *Proceedings,* 1956, pp. 556-57. Galatians 3:28 is frequently cited as the keystone of Christian feminism in that it supersedes differentiation by categories. Select citation of Bible passages in support of a particular position is known as proof-texting. Its widespread misuse only adds to the polarization of theological and hermeneutical debates in which each side cites selected texts in support of its point. Additionally, proof-texting generally excludes counter-texts from consideration, as was the case in a conversation in which a Missouri Synod layman asked a pastor who was declaring his theological conservatism how he understood Galatians 3:28. "We have a gentlemen's agreement not to discuss it," replied the pastor. Daniel Hildebrandt, personal statement to the author, June 25, 1995, Kansas City, Missouri.

The report then goes on to cite the passages that stress the order of creation — 1 Corinthians 11:2-16, 1 Corinthians 14:33b-38, and 1 Timothy 2:11-15. Its exegesis of the Corinthians passage on head coverings in chapter 11 understands the writer, the apostle Paul, to be referring less to the custom of head covering than he is to the concept of headship, or graded orders of subordination: God/Christ/man/ woman. Acceptance of this principle affirms that "it is not degradation but nobility to take one's place in the position assigned by God and through faithful and loyal service in that position," and further, that "the offices of man and woman in the mundane economy are not competitive, but concordant and counterpart. Each sex is incomplete without the other."[51]

The Corinthians passage in chapter 14 is specific to order in the church, and woman is enjoined from speaking there, because to do so would violate the order of creation and man's headship. Verse 34 reads: "Women should keep silence in the churches. For they are not permitted to speak, but should be subordinate, even as the Law says." "Silence," according to the suffrage committee, "means just that" and "clearly pertains to the teaching-learning aspects of the regular public [worship] service."[52] The Timothy passage serves to reinforce the Corinthians teaching by stating: "I permit no woman to teach, or to have authority over man; she is to keep silent."[53] The committee preferred the American Standard Version of 1902 rendering of this text, which uses the phrase "have dominion" rather than the King James Version's "usurp authority," because the Greek word *authentein* is used only in this one place in all of scripture. The report objected to the word's "opprobrious connotation," and compared it to the current and "vulgar" phrase "to wear the pants." Paul chose this word, they believed, "because of his horror at contemplating any person willfully stepping out of line and forsaking his or her place in the Creator's scheme of things."[54]

Following its explication of the scripture passages, the committee posed to itself some of the questions it had been asked in correspondence and responded to them. The first queried whether Paul's pro-

---

51. Missouri Synod, *Proceedings,* 1956, p. 558.
52. Missouri Synod, *Proceedings,* 1956, pp. 560-61.
53. Revised Standard Version (1946).
54. Missouri Synod, *Proceedings,* 1956, pp. 563-64.

scriptions were meant only for the first-century churches to whom he wrote his letters, especially as Paul uses the first-person pronoun, implying personal preference but not an imperative with which others must concur. To this the committee replied firmly that

> the principles enunciated are . . . of universal and abiding validity and the injunctions dare not be set aside as vetoes superseded by current sociological and theological trends. They express the mind and purposes of God.[55]

In addition, the committee understood the principles to apply to all women, not only married women as some interpreters had argued.[56]

Finally, the committee returned to its original assignment and addressed specific problems, particularly woman suffrage in the church. Admitting that its task had not been to discuss the ordination of women (which would have "led to an unequivocal NO!"),[57] the suffrage committee concluded that, because "it has been the general practice of our congregations to withhold voting privileges from women," and because "our church has prospered under this system," that "we can foresee only evil results in any change of the polity under which our church has been so signally blessed for more than a century."[58] Significantly, after focusing entirely on scripture in its report, the committee relied entirely on tradition in making its recommendations, which appealed for retention of the status quo of male-only voters' meetings.

The synod, after consideration of the committee's report, extended its thanks to the members, but noted in a lengthy resolution that the suffrage question really had not been settled:

> the committee does not state that it finds woman suffrage in our congregations forbidden in express words in the Scriptures, but emphatically warns against any anti-Scriptural practice whereby the headship of man to woman in the affairs of the church would be surrendered; and . . .

55. Missouri Synod, *Proceedings,* 1956, p. 564.

56. The single woman remains a problem for biblical interpreters. The question is especially arguable in the New Testament household codes, where there are references to wives and husbands and women and men. Does a restriction or an admonition to married women necessarily extend to all women?

57. Missouri Synod, *Proceedings,* 1956, p. 566. Emphasis in the original.

58. Missouri Synod, *Proceedings,* 1956, p. 568.

We recognize the problems involved in applying these texts of Scripture to woman suffrage in our congregations and all the issues involved therein; . . . [resolved that]

A standing committee of three members be appointed by the Praesidium of Synod which will continue to study this entire area of the place of woman in the church and which will provide guidance and direction through pamphlets, brochures, books, correspondence, and direct consultation wherever desired.[59]

Ten delegates voted against this resolution and were encouraged to state their reasons for the record to the secretary of synod.[60]

One Man's Stand Against a Standing Committee

Had it not been for a hospital chaplain in New Orleans, Russell C. Prohl, the standing committee on woman suffrage mandated by the St. Paul convention would have had little to do. President Behnken had appointed three men to serve on the committee: Walter W. Stuenkel, president of Concordia College, Milwaukee, Bernhard G. Mueller, then president of the North Dakota District, and Walter H. Wente, academic dean of Concordia Senior College in Fort Wayne. At their first meeting in June 1957, Stuenkel was elected chairman and Wente secretary of the group. They studied the 1956 report and determined that they should procure the records of the previous committee.[61] The committee had been put on notice by Behnken that they would be asked to meet with representatives of the National Evangelical Lutheran Church (Finnish),

---

59. Missouri Synod, *Proceedings,* 1956, pp. 570-71.

60. Missouri Synod, *Proceedings,* 1956, p. 571. In 1969, Richard Jungkuntz, Executive Secretary of the Commission on Theology and Church Relations, attempted to discover the identity of the negative voters and their reasons, but was unable to find any evidence at either the Concordia Historical Institute or synod headquarters. Letter from Richard Jungkuntz to Walter Stuenkel, May 1, 1969. Stuenkel papers.

61. Victor Bartling, chair of the 1953 committee, responded to Stuenkel's request for materials with a packet and a letter in which he wrote: "Most of the material in my files concerned itself with the preliminary work of our committee which finally resulted in our report. Much correspondence from various quarters that offered us free advice is dated and hardly deserves preservation." Letter to Stuenkel from Victor Bartling, June 20, 1957. Stuenkel papers.

which wished to join the Missouri Synod. The Finns, who had practiced woman suffrage (but not women's ordination) since 1910, wanted to discuss the issue with the suffrage committee in an attempt to somehow reconcile the difference in the two synods' practices.[62]

The three men met again in November 1957, at which time Mueller suggested, following a discussion, that "the eventual solution lies with the women of the church, for whom there should be an educational effort to bring out and disseminate the right scriptural teaching; in this effort the cooperation of the LWML [Lutheran Women's Missionary League, official auxiliary of the synod] should be enlisted."[63] But Mueller's recommendation, remarkably, was never acted upon. At no time during the thirty years between the first resolution raising the suffrage question in 1938 and the eventual acceptance of women's voting rights in 1969 did the synod seek the opinion of women.

As a means of restating the position of the synod, the three men decided to incorporate their conclusions into a set of theses. The theses contained nothing that not had already been said. Combining the "best judgment" of the 1956 committee report and portions of the synodical resolution at that same convention, these standing committee theses served as the official Missouri Synod position on women in the church for twelve years.

Before the committee met again, a storm broke. In 1957 Russell Prohl published *Woman in the Church: A Restudy of Woman's Place in Building the Kingdom*. Originally developed as an essay assigned to him by his pastoral conference in Texas, Prohl's paper had been advertised in both the *Lutheran Witness* and the *Lutheran Laymen,* and four hundred copies had been distributed. After he expanded it into a Bachelor of Divinity thesis at Brite College of the Bible at Texas Christian University, Prohl contacted several publishers, one of which was Concordia Publishing House, who "indicated its editorial committee was ready to recommend publication."[64] Instead, the book was published by the William B. Eerdmans Company in Grand Rapids, Michigan.

Woman in the Church takes issue with any church body that does

---

62. Letter from Behnken to Stuenkel, May 16, 1957. Stuenkel papers.

63. Minutes, Committee on Woman Suffrage, November 20, 1957. Behnken Papers, Box 24, CHI. There is no reference to any cooperative venture with the LWML in the Committee's records.

64. Minutes, Woman Suffrage Committee, August 22, 1958. Stuenkel papers.

not recognize the full value of women and their potential for service to the church. In particular, Prohl questions the 1956 decision of his own Missouri Synod in which the practice of denying women the right to vote in congregational meetings was upheld, arguing that it was based on tradition and not on scripture. Prohl disputes Zerbst's contention that "the order of creation must remain for the duration of the present age," and that the church must uphold that order by its limitation on women's service to only those activities which do not challenge male headship. He instead subscribes to Emil Brunner's understanding in *The Divine Imperative* that the order of creation has been transcended by the order of redemption, and for that reason definition of activity by gender is no longer appropriate.[65]

While Prohl agreed with Zerbst that the question of woman's service in the church was not addressed in the Lutheran confessions, his primary objection to Zerbst focused on the latter's extension of male headship in marriage to gender relations in general. Following his exegesis of the same three New Testament passages discussed by Zerbst and a chapter on women in the Old Testament, Prohl concludes that "It is not true, as many believe, that the Bible subordinates woman as a sex to man as a sex. There is no law of creation which makes women in general subordinate to men in general."[66] He argued that the laws invoked by the early church on women's activities were customary laws that do not apply in today's society. In his last two pages Prohl addressed specifically his own Missouri Synod:

> Our church has a vast reservoir of talent in our devoted and highly qualified women. To keep this treasure in storage is poor stewardship. It is time for us to put to use, to the fullest extent, the mission potential we have in our women.[67]

Women should be not only voting members of congregations, he believed, but synodical convention delegates and even seminary students. Suggesting that Lutherans should follow the lead of the Presbyterians in 1955 and ordain women to the public ministry, Prohl concluded his

65. Russell C. Prohl, *Woman in the Church: A Restudy of Woman's Place in Building the Kingdom* (Grand Rapids: Wm. B. Eerdmans Publishing Co., 1957), pp. 21-22.

66. Prohl, *Woman in the Church,* p. 47.

67. Prohl, *Woman in the Church,* p. 79.

68. Prohl, *Woman in the Church,* p. 80. Prohl's reference is to certain transla-

book with a prayer that "the host of women preachers will be great indeed."[68]

For a Missouri Synod clergyman to speak or publish views dissonant with those of the synod was not unheard of prior to Russell Prohl's manifesto, but such a practice had always involved substantial risk-taking. Prohl claimed he wrote his book "not so much as a definitive statement as rather a contribution to the study of the subject."[69] But that was not how the book was received. Walter Stuenkel ordered a copy in January 1958 and immediately knew his committee would be asked for an opinion. He promptly wrote Mueller and Wente regarding the strategy they might pursue in preparing their response. In a follow-up letter to Mueller, Stuenkel expressed an openness to dialogue about the issues Prohl raised:

> Since we have here a man who has an honest difference of opinion and is willing to express it, it will give us a fine opportunity to look at the reasoning and conclusion of such people that disagree with our traditional position.[70]

He specifically did not respond to an earlier comment of Mueller's about Prohl's "exegetical contortions."[71]

In his pursuit of opinions, Stuenkel also wrote to Roland Wiederaenders, at the time president of the Texas District of the Missouri Synod. Prohl had been a pastor in Texas, though in an English District congregation,[72] prior to entering the institutional chaplaincy in New

tions of Psalm 68:11, which read: "Great is the company of the women who bore the tidings."

69. Minutes, Committee on Woman Suffrage, August 22, 1958. Stuenkel papers. Prohl's son suggests that his father became interested in the issue of women's service in the church while serving a vacancy parish in North Vernon, Indiana, around 1950. Because men of the congregation had abdicated leadership roles, women filled the vacuum, demonstrating "dynamic leadership." This experience was the beginning of Prohl's study of scriptural references to women's service in the church. John Prohl, telephone conversation with the author, January 13, 1996.

70. Letter from Walter Stuenkel to B. G. Mueller, March 3, 1958. Stuenkel papers.

71. Letter from B. G. Mueller to Walter Stuenkel, February 24, 1958. Stuenkel papers.

72. The English District is a nongeographical district within the Missouri Synod. Its congregations have historically been located in urban areas and have

Orleans. Stuenkel asked Wiederaenders for his "personal reaction."[73] Wiederaenders was frank in his appraisal of Prohl's book: "I felt as though I was walking in my sleep. I felt very uneasy. I hoped I would wake up and find what I feared was not so."[74] He went on to cite three specific complaints with the book: Prohl's careless use of quotations, scripture-twisting, and lack of evidence for premises made. Wiederaenders's summary of Prohl's book became the paradigm for its general reception by synodical leaders. Vague charges could remain unsubstantiated because the broad brush of the misuse of scripture underlay them all. Wiederaenders reported that he had already asked another Texas pastor, Vernon Harley, to write a critique of *Woman in the Church*.

When the suffrage committee met in early April, its conclusions were similar to Roland Wiederaenders's concerns, that quotations were used out of context, that Prohl did not properly understand the distinctions between the orders of creation and redemption, and that his biblical exegesis was inadequate. Stuenkel, Mueller, and Wente decided to publish their earlier theses in the *Lutheran Witness* along with a statement on the Prohl book in November. And Stuenkel was to contact Prohl's district president, Edgar Homrighausen, to inquire about any action or reaction in the Southern District.[75] In correspondence, the two agreed to keep each other informed on the Prohl matter.[76]

In July, synod president John Behnken wrote to Walter Stuenkel:

> The author of *Woman in the Church* certainly deserves some rather severe slaps on the fingers. It is a pity a man like Pastor Prohl rushes into print when two conferences sought to correct his error, but he would not listen to them. We must realize, too, that he had the book published by Eerdmans Publishing Company and not by Concordia Publishing House. He surely realized it would never have passed cen-

---

been scattered throughout twenty states. See chapter 3 for its early history and entrance into the synod.

73. Letter from Walter Stuenkel to Roland Wiederaenders, April 8, 1958. Stuenkel papers.

74. Letter from Roland Wiederaenders to Walter Stuenkel, April 16, 1958. Stuenkel papers.

75. Minutes, Committee on Woman Suffrage, April 8, 1958. Stuenkel papers.

76. Letter from Walter Stuenkel to Edgar Homrighausen, April 23, 1958. Homrighausen to Stuenkel, May 5, 1958. Stuenkel to Homrighausen, May 12, 1958. Stuenkel papers.

sorship. The very sad part about it is that he is another one of those men who disturb the church by his independent action.[77]

Whether Behnken's letter was the spark that moved the committee to action remains uncertain, but by early August the suffrage committee determined that Prohl's book was "causing disturbance in the church and that action should be taken."[78] In a meeting that Behnken attended, it was decided that Prohl be asked to cease distribution of his book. But no mention was made of meeting with Prohl until the following day, when Homrighausen strongly urged Stuenkel to consider doing so as "Prohl is very determined in his position."[79] By the end of the week, when Stuenkel returned to Milwaukee, he found in his mail an advertisement for Prohl's book, which consisted of eight anonymous endorsements from pastors, "veterans of the Cross," a laywoman, a college president, and a synodical board member — "what some of your fellow Lutherans are saying about my new book," Prohl wrote. Prohl had pursued an active campaign of seeking endorsements as well as promoting his book.[80] Stuenkel had had enough. He immediately wrote Prohl and asked him to cease and desist from further mailings until the committee could meet with him.[81] A meeting was arranged for August 22nd in St. Louis at synod headquarters.

At the meeting, attended by the suffrage committee, Prohl, Homrighausen, and his first vice president, William Kennell, Prohl was given the floor to make an explanatory statement. He gave a background of *Woman in the Church,* how it grew from an assigned conference paper to a student thesis to a published book. He added that he thought of his

77. Letter from John Behnken to Walter Stuenkel, July 8, 1958. John W. Behnken Papers, Box 24, CHI. Behnken's use of the term "censorship" refers to the synod's anonymous doctrinal review process through which every manuscript submitted to Concordia Publishing House must pass.

78. Minutes, Committee on Woman Suffrage, August 4, 1958. Stuenkel papers.

79. Letter from Walter Stuenkel to Walter Wente, August 11, 1958. Stuenkel papers.

80. Prohl's personal papers contain numerous notes and letters asking if he might quote positive comments he received from readers. In addition, he sent complimentary copies of the book to college, university, and seminary libraries nationwide. Russell Prohl papers, possession of Prohl family. Used with permission.

81. Letter from Walter Stuenkel to Russell Prohl, August 11, 1958. Stuenkel papers.

work as a contribution to ongoing study of the subject. Next, the committee read and discussed an analysis of the Prohl book that member Bernhard Mueller had prepared for an earlier meeting. Rather than dialogue about the issues, as Stuenkel had earlier expressed an interest in doing, the committee decided to ask Prohl to "discontinue the dissemination of the book." And they reaffirmed their plans to issue a statement in the November 4th issue of the *Lutheran Witness*.[82]

The statement Stuenkel prepared for publication in the *Witness* was brief but straightforward regarding the committee's opinion. Prohl assumed, but did not prove by scripture, certain premises that led him to believe that women should not only be allowed to vote in congregational meetings and hold parish office but also be ordained to the ministry. While Stuenkel suggested that Prohl's arguments were not new, but were the same used by "other protagonists for woman suffrage in the church," he did state that Prohl offered his findings as "problems to be discussed rather than as final conclusions reached." But, Stuenkel warned that Prohl's "personal findings may confuse and mislead the reader who is not able to check the quotations and Scripture interpretations carefully." His suggestion, therefore, was that anyone reading Prohl's book should also read Zerbst's. Finally, he restated the eleven theses that represented the synod's position on the place of woman in the church.[83]

Subsequently, several readers responded to the committee's published statement in letters to the editor of the *Lutheran Witness*. One man in Pennsylvania said the article disgusted him:

> Your arguments, me thinks, smack of German authoritarianism and are akin to those grasped by segregationists. What a field day the segregationists are having in supporting their "righteous" stand by quoting from the Bible! Could there be a parallelism in the instant case?[84]

Another male reader in Colorado argued that "the committee members should honestly accept the fact that women are not threatening scrip-

82. Minutes, Committee on Woman Suffrage, August 22, 1958. Stuenkel papers.

83. *Lutheran Witness* 77 (November 4, 1958): 21.

84. Letter from Sheridan Stroup to the *Lutheran Witness*, November 21, 1958. Stuenkel papers. Stroup closed his letter with an odd postscript: "P.S. I think I'm a man."

tural revelation but are threatening the status needs of men in the church." Accusing the committee of poor logic, the reader found "the historical position of a religious body . . . a totally inadequate criterion for dogma as Martin Luther demonstrated so well in the early sixteenth century."[85] A woman wrote to Oswald Hoffmann, Lutheran Hour speaker, to say that after reading Stuenkel's comments in the *Witness,* she bought Prohl's book, and found his position compelling. Hoffmann responded to the writer, but also wrote to Walter Stuenkel, asking his seminary classmate to tell him "in the plainest terms how this problem looks to you," as Hoffmann had promised the woman a more thoughtful reply. In his reply to Hoffmann, Stuenkel referred to Prohl's "very irritating" book, calling the author "a very sincere individual but certainly not very scholarly." Hoffmann's letter writer, Adelia Weis, a professor at Colorado State University, continued to pursue the issue in letters to committee members Stuenkel and Mueller, in which she enclosed copies of the Prohl book. Stuenkel was gracious in his reply, as was Mueller, who wrote: "My experience has been that women have more opportunity to serve in the church than can adequately be taken care of." Privately, Mueller disparaged "spinsters" like Weis, who he felt were agitating on the suffrage issue.[86] And he sent the book back.

Adelia Weis also corresponded with Russell Prohl. Very close to leaving her Missouri Synod congregation because of the synod's continued refusal to consider woman suffrage, Weis took heart upon discovering Prohl's book. She supported him by offering marketing suggestions, and on several occasions sent a check to be used at Prohl's discretion in the distribution of the book. He supported her by encouraging her to think through her decision about church membership carefully.[87]

85. Letter from Donald G. Miles to the *Lutheran Witness,* November 4, 1958. Stuenkel papers.

86. Letter from Adelia Weis to Oswald C. J. Hoffmann, March 1, 1959. Hoffmann to Walter Stuenkel, March 5, 1959. Stuenkel to Hoffmann, March 18, 1959. Weis to Stuenkel, May 15, 1959. Stuenkel to Weis, June 10, 1959. Weis to Mueller, May 16, 1959. Mueller to Weis, June 16, 1959. Stuenkel papers.

87. Adelia Weis to Russell Prohl, May 16, 1959. Prohl to Weis, June 12, 1959. Weis to Prohl, July 6, 1959. Prohl to Weis, August 18, 1959. Weis to Prohl, September 1, 1959. Weis to Prohl, September 13, 1959. Weis to Prohl, March 21, 1960. Prohl to Weis, April 1, 1960. Weis to Prohl, April 10, 1960. Prohl to Weis, June 14, 1960. Prohl to Weis, n.d. Prohl papers.

With the Prohl matter seemingly resolved by Stuenkel's article in the *Lutheran Witness,* the substance of the suffrage committee's work in 1959 revolved around correspondence. At the synodical convention in San Francisco in June, the synod voted to reaffirm its historic position and once again encouraged any congregations practicing woman suffrage to reconsider in light of the synod's stance.[88] This action attracted little notice with the exception of a letter to the editor of the *Lutheran Witness* from an angry woman in Maryland who referred to the "damaging influence" of the Missouri Synod — "the church of the male sex" — which had "crippled so miserably" its women.[89] Stuenkel inquired of Behnken whom he would be appointing to the suffrage committee for the next triennium, as synodical committees serve from convention to convention. Behnken responded by reappointing all three men to another term.

The suffrage committee found no reason to meet and there had been no further developments in the Prohl matter, until Russell Prohl wrote Walter Stuenkel on the seventh of October:

> A generous gift from an interested party is making it possible to send copies of my book . . . to all the circuit counselors of Synod. . . . I trust you will welcome this means of encouraging continued study of this controversial subject.[90]

Stuenkel was furious. He accused Prohl of breaking his promise from August 1958 that he would stop "making any propaganda" for his book,[91] and then he confronted the real issue: "This becomes a very serious matter as far as your synodical loyalty and affiliation are concerned." Appalled at Prohl's suggestion that Stuenkel might "welcome" his action, the chairman concluded with the hope that Prohl could see "the gravity of the situation which you have created."[92] The next day

---

88. Missouri Synod, *Proceedings,* 1959, pp. 190-91.

89. Letter from Ida R. Otte to the *Lutheran Witness,* July 3, 1959. Walter Stuenkel to Otte, July 24, 1959. Stuenkel papers.

90. Letter from Russell Prohl to Walter Stuenkel, October 7, 1959. Stuenkel papers.

91. Stuenkel's letter reads, "You promised . . . ," but the minutes of the meeting, which Prohl attended, record only "that Pastor Prohl be requested to discontinue the dissemination of the book." Minutes, Committee on Woman Suffrage, August 22, 1958. Stuenkel papers.

92. Letter from Walter Stuenkel to Russell Prohl, October 9, 1959. Stuenkel papers.

Stuenkel wrote to John Behnken about Prohl's letter: "He is spreading false exegesis and with that, of course, as a result false doctrine."[93] Bernhard Mueller also wrote Behnken with his own suspicions:

> The other day I received a form letter from Pastor Proehl [sic] stating that he is sending a copy of his book to each visitor. Someone — I suspect a spinster — made this money available. It seems to me we'll have to answer that kind of propaganda somehow.[94]

Behnken decided to put the matter in the lap of Prohl's district president, Edgar Homrighausen: "Someone furnished some money to Pastor Russell Prohl to send his book to all circuit counsellors. . . . This is a matter which will need your careful and prayerful consideration."[95] Homrighausen met with Prohl and asked him to stop sending out his book, but the district president was torn. He wrote Stuenkel that he could see Prohl's side in "making a sincere and honest effort to further discuss the problem of woman in the church," and that he was "not at all sure that we have a right to silence a man who approaches a problem in the manner Russell Prohl did."[96]

Prohl, in the meantime, continued to repeat his position that the issue of women's place in the church was not a confessional issue and that he had not broken his clerical vows by stating his opinion. He also contended that he had made no promise to the committee about suspending mailings regarding his book.[97] Bernhard Mueller was irritated by Prohl's position that the question of women's service was not a con-

93. Letter from Walter Stuenkel to John Behnken, October 10, 1959. Stuenkel papers.

94. Letter from B. G. Mueller to John Behnken, October 14, 1959. Unprocessed files of the Commission on Theology and Church Relations, 1962-1969, CHI. There is no record of who made the "generous gift" available to Prohl, though correspondence hints that it was very likely a gift from Adelia Weis. John Prohl recalls that the Prohl family lived on the usual clergy shoestring, and that his father had borrowed against his children's insurance policies and his daughter's wedding funds to enable the distribution of his book. John Prohl, telephone conversation with the author, January 13, 1996.

95. Letter from John Behnken to Edgar Homrighausen, October 17, 1959. John W. Behnken Papers, Box 24, CHI.

96. Letter from Edgar Homrighausen to Walter Stuenkel, October 26, 1959. Homrighausen to Stuenkel, November 13, 1959. Stuenkel papers.

97. Letter from Russell Prohl to Walter Stuenkel, December 7, 1959. Stuenkel papers.

fessional issue and said so to Stuenkel. The committee decided it needed another meeting with the chaplain. Prohl was summoned to Concordia Senior College at Fort Wayne on February 20, 1960. He was told by Stuenkel to be prepared to defend his position as stated in his book, and that the committee wanted "to deal with you in all love and kindness but at the same time with steadfast firmness."[98]

When Prohl met with the suffrage committee, he was handed and read charges of transgressing basic principles of scriptural interpretation and of proper ministerial conduct, with specific reference to six contested items in his book.[99] Stuenkel laid his case before the chaplain, citing the synodical constitution: "Unless you admit these and repent of them, it seems to me that it will not be possible for you to continue to serve as a pastor of The Lutheran Church–Missouri Synod."[100] It was because Russell Prohl refused to back down from his position — to stand by what he had written — that he stood accused. As the committee took up its list of issues, the four men engaged in hermeneutical jousting and contextual challenges. Prohl was asked to remove certain sentences, change words, add footnotes. Prohl's own notes of the meeting are indicative of the standoff between the pastor and the committee. He was accused of "incorrect hermeneutics" in, one, "the way I interpret Scripture," and, two, "honesty of quotations."[101] His only other legible notations include in quotation marks, "Passages of Paul are infinitely puzzling," and "Stuenkel says must be according to 'analogy of faith.'"[102] Mueller objected to Prohl's reference to the Missouri Synod as a tradition-bound church. Wente reminded Prohl that the basic frame of reference — the order of creation — had to be central to any discussion of the question of women in the church. There is no record in the minutes of Prohl's response to Wente. On some of the procedural issues Prohl yielded, such as

98. Letter from Walter Stuenkel to Russell Prohl, January 21, 1960. Stuenkel papers.

99. These were just from Stuenkel; Mueller and Wente had seven items each on which they challenged Prohl.

100. Document, "Discussion of the Following Points in *Woman in the Church*," n.d. Stuenkel papers.

101. "Discussion of the Following Points in *Woman in the Church*," n.d. Prohl papers.

102. "Discussion of the Following Points in *Woman in the Church*," n.d. Prohl papers. Analogy of faith is an expression meaning that the interpretation of scripture should be done so that it is in harmony with the whole of scripture.

agreeing to remove or add a citation or drop a sentence; on others he refused. In the end, he asked the committee for "time to reconsider" and to respond to particular items from Stuenkel's list, while agreeing to suspend for the time being his plans to distribute his book to the synodical praesidium and the College of Presidents. The committee agreed while expressing fear that "the book will exert harmful influence, also outside of our Synod, in addition to confusing the thinking of lay people and also pastors in the church."[103] Walter Wente concluded in his minutes of the meeting that, because the order of creation must remain central to any discussion of the woman question, "against this background it is impossible to maintain the basic theses of Pastor Prohl's book."[104]

On March third Prohl wrote Walter Stuenkel a letter asking a simple question: "What am I to admit and repent?" He had been reading the synod constitution and weighing the three options given him by the suffrage committee — to "admit" and "repent," to withdraw from Synod, or to have action initiated against him.[105] He was sincerely asking Chairman Stuenkel for a clear statement of his offense. Stuenkel replied that there were two matters: one, that Prohl persisted in offensive conduct by using misquotations and quoting out of context in his book, and two, that he misused scripture. They expected him to admit and repent of both. Without agreement on this point, Stuenkel said, there could be no further discussion.[106] On March 14th, Prohl advised Stuenkel that he had a meeting planned with Homrighausen for March 29th and would inform him of his plans after that meeting.[107] There is no further correspondence in Stuenkel's files until July 1960, when Walter Wente wrote to Stuenkel:

> Now the situation has settled down to one simple and definite issue, namely, the ordination of women into the ministry. I keep wondering

103. Minutes, Committee on Woman Suffrage, February 20, 1960. Stuenkel papers.
104. Minutes, Committee on Woman Suffrage, February 20, 1960. Stuenkel papers.
105. Letter from Russell Prohl to Walter Stuenkel, March 3, 1960. Stuenkel papers. There is no mention in the minutes of the February 20 meeting of any options offered Prohl.
106. Letter from Walter Stuenkel to Russell Prohl, March 10, 1960. Stuenkel papers.
107. Letter from Russell Prohl to Walter Stuenkel, March 14, 1960. Stuenkel papers.

whether our respondent fully realized what he was advocating when he published his book. I can hardly imagine that he is willing to uphold such a position when he realizes the full implications, and that it should be possible to persuade him to refrain from further agitation on this basis.[108]

Less than a month later Wente again wrote Stuenkel about Prohl. The committee had met in the meantime, and Stuenkel had related to the others that President Behnken was reluctant to take further action against Prohl, as Behnken considered him simply "a man who had gone off on a tangent." Wente also advised caution, particularly in light of "the man's physical condition and Dr. Behnken's apparent attitude," suggesting that Prohl's desire to distribute his book stemmed more from

> pride of authorship rather than from a desire to agitate the question and disturb the Church. It is not as though he were a violent millennialist seeking to make converts, as, if I remember correctly, there once was in the history of our Church.[109]

Stuenkel passed Wente's comments along to Mueller, the more hardline member of the trio, adding only that he wanted Prohl to make a statement in writing that "will indicate that he see this matter is of some consequence."[110] Mueller, complaining that Wente had always seemed "a bit hesitant to dig into the problem of our committee and to commit himself," felt that any action had to come from Prohl's district, which would be appropriate, as a synodical committee has no power to take action against any member of the synod. Mueller obviously wanted the matter settled: "I think the Lord wants us to close ranks on the basis of His Word."[111]

There is no further correspondence in the committee files on the Russell Prohl matter after late August 1960. But Prohl's own

108. Letter from Walter Wente to Walter Stuenkel, July 11, 1960. Stuenkel papers.

109. Letter from Walter Wente to Walter Stuenkel, August 9, 1960. Stuenkel papers.

110. Letter from Walter Stuenkel to B. G. Mueller, August 12, 1960. Stuenkel papers.

111. Letter from B. G. Mueller to Walter Stuenkel, August 17, 1960. Stuenkel papers.

correspondence reveals that within weeks after his meeting with the committee, he had become convinced that his only recourse was to resign from the synod. On March 29th he submitted a letter of resignation to Homrighausen and the others with whom he had been meeting in the Southern District. That same day Prohl contacted the president of the Texas District of the United Lutheran Church in America (ULCA) in order to arrange a meeting, as he wished to pursue a call in the ULCA. Those plans never materialized because Homrighausen refused to accept Prohl's resignation, arguing that "this does not pertain to any saving doctrine." Instead the district president continued working to arrange some sort of compromise between his chaplain and the suffrage committee. No agreement was ever reached.[112] In October Prohl entered the hospital in New Orleans for ulcer surgery, but had a difficult recovery due to an underlying condition of leukemia. On November 26th, following further surgery, Russell Prohl died at age fifty-three. With his death the most vocal spokesman for a change in the status of women in the Missouri Synod was silenced, and the church was spared having to take definitive action against a dissenter. Walter Stuenkel recalls that "after Prohl's death in 1960, discussion of his book practically ceased."[113]

Stuenkel may have been correct about official Missouri Synod circles, but Russell Prohl's legacy was to survive through influence. In 1969, when the American Lutheran Church was considering the question of the ordination of women, its president appointed an ad hoc committee to study the issue and make a recommendation to the ALC Church Council the following June. Margaret Barth Wold, one of two women appointed to that committee, recalled that, despite other helpful reading, "it was a Missouri Synod pastor's study of the relevant

112. Russell Prohl to A. T. DeGroot, March 4, 1960. Gene Harrison to Philip Wahlberg, President of the Texas and Louisiana Synod of the ULCA, March 18, 1960 (letter of introduction). Philip L. Wahlberg to Russell Prohl, March 23, 1960. Prohl to Wahlberg, March 27, 1960. Prohl to Homrighausen, O. H. Reinboth, and William Wedig, March 29, 1960. Reinboth to Prohl, March 31, 1960. Prohl to Wahlberg, March 31, 1960. Homrighausen to Prohl, April 2, 1960. Prohl to Homrighausen, April 6, 1960. Prohl to Wahlberg, April 6, 1960. Wahlberg to Prohl, April 8, 1960. Homrighausen to Prohl, April 11, 1960. Prohl to Homrighausen, April 14, 1960. Prohl papers.
113. Walter W. Stuenkel, letter to author, December 19, 1994.

scriptures that had motivated my own journey most significantly," citing Prohl's *Woman in the Church*.[114]

The Committee on Woman Suffrage served the remainder of its second term in relative peace as compared with the tensions that prevailed during the lengthy Prohl episode. Walter Stuenkel wrote an article for the *Lutheran Witness* in 1962 in which he replied to correspondence received by the committee he chaired, much of which challenged the synod's position on women in the church. Because the synod had not changed that position, Stuenkel could add little on the subject other than to reiterate the scriptural proscriptions and rehearse again the order of creation/order of redemption teaching. While again reminding readers that

> the Synod has not said that the Bible definitely forbids woman suffrage in the church, Synod has emphatically stated, however, that God has through the tradition of our fathers given us a system of church government which is in the spirit of all that Scripture says on woman's position in the church.
>
> Voters' meetings are concerned with matters vitally connected with the church's life and welfare, matters "which can be disassociated from the church's worship service only with great difficulty." It follows therefore, according to the adopted resolution, that the Scriptural principles governing public worship apply also to voters' meetings. "Consequently it has been the general practice of our congregations to withhold voting membership from women."
>
> Synod has resolved not to give up this position unless very powerful reasons are advanced for adopting superior administrative patterns that are also in complete harmony with the Scriptures.[115]

Here Stuenkel, by linking the question of suffrage to church governance and administration, appeared to reduce the issue to a matter of church polity alone, and to a polity based on tradition. Russell Prohl was no longer around to challenge him on the larger issue of women's

114. Margaret Barth Wold, "We Seized the Spirit's Moment," in *Lutheran Women in Ordained Ministry, 1970-1995: Reflections and Perspectives*, ed. Gloria E. Bengston (Minneapolis: Augsburg Fortress, 1995), p. 19.

115. Walter W. Stuenkel, "Woman Suffrage in the Church," *Lutheran Witness* 81 (March 20, 1962): 6-7. Stuenkel was quoting the report of the Committee on Woman's Suffrage to the 1956 synodical convention. See Missouri Synod, *Proceedings*, 1956, p. 568.

service in the church. Stuenkel received the usual letters from laypeople in response to his article, several of which advocated that synod leave the matter of suffrage up to the local congregations, on which the polity of synod is based. One woman suggested further study was indicated and asked that women be included on the study committee. Several asked to be directed to congregations that practiced woman suffrage.[116] At the synodical convention in Cleveland that summer, the only action pertaining to women appeared in three resolutions with regard to women teachers. Since women had by 1954 become the majority of teachers in the synod's parochial school system,[117] new questions arose as to their status. The convention established a committee to study that status, resolved to address procedures regarding nonsynodically trained women teachers, and asked the College of Presidents for guidelines for the "orderly transfer of women teachers."[118] There was no report from the standing Committee on Woman Suffrage.

The Scripture Debate Begins in Earnest

The Prohl episode, which consumed the Committee on Woman Suffrage between 1958 and 1960, was probably considered nothing more than a nuisance by contemporaries compared to a more central controversy then emerging in the synod. The story drawing far more attention featured Martin Scharlemann, a professor at Concordia Seminary, St. Louis, who in 1958 prepared an essay to be presented to the seminary faculty for discussion. Entitled "The Inerrancy of Scripture," Scharlemann began his essay by proposing "to defend the paradox that the Book of God's Truth contains 'errors.'"[119] Scharlemann wrote as a self-proclaimed "volunteer" out of the conviction that "part of our task — possibly even part of our cross" was to look at scripture, in particular at

116. Letters addressed to the editor of the *Lutheran Witness* dated March 19, 1962; March 20, 1962; March 28, 1962; March 30, 1962. Stuenkel papers.

117. *Statistical Yearbook of the Lutheran Church–Missouri Synod for the Year 1954* (St. Louis: Concordia Publishing House, 1955), p. 248.

118. Missouri Synod, *Proceedings*, 1962, resolutions 1-66, 1-67, 1-68.

119. "The Inerrancy of Scripture," unpublished manuscript, mimeographed copy, dated February 25, 1958. Martin Scharlemann papers, Supplement III, Box 14, CHI. The bulk of the Scharlemann papers are sealed until the year 2008.

the "human side" of revelation. The object of his exploration was the first paragraph of the synod's Brief Statement, which Scharlemann believed had not been very thoroughly examined before being adopted:

> We teach that the Holy Scriptures differ from all other books in the world in that they are the Word of God. They are the Word of God because the holy men of God who wrote the Scriptures wrote only that which the Holy Ghost communicated to them by inspiration. We teach also that the verbal inspiration of the Scriptures is not a so-called "theological deduction," but that it is taught by direct statements of the Scriptures. Since the Holy Scriptures are the Word of God, it goes without saying that they contain no errors or contradictions, but that they are in all their parts and words the infallible truth, also in those parts which treat of historical, geographical, and other secular matters.[120]

He thought the synod's official position on scripture a "pure rationalization, built on the assumption that our Scriptures are, like the Book of Mormon, a gift that fell straight from heaven, when in fact, it is the book of the people of God, with all that such a statement implies." Scharlemann considered such a narrow understanding of verbal inerrancy incomplete, an approach "concerned almost exclusively with the verbal side of Biblical revelation." As such, inerrancy was an oversimplification, one that not only was "quite out of keeping with the nature of Biblical revelation," but also "stunts the message of the Bible." Concerned that the graduates the seminary faculty was preparing would "be fighting the battles of God on the wrong fronts," Scharlemann, a former military chaplain, saw discussion of inerrancy "strictly a diversion." He thought it entirely possible, as he suggested in one of his seven theses on the interpretation of scripture, for interpreters of scripture to differ in their exegesis without being in doctrinal disagreement.

Scharlemann's essay was intended as an internal document for faculty discussion only, but it was not long before the paper had been leaked to conservative critics outside the seminary.[121] That action be-

---

120. *Brief Statement of the Doctrinal Position of the Missouri Synod* (St. Louis: Concordia Publishing House, 1932), p. 3.

121. Richard Donald Labore, "Traditions and Transitions: A Study of the Leadership of the Lutheran Church–Missouri Synod During a Decade of Theological Change, 1960-1969" (Ph.D. diss., St. Louis University, 1980), pp. 130, 203n20. La-

gan a series of skirmishes that would last almost four years, in which the professor fought to defend his "exploratory" studies and those who opposed him fought to expose what they considered the dangerously liberal and modernist tendencies of the faculty at the St. Louis seminary. Eventually officially settled, though unsatisfactorily resolved in the conservatives' mind, this episode foreshadowed far more contentious developments in the synod in the next decade.

Scharlemann's intention in presenting this essay, and three more the following year, was "to invite the pastors of the Church, as his peers, to a reexamination of certain issues."[122] His postgraduate studies at Union Theological Seminary had contributed to his sense that someone needed to raise the questions that were arising out of current biblical scholarship, and that not only the pastors, but the faculties training future pastors, needed to be involved in study of those questions:

> When I came to the seminary, '52, our theology was pretty frozen. No new question had been asked for decades . . . because there was a kind of assumption that all the questions had been answered, when in fact new questions arise in theology all the time, and this was a very, very unwholesome atmosphere in which to live. So I began to write some of those essays. . . . I took up the question of inerrancy. . . . My own idea was that we ought not even use the word because it has a Reformed background and usually misleads people when they read it. In fact, it often keeps people from reading the Bible because they're scared to run into some problem, since inerrancy suggests that everything is in neat order, which, of course it isn't, in Scripture. Well, of course, as soon as you start tinkering with the word "inerrancy" you get into trouble.[123]

---

bore, who devotes a chapter of his dissertation to "The Martin H. Scharlemann Case," in 1977 interviewed Scharlemann, who indicated that the paper was leaked by Robert Preus, another member of the St. Louis faculty. Preus and his brother Jacob had in the late 1950s joined the Missouri Synod as faculty members at its seminaries, Robert at St. Louis and Jacob at Springfield. Both were originally members of the Little Norwegian Synod (the Evangelical Lutheran Synod), known for its ultra-conservative position, and which in 1955 had suspended its relationship with the Missouri Synod for Missouri's tolerance of doctrinal error, such as the position of the "Forty-four."

122. Labore, "Traditions and Transitions," p. 125.

123. Martin H. Scharlemann, interview transcript (1980), Archives of Cooperative Lutheranism ALC-AELC-LCA Oral History Collection, ELCA Archives, Chicago, pp. 34-35.

Like Russell Prohl, he believed he was offering his musings to the church in the spirit of honest study. The church, it seems, was ready for neither of them.

Invited to present essays at several district pastoral conferences in 1959, Scharlemann used those opportunities to continue introducing his thinking on biblical interpretation to the clergy. In April he read "The Bible as Record, Witness and Medium" to Northern Illinois District pastors.[124] Suggesting the term "reliability" was preferable to inerrancy, he stressed the role of scripture as a medium of God's revelation, though not a revelation itself. It follows, then, that use of the Bible as the infallible rule of faith and practice is not the same as insisting that every piece of information contained within it is factually accurate. The historical moments in which the biblical writers wrote necessarily imposed limitations on the authors. The one point Scharlemann repeated often in these essays was that the revelation of God came in the actions of God, not in words: "Revelation does not consist in unveiling timeless truths. God did not hurl His absolutes out into the universe at random."[125]

In October 1959 Martin Scharlemann read the third of his essays to the Western District pastoral conference. In this paper, "Revelation and Inspiration," he set about to differentiate the Lutheran view of scripture from that of what he called Reformed Fundamentalism.[126] Acknowledging that the Lutheran confessors had never developed a doctrine of the Word, by which the church would know more definitively how to understand and interpret scripture, Scharlemann began his remarks by declaring his own commitment to the doctrine of verbal inspiration. His disclaimer had come at the suggestion of Alfred Fuerbringer, president of the St. Louis seminary, who, while supporting Scharlemann, was also quite aware of the growing reaction against his professor's current work.[127] Revisiting many of the points made in his earlier essays, Scharlemann focused his concern again on the Brief Statement, which he believed had been adopted hastily, giving rise to fundamentalist interpretations, that *because* scripture was verbally inspired, it therefore *was* the

124. "The Bible as Record, Witness and Medium," unpublished ms., mimeographed copy, n.d. Scharlemann papers, CHI.
125. "The Bible as Record, Witness and Medium."
126. "Revelation and Inspiration," unpublished mimeographed copy, n.d. Scharlemann papers, CHI.
127. Labore, "Traditions and Transitions," p. 141.

Word of God: "It is this particular emphasis that has misled may Christians into believing Christian faith is a belief in a book."[128]

In a letter of response to questions from pastors who had heard him speak at Pocono Crest, Pennsylvania, earlier that year, Scharlemann summarized the principal argument of all three of his essays: "As the Word of God the Bible is authoritative. To apply the notion of 'inerrancy' to it is applying a yardstick which is quite foreign to the Bible itself."[129]

To synod conservatives, here was more than enough evidence that "Dr. Martin Scharlemann is spearheading a movement to rid the Missouri Synod of the doctrine of the inerrancy of Holy Scripture, and, with that, of its Plenary and Verbal Inspiration as confessed by the Missouri Synod e.g. in the Brief Statement."[130] In response to charges of unorthodoxy by one of their members, the seminary faculty prepared "A Statement on the Form and Function of the Scriptures" in the spring of 1960.[131] Sides were drawn.

This furor over Scharlemann's bold declarations regarding inerrancy and the Brief Statement was exacerbated by the context into which they were set. At its San Francisco convention in the summer of 1959, the synod had passed as Resolution 3-09 that "pastors and teachers and professors are held to teach and act in harmony with" synodically adopted doctrinal statements.[132] By effectively elevating the Brief Statement to doctrinal status, Resolution Nine, as it came to be known, formally altered the confessional base of the synod. This action raised grave concern among many in the synod about where this new imposition of legalism and absolutism — as they understood the nature of a binding resolution — might lead. One pastor, a signer of *A Statement* in 1945, found echoes of synodical actions that had impelled the "Forty-four" to their protest. He summarized his worry about the advisory synod's grasp of legislative power:

> It is a terribly precarious procedure to elevate human deductions, interpretations, applications to the level of a divine, infallible truth. . . .

128. "Revelation and Inspiration," pp. 19-20.
129. Duplicated letter, December 16, 1959. Scharlemann papers.
130. "What the Missouri Synod Is Really Facing Today," *The Confessional Lutheran* 20 (November 1959): 109-10.
131. Published in *Concordia Theological Monthly* 41 (1960): 626-27.
132. Missouri Synod, *Proceedings*, 1959, pp. 191-92.

   No matter how seriously concerned Synod may be about the safe-guarding and preservation of truth, it will never be justified on the basis of the Scripture or of the Reformation principle "Sola Scriptura" to establish doctrine binding on men's souls by means of resolutions passed by a majority vote at a synodical convention.

   Only God can establish doctrine and reveal divine truth. This cannot be achieved by convention resolutions.

   Only the Spirit of God can persuade man of divine truth. This cannot be achieved by convention resolutions. . . .

   We are always trying to play God in one way or another. . . .

   We ought most meekly remember: "We now see as through a glass darkly. We know in part." 1 Cor. 12:12. Persons with such sketchy knowledge should not make like God.[133]

The decision to withdraw *A Statement* as basis for discussion had allowed the "trends and tendencies" that alarmed its signers to continue. As the decade turned, the Missouri Synod found itself experiencing symptoms of unraveling.

Changes in Leadership and Direction

The synodical convention held in Cleveland in 1962 marked several significant changes for the church. John Behnken retired from the presidency after serving for twenty-seven years, and Oliver Harms was elected to succeed him. Martin Scharlemann publicly withdrew his essays and, despite many calls for his suspension from the seminary, was forgiven by the assembled church body.[134] The by-now infamous Resolution Nine adopted by the previous convention had been declared unconstitutional by the Commission on Constitutional Matters (CCM) for having amended the synod's constitution without proper procedure. By this ruling a question critical to the identity of the synod, that of the imposition of public doctrine, was removed from discussion; dis-

133. Unsigned manuscript, "Resolution Number Nine," n.d. Files of O. A. Geiseman, Grace Lutheran Church Archives, River Forest, Illinois. The two-part essay is likely Geiseman's own very negative reaction to Resolution Nine.

134. For a detailed narration of the Scharlemann episode, see Jack Howard Greising, "The Status of Confessional Conservatism: Background and Issues in the Lutheran Church–Missouri Synod" (Ph.D. diss., St. Louis University, 1972), pp. 121-23.

missed on legality, it would have been preferable had the convention confronted head-on a matter that had generated such tremendous controversy for three years prior. Instead, it was left to smolder. But the issue of binding resolutions would not go away.

Despite its eventual overthrow, Resolution Nine had set a dangerous precedent. It had shown that major changes in doctrine could be effected by a majority vote of the delegates to a synodical convention. And exactly that happened at the 1962 convention as a significant change in the synod's doctrine of ministry was accepted by the passage of three resolutions on constitutional, not doctrinal, matters.[135] Missouri's long-held understanding that the office of public ministry required a call from a congregation was redefined, so that a call was now attached to the office a man served, whether pastor, professor, district or synod executive, missionary, or military chaplain. The College of Presidents had initiated the change, necessitated, they felt, by the vast increase in the number of administrative positions created as a result of the synod's postwar growth, as well as a need to clarify ordination for the federal government with regard to military chaplains and authorization to perform marriages. This administrative rationale, however, obviated recognition by the synod of a very real change in its doctrine of public ministry, one that allowed the synod itself, no longer only the congregation, to determine the definition of the pastoral office.[136]

One lesson learned in the interim between conventions was that there was a need for some more permanent agency within the church to deal with such primary theological questions. Accordingly, the Cleveland convention passed a resolution establishing a new synodical Commission on Theology and Church Relations (CTCR) to serve as an advisory body to the synod on matters of doctrine and relationships with other church bodies. The creation of the CTCR effectively merged earlier committees, such as the Committee on Woman Suffrage, which had been appointed on an as-needed basis into "a single, unified voice."[137] At the same time, the Commission replaced the long-standing practice of consulting seminary faculties for theological opinions. Was the CTCR simply an example of bureaucratic efficiency as required by a growing synod,

135. Missouri Synod, *Proceedings,* 1962, pp. 130-31.
136. For the history of this development, see John C. Wohlrabe, Jr., "An Historical Analysis of the Doctrine of the Ministry in the Lutheran Church–Missouri Synod until 1962" (Th.D. diss., Concordia Seminary, St. Louis, 1987).
137. Missouri Synod, *Proceedings,* 1962, pp. 55, 123-24.

or was there also concern, in light of the Scharlemann case, over the direction the seminary faculty was leaning in its scholarship?

The question of woman suffrage was referred to the new commission. But woman suffrage was not the pressing issue in the church in 1962.[138] Following announcement of the Commission's appointment, pastors and people sent requests for clarification on questions about Bible teachings, what was being taught at the seminaries — specifically the Scharlemann matter — the teaching of evolution, confirmation, baptism, the Boy Scouts,[139] and charges that the Missouri Synod was becoming a "church of the clergy," the CTCR serving as prime example. Additionally, there were increasing calls for "official interpretations" of scripture passages, despite the synod's long history of accepting "variant Interpretations."[140] Woman suffrage, while on the list, was hardly near the top. The list itself indicates not only the accumulation of issues with which the church was confronted, but the inadequacy of the synod to address doctrinal issues, particularly over against sociocultural change.

With no magisterium or primary teaching office other than its ordained ministry in a congregational polity, and a tradition of appealing to seminary faculty for learned opinion, the establishment of a Commission on Theology and Church Relations represented an attempt to direct much of this controversy to an advisory body for study and opinion. Like the synod itself, synodical commissions are only advisory bodies, and action may only be taken by the synod in convention. But the creation of the CTCR was significant in another way. A permanent commission on theology was an admission that the synod's "unmoving theology" — perhaps also its congregational polity — was not adequate to address either the multiple issues of modern society, or the inconsistency in congregational practices inherent in the synod's polity, an inconsistency that had been compounded by the synod's remarkable growth in the postwar years. Since 1945 the number of baptized members had nearly doubled and the synod had added half again as many congregations.[141]

138. Executive Office files, Box 68, CHI.

139. Scouting was challenged over its use of the Boy Scout oath and its ecumenism, which threatened the synod's strict posture against unionism.

140. John Constable, "Of Congregational and Synodical Authority," *Concordia Theological Monthly* 43 (1972): 224-31.

141. In 1945 the synod had 1,532,702 baptized members and 3,816 congregations. In 1965 the baptized membership was 2,944,675 in 5,825 congregations. *Statistical Yearbook of the Evangelical Lutheran Synod of Missouri, Ohio and Other States for*

Thinking About Things Differently:
The CTCR and the Suffrage Question

Yet, despite the centrality of the scripture issue, the CTCR also found that the woman suffrage issue had not disappeared. In 1963 the Commission on Constitutional Matters (CCM) sent a request for consideration of the issue to the CTCR. The CCM, which had been receiving appeals from congregations who were being denied membership in the Missouri Synod because of suffrage clauses in their constitutions, believed suffrage to be a theological matter.[142] The CTCR itself received repeated letters and requests for clarification on the synod policy from both congregations and districts. Letters from individual members of the synod were forwarded from the *Lutheran Witness*. Various questions emerged, such as Theona von Lorenz's:

> How long does the Missouri Synod intend to put off the right to vote on the part of women in our church? . . . I have waited twenty-five years for the right to say "yes" or "no" on a ballot in a Missouri Synod church. I tithe. I have pledged. I continue to tithe, but I refuse to pledge to a church that stubbornly refuses to withhold this privilege from a large group of its membership. This is a form of segregation. It is wrong.[143]

The letter writer embedded her demand for suffrage in the civil rights language of the times, arguing that the synod practiced segregation by disallowing women voting privileges in their congregations. Like the earliest suffragist arguments in the nineteenth century, she saw suffrage as a justice issue, thereby challenging the long-held position of the church that the genders had different roles to play. A woman from Cincinnati was so annoyed with the synod's insistence on the maintenance of gender spheres and its "faulty emphasis on women from Mis-

---

the Year 1945 (St. Louis: Concordia Publishing House, 1946), p. 140; *Statistical Yearbook of the Lutheran Church–Missouri Synod for the Year 1965* (St. Louis: Concordia Publishing House, 1966), p. 180.

142. Letter from the Commission on Constitutional Matters to the Commission on Theology and Church Relations, May 13, 1963. Unprocessed files of the CTCR, 1962-1969, CHI. Correspondence from congregations regarding membership is in the CCM files, Executive Office files, CHI.

143. Letter from Theona S. von Lorenz, Minneapolis, to the editor of the *Lutheran Witness*, February 3, 1964. Unprocessed files of the CTCR, CHI.

souri Synod teachings taken out of context"[144] that she sent both a letter and a telegram to Oliver Harms on the same day. Her appeal echoed the civil rights argument of the earlier writer but said it more bluntly: "Life is moving at a tremendous rate. Since the Missouri Synod has discovered Boy Scouts, nice pictures of Negroes and whites together, will women ever get off their milk stool?" The writer concluded by reminding Harms that there would be no sexes in heaven.[145]

The new commission had to assign some priority to the many issues and requests it received. Some questions seemed predetermined either by prior synodical action or long-standing synodical position. One of those predetermined issues was the ordination of women to the public ministry. There is no indication of the source, but the minutes of the October 1963 meeting of the CTCR contain a formal resolution that states that "the question of the ordination of women has been laid before the CTCR." The CTCR deferred placing the issue on its immediate agenda and was specific as to its reasons — not only did "clear passages of Scripture forbid women to speak and to teach in the church," but "the question of the ordination of women does not appear to be a problem facing our synod at this time." The position of the church on this issue seemed self-evident. The Commission also declined a second resolution requesting a restudy of woman suffrage, citing the fact that there had been no new evidence to warrant a restudy, and expressing its position that the synod had "declared itself officially and in detail" on the question of suffrage.[146]

At the 1965 synodical convention in Detroit, a resolution to adopt a statement on woman suffrage appeared to modify the resolutions of the 1956 and 1959 conventions. Again complaints surrounded the lack of clarity as to what was meant by the scripture passages cited by the earlier committees. While the resolution reasserted the order of creation and reaffirmed the Pauline teachings forbidding women from publicly preaching, teaching men, holding office, or voting "where this involves exercising authority over men," it stated that "we consider woman suffrage in the church as contrary to Scripture only when it violates the above-mentioned Scriptural principles."[147] The convention

144. Letter from Elsie Ayer to Oliver Harms, April 2, 1964. Unprocessed files of the CTCR, CHI.
145. Telegram from Elsie Ayer to Oliver Harms, April 2, 1964. Unprocessed files of the CTCR, CHI.
146. Minutes, CTCR, October 21-23, 1963. CHI.
147. Missouri Synod, *Proceedings,* 1965, p. 103.

adopted the resolution, leaving the question of just when and where woman suffrage could be practiced still unresolved in many Missouri minds. The ambivalence of the Detroit convention on woman suffrage contrasted to other convention action, which included a reaffirmation of both the synod's "unwavering loyalty to the Scriptures as the inspired and inerrant word of God,"[148] and its "conviction that the events recorded in the book of Jonah did occur."[149] In addition to actions asserting its position on scripture, the synod also agreed "to uphold and honor the doctrinal content of synodically adopted statements," a resolution in response to the festering question of the status of the Brief Statement.[150] Amid this restatement of the church's prior posture, the Detroit convention took two very positive steps forward. Delegates received with thanks the Mission Affirmations, a visionary report that was the result of an extensive study by Martin L. Kretzmann, a former missionary,[151] and enthusiastically approved the synod's membership in the new pan-Lutheran cooperative agency, the Lutheran Council in the USA (LCUSA).[152]

The CTCR was made up of appointed faculty representatives from each of the synod's two seminaries as well as elected clergy and lay members, all male. It divided its work into two committees, Committee One on theology and Committee Two on church relations, matters of ethics, and polity. Subcommittees were formed as needed. In 1967 Martin Scharlemann — recently himself the subject of one of the first controverted issues the CTCR had to address — was appointed to the CTCR as a representative of the St. Louis seminary faculty. In late 1964 the Commission elected its first Executive Secretary, Richard Jungkuntz, who had been an original member of the CTCR as a faculty representative from Concordia Seminary, Springfield.

Personally interested in the issue of woman suffrage — "a couple of us thought it was one of the things the Missouri Synod could move forward on" — Jungkuntz presented at its meeting in January 1967 a working paper he had prepared for the Commission.[153] Written around

148. Missouri Synod, *Proceedings,* 1965, p. 94.

149. Missouri Synod, *Proceedings,* 1965, p. 100.

150. Missouri Synod, *Proceedings,* 1965, p. 96.

151. Missouri Synod, *Proceedings,* 1965, p. 88.

152. Missouri Synod, *Proceedings,* 1965, pp. 69, 106-10.

153. Richard P. Jungkuntz, interview by author, January 18, 1995, tape recording.

a series of rhetorical questions to promote discussion, the paper grounded the question of suffrage in just how the issue should be treated — does it fall under the rubric of Law, Gospel, or both, or neither? Or is it an *adiaphoron,* an "indifferent thing" which is neither commanded nor forbidden by scripture? Jungkuntz then addressed the usual New Testament passages cited in regard to women's place in the church before he examined the orders of creation and redemption. Arguing that the 1956 report on suffrage was inconsistent both in its definitions of speaking and silence and in its treatment of scripture, Jungkuntz concluded that

> The traditional position of our church on Woman's Suffrage is not as clearly or securely grounded in Holy Scripture as has generally been supposed. There does not appear to be adequate Biblical reason for categorically denying women the privilege of voting in the congregation on any question that legitimately comes before it. Similarly, there appears to be no Biblical reason for excluding women from service on any church board or committee. . . . The issue of Woman Suffrage . . . is a genuine adiaphoron and is to be dealt with in the freedom with which the Gospel frees us.[154]

Jungkuntz's position reflected a more broadly conceived interpretation of the scriptural passages on which the synod had based its prohibition of woman suffrage than that used in the 1956 report. After he had finished his presentation to the Commission, considerable discussion followed. Jungkuntz recalled:

> Just as the discussion was drawing to a close, Dr. Scharlemann observed, "But if those positions that Jungkuntz has taken, and his arguments in support of them, if they are valid, that means that women's ordination should be permitted." And I said, "Well, you're the one who said it," and I did not pursue it further, because that would have led us down this other path and utterly derailed the suffrage question. My feeling (and that was a political choice) was that if we can get suffrage in, at least there's a foot in the door or a camel's nose under the tent.[155]

154. Richard P. Jungkuntz, "Observations on the Question of Woman Suffrage in the Church," January 12, 1977. Unprocessed files of the Commission on Theology and Church Relations, CHI.
155. Jungkuntz interview.

This story provides yet another example of a pattern that had emerged in Missouri already during the Prohl episode — in every discussion of the service of women in the church, the theologians' reticence to discuss fully the dimensions and implications of that service left the woman question unsatisfactorily unresolved.

Nevertheless, at that same meeting, the Commission recommended that a special subcommittee be appointed to "undertake Biblical and exegetical studies to provide a scriptural basis for 'The Position of Women in Relation to the Public Administration of the Office of the Keys.'"[156] Four men were appointed: Jungkuntz, Victor Bartling, his son Walter Bartling, and Armin Moellering.[157] Despite the assignment given, the subcommittee would examine the question of woman suffrage and only that question.

Since the synod moved from triennial to biennial gatherings in 1965, another synodical convention met in New York City in the summer of 1967. Prior to the convention, President Harms reported to the CTCR on "some disturbances in the church on the question of women," and was advised by the Commission to refer questioners to the previous convention resolutions.[158] In New York the convention passed a resolution admitting the confusion and disagreement within the church over the 1965 convention resolution on suffrage and agreeing to "wait in patience" for the report of the Commission on Theology and Church Relations, which would be complete by the 1969 convention. A second resolution declared women eligible to serve as advisory members of synodical boards and commissions, with the question of their full membership referred to the CTCR for study.[159] And like the Detroit convention, the New York convention again reaffirmed the synodical position on scripture,[160] its teaching on the creation and fall as well as its doctrinal stance on Christ's resurrection and atonement.[161] One observer worried, however, that the church body had "adopted some of the most fundamentalistic resolutions in the area of biblical interpretation that the Synod had ever

156. This reference to the office of ordained ministry as the public administration of the office of the keys is both unusual and unexplained in the minutes.
157. Minutes, CTCR, January 17-19, 1967. CHI.
158. Minutes, CTCR, May 31-June 2, 1967. CHI.
159. Missouri Synod, *Proceedings,* 1967, p. 89.
160. Missouri Synod, *Proceedings,* 1967, p. 92.
161. Missouri Synod, *Proceedings,* 1967, p. 95.

known."[162] In other action, Missouri moved as close as it ever had to fellowship with the American Lutheran Church, anticipating that a vote would follow at the next convention.[163] Again the church seemed to be going in two directions at once.

By October 1967 the special committee on woman suffrage had finished its report. It had studied all prior activity in the synod on the subject, and had read the Zerbst book on woman in the church on which the 1956 committee had so heavily relied, but which Richard Jungkuntz personally considered "not an impressive document, not then, and not now."[164] The conclusion of the committee was that, although

> the Synod has seen a limitation of some kind on the practice of woman suffrage in the church, . . . it has had difficulty in specifying the practical implications of this limitation. The reason for this difficulty seems to be the fact that there is no clear or necessary connection between the apostolic teaching of these passages and the issue of woman suffrage as such.[165]

The subcommittee had benefited from the contribution of a newly appointed lay member of the Commission, David Leege, a young professor of political science with an expertise in voting behavior. Leege recalls that the CTCR discussion revealed two differing positions on the issue of authority: the broad constructionist "assumed that any kind of action involving men and women where women had authority equal to that of men was circumscribed by the biblical texts," while the strict constructionist looked at the context of those texts and argued that references to authority had to do with the public office of pastoral ministry, which was not allowed to women, but said nothing at all about exercising the franchise.[166] Leege helped the Commission delineate the difference between women voting and their holding the office

---

162. Larry W. Neeb, "Historical and Theological Dimensions of a Confessing Movement within the Lutheran Church–Missouri Synod" (D.Min. diss., Eden Theological Seminary, 1975), p. 92.

163. Missouri Synod, *Proceedings,* 1967, 102-3.

164. Jungkuntz interview.

165. "Report of the Special Committee on Woman Suffrage," Commission on Theology and Church Relations, October 21, 1967. Unprocessed files of the CTCR, CHI.

166. David Leege, interview by author, October 10, 1995, tape recording.

of public ministry.[167] He had helped Jungkuntz develop a set of "Theses on the Significance of the Franchise in LC-MS Polity," which began by reiterating the standard synodical position, that church polity itself was an *adiaphoron*.[168] By arguing that the real problem was the significance of the franchise in church polity, the committee concluded that the authority exercised in a democratic polity is the will of the whole body as expressed by the majority, not the will of any individual over others, and that "it was really stretching something to say that women were usurping or exercising authority" in voting.[169] The authority of the majority would shortly become a critical issue for Missouri, but the location of authority as here interpreted by the CTCR turned on its head the synod's earlier opinion that "to vote is to rule." The Commission had in its mind successfully separated the issues of woman suffrage and women's ordination. This distinction was important. In a time when the term "domino theory" was frequently heard in public discourse about the war in Vietnam, many in the church had appropriated the term and applied it to the synod's theology.[170] Worried conservatives wondered if women got the vote, could women pastors be far behind?

To that end, the subcommittee report restated the founding principle of Missouri Synod governance — congregational right to establish its own polity — and concurred that woman suffrage was not forbidden in the church, although neither was it required. Because the issue of authority is not involved in exercise of the franchise, there was no reason

167. This distinction was not universally agreed upon at the time. See Krister Stendahl, *The Bible and the Role of Women: A Case Study in Hermeneutics* (Philadelphia: Fortress Press, 1966), pp. 39-43. Stendahl's essay, first published in 1958 when he was Bishop of Sweden, argues that a false separation exists between church and world. Ordination, therefore, is not a "special problem," but a question about the right relationship between man and woman in Christ. Stendahl has maintained his position; see "There Was More to It than I Thought and There Is Even More to Come: Retrospective Prospects," in *Lutheran Women in Ordained Ministry, 1970-1995: Reflections and Perspectives,* ed. Gloria E. Bengston (Minneapolis: Augsburg Fortress, 1995), pp. 137-47.

168. Mimeographed document dated October 21, 1967 and attached to the "Report of the Special Committee on Woman Suffrage." Unprocessed files of the CTCR, CHI.

169. Leege interview.

170. Leon Rosenthal, interview by author, August 23, 1995, River Forest, Illinois, tape recording.

to bar women from serving in elected office in the congregation. The report concluded with a caveat that local congregational franchise is "limited to matters that do not involve doctrine or conscience" and denied that the question of the ordination of women was part of their assignment or was addressed by their report.[171] In fact, as the minutes of the CTCR make clear, this was not so.[172]

The report of the special committee went through repeated recommittals to the subcommittee before it was finally accepted by the entire Commission and prepared for synodical distribution. In the spring of 1968 Martin Scharlemann was appointed to the subcommittee on suffrage when it became clear that the final draft would need to include scriptural exegesis.[173] The formerly moderate Scharlemann had reversed his former position by the end of the decade and now represented the conservatives who had once attacked him for his writings on biblical interpretation. He became the most significant influence on the suffrage report that would finally emerge from the CTCR. Leege, in recalling that "Martin in effect took over the document at that point," believes that Scharlemann was driven by a need for order, that "it was just his nature to look for something about order."[174] The reserve military chaplain had suffered personal anguish when the antiwar movement at the seminary came to include his own son. Scharlemann's concern for order marked another document that he was drafting at the same time on guiding principles of Christian citizenship.[175] Scharlemann found in the orders of creation what he was looking for regarding the role of women in the church. Leege believes that Scharlemann's position was a direct result of the events in which he had been involved a decade earlier:

171. "Report of the Special Committee on Woman Suffrage." Leege took issue with one of the conclusions of the Report, which stated that "woman suffrage is not demanded by the inherent nature of democratic polity." He felt this statement contradicted the principle of popular sovereignty by limiting the franchise. He was, however, overruled by the majority of the CTCR, who felt that limiting the franchise under certain circumstances might be appropriate, though they did not articulate what circumstances.

172. Minutes, CTCR, January 17-19, 1967. CHI. See note 156.

173. Leege interview.

174. Leege interview.

175. "Guidelines for Crucial Issues in Christian Citizenship," Missouri Synod, *Workbook*, 1969, pp. 511-13.

Martin had introduced principles of literary criticism to theological study at the seminary and he had seen the kind of response that people gave to that and he was a little unsteady about that himself. . . . Just everything that was going on in American society in the 1960s cried out for some principles of order again. . . . Martin evolved in part as a person interacting with a society where he thought maybe he'd gone a little bit too far in breaking up an old order.[176]

Thus the document adopted by the CTCR on December 7, 1968, differed dramatically from the report filed fourteen months earlier by the original subcommittee. Essentially the work of Martin Scharlemann, the final version retained the basic conclusion of the November 1967 report, but as Leege recalls, "the theological argumentation was very far away."[177] It was *so* different that Richard Jungkuntz believes he would have submitted a minority report if his position of Executive Secretary had been authorized a vote on the Commission regarding reports or recommendations to be presented to the synod.[178]

At no time during this entire study did the CTCR consider consulting women members of the Missouri Synod. According to Leege, "women in the synod simply didn't count . . . a quarter century ago."[179] To have consulted them would not have been considered germane to the issue, especially in the male environment of the synod as represented by the men of the CTCR.

Sometime after the final report had been drawn up, Jungkuntz found what he considered supporting evidence for his own position on women in the church. His research took him back to the Adiaphoristic Controversy of the sixteenth century, a situation in which Lutherans divided in 1549 over the restoration of Roman Catholic ceremonies imposed by the Emperor. Leading the Adiaphorists was Philipp Melanchthon, who regarded as harmless the restoration of Roman ceremonial form in the celebration of the mass. Matthias Flacius opposed Melanchthon, to the point of accusing him of treason against the truth of the Gospel. Flacius held to the rigidly conservative position that to concede on any issue to the "Romanists" was to deny being the Evan-

176. Leege interview.
177. Leege interview.
178. Richard Jungkuntz, note to author, January 19, 1995.
179. Leege interview.

gelical Church.[180] Flacius argued that certain sacred rites and usages, including preaching the Word and administering the sacraments, were divinely commanded, but all other issues, including polity and ceremonies, were *adiaphora*. God required only that all things be done in decency and order and to the edification of the church. In his list of *adiaphora*, Flacius indicated preference for, but not insistence on, certain matters: "It is more fitting that men speak in the church and perform all functions than women, as Paul prescribes."[181] Flacius was joined in his position by the Hamburg Ministerium.[182] Melanchthon eventually backed down and agreed with those who had opposed him. Jungkuntz found these references "fascinating" as well as further evidence of the posture he had assumed in the working paper he had presented to the CTCR in 1967.[183] The irony of this vignette lies in the fact that the evidence used to support the more progressive position on the woman question came from one of the most conservative voices in Lutheran history, Matthias Flacius.

Jungkuntz was also convinced that it was most important to keep the issues of suffrage and the ordination of women separate. Suffrage, as he — and likely many Missourians of those days — understood it, had nothing to do with the Office of the Keys or the ordained ministry. Suffrage was an issue of church polity and administration. But as long as the same arguments and the same Bible passages emerged each time the synod addressed the question of what women were allowed to do in the church, the issues became conflated. It was not surprising, therefore, that the CTCR took a very cautious stance when invited to hear the report of a study just completed by theologians of the three major Lutheran synods on the ordination of women. This joint study was being conducted by the Division of Theological Studies of the new Lutheran Council in the USA during the same period the CTCR was refin-

180. F. Bente, *Historical Introductions to the Book of Concord* (St. Louis: Concordia Publishing House, 1965 reprint from the Concordia Triglotta, 1921), pp. 107-12.

181. Matthias Flacius, *Omnia latina scripta hactenus sparsim contra Adiaphoricas fraudes et errores aedita, #10. Liber de veris et falsis Adiaphoris, quo integre propemodum adiaphorica controversia explicatur* (Magdeburg, 1549).

182. Epistola Hamburgensium ad Melanthonem, 1549, *Corpus Reformatorum* VII, no. 4516, col. 372.

183. Letter from Richard Jungkuntz to Walter Stuenkel, April 9, 1968. Stuenkel papers.

ing its report on woman suffrage. Jungkuntz went to hear the report as a courtesy, believing it would be "politically imprudent" to get further involved with the joint study when the Missouri Synod wasn't even straight on suffrage yet.[184]

When the Commission on Theology and Church Relations issued its report on Woman Suffrage in the Church prior to the 1969 synodical convention, its recommendations did not differ from those of its four-man subcommittee. Its reasons for making the recommendations did. Whereas Jungkuntz and the other subcommittee members had argued that suffrage was really an issue of polity, and in a democratic polity the authority of an individual was not at issue, the writers of the CTCR report to the Denver convention harked back to the 1956 suffrage committee report as a point of reference. The central feature of the 1969 report remained the order of creation. Focusing on the perceived danger of usurpation of authority by women, the authors concluded that elective franchise alone was likely not "an instrument of usurpation." Rather it was a means of delegating authority and affirming elective office as a means of service. What was previously discouraged, therefore, was now in fact being almost recommended by the advisory Commission on Theology, as long as the order of creation was not violated.[185] The 1965 convention had repudiated woman suffrage as contrary to scripture when it involved the exercise of authority over men.[186] But in 1969 the synod's advisory Commission on Theology and Church Relations stated:

> We find nothing in Scripture which prohibits women from exercising the franchise in voters' assemblies.
>
> Those statements of Scripture which direct women to keep silent in the church, and which prohibit them to teach and to exercise authority over men, we understand to mean that women ought not to hold the pastoral office.[187]

---

184. Jungkuntz interview. The relationship between the Missouri Synod and the Lutheran Council (LCUSA) was an odd one: "We went to the prom with them but we wouldn't get on the floor and dance."

185. "Woman Suffrage in the Church," Report of the Commission on Theology and Church Relations, 1969.

186. Missouri Synod, *Proceedings,* 1965, 103.

187. Report of the Commission on Theology and Church Relations, "Woman Suffrage in the Church," Missouri Synod, *Workbook,* 1969, 514-22.

The convention adopted the resolution based on the Commission's report, refusing to consider a more conservative substitute motion that the synod's position on woman suffrage not be changed.[188] It had been thirty-one years since the first request had been made at a synodical convention to study the question of woman suffrage. Only by reinterpreting its understanding of authority did the synod allow its women participation in their congregations' governing process. Now it would be up to those congregations to put suffrage into practice.

Conclusion

In 1969, the year the synod finally passed woman suffrage, women were allowed to attend voters' meetings in only 10 percent of Missouri congregations and to vote in only 1 percent of the synod's churches.[189] Following the Denver convention, many congregations were quick to change their bylaws to allow women the right to vote and hold office. But not all followed suit. By the mid-1980s, when congregations of the synod were surveyed on the question, its was reported that women were still prohibited from voting in 20 percent of synodical congregations.[190] The synodical polity that allows each congregation to establish its own bylaws as long as they are not in conflict with those of the synod explains the differential, as do the persistent voices that continue to call for woman suffrage to be rescinded.[191]

Patterns but not consistency marked the long history of Missouri's response to woman suffrage, the question that ultimately required the synod to rethink its understanding of authority. The par-

188. Missouri Synod, *Proceedings,* 1969, 88-89.

189. Margaret Sittler Ermarth, *Adam's Fractured Rib: Observations on Women in the Church* (Philadelphia: Fortress Press, 1970), p. 115.

190. *God's Woman for All Generations,* Report of the President's Commission on Women, 1986. No statistics have been gathered since the survey conducted for this report, though observers speculate that 20 percent is still an appropriate figure.

191. Laurence L. White, "The Role of Women in The Lutheran Church–Missouri Synod: A Study in Historical Development and Theological Change," unpublished ms., 1991, CHI. White is an LCMS pastor. See also Douglas Judisch, "Theses on Woman Suffrage in the Church," *Concordia Theological Monthly* 41 (1977): 36-45. Judisch is a professor at Concordia Theological Seminary, Fort Wayne.

ticular scripture passages cited in reference to woman suffrage remained the same passages cited in every case addressing women's service and place in the church, yet the interpretation of those passages came to vary over time. Woman suffrage and office holding in congregations, long considered by the synod to be prohibited by the Pauline proscriptions on the role of women in public assemblies, came in time to be seen as activities that did not challenge the mandate that women not exercise authority over men. Yet because the synod has always based its justification for limitation of women's service on only two proof-texts, every activity in which women wished to be involved was construed in light of the ultimate threat, the activity of ordained women. Walter Wente therefore identified the entire Prohl controversy as having come down to: "one simple and definite issue, namely, the ordination of women into the ministry."[192] The synod, after two and a half years of dispute with Prohl, was spared having to address the issue of ordination of women by the chaplain's sudden death in 1960. Even had he lived, Missouri would likely have been able to avoid the issue, as Prohl and the suffrage committee had reached an irreconcilable impasse that Prohl believed could be resolved only by his resignation from the clergy roster. Individual dissidents are easily dismissed when their position is radically at odds with that of the church body, as Russell Prohl's was.

Between 1955 and 1969, the order of creation argument became key to the synod's position on woman's place in the church. Most curious is the fascination of certain Missouri Synod theologians with Fritz Zerbst's use of the term. It had not been a primary frame of reference for either Luther or Walther. As Edward Schroeder pointed out following his inquiry into the 1956 committee on woman suffrage report,

> Zerbst thinks he is in harmony with the Lutheran tradition, but curiously enough he only cites Luther twice — and that for rather weak support of his position. The theologian from the 16th century who is cited over and over again is John Calvin. . . . [An] overarching Calvinism . . . shapes Zerbst's mode of exegesis and, above all, his notions of redemption and the will of God.[193]

192. Letter from Walter Wente to Walter Stuenkel, July 11, 1960. Stuenkel papers.
193. Schroeder, "The Orders of Creation," p. 170.

Schroeder underscores the contrast between Calvin's rigid sense of creation and Luther's sense that creation is ongoing. Zerbst argued a fixed order of creation.[194] Both the 1956 and the 1969 reports on woman suffrage, though they came to different conclusions as to its practice, relied heavily on Zerbst's use of the order of creation as justification for what might or might not be allowed women in Missouri Synod congregations. Yet the concept they considered so essential to maintain was one they did not draw from their own, oldest Lutheran approach to the reading of scripture.

The primary contested issue in the history of the Missouri Synod has always been authority — of scripture, of synod, of the congregation, of the pastoral office, of woman, of man. In the various arguments on whether women should be granted the right to vote in congregational meetings in the synod, the fear consistently surfaced, beginning with the 1916 Dau opinion, that conceding voting rights to Missouri's women gave woman authority over man. Repeated reference to a single passage, 1 Timothy 2:12 ("I permit no woman to teach or to have authority over a man"), closed the scriptural argument on the question. Yet, the twentieth-century theologians had to determine what activities of a woman in the church might be considered as having authority — voting, holding office, teaching, preaching?

The question became even more complex as Missouri faced tensions in its own tradition around the issue of synodical and congregational authority. Despite its foundational adherence to a polity based on the autonomy of the individual congregation, the church in the second half of the twentieth century became increasingly centralized and dependent on what are supposedly advisory-only bodies — the synod itself, its boards and commissions. The democratic polity, by its very nature, insures a built-in inconsistency, as six thousand parishes can hardly be autonomous if they are expected to conform to synodical mandates, even on issues that are not doctrinal. Yet the growing dependence on the CTCR for clarity on just what is and is not allowed is entirely due to the confusion created by that inherent inconsistency. In turn, it has become the paradoxical and inevitable result of the synod's congregational polity. Repeated calls for reaffirmation of previously adopted positions have conveyed a mood of un-

---

194. Edward Schroeder, telephone conversation with the author, January 8, 1995.

certainty, fear, and a need for insistence on required conformity in all matters.

C. F. W. Walther, father of the congregational governance unique to Missouri Synod Lutheranism, commented in 1881 on Article VII of the synod's constitution, repeating its first line: "No resolution is binding on any congregation. If we ever made resolutions binding, we would be nothing but the German consistorium."[195] Binding resolutions must have reminded Walther of enforced pledges of subjection, a lesson he carried with him from early in his ministry. But what did he have in mind in insisting on an advisory synod that could pass resolutions to which no congregation had to subscribe?

The Reformation principle of *sola scriptura,* coupled with the Lutheran confessions as a lens through which scripture is read, were intended to provide Lutherans the necessary consistency for resolving doctrinal issues. Inconsistency arose from *how* scripture was interpreted. Though the synod had never before accepted "official" interpretation of scriptural passages, twentieth-century developments within the church seemed increasingly resolvable only by synodical declaration of a particular method of interpretation to the exclusion of all others. The question of women's service in the church — whether as parochial school teachers, congregational voters or office holders, or in the pastoral ministry — was only ever addressed through a verbally inspired interpretation of two Pauline passages. Yet, as the meaning of the notion of authority shifted, the question of scripture and the authority of its interpreters and their methods could be avoided no longer.

Since mid-century, when some in Missouri started to call for specific interpretations of scripture passages in response to disagreements on synodical policy, the boundaries between these various authorities began to collapse. In the postwar years, the "Forty-Four" had challenged the authority of an advisory synod and of its traditions. In responding to the question of woman suffrage in the 1950s and 60s, the church had to examine and eventually redefine its understanding of the very notion of authority. On the heels of this episode would come the most serious challenge in the synod's history, one over the authority of scripture itself.

195. C. F. W. Walther, *Der Lutheraner* 37 (June 15, 1881): 90. Quoted in John Constable, "Of Congregational and Synodical Authority," *Concordia Theological Monthly* 43 (1972): 230.

Each challenge added new questions while underlining the old and never satisfactorily answered: What authority does an advisory synod have over its member congregations? What authority is vested in it over its member pastors, teachers, and professors? What authority is granted doctrine? scripture? women? men? clergy? laity? And by what authority is any of this determined?

As the synod turned from an era in which the woman question focused on suffrage to an era in which a larger question loomed, that of women in public ministry, those questions would be asked over and over again. At bottom, the question would be: Is the prohibition of women from the pastoral office scripturally mandated — because the Bible says so — or synodically mandated — because the synod says so — or is it because the synod says the Bible says so?

6

"Not in God's Lifetime": The Significance of the Ordination of Women

D uring the summer of 1969, while Missouri's delegates in Denver were debating whether to allow women full participation in their local congregational meetings, Missouri's representatives to the Lutheran Council meeting in New York were debating whether women could be ordained into the ministry. The irony of this situation reflects the depth of the divisions evident by the late 1960s in the Missouri Synod.

Since 1962, when Oliver Harms was elected president of the synod, a conservative opposition had been gathering strength. Missouri was not alone in experiencing a renewed conservative activism, as Ronald Flowers has observed about American religion in the 1960s: "Conservatives organized themselves into pressure groups to try to move the entire denomination to a more orthodox position."[1] Harms was a vocal advocate of Lutheran unity, and "unionism" had always been a term that raised a red flag in Missouri. "Union" referred to the practice of pulpit and altar fellowship, based on sufficient doctrinal agreement between two church bodies that both preachers and people were welcome to worship in the other's churches. "Unionism,"[2] on the

1. Ronald B. Flowers, *Religion in Strange Times: The 1960s and 1970s* (Macon, Ga.: Mercer University Press, 1984), p. 41.
2. The term originated in Germany at the time of the Prussian union.

other hand, was a pejorative referring to *any* dealings with a church — usually referred to as heterodox as opposed to orthodox — pursued by those eager for fellowship but without the proper preliminary agreement in doctrine. Missouri had always been deliberately cautious about its involvement with other Christians, including other Lutherans, and, other than its involvement in the Synodical Conference since 1872, had succeeded in maintaining a relatively insular existence since the 1920s by insisting on full doctrinal agreement prior to any kind of inter-Lutheran fellowship. But the years following World War II brought renewed pressure from other Lutheran churches to join in cooperative ventures.

Despite this apparent rigidity in its historic position on fellowship, the synod in the postwar years began to relax its resistance to cooperating with other Lutherans. Missouri's participation in a new inter-Lutheran agency would be the culmination of its more progressive leaders' dreams. Yet there were others who saw in such action a danger signal. Conservatives in Missouri were concerned chiefly about retaining the absolute authority and verbal inerrancy of the Bible as called for by Pieper against the increasingly popular historical-critical method of biblical scholarship employed by the more moderate clergy. By the 1960s, the moderates included a good portion of the St. Louis seminary faculty. The right wing, which had begun to organize in the early 1960s, was by 1967 determined to challenge Harms's re-election bid at the 1969 convention. Not only were the conservatives unhappy with Missouri's cooperative venture with other Lutherans, but they were also disturbed by the discussions that had been underway since 1964 with the American Lutheran Church for full altar and pulpit fellowship between the two synods. In the isolationist eyes of the Missouri right, fellowship signaled a "dangerous move to the left."[3]

Had the church changed? In 1963, in an essay to the College of Presidents, synodical vice president Roland Wiederaenders dramatically described the dilemma in which the synod found itself as a result of its historic and persistent claim to an unmoving theology:

Despite repeated efforts we have not dealt honestly with our pastors and people. We have refused to state our changing theological posi-

3. E. Clifford Nelson, ed., *The Lutherans in North America,* rev. ed. (Philadelphia: Fortress Press, 1975), p. 528.

tion in open, honest, forthright, simple and clear words. Over and over again we said that nothing was changing but all the while we were aware of changes taking place. Either we should have informed our pastors and people that changes were taking place, and if possible, convinced them from Scripture that these changes were in full harmony with "Thus saith the Lord!" or we should have stopped playing games as we gave assurance that no changes were taking place. With increasing measure the Synodical trumpet has been given an uncertain sound. . . . Quite generally our pastors and almost entirely our laity became more and more confused. Confusion led to uncertainty. Uncertainty led to polarization. Polarization destroyed credibility. Loss of credibility destroyed the possibility for meaningful discussion. The loss of meaningful discussion set the stage for head-on collision.[4]

Wiederaenders's prophetic remarks portended the developments of the coming decade, during which the central issue would again be the identity of the church, the nagging question that had to be answered before any efforts at fellowship could proceed. Two very different opinions on how that question should be answered took shape in the 1960s, but in the end only one opinion would prevail.

As the conservative opposition to Harms grew, its supporters found a candidate to challenge him in Jacob A. O. Preus, president of Concordia Seminary in Springfield, Illinois. Preus had come to Missouri from the Evangelical Lutheran Synod (ELS) just a decade earlier. While it was evident in the synod that the right had been gathering strength since 1962 by gaining positions on synodical boards and committees, the moderates were clearly unprepared for the coup staged at the Denver convention. Taken by surprise at the strength of the opposition and objecting loudly to the blatant politicking that they considered so foreign to church proceedings, they reacted in shock to Harms's loss and the portent of what was to come in their church.[5]

4. Roland Wiederaenders to the College of Presidents, December 2, 1963. Quoted in Larry W. Neeb, "Historical and Theological Dimensions of a Confessing Movement within the Lutheran Church–Missouri Synod" (D.Min. diss., Eden Theological Seminary, 1975), pp. 7-8.

5. The election of the president is the first significant order of business at synodical conventions. The drama of the 1969 election is described in James Adams, *Preus of Missouri and the Great Lutheran Civil War* (New York: Harper & Row, 1977). Adams, a journalist for the St. Louis *Post-Dispatch,* writes as an outside ob-

If Preus's election signified a move to the right, it was not apparent in the two other major actions taken at the Denver convention. Over Preus's objections, delegates voted to enter into fellowship with the ALC. And, in what was the most progressive action ever taken on women's issues, the synod accepted woman suffrage within the church's governing bodies, finally acting on a question that had been discussed and dismissed for thirty years. In hindsight, the paradox of Denver was the first tangible evidence of a church body on the verge of fissure. The primary site of contention for the next several years would be the St. Louis seminary, but the underlying issue was again authority. This time the struggle would center on the authority of scripture.

Cooperative Efforts

The majority of Lutherans in the United States in the 1960s belonged to three church bodies: The American Lutheran Church (ALC), the Lutheran Church in America (LCA), and The Lutheran Church–Missouri Synod (LCMS) — the differences among them centering on ethnic heritage and doctrinal fine points. Both the ALC and the LCA were products of recent mergers of smaller ethnic Lutheran synods. But other small ethnic synods wished to avoid catching the amalgamation fever spreading among Lutherans during the 1950s. Missouri's only remaining partners in the Synodical Conference, the Wisconsin Synod and the Evangelical Lutheran Synod (ELS, also called the Little Norwegian Synod), had withdrawn from the Conference in 1963 due to what they considered Missouri's rising syncretism.[6]

---

server. See also Bryan V. Hillis, *Can Two Walk Together Unless They Be Agreed? American Religious Schisms in the 1970s* (New York: Carlson Publishing Inc., 1990). For partisan accounts of the decade, see John H. Tietjen, *Memoirs in Exile: Confessional Hope and Institutional Conflict* (Minneapolis: Fortress Press, 1990), Frederick W. Danker, *No Room in the Brotherhood: The Preus-Otten Purge of Missouri* (St. Louis: Clayton Publishing House Inc., 1977), Neeb, "Historical and Theological Dimensions of a Confessing Movement," and Kurt E. Marquardt, *Anatomy of an Explosion: Missouri in Lutheran Perspective* (Fort Wayne, Ind.: Concordia Theological Seminary Press, 1977). No comprehensive history of this chapter in synodical history has yet been written.

6. Erwin L. Lueker, ed., *Lutheran Cyclopedia,* rev. ed. (St. Louis: Concordia Publishing House, 1975), p. 749.

Increasingly, a climate of cooperation and concord overspread the decade. The *aggiornamento* spirit of Vatican II — to "bring the church up to date"[7] — was not limited to Roman Catholics; its contagious mood led to an openness among Lutherans to discuss a variety of issues previously considered closed to debate. In 1965 the ALC and the LCA joined with the Missouri Synod to form the Lutheran Council in the United States (LCUSA). As a pan-Lutheran agency, LCUSA was intended to facilitate further cooperation and unity through theological study and Christian service,[8] "a place to do things in common without compromise," according to Ralph Bohlmann, later president of the Missouri Synod.[9] Missouri, traditionally the doctrinal "conscience"[10] of American Lutheranism, had insisted that the structure of the agency include a Division of Theological Studies [DTS], and it was to this group of theologians that key questions facing the church were assigned.

Renewed efforts at unity were welcomed by those in the Missouri Synod who saw more need for common ground than division among Lutherans. Critics of unity, however, worried over the contamination of the synod's pure doctrine *(reine Lehre)*, since to the conservatives even cooperative discussion presaged the dreaded unionism. One pastor who became a key player in the struggle of the 1970s later reflected on this long-standing difference of opinion and division within the church:

> [H]istorically, there have always been people in the Missouri Synod who were more mindful of good inter-Lutheran relationships and a larger number who were separatists. You have a fair number that are high church liturgically and others who are very low liturgically. There are people within Missouri who believe you have to have a

7. Jay Dolan, *The American Catholic Experience: A History from the Colonial Times to the Present* (Garden City, N.Y.: Image Books, 1985), pp. 424-26.

8. Richard Labore, "Traditions and Transitions: A Study of the Leadership of the Lutheran Church–Missouri Synod During a Decade of Theological Change, 1960-1969" (Ph.D. diss., St. Louis University, 1980), pp. 344-45.

9. Ralph A. Bohlmann, interview transcript (1979), Archives of Cooperative Lutheranism ALC-AELC-LCA Oral History Collection, ELCA Archives, Chicago, p. 9.

10. Fred W. Meuser, interview transcript (1977), Archives of Cooperative Lutheranism ALC-AELC-LCA Oral History Collection, ELCA Archives, Chicago, p. 7.

highly trained clergy and others who have feelings that we really ought not to get too deep in that academic world. But we have always had . . . a recognition of the differences among us and a respect for one another and a willingness to accept one another, and let God use the church to achieve His will.

. . . [W]hen it appeared as though Missouri Synod might move out of its shell through membership in the Lutheran Council, through potential membership in the Lutheran World Federation, and out of its attitude of self-deception, hypocrisy . . . when we were beginning to lose our isolation and separatism, and were learning to accept one another across the denominational line, that's when people began to build up the opposition.

. . . Missouri's tragedy was developed deliberately by conservatives who wanted to take control, to prevent the improving of inter-Lutheran relations, to prevent what they considered watering down theology, and to prevent the "loss" of what they believed was *the true visible church*.[11]

The Missouri Synod is a church body whose history is wrapped tightly around its professed consistency in theology and actions. The synod's willingness, indeed, insistence on theological dialogue in its new cooperative venture reflected a posture very different from its historic fear of union. Without hesitation or consultation with their individual church bodies, the LCUSA theologians began their studies, one of which centered on the ordination of women. And while Lutheran unity and the ordination of women were entirely separate issues in no way binding on one another, there was hardly a hint as the study began that the two issues might be incompatible. By the end of the 1970s, however, "the woman question" had made Lutheran unity an impossibility. The ordination of women would come to serve as the most visible symbol of a church body's understanding regarding the authority of scripture. Missouri made its mind up and its position clear in 1970 when the other Lutheran synods voted to ordain women to the ministry and it did not.

Lutherans as a whole have struggled with their understanding of the nature of the public ministry, and have not yet reached a satisfac-

11. William H. Kohn, interview transcript (1977), Archives of Cooperative Lutheranism ALC-AELC-LCA Oral History Collection, ELCA Archives, Chicago, pp. 36-37. Emphasis in the original.

tory conclusion, let alone doctrine, on which to base their practice.[12] But only at the end of the joint Lutheran study on the ordination of women did it become apparent that the various synods should first have studied the larger question, the nature of the ministry. Because that did not happen, the study of the ordination of women was examined as an issue unto itself. The problem with that approach was that many in the Missouri Synod saw the ordination of women as a woman's issue, and reacted as Missouri usually did to women's issues — defensively. The synod's recognized conservative posture extends to social issues as well as theological ones, and its historic response to social change has been one of rejection, couched in cautious talk about the church being in the world but not of the world. Alan Graebner, historian of Missouri's laity, notes that the synod's "typical attitude toward contemporary society was negative, the typical response was to attack it."[13] As woman's right to vote in federal political elections since the 1920s had not transferred to her a similar right in her local church by the 1960s, so the changes introduced into society by the second wave of feminism would not extend readily into Missouri parishes.

"Called to Consider Anew
What We Have Readily Assumed"

When The American Lutheran Church, which had admitted women to its seminaries since the early 1960s, asked the newly organized Lutheran Council in 1967 to study the question of ordination of women to the ministry, it did so with the hope of agreement on the issue by the major synods.[14] Already at its formation, LCUSA had been asked by the ALC to study ecclesiology — the theology of the church — and ordination. Now the impetus was the presence of several women students who were nearing the end of their studies in ALC seminaries and a reluctance on the part of the ALC governing council to make a recommen-

12. Eric W. Gritsch, "Convergence and Conflict in Feminist and Lutheran Theologies," *Dialog* 24 (Spring 1985): 15-17.
13. Alan Graebner, *Uncertain Saints: The Laity in the Lutheran Church–Missouri Synod* (Westport, Conn.: Greenwood Press, 1975), p. 110.
14. Gracia Grindal, "Getting Women Ordained," in *Called and Ordained: Lutheran Perspectives on the Office of the Ministry,* ed. Todd Nichol and Marc Kolden (Minneapolis: Fortress Press, 1990), p. 164.

dation for its church body alone.[15] In a letter to LCUSA general secretary C. Thomas Spitz, President Frederik A. Schiotz of the ALC stressed his church council's "feeling that it is highly desirable that Lutherans act together on this."[16]

Until the 1960s, Lutheran churches throughout America had resisted many of the changes in women's roles that were taking place both within society and elsewhere in mainstream Protestantism. Only in postwar Europe did Lutheran churches allow women to serve as pastors.[17] So, despite the acceptance of women into the ministry of major Protestant denominations beginning in the mid-1950s, within the various Lutheran church bodies the question had been not only undebated, it had been undebatable. Lutheran theology had always understood scripture to say that women should be silent in the churches.[18] The issue is never addressed in the Lutheran confessions; Luther himself was inconsistent in his references to women, though he was of the opinion that women should preach if there were ever a shortage of men.[19]

It took a year and a half for a subcommittee of representatives from each member church to analyze the four categories of argument generally raised in objection to the ordination of women: biblical, theological, practical, and ecumenical. The exhaustive study was presented to the standing committee of the DTS in March 1969, having accepted the challenge that

---

15. "The Ordination of Women: A Study Conducted Under the Auspices of the Division of Theological Studies, Lutheran Council in the U.S.A., 1968-1970," hereinafter referred to as the protocol document. Letter from Frederik A. Schiotz to C. Thomas Spitz, July 6, 1967. ELCA Archives, Chicago.

16. Protocol document, letter from Frederik A. Schiotz to C. Thomas Spitz, June 24, 1968.

17. Scandinavian state churches were the first to permit the ordination of women, beginning with Norway in 1938 (though a woman was not ordained there until 1961), Denmark in 1947, and Sweden in 1959. Churches on the continent followed suit in the 1960s. See John E. Lynch, "The Ordination of Women: Protestant Experience in Ecumenical Perspective," *Journal of Ecumenical Studies* 12 (1975): 183-86.

18. 1 Corinthians 14:34-36; 1 Timothy 2:8-15.

19. Luther did expect, however, that God would always provide an ample supply of men to preclude this possibility. For his reference to women preaching, see "The Misuse of the Mass (1521)" in *Luther's Works,* American edition, ed. Jaroslav Pelikan and Helmut T. Lehman (St. Louis and Philadelphia: Concordia Publishing House and Fortress Press, 1955-1986), 36:152.

> It is necessary to ask from time to time whether areas of the church's life such as practices regarding the ordained ministry do properly reflect the Gospel and the will of the Church's Lord amid new situations. . . . Lest we miss the ongoing work of God and promptings of his Spirit, we are called to consider anew what we have readily assumed.[20]

Their conclusion was inconclusive. Scripturally, and therefore theologically, the subcommittee found that "there are no conclusive grounds for forbidding the ordination of women and no definitive ones for demanding it."[21] In terms of the practical and ecumenical objections, they felt that "social and other factors could allow churches to have differing practices but still remain in fellowship."[22] The report offered no clear direction, as subcommittee members knew their recommendation was only a nonbinding response to a requested study; the individual church bodies would have to wrestle with the results themselves. And so, as their chairman recalls, they had deliberately taken a bland approach, out of "a kind of pastoral concern" for the obvious differences among the churches.[23] Still, the authors did note prophetically the problem of conceiving the question narrowly: "We have been forced to observe again and again in our study that the ordination of women is part of larger questions," specifically those having to do with the ministry and Lutheran differences in the interpretation of scripture.[24] The committee recommended that an inter-Lutheran consultation be scheduled for September when the results of the study could be presented to a larger gathering. Between March and August 1969, however, a change in Missouri Synod leadership redirected the course of Lutheran unity unalterably.

Because of the dramatic changes voted into being at the Missouri

20. Protocol document, Report of the Subcommittee on the Ordination of Women, March 7-8, 1969.

21. Protocol document, Exhibit B: minutes of DTS Standing Committee, March 7-8, 1969, Report of the Subcommittee, p. 3.

22. John H. P. Reumann, *Ministries Examined: Laity, Clergy, Women, and Bishops in a Time of Change* (Minneapolis: Augsburg Publishing House, 1987), p. 18.

23. John H. P. Reumann, interview transcript (1977), Archives of Cooperative Lutheranism ALC-AELC-LCA Oral History Collection, ELCA Archives, Chicago, pp. 52-53.

24. Protocol document, Exhibit B, March 7-8, 1969, Report of the Subcommittee, 4.

Synod convention in Denver, the inter-Lutheran consultation on "The Ordination of Women in Light of Church and Ministry" met in Dubuque, Iowa, in September 1969 facing an uncertain reception from its Missouri delegation. Participants in the DTS study observed a change in the mood of the synod after Preus's election, as Fred Meuser recalled:

> In the early years of the Harms presidency . . . people who were of a particularly open and trusting kind of spirit were chosen. . . . When Jack Preus became president, the Missouri Synod's representation changed. Then the whole spirit of the work of the Division of Theological Studies changed.[25]

But Preus himself offered a different perspective, implying that the Missouri Synod representatives to LCUSA were from a different camp than he: "Had other people been appointed at that moment to the subcommittee another opinion would have been forthcoming. . . . The power of appointment is extremely important."[26] He meant what he said. New representatives to LCUSA were only part of the housecleaning the synod underwent in the months following the Preus coup. Moderates were replaced with conservatives who were eager to take back the synod from those they believed had "sold out the Missouri Synod position."[27] Robert Bertram, professor at Concordia Seminary, St. Louis, and Missouri Synod member of the DTS, belonged to the moderate faction. To represent the new administration, and quite intentionally to offset Bertram's moderate leanings, Jacob Preus appointed Martin Scharlemann to represent Missouri at the Dubuque consultation, replacing the already slated Herbert Mayer, another St. Louis professor. The other members of the Missouri delegation were Edward Schroeder, chairman of the theology department at Valparaiso University, and Fred Kramer, professor at Concordia Seminary, Springfield, Illinois, and a member of the CTCR from its creation in 1962.

25. ArCL/ALC-AELC-LCA/OHC: Fred W. Meuser, p. 13.

26. J. A. O. Preus, interview transcript (1978), Archives of Cooperative Lutheranism ALC-AELC-LCA Oral History Collection, ELCA Archives, Chicago, p. 25. Used by permission.

27. Paul D. Opsahl, interview transcript (1982-83), Archives of Cooperative Lutheranism ALC-AELC-LCA Oral History Collection, ELCA Archives, Chicago, p. 27. Used by permission. Opsahl was a LCUSA staff member assigned to the DTS subcommittee.

The Dubuque gathering was held to provide an opportunity for representatives from each of the synods to hear the report of the DTS and respond to it. Not surprisingly, the consensus of the consultation remained an agreement to disagree. About one issue there was consensus, that a larger question was involved — the nature of the ministry itself.[28] The two-and-a-half day meeting was not a forum at which papers were presented, but rather, the ten invited participants were asked to "react directionally" to specific questions about how the report reflected the situation in their various church bodies and what larger questions on ministry were raised by the study.[29] DTS staff members present filed a summary of the consultation, noting that

> Ordination of women is not the basic issue. More basic are 1) relationship of men and women all across the board; 2) shape of the ministries of the church; 3) role of the laity. The revolution in women's affairs is deeper and broader than most people imagine. When churches get around to a position on this it will probably already be too late. "Equality" terminology is not the best.[30]

As the group responded to the questions, several themes continued to be problematic. Primary among those was the order of creation as raised by Martin Scharlemann, who spoke of the need for a *kephale* (headship) structure, to which he felt no one had given much thought.[31] Scharlemann continued to press the issue, and as often as he did, Robert Bertram proposed an alternative *kephale* model. Convinced that Scharlemann was inaccurately reading the Lutheran tradition, Bertram thought that "the kind of appeal Scharlemann was making was a contradiction of the confessional understanding of the two kingdoms."[32] Bertram also wanted it on the record that the Concordia seminary faculty did not speak with one voice. While he accepted the

28. Robert Bertram, interview by author, October 27, 1995, tape recording. Bertram, then a professor at Concordia Seminary, St. Louis, was the Missouri Synod representative on the Division of Theological Studies.

29. Protocol document, DTS Subcommittee on the Ordination of Women, letter to participants from Paul Opsahl, August 4, 1969.

30. Protocol document, Exhibit A, Report of a Consultation: The Ordination of Women in Light of Church and Ministry, September 20-22, 1969, Dubuque, Iowa, 82.

31. Protocol document, Exhibit A, Report of a Consultation, 87.

32. Bertram interview.

occasional need for a headship in which one exercised authority over another — as in the parent-child relationship — Bertram's preferred model was that of a servant-like authority, the model of Christ. Hoping to "smoke out the larger question of what is the nature of ministry in the first place," Bertram believed it was important to rephrase the question. He suggested they not ask, May women be ordained? but instead ask, To what kind of ministries may women be ordained?[33] Many of the consultation participants agreed, even as they continued to focus on the topic at hand: the ordination of women.

Edward Schroeder recalled being surprised at what he called "Martin's new red herring," Scharlemann's use of the *kephale* structure argument in Dubuque.[34] Both Schroeder and Bertram credited Scharlemann's well-known military history as the primary reason he valued order and authority so highly. What was more difficult to understand was the change that had come over Martin Scharlemann. In less than a decade, the man who had lit a firestorm in the church by introducing new ideas and scholarship on biblical interpretation had become a spokesman for the church's new conservative administration. Bertram ventured a hunch that

> At least at the conscious level, he began to realize, maybe to his horror, that he might have created a hole in the dike, never guessing what a floodtide would rush through there. And this is how he would see it, and somehow regretted that and then joined the forces of resistance to try to close the hole in the dike.[35]

Schroeder, Scharlemann's brother-in-law, added that it was difficult for Scharlemann to see some of his own students return to the seminary to teach after graduate school, newly infused with the political liberalism of the 1960s. The anti-authority mood in America, in particular the growing opposition to the Vietnam war — a war he considered "one of the most just wars in which the United States was ever engaged" — was disconcerting to Scharlemann, a Brigadier General in the Air Force reserves.[36] "He was marvelously objective in his scholarship (almost lib-

33. Bertram interview.
34. Edward Schroeder, interview by author, November 2, 1995, tape recording.
35. Bertram interview.
36. Martin H. Scharlemann, interview transcript (1980), Archives of Cooperative Lutheranism ALC-AELC-LCA Oral History Collection, Chicago, pp. 62-63.

eral), but with a military mentality. He could brook no opposition and hated those who would flout authority," recalled one pastor who had been a student of Scharlemann's in the 1950s before the controversy had broken out over his essays.[37] In addition, Martin Scharlemann had become deeply embittered since May 1969, when John Tietjen, head of public relations for LCUSA[38] and a pastor in the synod's English District, was named the new president of the St. Louis seminary. Scharlemann had actively sought that position himself and had been "antagonistic toward Tietjen even before the new president had taken office."[39]

Throughout the weekend in Dubuque, Martin Scharlemann held his ground, repeatedly raising the notion of orders of creation and its relation to the ordination of women. But the order of creation debate remained between the members of the Missouri delegation. The few comments by other participants tended to be dismissive of the "variously used and misused" concept, as one ALC representative reflected:

> In my opinion there is no biblical reason against the ordination of women to the ministry of the word. . . . The chief argument seems to be the "orders of creation" argument. However, this seems to be dogmatics telling the Scriptures what to say rather than the other way around.[40]

Yet in the end, after subcommittee chair John Reumann had summarized the two-day discussion, Scharlemann reminded the gathering of a larger problem that would not be solved even if one of the Lutheran church bodies acted to ordain women. That problem was hermeneutical: How was scripture to be interpreted? Looking back, Robert Bertram would agree profoundly with Scharlemann's assessment, as he sees now how much "the issue of the ordaining of women was a precipitant in the real blowup in the Missouri Synod over . . . the issue of the authority of scripture."[41] The inter-synodical consultation at

37. Garth Ludwig, personal correspondence with author, September 1, 1995.
38. Hillis, *Can Two Walk Together Unless They Be Agreed?* p. 52.
39. Neeb, "Historical and Theological Dimensions of a Confessing Movement," p. 122. Scharlemann had sent a confidential letter to the seminary faculty in which he cited Tietjen's own writings to argue that Tietjen lacked "confessional commitment" and therefore should not head the seminary.
40. Protocol document, Report of a Consultation, Responses to Questionnaire re Ordination of Women, September 20-22, 1969, pp. 87, 89.
41. Bertram interview.

Dubuque made public the growing intra-synodical standoff within Missouri.

Following the Dubuque meeting, hope that Lutherans in the United States would take the step to ordain women together grew dimmer, though there would be one last opportunity when the presidents of all three church bodies met at the annual meeting of LCUSA in February 1970.[42] In the end there would be no unanimity among the leaders of the churches. The only action agreed to regarding the ordination question was that the report be transmitted back to each church body for "further study and consideration."[43] The official record of the meeting does not indicate that in reaching that decision the presidents disagreed substantively on the issue. But their comments, as recalled by observers, suggest otherwise. Jacob Preus stated that "he would have a tough time holding his troops together if one or the other of the church bodies should decide to ordain women. He made it clear that that would become a very, very tough thing for Missouri to handle."[44] Preus's remarks that the issue could be disruptive of fellowship were countered by those of ALC president Frederik Schiotz, who stated definitively that he saw his church body moving in the direction of ordination.[45] The battle lines on unity had been drawn.

Because of the length of the protocol document, which included all of the subcommittee's research, it was decided that a condensed, popularized edition of the report should be drafted for each church body to send to its clergy. The summary was to be written by Raymond Tiemeyer, a staff member with the LCA Board of Parish Education. In his cover letter to the Tiemeyer mailing, Preus wrote to Missouri's pastors that he was sending the report out reluctantly because it treated scripture in a "rather flippant" manner. Dissatisfied because the DTS report "seems to negate" the concept of the orders of creation, Preus also complained that it "did not reflect the seriousness which the question of the ordination of women requires."[46] But

42. Protocol document, DTS Standing Committee minutes, October 9-11, 1969, 49.

43. Protocol document, LCUSA Annual Meeting minutes, February 3-4, 1970, 10.

44. ArCL/ALC-AELC-LCA/OHC: Paul Opsahl, 53.

45. ArCL/ALC-AELC-LCA/OHC: Paul Opsahl, 53.

46. Letter to the clergy from J. A. O. Preus, June 17, 1970. Files of the Office of the President, CHI. The last sentence of Preus's letter contains a typographical

his comments to the clergy differed from his reaction to the original report. In a later conversation with Fred Meuser, Preus admitted he was encouraged that the subcommittee had taken scripture so seriously.[47]

Each of the three principal players in the Lutheran Council received the Division of Theological Studies report differently. At their 1970 conventions, first the Lutheran Church in America, by means of a simple change in the wording of its bylaws, and then The American Lutheran Church, took action to approve the ordination of women, and before the end of the year, each had ordained its first woman to the ministry.[48] In the Missouri Synod, the Systematics Subcommittee of the Commission on Church Literature arranged for Concordia Publishing House to publish in booklet form a 1959 article by German theologian Peter Brunner entitled "The Ministry and the Ministry of Women."[49] Brunner, professor of systematic theology at Heidelberg and a member of the Commission on Theology of the Lutheran World Federation, like Zerbst found no confessional evidence for a prohibition on women in ordained ministry. Admitting that the question was additionally complicated by the issue of the authority of scripture, Brunner claimed that the final analysis had to rest on two issues: "the theological doctrine of the sexual difference between man

---

error that must have raised at least a few clergy eyebrows: "We need to give careful thought to giving women the fullest possible *rule* for service to the church . . ." (emphasis added).

Two professors from the Fort Wayne senior college took issue with the tone of Preus's letter, suggesting he had "not read carefully," and that "unfortunately many clergy in our church will not read the whole document and will take your criticism of it as fair and accurate." Letter from John C. Gienapp and Neil V. Naumann to J. A. O. Preus, July 3, 1970. Executive Office files, Box 42, CHI.

47. ArCL/ALC-AELC-LCA/OHC: Fred Meuser, 23.

48. Reumann, *Ministries Examined*, pp. 122-23. See also Grindal, "Getting Women Ordained," pp. 161-79.

49. Executive Office files, minutes of the Commission on Church Literature, December 1969. There appeared to be a deliberate effort to locate texts to support Missouri's position. In a letter from J. A. O. Preus to O. A. Dorn, December 15, 1970, Preus asked Dorn, then manager of Concordia Publishing House, for a manuscript on the ordination of women that had been referred to him. The author, a professor of classics in Nova Scotia, believed "a deviation from the New Testament practice seems to imply heretic Christology and will cause, as it has already done in Sweden, a major crisis of authority in the Church." Executive Office files, Box 42, CHI.

and woman," and "what we understand by the ministry."[50] Brunner supported Zerbst's contention that the orders of creation determine the relationship between men and women, "a God-given ontological structure." On that basis, Brunner located the prohibition of woman from the pastoral office in "a basic existential conflict with her created being as woman."[51] A female pastor, therefore, is a contradiction not only in terms but in its very possibility, rooted deeply in a violation of the ordered *kephale* structure of God's creation. The appearance of Brunner's little book in 1971 as part of the synod's new "Contemporary Theology Series" effectively announced Missouri's response to the joint study on the ordination of women.

Missouri Goes Its Own Way

The signals given by Jacob Preus at the February 1970 LCUSA meeting were clear indicators of the direction the Missouri Synod would take not only on the issue of women's ordination, but on the issue of scriptural authority as well. Always more comfortable in an insular position, the church set out to declare the parameters of its tolerance.

The most pressing and problematic issue was the altar and pulpit fellowship that Missouri had declared in Denver in 1969 with The American Lutheran Church. In October 1970, the ALC convention, agreeing with "Luther's conclusion, namely, that God has left the details of the ministerial office to the discretion of the church,"[52] voted to admit women to the ordained ministry, and Missouri's already reluctant fellowship with the ALC at once became far more contentious than either synod had ever imagined. Ralph Bohlmann identifies the larger context of the ALC decision as being the difference between the two synods over the authority of scripture:

> It certainly caught Missouri by surprise, I think. We didn't think that was going to happen. And immediately it injected a new element into the Missouri Synod. . . . It was an upsetting factor, and since the great

50. Peter Brunner, *The Ministry and the Ministry of Women* (St. Louis: Concordia Publishing House, 1971). First published in English translation in *Lutheran World* 6 (1959): 13, 15.

51. Brunner, *The Ministry and the Ministry of Women,* pp. 34-35.

52. Grindal, "Getting Women Ordained," p. 173.

scare was authority of Scripture, you know, that this decision might mean that what the American Lutheran Church was really saying was that those Bible passages that speak of the role of men and women in the church, you know, in the Pastorals and in Corinthians, that these were simply so culturally conditioned that they no longer had relevancy and that what the American Lutheran Church was doing was sort of throwing out the Apostolic Word, and all of the grim spectres of anti-biblical authoritarianism really reared their head. So in that sense I think that decision, which happened after 1969, has had the effect of intensifying Missouri's fears of long standing that many in the American Lutheran Church did not have the same strong view of biblical authority that we did.[53]

The CTCR subcommittee on fellowship, of which David Leege was chair, began to suspect that the ALC decision to ordain women would be a coffin nail in the previously declared fellowship between the two church bodies. Leege remembered a discussion about the ordination of women in which "people were saying that this, too, was *adiaphoron*. . . . It really resolved on the principle of good order rather than on doctrine." He recalled a very agitated Jacob Preus "pacing the floor in the back of the meeting hall and [saying], 'Well, it may not be a doctrinal matter, but this church sure isn't ready for it.'"[54] Leege noted that Preus's comment seemed to end the discussion. Robert Bertram regrets that:

> When the discussion of the ordination of women came to an end, and effectively it came to an end when women began to be ordained . . . the real loss was that this discussion that we had started to undertake — about the nature of authority in the church, the nature of ministry and so on — disappeared. It's a discussion that is sorely needed today.[55]

While substantively the discussion about the ordination of women and the larger questions of ministry and ecclesiology did not continue among the church bodies that had cooperated in the LCUSA study, a limited conversation on the issue did continue. The ramifications of the ALC action to approve the ordination of women were im-

53. ArCL/ALC-AELC-LCA/OHC: Ralph Bohlmann, 41.
54. Leege interview.
55. Bertram interview.

mediately raised in the ALC-LCMS Commission on Fellowship, a joint body of the presidents and representatives of the two churches. Reminded that the LCUSA study had stated that the ordination of women should not be divisive of church fellowship, the presidents nevertheless clearly disagreed on the question. Preus read the ALC decision to ordain women as an "anti-Missouri" vote, while Schiotz of the ALC claimed his church body simply did not believe the issue was serious enough to threaten fellowship.[56] A similar discussion was held at the next meeting of the Commission, with new ALC president Kent Knutson replacing Schiotz but making essentially the same appeal, that the ALC did "not see its position as 'flying in the face of Scripture.'" Jacob Preus repeated the seriousness of the issue, and asked what the ALC would do if the upcoming convention of the Missouri Synod asked the ALC to rescind its decision.[57] The ALC commissioners replied that the Church Council would hear such a request and determine appropriate action. But, while assuring Missouri that the ALC would take its request seriously, any "actual reconsideration" would have to wait until the ALC's 1972 convention. And they gave no guarantees that the ALC would agree to reconsider its position.[58]

At Missouri's 1971 convention in Milwaukee, eight resolutions were submitted to protest the ordination of women, some insisting that the state of fellowship with the ALC be terminated. The position of those opposed to the action taken by the other Lutheran synods is reflected in a resolution submitted to the convention by an Illinois congregation:

> A church body that chooses to chance into experimentation against a clear scripture doctrine has "queered" its integrity as a responsible and reliable steward of the mysteries of God. We owe them our assistance and resistance.[59]

56. Minutes, Commission on Fellowship, November 18, 1970. Executive Office files, CHI.

57. Minutes, Commission on Fellowship, March 19, 1971. Executive Office files, CHI.

58. Minutes, Commission on Fellowship, March 19, 1971. Executive Office files, CHI.

59. Missouri Synod, *Workbook,* 1971, 93. Not all members of the congregation who submitted this resolution agreed, however. A minority report was filed by those who supported further study of the issues.

Seven other resolutions asked that suffrage granted at the previous convention to women in the Missouri Synod be rescinded, cautioning about "dangerous doors" (no doubt in the direction of ordination) that suffrage could open.[60] The most reactionary of those urged the synod to retain "the institutions of our Lord unaltered," since

> Some individuals today are advocating the use of elements other than those ordained by God for His holy institutions, such as the use of (a) Coke and pizza, donuts and coffee, etc., for the eucharist, (b) homosexuals or lesbians for marriage, (c) women for ordination to the holy ministry.[61]

The exaggerated fears expressed in this resolution equating serious sacramental or ethical questions with women's ordination attest to the stridence of the opposition to the ordination of women.

The convention's official statement on women was to reflect that opposition as the synod, expressing its "strong regret over The American Lutheran Church's action on the ordination of women to the pastoral ministry," voted to ask the ALC to reconsider its decision.[62] In an emotional address to the convention, Kent Knutson, president of the ALC, appealed for acceptance of the differences in the decisions of the various church bodies, asking, "What shall we do when we both act out of our conviction of what is taught by the Bible?"[63] The answer would come in time, but from this point on, the question of fellowship between the two synods would be in jeopardy, linked but not limited to the ALC's decision to ordain women, a position the ALC voted overwhelmingly to reaffirm at its 1972 convention.

Polarization and retrenchment followed. Whether stung by the dashed hopes for unity or in need of respite from the intensity of the early LCUSA efforts at cooperative projects, each of the church bodies retreated to the affairs of its own household. The ALC and the LCA began to monitor the entrance of women into the pastoral ministry as female enrollments increased at their seminaries. The Missouri Synod, too, focused on its seminaries, particularly Concordia Seminary in St. Louis, where a showdown had begun over the synod's keystone insis-

---

60. Missouri Synod, *Workbook,* 1971, p. 96.
61. Missouri Synod, *Workbook,* 1971, p. 113.
62. Missouri Synod, *Proceedings,* 1971, p. 136.
63. Missouri Synod, *Proceedings,* 1971, p. 102.

tence on the authority and verbal inerrancy of the Bible. The climax came in 1974 with the self-imposed exile of forty-five of the fifty faculty members and most of the students of the seminary.

Struggle and Schism

A mood of growing intolerance and foreclosed debate had been spreading through the synod over most of the decade despite evidence to the contrary, such as Missouri's participation in LCUSA and its action on woman suffrage. Unresolved history continued to haunt the church, and haunts it still.

Missouri's struggle was political — on the one hand were those who called themselves moderates (but who the conservatives considered liberal) and on the other hand were the conservatives (extremists in, or on, their own right, as far as the moderates were concerned). Since Jacob Preus's election in 1969, the conservatives had held the leadership positions in the synod while the moderates continued to dominate the St. Louis seminary. Because the synodical old-line had always been the only line, Alan Graebner found "no tradition of a loyal opposition" in the synod.[64] And though there had been opposing camps at various times in the synod's history — most recently and most virulently over the Statement of the Forty-Four — Missouri had not experienced such bitterness and division since the Stephan episode that led to its founding. Now again, a crisis of authority was to prevail, and to preclude other issues, in what James Adams of the *St. Louis Post-Dispatch* has called "the great Lutheran civil war."[65]

The seeds of the impending crisis — dormant since the less than satisfactory resolution of the Forty-Four episode — were fertilized in 1962 with the appearance of a new unofficial publication called *Lutheran News,* renamed *Christian News* in 1968. Its editor-publisher, Herman Otten, a 1957 graduate of Concordia Seminary, St. Louis, had been denied certification for ordination by the seminary faculty following Otten's criticism of certain professors there. Despite his unrostered status, Otten was called to pastor a Missouri Synod congregation west of St. Louis, where he still serves and from where he continues to publish his disproportion-

64. Graebner, *Uncertain Saints,* p. 196.
65. See Adams, *Preus of Missouri,* and Danker, *No Room in the Brotherhood.*

ately influential publication.[66] Alan Graebner identifies the role Otten and his paper played in the evolving polarization of the synod:

> Otten did not cause the conservative resurgence of the 1960s, nor was he its chief tactician. He was not even the first to raise the alarm. But he was the main publicist of the movement. His paper, intended for laity as well as clergy, was an essential instrument for arousing the disgruntled to action, for putting them in touch with one another, and for maintaining morale.[67]

The *News* allowed discontent among conservatives — in particular laymen — to simmer, stirred by anti-intellectual outrage over theological trends emerging from the synod's institutions of higher learning. The St. Louis seminary in particular was a ready target, with frequent calls for investigation of what was being taught there and who was doing the teaching.

At the end of the convention at which he was elected president of the synod in 1969, Jacob Preus said that the primary issue facing Missouri was not the fellowship with the ALC that he and the conservatives had so vigorously opposed, but "the proper understanding of and adherence to the doctrine of the inspiration and inerrancy of Scripture."[68] It did not take him long to make it so. Division between the Preus camp and the majority of the seminary faculty led Preus to authorize an investigation of what was being taught at the seminary in late 1970 and early 1971. Central to the controversy was the standard by which the faculty was being judged — against scripture and the confessions or against the synod's doctrinal statements, in particular the Brief Statement.[69] Preus proceeded to appoint a Fact-Finding Committee to interview each faculty member and report back to him on their theological fitness.

Concern was growing over the spirit of suspicion overspreading the synod. In January 1970, a group of St. Louis pastors and laity called Lutherans for Openness and Trust adopted a position paper. "A Call to Openness and Trust" was "an appeal for an attitude we think is needed

---

66. Not all articles in *Christian News* address theological concerns. Entire pages are frequently devoted to social issues as well. During the Cold War Otten was strongly anti-Communist. Recent issues have warned readers against the claims of psychology and have given extensive copy to articles on topics as disparate as antifeminism, anti-Catholicism, and Holocaust denial.

67. Graebner, *Uncertain Saints,* p. 190.

68. Adams, *Preus of Missouri,* p. 143.

69. Tietjen, *Memoirs in Exile,* p. 64.

in the Church in our time." Speaking for "freedom: diversity in unity," the document argued against an imposed conformity in doctrinal positions that "would make the doctrines rather than God Himself the object of faith." Finally, the group called for putting people over organizational structures, declaring that their intent was merely

> to state freely and clearly what it means to follow Christ in our time. We desire to form no new church body but only to increase freedom and responsibility in the church in which our Lord has placed us. To that end we ask only that our conscience not be bound, except by God, and that our freedom to speak, write and act not be arbitrarily curtailed.[70]

This early appeal for diversity summarized eloquently the essence of the synodical struggle to come.

In July 1971, the synodical convention in Milwaukee declared that the synod's doctrinal statements, as confessions of scripture, should be honored and upheld.[71] It did not go so far as to make them binding on pastors, teachers, and professors, as Preus had desired. But Preus eventually prevailed in his intention to hold the professors to his own standard of orthodoxy, and in 1972 he presented a document against which the seminary Board of Control could judge its faculty. "A Statement of Scriptural and Confessional Principles" was Jacob Preus's own Brief Statement, a six-part explication almost entirely devoted to Preus's own doctrine of scripture, with particular reference to its inspiration, infallibility, authority, and interpretation.[72] In her analysis of the rhetoric of the synod's controversy, Laurie Ann Schultz Hayes describes Preus's document as "a brief unsolicited statement of orthodoxy that implies accusation."[73] His "Statement" became Jacob Preus's attempt to return

---

70. "A Call to Openness and Trust," Independent Groups and Movements Collection, Lutherans for Openness and Trust file, CHI.

71. Missouri Synod, *Proceedings,* 1971, 119.

72. "A Statement of Scriptural and Confessional Principles," St. Louis, 1972. The document was written by Ralph Bohlmann, then Executive Secretary of the CTCR, who later said about it: "I never thought it would be picked up by people and made into some comprehensive statement of belief. It was intended as a tool." ArCL/ALC-AELC-LCA/OHC: Ralph Bohlmann, 64.

73. Laurie Ann Schultz Hayes, "The Rhetoric of Controversy in the Lutheran Church–Missouri Synod with Particular Emphasis on the Years 1967-1976" (Ph.D. diss., University of Wisconsin-Madison, 1980), p. 322.

to the Walther-Pieper model in which the office of synodical president and that of chief theologian were collapsed into one man.[74]

The seminary faculty, however, disagreed with Preus's document, calling its spirit "alien to Lutheran confessional theology," imposing on scripture "a set of human criteria when it lists certain theoretical and abstract qualifications that Holy Scriptures must have, but which the Holy Scriptures do not claim for themselves — such as, inerrancy...."[75] It was the opinion of Arthur Carl Piepkorn, chair of the systematics department, that the "superfluous" and "defective" document "breathes a Reformed fundamentalist spirit."[76] For Piepkorn and his colleagues, adherence to scripture and the synodical constitution was enough, and they took objection to Preus's distribution of his Statement to the synod, an action they saw as nothing but divisive.

When the report of the Fact-Finding Committee was released in September 1972, there was no finding of false doctrine among the seminary faculty. What Jacob Preus found, instead, was a false view of scripture.[77] The question had become focused on biblical authority and interpretation — was there but one way to understand scripture or would diverse viewpoints be tolerated? Only a few years earlier, sociologist Jeffrey Hadden had identified this as the "critical and all-embracing question" of what he called *The Gathering Storm in the Churches:*

> Are the institutional structures of the church broad enough to accommodate persons who are widely divided on the doctrinal basis of the faith and on the very meaning and purpose of the church, or are the divisions already so deep and entrenched as to make accommodation impossible?[78]

Hadden's question was one Missouri would need to answer.

74. See Hillis, *Can Two Walk Together Unless They Be Agreed?* p. 132.
75. "Response of the Faculty of Concordia Seminary, St. Louis," *Lutheran Witness* 91 (April 30, 1972): 28-31.
76. Letter from Arthur Carl Piepkorn to the Faculty Advisory Committee, March 10, 1972. Piepkorn papers, Box 111, ELCA Archives.
77. *Report of the Synodical President to the Lutheran Church–Missouri Synod (In Compliance with Resolution 2-28 of the Forty-Ninth Regular Convention of the Synod)* (St. Louis: Concordia Publishing House, September 1, 1972), p. 21.
78. Jeffrey K. Hadden, *The Gathering Storm in the Churches: The Widening Gap Between Clergy and Laymen* (Garden City, N.Y.: Doubleday & Company, 1969), p. 223.

The faculty became proactive on its own behalf and in January 1973 issued a document entitled *Faithful to Our Calling, Faithful to our Lord,* in which they responded to Preus's claims about their subscription to scripture.[79] Both individually and collectively, the professors expressed their confessional basis. That same month, the seminary Board of Control found no need to correct any faculty member; instead, all were to be "commended."[80] Preus was discouraged but not defeated; the upcoming synodical convention would decide the matter.

When the synod met in convention in New Orleans in 1973, the church had reached what its president considered a "doctrinal crossroads."[81] The critical concerns centered on the worsening seminary struggle. After re-electing Jacob Preus, the convention (tagged by many "the battle of New Orleans") officially accepted his "A Statement" as "a more formal and comprehensive statement of belief" that "expresses the Synod's position on current doctrinal issues,"[82] thereby giving the president a measure by which to continue his case against the seminary. And the convention determined that Article II of the synod's constitution — its doctrinal basis — allowed the adoption of additional doctrinal statements for clarification of controverted positions, and that such statements would be binding on all members.[83] The issue of the recalcitrant faculty was referred back to the Board of Control.[84] Their president, John Tietjen, was soon to become the principal target.

In the months following the New Orleans convention, moderate clergy and laypeople concerned about the direction their church was moving met in Chicago to form Evangelical Lutherans in Mission (ELiM), believing they could stay and stake out their claim to be "a movement of confession and protest"[85] removed from political infighting, whose purpose was to "go forward in the church, not out of the synod."[86] Echoing the earlier "Call to Openness and Trust," ELiM dis-

---

79. *Faithful to Our Calling, Faithful to Our Lord: An Affirmation in Two Parts by the Faculty of Concordia Seminary, St. Louis, Missouri* (St. Louis: s.n., 1973).

80. Missouri Synod, *Workbook,* 1973, pp. 99-100.

81. Missouri Synod, *Proceedings,* 1973, p. 63.

82. Missouri Synod, *Proceedings,* 1973, pp. 127-28.

83. Missouri Synod, *Proceedings,* 1973, pp. 114-15, known as Resolution 2-12.

84. Missouri Synod, *Proceedings,* p. 139.

85. "Group of 800 Gathers and Organizes 'Confessing Movement' Within Synod," *Lutheran Witness* 92 (September 16, 1973): 22.

86. *Missouri in Perspective* 1 (October 22, 1973): 2.

senters rejected the idea of forming a new church, believing there was room in Missouri for differing opinions. But the Commission on Theology and Church Relations thought differently, issuing within months an opinion that dissenting groups threatened the unity of the synod.[87] By that time, ELiM had begun publication of a biweekly periodical, *Missouri in Perspective,* to represent and publicize the moderate point of view on the growing controversy.

The crisis at the seminary had increasingly focused on efforts of the Board of Control to suspend President John Tietjen. In January 1974 they succeeded, accusing Tietjen of false doctrine and removing him from office. The campus community, fearing the eventuality of this development, had discussed various contingency plans. The day after Tietjen's suspension, students declared a moratorium on classes until such time as the Board of Control could tell them which "members of the faculty, if any, are to be considered false teachers and what Scriptural and Confessional principles, if any, have been violated."[88] The faculty laid plans to resume teaching off-campus as a seminary-in-exile. On February 19, students in solemn procession left the grounds of Concordia Seminary, followed by the majority of their professors.[89] "Seminex" would reconvene for classes the next day at St. Louis University and Eden Seminary.

A "battle for the Bible" had characterized the synodical controversy to this point, but after the walkout, the principal issue would not be the authority of scripture but the authority of the synod itself, as located in the office of its president. What was to be done with the graduates of a seminary that had removed itself from its church body? Shortly after the exile, Missouri's Commission on Constitutional Matters had declared that any congregation issuing a call to a Seminex graduate would forfeit its membership.[90] But what of the role of congregational autonomy, central to the identity of the synod from its founding? ELiM issued a pamphlet by a Seminex professor that located the problem: "Today, congregational rights face the most serious chal-

87. CTCR, "Opinion on Dissenting Groups," 1973.

88. Danker, *No Room in the Brotherhood,* p. 199.

89. Hillis, *Can Two Walk Together Unless They Be Agreed?* p. 71. Eighty-five percent of the student body and 90 percent of the faculty left the seminary campus that day.

90. Notice of official rulings were printed in the *Lutheran Witness* 93 (April 7, 1974): 27.

lenge yet in Missouri Synod history," wrote John Constable, in reminding his readers of Walther's insistence on the advisory nature of synod.[91] Was it not the right of a congregation to call the pastor of its choice? That became the underlying argument of eight district presidents who authorized the ordination of Seminex graduates.

Jacob Preus disagreed. To Preus, synodical structure and order required adherence to the rules. By the time of the 1975 convention in Anaheim, California, Preus felt his church body had reached a state of "organizational anarchy" after "two decades . . . of two opposing theologies, particularly with reference to the doctrine of Holy Scripture. No church body can long support two theologies which are in conflict." Despite his claim that "The Synod welcomes dissent," it was time, he believed, that dissenters cease and desist, "teach in conformity with our doctrinal position" or go elsewhere. Missouri's president was convinced that his church would "go down in history not just as a bunch of contentious and quarrelsome nit-pickers, but as a church that cared about its teachings and its faith and ultimately prevailed."[92] The convention went on to support Preus's position: it condemned ELiM as schismatic[93] and determined that district presidents who refused to follow synodical procedure were to be removed from office.[94]

By the following spring, events had reached the point of no return. Missouri's civil war ended not in reunion and reconstruction, but with secession. In this controversy over "control of belief,"[95] the most moderate members left the synod after 1976, unable to stay in a church that either lacked the tradition of a loyal opposition or had no desire whatsoever to tolerate one. Eight district presidents lost their positions in a purge that began in the spring of 1976 — they had challenged the authority of the synodical president and, in accordance with the will of the Anaheim convention, he removed them from office. In the end, one hundred and fifty congregations joined the seminary exiles in the formation of the Association of Evangelical Lu-

91. John Constable, "Synod: More than Advisory?" (St. Louis: Evangelical Lutherans in Mission, n.d.).

92. Missouri Synod, "President's Report," *Proceedings*, 1975, pp. 58-59, 61.

93. Missouri Synod, "President's Report," *Proceedings*, 1975, pp. 96-99.

94. Missouri Synod, "President's Report," *Proceedings*, 1975, pp. 122-24.

95. Hayes, "The Rhetoric of Controversy in the Lutheran Church–Missouri Synod," p. 479.

theran Churches (AELC).[96] Their goals were few other than support of Christ Seminary-Seminex and unity with other Lutheran church bodies. While the ordination of women was not a clearly stated objective of the new church, initiators of the breakaway movement asked for recognition of "the full participation of women in the whole ministry of the church, including the pastoral office."[97] A woman, Jan Otte, had graduated that spring from Seminex and had been certified by its faculty for ordination. The presence of women in the seminary meant the discussion of women in ministry was ongoing, and change seemed almost inevitable, according to Leon Rosenthal, a classmate of Otte's: "It was only a matter of how and when."[98] There are those who would say the decision to ordain women in the AELC was hasty, given its Missouri roots, taken without much thought as to what it would mean either for women or for congregations. But the decision was vital in establishing the identity of the new church, for it declared more clearly than any other action who these Lutherans were not — a Missouri Synod now firmly in the grip of its conservative wing and insistent on a verbally inerrant scripture.

In the polarized climate of the 1970s, the Missouri Synod — the church body other Lutherans often considered "people weaned on this assumption that they really are the cream of God's crop"[99] for its historic claim to be the true church — encountered the greatest challenge in its history. Now, with the dissidents gone, Missouri's past would become its security. But what Theodore Graebner had in 1948 called the synod's "burden of infallibility" began to grow heavier.[100] As Alan Graebner observed,

96. From its beginning, the AELC sought unity with the other Lutheran synods. In 1987, the LCA, ALC, and AELC agreed to merge into the Evangelical Lutheran Church in America. See Edgar R. Trexler, *Anatomy of a Merger: People, Dynamics, and Decisions that Shaped the ELCA* (Minneapolis: Augsburg Fortress, 1991).

97. *Missouri in Perspective* 3 (July 19, 1976): 7. The acceptance of women in public ministry in the AELC is recounted in Mary Todd, "Now Is the Kairos — the Right Time," in *Lutheran Women in Ordained Ministry, 1970-1995: Reflections and Perspectives,* ed. Gloria E. Bengston (Minneapolis: Augsburg Fortress, 1995), pp. 28-32.

98. Leon G. Rosenthal, interview by author, August 23, 1995, River Forest, Illinois, tape recording.

99. ArCL/ALC-AELC-LCA/OHC: Fred Meuser, 8.

100. Theodore Graebner, "The Burden of Infallibility: A Study in the History of Dogma," mimeographed copy 1948, reprinted in *Concordia Historical Institute Quarterly* 38 (1965): 87-94.

The emphasis on pure doctrine and on a Bible inerrant in all matters molded a cast of mind in which "truth" once articulated could no longer be debated. To admit in public that past pronouncements were mistaken pointed to the possibility that present statements might be. The only way out of the dilemma was silence.[101]

Keeping the Woman Question Alive

Almost ignored on the agenda at the 1973 convention was a proposal from the Commission on Theology and Church Relations that the synod establish a task force on the role of women in the church, "with adequate representation by women."[102] Since the business of the synod at New Orleans was about issues crucial to its very existence, the approval of this proposal is a curious development, likely intended to appear that the synod recognized the implications of feminism then beginning to sweep across America. Its surprising passage meant that the "woman question" would stay alive in Missouri, at least for the next two years.

Considering the internecine struggle going on in Missouri, it is no surprise that it took a while for the Task Force on Women to come to life. The first meeting was held a year later, in 1974. President Preus had appointed seven women and three pastors, who according to Jean Garton, elected chair of the Task Force, provided a balance between those "perceived to be moderates in the church and those who were perceived to be conservatives."[103] The group met with a staff member of the Commission on Theology who presented suggestions for possible projects proposed by Ralph Bohlmann, executive director of the CTCR. The suggestions included holding conferences and workshops, reviewing materials of the synodical publishing house, researching the current status of women in the synod, encouraging the CTCR to complete its work on the theology of male-female relationships, and producing "materials and articles that continue to honor motherhood, homemaker, teacher of [the] next generation."[104] Discussion of women's ordination was not on the list, as Ralph Bohlmann remembers, not because it was not an issue, but because the issue was "almost always

---

101. Alan Graebner, *Uncertain Saints,* p. 170.
102. Missouri Synod, *Workbook,* 1973, pp. 31, 61-62.
103. Jean Garton, interview by author, March 7, 1991, tape recording.
104. Task Force on Women, minutes, July 29, 1974.

utilized then as an instance of a differing concept of biblical authority," and the authority and interpretation of scripture was the overpowering theological issue for the synod in the 1970s.[105]

But at their first meeting, the members of the Task Force talked about the ordination of women anyway, before deciding that they would not address the issue because it was a theological one.[106] Alvin Schmidt, then a sociology professor at Lenoir-Rhyne College, fully expected the topic would be discussed, though "everybody knew at that time how much the Synod was opposed to it."[107] Both Schmidt and Harold Haas, a synodical college professor who had served as a consultant to the LCUSA subcommittee that studied the ordination question, commented that the Task Force certainly could not avoid the issue, adding that men needed help in understanding it.[108] But the women carried the day; the issue would be avoided, beginning a pattern by which loyal Missouri women deferred to their church's contention that the ordination of women was a subject not even to be discussed.

Perhaps the most acute observation about the uncertainty with which the Task Force began its work was made by Florence Montz, then president of the official synodical women's auxiliary, the Lutheran Women's Missionary League (LWML). Montz, who felt that the group started with strikes against it, commented that

> the seventies were unsettling years. It was not a good time for that Task Force to be working because there really was not much support nor was there much interest from the church at large. . . .
>
> The church at that time was not ready to look at anything except getting itself out of the mess it was in as far as the conflict.[109]

105. Ralph Bohlmann, interview by author, November 6, 1995, tape recording.

106. Louise Mueller, interview by author, February 23, 1991, tape recording.

107. Alvin J. Schmidt, interview by author, March 16, 1991, tape recording. Schmidt admits to an "old-line" conservatism and strong opposition to the ordination of women when he joined the Task Force. His experience on the Task Forces and his own subsequent study has led him to the opposite position. See Schmidt, *Veiled and Silenced: How Culture Shaped Sexist Theology* (Macon, Ga.: Mercer University Press, 1989).

108. Task Force on Women, minutes, July 29, 1974.

109. Florence Montz, interview by author, March 21, 1991, tape recording. In 1983 Montz became the first woman ever elected to the Board of Directors of the Missouri Synod. She served the maximum term of twelve years until 1995.

Despite the lack of a defined assignment, the men and women of the Task Force on Women created an agenda and spent the next nine months engaged in data gathering and study. Their most important work was a survey on the status of women in individual congregations throughout the synod, and the preparation of an extensive report on their efforts for the next convention to be held in Anaheim, California, in 1975.

Most of the members of the Task Force agreed that they had not had adequate time to complete their task and asked the convention to grant them an extension. Without consulting her fellow members, Jean Garton initiated a resolution to a floor committee that the Task Force be disbanded and its work picked up by the CTCR. When Preus asked Florence Montz if she wished to speak to the resolution, she spoke against it, suggesting that the Task Force had just "come of age."[110] The question failed, but the hostility that resulted from its own chairman's actions set the tone for an unproductive second term for the Task Force on Women. This episode, however, was typical of the actions of the Anaheim convention, during which the synodical crisis grew closer and closer to schism.

When the Task Force resumed its work in September 1975, Preus suggested that they include in their efforts the concerns of three groups: "lady teachers, deaconesses and youth."[111] Accordingly, two members were added to the group in 1975, one a parochial school teacher and the other a deaconess. Florence Montz was asked to become a permanent member, as her term as LWML president had ended and the new president, Helen Morris, automatically became an advisory member of the Task Force. Though the group again met six times over the next two years, attendance was irregular and participants recall Task Force II as a frustrating experience. "The sizzle went out," said Jean Garton.[112] She felt her attempt to disband the Task Force had been vindicated by the burnout she observed. It is more likely that her Anaheim action had instead become a self-fulfilling prophecy.

110. Montz interview.
111. Task Force on Women, minutes, September 16-17, 1975. The Missouri Synod has the largest number of women parochial school teachers after the Roman Catholic Church. Deaconesses are professional parish workers who are consecrated but not ordained. See above, chapter 4.
112. Garton interview.

Although they had done little to advance the cause of women in the Missouri Synod, members of the Task Force felt they could at least point to several catchwords they had chosen as goals: "sensitize," "recognize," "utilize," and the most often cited, "inclusive language." The focus of their efforts had been to raise the synodical consciousness about women, to point out discrepancies in salaries between male and female Lutheran school teachers, to identify areas of service available to women, and to report that women constituted 54 percent of Missouri's membership and were voting members in almost 64 percent of congregations in 1975, only six years after suffrage had been granted.[113] Al Schmidt believes the existence of the Task Force alone was enough; it said to the church at large that there *were* women's issues in the church.[114] But several other members were concerned that turning women's issues back to the Commission on Theology, which the termination of the Task Force effectively induced, would bury those issues.[115] Their fears were probably justified, although in the thick of the Lutheran civil war a good many issues were neglected. The 1977 convention, after re-electing Jacob Preus to a third term as president, commended the Task Force for its work and charged the CTCR with the ongoing work of studying women's issues in the church.[116]

For some reason Jacob Preus still seemed concerned about the women of the church. He approached Helen Morris, LWML president from 1975 to 1979, and said that he wanted an appointed synodical representative to sit on the LWML Board of Directors. From its founding, the women's auxiliary has had elected pastoral counselors, who serve on the board without a vote. But Preus wanted to appoint his own representative in addition. Morris took his request back to her Executive Committee, who rejected the idea. One of the women, however, suggested facetiously that if the synod would allow an LWML representative on the synodical Board of Directors, they might reconsider their decision.[117] The women stood up for themselves and

113. Missouri Synod, *Workbook,* 1975, Report of the Task Force on Women, pp. 57-63.

114. Schmidt interview.

115. Olive Spannaus, interview by author, March 3, 1991, tape recording, and Mueller interview.

116. Missouri Synod, *Proceedings,* 1977, pp. 129, 134.

117. Helen Morris, personal statement to author, June 23, 1995, Kansas City, Missouri.

their autonomy as an auxiliary, and Preus accepted their decision without animosity, but the episode serves as a telling example of the president's need to maintain control over his synod in those most contentious days.

Given the limitations of the situation and the uneasy times, the men and women who participated in the Task Force on Women during this time felt they had done what they could. There would be no official action on women's issues for another six years. The matter had been put to rest with the departure of so many of Missouri's moderate voices.

Once cleansed, the synod settled down to a restatement of its orthodoxy. The lingering woman's issue was the synod's position on the proposed Equal Rights Amendment. The CTCR in 1980 reissued its 1976 "Report on Equal Rights Amendment," in which the theologians seemed primarily concerned with what they called the "*absolute* character" of the amendment.[118] But to some laymen, the ERA posed a very real threat to Missouri's policy against the ordination of women. Their fears were addressed by one Indiana congregation:

> One of the gravest attacks on the churches of our land today comes in the form of the proposed Equal Rights Amendment (ERA) to the Constitution. . . . The ERA, if it becomes law, would empower the government to require our Synod, contrary to the teaching of . . . Sacred Scripture, to call women as professors to our theological seminaries and to ordain women as pastors for our Synod's congregations.[119]

The resolution went on to call for disobedience to the law and even hinted at a mild martyrdom if the amendment were ratified: "If our obedience to our God brings forth censures and penalties from our

118. CTCR, "Report on Equal Rights Amendment," August 1980. Emphasis in the original. "Constitutional absolutes are dangerous in a free society. . . . The amendment proceeds from the assumption that a particular solicitude for women is inherently an insult to their humanity. . . . We have major reservations about absolutist legal prescriptions, however well intentioned, which fail to recognize generic differences inherent in the created order and also affirmed by the Holy Scriptures."

119. Missouri Synod, *Workbook*, 1977, p. 95.

government and the persecutions of men . . . we shall gladly bear them."[120] But with the 1982 expiration of the Congressional extension for ratification of the amendment, the synod no longer had to worry about government interference in its prohibition of women from the ministry. Ironically, the energy spent in that worry was unnecessary in the first place, since the authors of this resolution failed to recognize that the First Amendment would likely preclude the ERA from affecting religious policy and practices.

In 1981 the CTCR Social Concerns subcommittee prepared and published a report entitled "Human Sexuality: A Theological Perspective," which framed its approach to sexuality on "the creation of man as male and female."[121] This report, requested by the 1973 synodical convention, was primarily concerned with sexuality within marriage, and with the principle of headship — a so-called "hierarchy of function" — which the Commission took care to note does not apply to men and women in general, but only in marriage. This latter point indicates a critical shift from the earlier CTCR position, firmly in place at the time of the suffrage debate, which bound itself to Fritz Zerbst's insistence on a universal rule of male superordination-female subordination. In the sexuality document the theologians were instead in agreement with Russell Prohl, who found the structure useful *only* within marriage. While not using the terminology of "orders of creation," the sexuality document admits to "a kind of inequality of authority" in a hierarchy of function.[122]

A third CTCR report issued in 1981 addressed the ministry. Amid the turmoil of the previous decade, questions regarding the ministry had centered on whether graduates of an exiled seminary could be certified for ordination in the synod. The final battle in the civil war had been waged over the answer to that question. The CTCR returned to the topic of the ministry in response to the usual requests for guidance from congregations and districts. The 1981 report entitled "The Ministry: Offices, Procedures, and Nomenclature,"[123] agreed with Walther's Theses of 1851, reiterating his emphasis on the

120. Missouri Synod, *Workbook*, 1977, p. 95.
121. CTCR, "Human Sexuality: A Theological Perspective," September 1981, p. 6.
122. "Human Sexuality: A Theological Perspective," pp. 29-32.
123. CTCR, "The Ministry: Offices, Procedures, and Nomenclature," September 1981.

one office of public ministry with the possibility for auxiliary or "facilitating" offices, "the most common" of which is the teaching ministry. Hereby the CTCR returned to the synod's original conception of the pastoral office, while granting that "inadequate definitions of terms tend to lead into a drift into practices that create confusion in the church and that may even contradict sound doctrine."[124] Misunderstanding — beginning with the word *ministry* itself — proliferated as congregations applied terms such as "elder" and "lay minister" to various offices with variant duties. The misunderstanding would only be compounded as women began to serve in some of those offices in the synod's congregations.

The President's Commission on Women

In 1981 Jacob Preus retired from the presidency of The Lutheran Church–Missouri Synod, and Ralph Bohlmann, president of Concordia Seminary in St. Louis, was elected to succeed him. This change in leadership, however, did not necessarily mean a change in synodical posture. The state of fellowship with the ALC, approved at the same convention at which Preus was elected in 1969, and under official protest since 1977 because of the ALC's decision to ordain women, was finally broken by vote of the delegates to the 1981 convention. The tenuous ties that held an admittedly distant hope for Lutheran unity had now been officially cut.

In 1983, in his first report as president of the synod, Ralph Bohlmann spoke to the issue of women in the church and of the need to expand their role. His previous involvement on women's issues had been limited to the suggestions he had transmitted to the Task Force in 1974. But by January 1984, he had taken the unprecedented action of appointing a President's Commission on Women (PCW).[125] No convention resolution had prompted his action. The woman question to Bohlmann was an important enough issue for him to make a unilateral decision to fund the Commission's work from his own presidential budget. He explains his decision: "It was the right thing to do for Missouri to begin asking

124. "The Ministry: Offices, Procedures, and Nomenclature," p. 5.
125. "God's Woman for All Generations," A Report of the President's Commission on Women, 1987, pp. 3-4. Hereinafter referred to as PCW report.

hard questions about the ministry of women in the church."[126] But Bohlmann did not mean the ordained ministry. The CTCR had already been assigned to draft a document on women in the church, and assignments — what Bohlmann calls "turf questions" — needed to be respected.

The President's Commission on Women differed from the Task Force in several significant ways. This ad hoc group would be comprised only of women. Bohlmann consulted people for recommendations, as he did not want to appoint "all academics, but ordinary, strong, parish-oriented LCMS women."[127] He received some criticism for limiting the new commission membership to women, but nevertheless pursued that course. At its first meeting Bohlmann presented nine women with six tasks outlining their assignment. These included reviewing the work of the Task Force as well as the current status of women in the synod, and recommending areas of service appropriate to women. None addressed the question of the ordination of women to the ministry — "there are more dimensions to the woman question than ordination"[128] — but Bohlmann did offer the Commission the opportunity to meet with the Commission on Theology "as it prepares its theological study on the service of women in the Church."[129]

The women who would work together over the next two and a half years had never met each other before their first meeting in July 1984. During an informal gathering prior to that session, Jean Garton, who became chair of this Commission as she had been of both Task Forces, suggested the members take a straw poll of their positions on the ordination of women. Marie Meyer recalled that no one spoke in favor of it: "It was a topic that was feared." The consensus of the group was firm: "We're all against it. We're not going to talk about it."[130] Nancy Nemoyer, then director of the deaconess program at Concordia College in River Forest, Illinois, agreed: "We determined that we were going to be behind our synod."[131] Garton claims that the Commission

126. Bohlmann interview.
127. Bohlmann interview.
128. Bohlmann interview.
129. PCW report, 4. The CTCR was directed by two conventions to give priority to its study of "both the extent and limitations on women's role in the church." Missouri Synod, *Proceedings*, 1981, p. 158, and *Proceedings*, 1983, pp. 157-58.
130. Marie Meyer, interview by author, February 23, 1991, tape recording.
131. Nancy Nicol Nemoyer, interview by author, March 6, 1991, Bridgeview, Illinois, tape recording.

felt no responsibility to deal with the ordination issue because it was a theological subject and not part of their assignment. She believed they were to be a data-gathering and recommendatory group only.[132] Once again the issue of the ordination of women had been addressed by remaining unaddressed.

What the women did address was the status of women in the Missouri Synod. Their most extensive effort was the development, distribution, and assessment of a survey, but unlike that prepared by the Task Force, the PCW's survey included both statistical and attitudinal questionnaires. Pastors, lay women and men, parochial school teachers, and professional church workers were asked about their congregational organization and makeup as well as about their understanding of gender limitations within the Missouri Synod. As in 1975, women continued to make up 55 percent of the membership of the synod, but the number of congregations in which women were voting members had increased to nearly eighty percent.[133]

Perhaps the most significant findings of the survey were the discrepancies between practice and posture with regard to women's service in key positions within the local congregation. Respondents reported that women's service was more limited in their churches than they felt it should be. It was apparent that, although restrictions on women's service had been eased, change was slow to come. When given a list of activities and asked which should be limited to males, the pastoral roles of preaching and presiding at the eucharist still tended to be seen as gendered roles by the majority of respondents, as did the position of elder, which is understood by Missouri to be a lay office of spiritual oversight.[134] How did those surveyed understand these limitations? In a key finding, far more believed that the limitations were synodically imposed than biblically mandated, particularly in the activities associated with the pastoral office.[135] The laity remained uncertain both about the scriptural references to women and the synodical prescriptions based on those references. Interestingly, women were more willing than men to admit they were unsure of the biblical position.[136] And when asked to comment on how change takes place in the

132. Garton interview.
133. PCW report, p. 12.
134. PCW report, p. 23.
135. PCW report, p. 25.
136. PCW report, p. 28.

church, 85.8 percent agreed that change in the church comes as a result of societal change — that culture shapes theology — yet 54.4 percent believed that the Missouri Synod would never permit women to serve as pastors.[137] The Commission let the statistics stand on their own as clear indication of the confusion and tension among those surveyed about women's place within the synod. Despite the synod's very public identification in the 1970s as a church that stood for a verbally inerrant scripture as the basis for its doctrinal positions, a representative sampling of its members ten years later showed a significant discrepancy between the synod's position and biblical teachings.

The interaction between the President's Commission on Women and the Commission on Theology and Church Relations provided the point-counterpoint in the 1980s of the debate within Missouri about women. Far more than a story of male theologians who were less than happy about consulting with a group of women at the behest of the synodical president, this interaction revealed the prevailing attitude of male clergy within the synod.

Bohlmann had tasked the Commission to consult with the CTCR as it was preparing its report on women's service in the church.[138] But had he asked the CTCR to consult with the women? Each PCW member had been given a draft of the proposed CTCR document. Jean Garton recalled that the PCW members felt a joint meeting of the two commissions to discuss the draft was important, but the women were told by the CTCR that such a meeting was not necessary. Garton sought Bohlmann's intervention, and several meetings between the CTCR standing committee and subcommittees of the PCW were arranged.[139] During the course of these meetings the women encouraged changes in the title, tenor, and language of the proposed document. Louise Mueller recalled that the women had trouble with the theologians' "flimsy argument" over the order of creation, the principle by which the CTCR claimed that subordination of women does not mean inferiority, but on which they based their entire argument regarding women's service in the church.[140] Nancy Nemoyer expressed the frustration of the women as they tried to be "helpful editors from a

137. PCW report, p. 26.
138. CTCR, "Women in the Church: Scriptural Principles and Ecclesial Practice," September 1985.
139. Garton interview.
140. Mueller interview.

woman's perspective" but were given no credit or credence. The PCW members attempted to help the men understand how such terms as "order" and "subordination" were demeaning to women, and suggested that new language be found to express the theological position in less condescending terms. But even when given an opportunity to be more sensitive to the women of the church by means of language, the CTCR coined no new words in issuing its report.[141]

Because the women's principal objection to the draft was its prohibitive, negative tone, PCW members asked the men to make it more positive. As a result of the dialogue between the two groups, the final draft of the CTCR document, *Women in the Church: Scriptural Principles and Ecclesial Practice,* was somewhat modified from the draft the women had first seen. A section on the affirmation of women was added on the PCW's recommendation. Nevertheless, "We did not completely and unreservedly endorse the CTCR document," said Mueller. And, Nemoyer added, "it still came out to be a prohibitive document about what women can't do."[142] When the long-awaited report was finally issued in 1985, it was not the ordination of women that was called for, but their subordination as the Missouri synod understood it. The message of the CTCR was that the synod would remain true to its unchanging theological perspective.

Throughout its term, the President's Commission on Women received letters and comments of criticism, complaint, and concern from both pastors and laity about its purpose and intent. Questions came from all corners, including several from women who believed that the existence of such a commission gave the impression that Missouri was addressing the problem of women's issues, when it was really addressing only the symptoms. Some comments suggested that there were political reasons behind the appointment of the Commission, that it was being "used" by Ralph Bohlmann to push for the ordination of women. Others complained of the sexist makeup of the PCW and called for the appointment of nine men to round out the group.[143] The most telling letters were those that challenged the inconsistency of the church in its teachings and practices, and the confusion in a church body that, despite its insistence on an unmoving theology, had a history of changing

141. Nemoyer interview.
142. Mueller, Nemoyer interviews.
143. PCW minutes, February 22-24, 1985, p. 1.

its mind. In an unusually forthright observation — the most prophetic in its lengthy report — the Commission noted starkly: "There is a concern that the inconsistencies and uncertainties of what women can do is resulting in a church that is on a collision course with itself."[144]

When it came time to produce its report, the PCW confronted its powerlessness. While pleased with their accomplishments, the women realized, as Nancy Nemoyer noted: "We'd become a well-informed group that had something to say and then all we could do was say it and not propose it."[145] The report would prove to be the undoing of the seeming harmony in the Commission. One member, Marie Meyer, wanted to include a minority report that would offer an affirmative statement about being a woman in the church.[146] Told by the chairman that she was the only dissenter and torn by wanting to be part of "something that would be approved and accepted," the situation left Meyer conflicted and Nemoyer unnerved. In the end the report was presented as unanimous, though Meyer remarked: "The PCW almost tried too hard to present a report which could be acceptable to the church and would not create a problem to the church. . . . I felt we were putting Band-Aids on."[147]

The report of the President's Commission on Women had presented the synod with a significant challenge in its forthrightness about the woman question in the church. However, some of the commission members wondered whether their candor had been welcome. Four of the nine women on the original Commission — "quiet subversives," Louise Mueller called them[148] — guessed that they would not be invited to return for a second term. Increasingly frustrated by the powerlessness of the Commission, the strictures imposed by their limited assignment, and the biases of the synod against women, these women had challenged the leadership in various ways, most often by pressing for discussion of theological issues. The administration's response was to reduce the membership of the President's Commission on Women in its second and third terms and to make it more homogeneous in composition. Another change would be noticeable: there would no longer be an automatic slot on the PCW for the president of the LWML,

144. PCW report, p. 57.
145. Nemoyer interview.
146. Meyer interview.
147. Meyer, Nemoyer interviews.
148. Mueller interview.

even though that organization, as an official auxiliary, claims to represent the women of the Missouri Synod. Now the PCW claimed to represent them as well, and a disagreement that hinted at competition for the women of the church ensued. The real question is whether either of these groups, while professing to speak for the women of Missouri, serves as their advocate.

During the remainder of his term in office, Ralph Bohlmann continued to appoint successively fewer women to the PCW. His disappointment over inadequate financial resources required him to scale back to a commission of only five women.[149] Each triennium he appointed Jean Garton to chair the Commission, and sought the recommendations of PCW members regarding new appointments, in particular younger women. In 1990 a part-time staff person was assigned office space at synodical headquarters in St. Louis, which Garton saw as indication that the PCW has finally been "built into the system."[150] But Florence Montz believes the creation of a staff position instead reflects the critical problem: the PCW is just "rehearsing the same thing over and over. As long as the commission is part of the synod, it's never going to say anything that the synod doesn't say."[151] Olive Spannaus, a member of the earlier Task Force, agrees with Montz that the official status of the PCW precludes it from being an effective change agent and suggests that the perpetual avoidance of discussing women's ordination means "now we're more threatened by ordination than we were."[152]

Ralph Bohlmann would likely disagree. He believes that a number of synodical leaders, particularly district presidents, became more open and sensitive to women's issues as a result of the work of the PCW. He blames constrained synodical resources for the lack of follow-through on Commission findings. But in the end, Bohlmann claims his own admitted preoccupation with the controversies that plagued his last five years in office "got in the way."[153]

By 1992, the ever-present ultraconservative forces of the synod

149. Bohlmann interview.
150. Garton interview.
151. Montz interview.
152. Spannaus interview.
153. Bohlmann interview. Bohlmann was embroiled in a dispute with Robert Preus, president of Concordia Seminary, Fort Wayne, over Preus's leadership of the seminary.

had grown impatient with what they perceived to be Ralph Bohlmann's increasingly moderate positions, one of which had to do with women in the church. The 1985 report of the CTCR, it seemed, had done nothing to clarify the question of women's service in the church. The 1989 synodical convention workbook included twenty-three overtures on the woman question, some requesting more study, others more guidance, others a new document altogether. The congregational polity of the synod assured that inconsistency would be the persistent state of the church, as local congregations made their own decisions about the limitations on women's service in the parish. But that inconsistency is exactly what unnerved the ultraconservatives, who reject any easing of the synod's position on women's service. Bohlmann, they said, was soft on the issue. He didn't think so, and said so in his report to the churches in the summer of 1991: "Contrary to what you may hear elsewhere, there is no clamor for the ordination of women to the pastoral office . . . or for any other diminution of our confessional stance."[154] Bohlmann's coupling of women's ordination with the synod's "confessional stance" is interesting in that the Lutheran confessions never address the question. Bohlmann admits to finding the order of creation argument, the linchpin of the synod's position on women's service in the church, less than compelling. But he recognized the implications of accusations against him regarding the woman question: "The woman's issue was a kind of a continuing hot potato in Missouri, mostly because of the far right network that stirs the pot and makes issues issues that aren't really issues for most people."[155]

Nevertheless, on the first morning of the synodical convention in Pittsburgh in 1992, Ralph Bohlmann lost in his bid for re-election by twelve votes to Alvin L. Barry, president of the Iowa East District. Waylaid by a concerted and well-financed political campaign to unseat him, Bohlmann cautioned his church body in his closing remarks: "All too often, The Lutheran Church–Missouri Synod is seen . . . as a church with tremendous resources . . . yet [one] that fights far too much, that focuses more attention on the faults of one another."[156]

As president emeritus of the synod, Bohlmann remains a popular

154. Ralph Bohlmann, "From the President's Desk: Districts in Mission," *Lutheran Witness* 110 (August 1991): 25.

155. Bohlmann, "From the President's Desk: Districts in Mission."

156. David Strand, "Eight Days in Pittsburgh," *Lutheran Witness* 111 (August 1992): 6.

speaker whose opinion on matters at issue within the synod is still sought. So, in 1994, when the CTCR was yet again dealing with a convention request that it clarify the synod's position on women's service to the church — in particular whether women might serve as congregational presidents and elders — several district presidents asked Bohlmann to comment on the Commission's proposed draft. Bohlmann developed a lengthy response paper in which he recommended the CTCR write in a scriptural and pastoral tone that would "avoid language that is condescending or defensive," and that it "demonstrate conclusions and recommendations from the Scriptures, rather than synodical resolutions and CTCR documents."[157]

The CTCR's first draft addressed the congregational offices of elder, chair and vice-chair, and district and synodical boards and commissions. In addition, it considered for the first time whether a woman might serve as "a teacher of theology in a class with students who are preparing for full-time work within the LCMS." In a concisely constructed response, the CTCR determined that, in cases where the description of such a teaching position does not require that the teacher be clergy, a layman or a laywoman may serve as a teacher of theology.[158]

Alvin Barry, too, was asked to comment on the proposed CTCR draft, and his response statement took issue with several aspects of the report. Worried that "the pastoral office could very well be subjected to the 'death of a thousand cuts,'" Barry expressed concern over a whittling down of the functions of the pastoral office. Complaining that the draft "seems to lack a definitive exposition of just what the pastoral office is and what its essential functions are," the president claimed that the CTCR's itemization of the functions of the pastoral office "lacks specificity." (The draft, consistent with the 1985 report, listed four functions of the pastoral office: preaching, leading formal worship services, public administration of the sacraments, and public administration of the office of the keys.) Citing Article XXVIII of the Augsburg Confession, the president included the judging and condemning of doctrine among pastoral duties. Barry also

157. Bohlmann Comments and Questions on the CTCR Draft: "The Service of Women in Congregational Offices," unpublished manuscript, September 23, 1994.

158. CTCR, "The Service of Women in Congregational Offices," first draft, n.d., but distributed to the Council of Presidents in spring 1994.

disagreed with the CTCR's assessment that women might serve on the CTCR itself, as he feels that "the CTCR is in reality an extension of the pastoral office carried out on behalf of the congregations and pastors of the Synod." Finally, he could not accept women as teachers of theology, a position he also considers "part of the function of the pastoral office." Reminding the Commission that "the future of the church depends, under God, upon 'matters of Biblical teaching,'" the synodical president encouraged the CTCR to consider his comments as they prepared their final draft.[159]

Ralph Bohlmann was again asked for his opinion, this time on President Barry's response to the first draft. Finding Barry's memo frankly "weak and worrisome," Bohlmann expressed concern for "our sisters in Christ, if his [Barry's] questionable opinions were given great weight by the CTCR simply because they come from the synodical president."[160] When the final draft of the CTCR report was issued a month later, it was "a little kinder," observes Bohlmann, but the entire question of women's service as teachers of theology had been left out. And for the first time in its history, a minority of the CTCR issued a dissenting opinion, albeit from the "conservative" position. The CTCR had concluded that women might serve as congregational chairs and vice-chairs, but that the office of elder was still to be understood as an adjunct of the pastoral office, and therefore one in which "the functions distinctive to the public exercise of the ministry of Word and sacrament" pertains.[161] Bohlmann contends that there is a blurring of terms which leads to much of the confusion around the role of elder. The problem centers on the scriptural use of "elder" in the New Testament, a use that should not, in his opinion, be used to refer to a lay office. Attempts to conflate the early church offices into contemporary categories of clergy and lay does not help in the determination of what the appropriate service of women might be. This lack of clarity is problematic for the church, whose doctrine of ministry argues a single pastoral office assisted by auxiliary offices created by the congregation as

159. Memorandum, A. L. Barry to CTCR, August 25, 1994.

160. Ralph Bohlmann, "A Brief Analysis of President Barry's 'Observations on the CTCR Draft Document' on the Service of Women," unpublished manuscript, October 3, 1994.

161. CTCR, "The Service of Women in Congregational and Synodical Offices," November 1994.

needed. The biblical model appears to present a more multilayered model of ministry. Bohlmann asks which it will be, reminding the CTCR that "we can't have it both ways."[162]

The five dissenting members of the Commission, all professors of theology, objected to procedural issues, claiming the majority had acted in haste and overridden its own usual processes. More significant was their complaint that "the present report challenges the repeated and historic position of the Synod regarding the service of women." Disturbed over the majority's "refusal to include the order of creation as a guiding concept in its argument," the minority urged further study.[163]

The majority came to its own defense in the workbook of reports prepared for the July 1995 synodical convention. Some in the synod were so upset over the CTCR report that they called for its dissolution. Forty overtures, or proposed resolutions, were submitted to the convention that directly referred to the woman question in the synod. Because the definition of the pastoral office is unclear, so is the definition of what constitutes support of the pastoral office. It should be no surprise that the question of women's service was again sent back to the Commission for study.[164] Ralph Bohlmann finds the whole matter distasteful:

> Missouri doesn't know how to conduct theological discussions anymore. We just don't. You simply assume apparently that if people are raising questions about our history, tradition or our usual interpretation, that they are disloyal, wild, trying to lead us into some abyss. And that's too bad.[165]

And he suggests that some of what is going on in the church today is related to its relatively recent contentious past: "We had our belly full of [controversy] in the 60s and 70s and people were doing almost anything to prevent arguing about anything. What we have to learn through all of this is something about Christian discourse." Bohlmann admitted that he has become "a lot less dogmatic" of late, and while he

162. Bohlmann, Comments and Questions, 10.
163. CTCR, "Dissenting Opinion on Women in Congregational Offices," November 1994.
164. Missouri Synod, *Proceedings*, 1995, Resolution 3-06.
165. Bohlmann interview.

still thinks scripture prohibits the ordination of women, he notes that he said "think. . . . There's a lot more gray than I ever imagined."[166]

Despite fears that Alvin Barry would discontinue the President's Commission for Women, the new president of the synod instead enlarged the PCW. The Commission in 1993 was tasked by Barry to "focus on those issues in our society and culture which impact the lives of the women of our church." Specific issues to be addressed included "sexual harassment and discrimination; sexual violence and abuse; marriage, divorce and death of spouse; abortion and other 'life' issues; women in the workplace and at home; and feminism and the 'women's movement.'"[167] Again the women were given "women's issues" to study, which kept them marginal to, if not completely removed from, the CTCR debate over women's service in the church. But as important is the synod's failure to recognize that the issues affecting its members are not gendered matters, but issues belonging to the whole church.

"What's a Bright Girl Like You Doing in a Church Like This?"

This question, posed humorously by a member of the President's Commission on Women to a young woman church worker during a PCW interview,[168] nevertheless presents a serious challenge to even the reluctant feminists in The Lutheran Church–Missouri Synod.

The increasing polarization between liberals and conservatives in many American denominations, particularly in the last two decades, has been well documented by sociologists of religion.[169] Reflective of an ideological disagreement embracing Americans at large over socioeconomic issues, questions of personal morality, and the limits of government intervention, the division is evident not only among Lutherans in general, but yet again within the synod whose conservative

166. Bohlmann interview.

167. LCMS *Reporter* 19 (January 18, 1993): 1.

168. Nemoyer interview.

169. Robert Wuthnow, *The Struggle for America's Soul: Evangelicals, Liberals, and Secularism* (Grand Rapids: Wm. B. Eerdmans Publishing Co., 1989); Wuthnow, *The Restructuring of American Religion: Society and Faith Since World War II* (Princeton: Princeton University Press, 1988).

takeover in 1969 quickly forced the hands of many of the more moderate voices in the church.

The "great Lutheran civil war" of the 1970s was a result of the polarization of the Missouri Synod, but it did not result in a complete purge of progressive voices. How else does one explain the persistent resolutions supporting the ordination of women presented to each synodical convention since the secession of the Association of Evangelical Lutheran Churches in 1976? Significantly, in 1989 there were more requests for renewed study on the issue of women's service in the church than calls for limitation on the basis of gender. Indeed, what is clear is the dissatisfaction of lay people, both progressive and conservative, with the response of the CTCR to women's issues. The confusion in Missouri is made both more and less muddy with the realization that significant theological issues of the synod can only be decided by a majority vote of convention delegates.

The Missouri Synod's public position on the ordination of women over the past twenty-five years has deteriorated from cooperative study to coopted silence. Perhaps the issue was really settled once and for all in 1970, when two of the three church bodies who had studied the question began to ordain women and Missouri did not. Many of the participants in the joint efforts toward Lutheran unity believed this was a defining moment at the time, and speak of Missouri's unwillingness to move from a given point or deal with an issue, its "foreclosure of imagination," its resistance to change.[170] The official actions of the synod on women's issues in the years since 1970 have given those comments further plausibility. Not only has the synod repeatedly restated its opposition to the ordination of women in convention, but the creation of both the Task Force on Women and the President's Commission on Women have reinforced Missouri's position on and attitude toward women. What might have been opportunities for serious study of the biblical references to women were foiled by the synodical prescriptions on woman's role — no redefinition of terms was allowed; exploration of alternative terminology was dismissed; women were invited to join in a game whose rules the men had already set.

That the women who participated in the advisory ad hoc groups appointed since 1973 played a role as unwitting partners in the synod's dogged resistance to even discuss women's ordination does not dimin-

170. Reumann transcript, p. 133.

ish their valuable contributions on the Task Forces and Commissions. The slow but steady progress in the inclusion of women on boards and committees at all levels of the church would not have been accomplished without the lobbying of the Task Force, for example. Nevertheless, women's presence in the synodical bureaucracy has been paradoxical. While providing service of positive value through their many tangible accomplishments, they have simultaneously provided synodical leaders a cover, giving the appearance that issues of substance were being addressed. If they were unaware of the part they were playing, the frustration of which they speak suggests that they were not entirely comfortable collaborators. Yet in their service to women they themselves reinforced women's silence. And it is the silence of women that has been called for most loudly, as the unofficial conservative weekly *Christian News* did when it responded to the 1986 PCW report not by reporting its findings, but by arguing that the synod should reverse its position on woman suffrage:

> Rarely have the social attitudes of the day clashed so directly with the traditional teaching of the church than on the role of women in the family and in the church. . . . Sometimes the times are wrong. Even a great church body like the Lutheran Church–Missouri Synod can make a mistake. . . .[171]

Despite the hopes of such conservatives, feminists who claim to see disparity between practice and preaching will continue to raise issues and ask for dialogue, and conservative churches like the Missouri Synod will find it increasingly difficult to defend sexist practices in scriptural terms or on the basis of synodical authority. Martin Marty, ex-veteran of Missouri, believes that the synod will have "a harder and harder time making sense of the exclusion," suggesting that Missouri is holding onto the ordination issue because it remains one of the clear "symbols of the revolution" that split Lutherans in the 1970s, and therefore gives the synod its distinctive identity.[172]

Oscar Wilde once said that a problem is not a problem if nobody is talking about it. It could be argued that the consistency of the Missouri Synod's public position against the ordination of women since

171. Rolf Preus, "Women in the Church," *Christian News* 24 (June 9, 1986): 21-22.

172. Martin E. Marty, letter to author, January 8, 1991.

1970 reflects a general consensus among the synod's members on the issue. Or it could be argued, as has been suggested here, that the synodical administration has enhanced its public position with a pretext of ongoing study of women's issues, including a significant amount of work done by women themselves. Conspicuous by its absence in all this study is the issue no one is talking about — the ordination of women to the ministry. To Missouri's leadership, that only proved it wasn't a problem in the first place.

But it is being talked about. Once hesitant voices are gaining strength and speaking aloud to the issue within the Missouri Synod. The first organized voices have been those of women, since charges of false doctrine and threats of litigation loom before pastors and professors who challenge the old line. In October 1989 a free conference called "Different Voices, Shared Vision" was held in St. Paul, Minnesota. The primary force behind this effort was Marie Meyer, who as a member of the first President's Commission on Women thought that the PCW had not gone far enough in its report to present a positive image to Missouri's women.[173] Interested in engaging the synod in dialogue on the portions of scripture most often used to defend synodical practice, the activists — now known as Voices/Vision — continue to lobby to gather support among both men and women in the synod through a newsletter and occasional conferences and workshops. The women are repeatedly vilified by the ultraconservative *Christian News* as the radical feminists of the Missouri Synod whose hidden agenda is the ordination of women.

Ralph Bohlmann observes how "the women on Missouri have been so exceedingly gracious and kind" about the synod's rigidity, when they could have been "angry and militant."[174] But some are losing patience, as was reflected in letters to the editor of the *Lutheran Witness* in response to a 1990 article entitled, "'Why *Can't* Women Be Pastors?'" Several writers spoke of Missouri's inflexible application of scripture and its offensiveness towards women, and one man wrote simply to thank the *Witness* for the article, as it had helped him make the decision to leave the synod.[175]

173. Meyer interview.
174. Bohlmann interview.
175. Dirk van der Linde, "'Why *Can't* Women Be Pastors?'" *Lutheran Witness* 109 (April 1990): 4-5, and reader response, July 1990, pp. 18-19.

Yet the women of Missouri themselves present the greatest obstacle to change. The structure of the synod allows for a broad range of experience, since local congregational autonomy is its guiding principle. And one's sense of community in her local congregation is usually far more important to the individual woman than synodical dictates or loyalty. There is still no organized community for either women or men outside the official auxiliaries. The Lutheran Women's Missionary League, official women's auxiliary of the synod, concentrates its efforts on a wide variety of mission efforts, but does not seek to advocate for women. Given the opportunity to take a position on the ordination question at its February 1991 Board of Directors meeting, when presented with two resolutions repudiating women's ordination, the LWML Executive Committee recommended against the Board of Directors taking any action. Discussion was curtailed by the president's explanation that ordination was a political question, and the LWML desires to remain apolitical.[176] As long as the synod continues, as in this instance, to frame theological issues as politics, it will remain confounded and unable to adequately address questions on which its congregations repeatedly call for clarification, such as women's service to the church, the pastoral office, and scripture.

Conclusion

Where the ordination of women has taken place in Protestant denominations in America since the mid-twentieth century, it has been a result of each church body reconsidering its previous historic prohibition of women in public ministry in light of sociocultural changes.[177] As Lutherans followed the same process, they looked to the source of Lutheran teaching, scripture and the confessional standards of expositing scripture, in search of an answer to the question — May women be ordained to the ministry of Word and sacrament? The summary conclusion of the study conducted by a subcommittee of the Division of Theological Studies of LCUSA was that scripture was inconclusive in

176. Minutes, ILWML Board of Directors, February 1-4, 1991, p. 13.
177. See, e.g., J. Gordon Melton, *The Churches Speak on: Women's Ordination. Official Statements from Religious Bodies and Ecumenical Organizations* (Detroit: Gale Research Inc., 1991), and Mark Chaves, *Ordaining Women: Culture and Conflict in Religious Organizations* (Cambridge, Mass.: Harvard University Press, 1997).

answering the question. While the theologians agreed that biblical references had been one basis for the exclusion of women from ordained ministry, they noted that scriptural injunction had not been the sole basis, and that "long-standing and inherited custom [and] sociological and psychological factors" had also contributed to the ban. The study left the question open: "No one argument or set of arguments settles the matter clearly one way or another." Therefore, "there are no conclusive grounds for forbidding the ordination of women and no definitive ones for demanding it."[178] While never using the word, the theologians concluded that the ordination of women was an *adiaphoron,* "a thing that makes no difference," just as the rigidly conservative Matthias Flacius had argued in the Adiaphoristic Controversy four centuries earlier.

Has Flacius' preference (but not insistence) — that men preach rather than women — become by virtue of long practice the church's custom? And is it to preserve tradition that the Missouri Synod's appeal to a verbally inerrant scripture is required? Arthur Carl Piepkorn, the synod's foremost authority on the Lutheran confessions, while participating in Lutheran dialogue with Roman Catholics in the early 1970s, argued forcefully that, as a church reviews its historic practice,

> The sacred scriptures do not provide an absolute guide to the rightness of a particular decision. Indeed, it is frequently their silence or the (at least apparent) ambiguity of the evidence that they do provide which necessitates a decision by the church or the church's leadership.[179]

Piepkorn's use of the "absolute" reflects his concern over an unconditional approach to the use of scripture that he believed denies the validity of historical development. Thus, he notes the importance of the category *adiaphoron* for those practices or customs that may be appro-

---

178. Protocol document, Report of the Subcommittee on the Ordination of Women, March 7-8, 1969, adopted by the Standing Committee, Minutes, March 7-8, 1969.

179. Arthur Carl Piepkorn, "*Ius Divinum* and *Adiaphoron* in Relation to Structural Problems in the Church: The Position of the Lutheran Symbolical Books," in *Papal Primacy and the Universal Church,* Lutherans and Catholics in Dialogue V, ed. Paul C. Empie and T. Austin Murphy (Minneapolis: Augsburg Publishing House, 1974), p. 125.

priate at one point in the history of "an essentially conservative institution like the church,"[180] but not necessarily for all time.

Theodore Graebner, one of the synod's most prolific writers as co-editor of the *Lutheran Witness* from 1918 to 1948, was also the church's staunchest defender of "the Scriptural concept of *adiaphora*," without which "the Gospel itself [is] perverted into a system of legalistic propositions."[181] Graebner was primarily concerned that the church retain the use of *adiaphora* in light of Missouri's insistence on full doctrinal agreement prior to fellowship, so that arbitrary differences in local practice did not become obstacles to union. But his broader application of *adiaphora* appeals for tolerance in the church: "Let us not make more sins than there are."[182] What matters, Graebner repeatedly invoked, is whether or not an issue is an article of saving faith. Maintaining a practice that is not essential to salvation because it is tradition, he held, is contrary to the principle of *sola scriptura*. Graebner held firmly to the Missouri teaching that there were no open questions of doctrine, but still cautioned against the elevation of what is rightly an adiaphorous issue to a level of confessional doctrine simply because it is "urged so insistently." Instead, he argued, "What is demanded is a much closer study of Scripture itself and the definite proof that something is against Scripture before we call it wrong."[183]

The Missouri Synod nevertheless chose to disagree with the findings of the DTS study, giving as its reason an unhappiness over the way scripture had been used by the scholars who studied the question. Had the leadership of the synod not so recently changed from the moderate Oliver Harms to the conservative Jacob Preus, the synod's response at the Dubuque consultation might have been less resolute. Missouri was surely not ready, having only just agreed to woman suffrage in its congregations, to welcome women into its seminaries and eventually its pulpits, but the synod might have been willing to explore further the underlying question of the ministry. And, while even the moderates in the synod tended to limit theological discussions to the clergy, there is a chance the laity might have learned of the discussions and asked to become involved.

180. Piepkorn, *"Ius Divinum* and *Adiaphoron,"* p. 125.
181. Theodore Graebner, *The Borderland of Right and Wrong,* 4th enl. ed. (St. Louis: Concordia Publishing House, 1938), p. iii, Preface to the Third Edition.
182. Graebner, *The Borderland of Right and Wrong,* p. 99.
183. Graebner, *The Borderland of Right and Wrong,* p. 71.

Since C. F. W. Walther wrote the first issue of *Der Lutheraner* in 1844, the synod has proclaimed itself the voice of confessional Lutheranism in America. To be truly confessional one could argue that the Missouri Synod must acknowledge the ordination of women to be an *adiaphoron,* a matter of evangelical freedom. Were that the case, under the synod's congregational polity, the decision whether to ordain a woman would be local, as it is in the Southern Baptist Convention. Yet that is not the sort of congregationalism the synod practices. Instead, hundreds of independent enclaves do more or less what they please depending on the theological positions of pastor and people, all loosely held together by an intentionally advisory, decentralized synod whose doctrinal positions are subject to majority vote in triennial convention.

No matter how circuitously Missouri tries to avoid it, the issue of the ordination of women remains. Three factors are at stake — the synod's understanding of scripture, of the pastoral office of ministry, and of women. Continuing to insist on a verbally inspired literal interpretation of the Bible will not suffice indefinitely. Yet the prohibition of women from the pastoral office remains the synod's most visible commitment to its stand on inerrancy, and inerrancy in turn serves, in sociologist Mark Chaves's term, as a "symbolic connection" to a more general posture of antimodernism.[184] To support its scriptural position on the service of women to the church, the synod relies on the "order of creation," but that reliance has led the synod to accept a more Calvinistic than Lutheran understanding of the activity of God as Creator. Bolstered by verbally inerrant scriptural evidence, some theologians in the synod have elevated the order of creation to doctrinal status. The church has no original texts of its own on the subject, so Missouri has had to depend on the work of German theologians to prove the rightness of its position. In the 1950s, Albert Merkens introduced the work of the little-known Fritz Zerbst as primary support for retention of the synodical ban on woman suffrage. Following its acceptance of suffrage in 1969 but its parallel rejection of the admission of women to public ministry, the synod arranged for the publication of Peter Brunner's article. Into more recent debate over the service of women, the synod has introduced an article by Jobst Schöne, bishop of

184. See Mark Chaves, "The Symbolic Significance of Women's Ordination," unpublished paper, and "Ordaining Women: The Diffusion of an Organizational Innovation," *American Journal of Sociology* 101 (1996): 868.

Missouri's partner church in Germany, the *Selbständige Evangelische Lutherische Kirche* (SELK).[185] Translated and published at the request of the synodical president's office, Schöne's argument differs little from Zerbst and Brunner in its representation of the "continuing validity" of the order of creation.[186] However, the bishop does pursue an additional line of argument in his emphasis on the maleness of Christ and his apostles and the corresponding image of God that is thereby presented to church and world.[187] The scriptural basis for Missouri's proscriptions on the role of women has been reduced to a narrow and literal use of a few selected texts. The "order of creation" argument simply offers a more sophisticated interpretation of the same texts used in the nineteenth century to define and justify woman's place in both church and society.

The ministry has been a continual subject of study throughout the synod's history, but never from a truly confessional basis. Instead, Walther has always been the starting point. Olive Spannaus, a member of the Task Force on Women, believes that the synod's members perceive the opinions of the advisory-only Commission on Theology as being "carved in concrete," but she finds hope in her observation that "the thing that brought about the change in woman suffrage was not that [the CTCR] looked at scripture in a different way, but that they took another look at what the franchise meant."[188] The DTS study was pointedly clear on the larger issue surrounding the question of the ordination of women — the doctrine and definition of the ministry itself. Spannaus's unspoken analogy suggested that study of the office of the ministry might possibly lead to a reconsideration of who may serve in the pastoral office. The CTCR's inability to adequately define pastoral ministry, at the root of its inability to define offices of pastoral support within the congregation, attests to the fact that the central question might not be about women at all, but about ministry.

On the subject of women, Missouri continues to express its usual ambivalence. The synod's record on women's issues since 1970 has

185. Jobst Schöne, "Pastoral Letter on the Ordination of Women to the Pastoral Office of the Church," *Concordia Theological Quarterly* 59 (1995): 301-16. Male modeling of Christ as a prerequisite to ordination has been a standard Roman Catholic, not Lutheran, argument.

186. Schöne, "Pastoral Letter on the Ordination of Women," p. 313.

187. Schöne, "Pastoral Letter on the Ordination of Women," pp. 307-12.

188. Spannaus interview.

been one of doing the "right" thing. While synodical conventions have consistently reaffirmed the church's theological position that women may not be ordained, in each decade the president of the synod has appointed an ad hoc task force or commission to study the question of women's service to the church. These groups, comprised since 1983 solely of women, have served to suggest to the church at large that the issues of the women of Missouri were being addressed. Yet behind the pretense of studying the issues lay maintenance of the status quo. More significant than the findings of commissions on women, however, is the reliance of the Commission on Theology and Church Relations on the order of creation argument to define woman's place in the church. Division on the CTCR since 1994, in particular the issuance of a conservative minority report that specifically demanded further study of the order of creation, raises questions about the durability of the principle as the basis of the synod's position on women in the church. Additionally, there is increasing dissonance between the theologians' emphasis on the need for a gendered order and the reality of women and men in church and society. Upon learning that the CTCR report based its findings entirely on a timeless order of creation hierarchy, one woman dismissively commented: "Nobody believes that anymore!"[189]

During the twenty-five years since Missouri and the "other Lutherans" agreed to disagree on the ordination of women to the public ministry, the synod has narrowed its position on scripture, restated its original understanding of ministry, and maintained that women are proscribed from ordained ministry by virtue of their subordination under God's timeless order of creation. But also during this period, increasing inconsistency of congregational practice has left the advisory synod unable to provide guidelines that adequately integrate its various positions on scripture, the ministry, and women. The synod maintains that it alone retains the correct teaching, as the Bible forbids women from any exercise of authority over men in the church. Will the issue of women's ordination, currently so central to the identity of the Missouri Synod, continue to distinguish it from other Lutherans in the future? In dealing with cultural change the synod's historic pattern has been its "statement of conservative position, then prudent silence when the position proved too difficult to maintain, and then accommodat-

189. Dorothy Hildebrandt, telephone conversation with author, March 14, 1995.

ing restatement."[190] Its conservative position has been restated over and over again — a combination of institutional orthodoxy and administrative measures designed to avoid the mere discussion of the issue — but Missouri's response to those voices pressing to open dialogue on the issue of the ordination of women will indicate whether the future will be a time of hopeful silence or one of unquestioning insistence on tradition.

190. Carl S. Meyer, ed., *Moving Frontiers: Readings in the History of the Lutheran Church–Missouri Synod* (St. Louis: Concordia Publishing House, 1964), p. 366.

7

The Problem of Authority

A t its 1995 convention, the synod authorized its Board of Directors to study the possibility of changing the name of the church body. Recommendations are to be presented to the 2001 synodical convention.[1] The synod had changed its name before, twice in fact — in 1917 when it dropped the word "German," and again in 1947, on the occasion of its centennial, when it became The Lutheran Church–Missouri Synod. On each of those occasions, the required two-thirds of the synod's congregations voted to accept the change, likely secure that they were doing nothing more than facilitating the business of the church.

But a name change is more than that. It has to do with the very identity of the entity whose name is, for whatever reason, no longer considered adequate. A name is not only that by which we understand ourselves, but how we tell others who we are. So what does it mean that the synod believes it is time to again adjust its identity? And what might it mean to the people who identify with a church curiously known as the Missouri Synod? What, for example, does the average layperson know of the synod and its workings? What loyalty to a name or a heritage impacts a congregation's level of interest, investment, or involvement either locally or beyond its own property? How does a congregation understand itself and its authority over against that of the institutional church, represented as an advisory synod?

1. Missouri Synod, *Proceedings,* 1998, pp. 102-3, referred from 1995.

In an increasingly multicultural and postmodern society, self-definition and identity are essential issues. Names are important as language is important. Attempts to modernize or popularize names created long ago often meet unanticipated resistance, not only because "we've never done it that way before," but because change is threatening and changing one's name cuts to the very core of one's identity. Yet there remains a sense among some in the synod that "many people in this society do not understand the international scope of a church body named 'Missouri' and have little, if any, understanding of the concept of a 'Synod' or the meaning thereof."[2] This claim from an overture to the 1998 synodical convention expresses a belief that the synod's name should reflect what it has become, an international Lutheran church.

Despite its remarkable longevity, the synod is hardly the same church it was at its founding. The difference lies in more than demographics. Missouri began as a transplanted German church in the American midwest that has, over the course of its 150-year history, become a truly American church. Able to retain its distinct identity for the first half of its history — best exemplified by its intentionality about speaking the language of the fathers — in the twentieth century the synod has had to respond to the same forces of change that have impacted the culture at large, the greatest of which has been the increasing diversity in American society. But what today makes Missouri distinct over against other churches? While none is by itself unique to this church body, four interrelated issues remain problematic for the synod: ministry, women, scripture, and church polity. Overarching all is the problem of authority.

The Problem of Ministry

The Missouri Synod is a clergy church. The authority of the church is vested in the office of public ordained ministry. Yet the hierarchy of pastors-then-people remains a curious one. The clergy are members of the synod, laypeople are not. Congregations are members, clergy and commissioned ministers of religion are members, but a layperson has neither voice nor vote except as an elected representative to a conven-

2. Missouri Synod, *Workbook*, 1998, p. 123.

tion. What does this suggest about the relationship between pastors and people in this church body? When laypeople depend too heavily on pastoral leadership, either out of deference for education and position or due to a dominant style and presence, the church becomes the pastors' church and partnership with the people is diminished. Lay leadership and responsibility for doing the work of the church rests in the hands of the very few, and the Lutheran paradox of ministry — wherein some are set apart but all are priests — seems to have been lost. Perhaps history can shed light on how that happened.

The emigrant community that left Saxony for Missouri in 1838 had organized and pledged itself to an episcopal form of governance that depended entirely on the person of the company's leader and bishop, Martin Stephan. Not only was Stephan senior in age to the other clergy in the emigrant band, but his vision dominated the enterprise. The community's commitment to an episcopacy seemed so unquestionable that, even after the expulsion of its leader, there was neither obvious need nor immediate demand that the episcopal structure be discontinued. The primary question was, who would replace Stephan?

Only following the direct challenge by a small group of laymen and the clergy's inability to answer effectively their charges did the vision of doing things differently take shape among the Saxons. Faced with Vehse's eloquent pietist argument for a polity based on the priesthood of baptized believers, the clergy abandoned their pursuit of an episcopacy but not their belief in it. Not until almost two years of crisis and impasse had racked the community did C. F. W. Walther offer a satisfactory defense of the company's continued existence in America as a church, a compromise made possible in the merger of Luther's doctrine of the church with the religious freedom America offered the Saxon Lutherans.

Walther's compromise satisfied the wary laity that they would never again fall under the domination of a clergyman as they had under Stephan and his doctrine of ministry. In response to that experience, the Saxons then developed a guarded clergy-lay relationship within their local congregations. It was through the founding of a synod of like-minded congregations that Walther was able to reclaim for the clergy some of the status and authority they had ceded in Perry County. Though the new synod was to be advisory only, and its representation equally divided between clergy and laity, its leadership with the exception of the treasurer would be clerical. Walther's doctrine of ministry evolved from his careful reconstruction of what remained after Stephan's exile — pastors and people. The solution he arrived at was practical, designed to meet the circumstances in which the Saxons found themselves. And, as long as the synod grew incrementally, in numbers of congregations, a doctrine of ministry that required the call of a congregation was adequate to its needs. Extenuating circumstances, beginning with the question of itinerant preachers, were resolved through appeal to a law of love that prevailed over a legalistic application of regulations. But in the twentieth century, when the synod began to grow institutionally, Walther's doctrine of ministry required adjustment.

In defining the pastoral office as the highest office in the church, Walther placed other offices of ministry, particularly the teaching office, in auxiliary positions. In so doing he also introduced a persistent tension between pastors and teachers as to role and status that has required redefinition of the ministry itself. But in the twentieth century, extenuating circumstances were not so easily met by a law of love when federal law required precise nomenclature regarding teacher and clergy status. Again the church met the exigency by adjusting its terms and thereby its doctrine. And, as women became the majority of the synod's teachers, the question only became more complicated, requiring further adjustment and resulting in not a little confusion. It seems self-evident that the definition of any facilitating or auxiliary office must begin with the definition of its office of origin, the pastoral office. Nevertheless, categories of ministry have been added, removed, and reclassified on a regular basis through convention action, all in response to an inadequate theology of both church and pastoral ministry that began in a pragmatic solution to an extreme situation. And the synod has still not made a comprehensive study of its doctrine of ministry in light of its claim to represent confessional Lutheranism. How can the synod understand itself within the continuity of the church catholic as long as it references its starting point in the nineteenth century? Reliance on such a truncated history imposes further limitations on a church body whose history is already one of self-imposed restrictions and boundaries.

Within the division of labor imposed by the synod's doctrine of ministry on clergy and laypeople, congregations and pastors negotiated leadership and support of the pastoral office. As long as the lay leadership included only men, the uneasy tension between congregational autonomy and pastoral authority was considered normative in the synod. The tension increased, however, when the question of women as voting members of congregations was raised. While male lay participation and leadership in congregations was not only assumed, but central to the synod's understanding of church and ministry, women's desire for participation in equal measure was cast in another light, that of authority and office. The synod's long and protracted debate over woman suffrage is further evidence of its ambivalent doctrine of church and ministry. Before the question of the ordination of women to the public ministry can be addressed by a church body, the question of lay leadership has to be answered.[3] It does not necessarily follow, however, that any request for gender equity in lay participation must be seen as a demand for pastoral office. The synod's conflicted understanding of the distinction between the universal priesthood and the nature of the public pastoral office becomes only further confounded by the gender question.

The Problem of Women

The Missouri Synod is a male church. History again can provide some background. Missouri's nineteenth-century roots, begun in Germany and transplanted to America, reflected the prevailing notion of the times regarding gender roles. Relegated by her biological nature to the domesticity of home and family, woman was praised for her nurturing abilities and her piety. A clearly delineated separation of spheres meant the synod had little reason to concern itself that its women would step outside their place.

And they did not. Only as women in American society began to demand equal rights in the national political process did Missouri theologians express their fears of what "feministic tendencies" might portend. And even then their worries did not translate to fear of a similar demand in the church. But once American women had won the

3. Barbara Brown Zikmund, "Winning Ordination for Women in Mainstream Protestant Churches," in *Women and Religion in America,* vol. 3: *1900-1968,* ed. Rosemary Radford Ruether and Rosemary Skinner Keller (New York: Harper & Row, 1986), p. 340.

right to vote, the synod realized its influence over its women was limited to their involvement within the church. As new opportunities for women began to be introduced in every dimension of society, Missouri recognized a need to more clearly define its position on women's service. It found justification for limitations on women's activities in an "order of creation," which required male headship and female subordination, according to two scriptural texts attributed to the apostle Paul. Applying this principle — "largely a theological attempt to say that biology is destiny"[4] — to service in the church, the synod has repeatedly prescribed limitations on woman by deriving them from her gendered nature.

Yet the order of creation argument retains an ambivalent status within the synod, since it holds primary status for some theologians while not for others. And the reality of women's service within congregations is rarely filtered through the lens of created order, but instead through local practice and need. Still, it is interesting to note that a church body that, ostensibly, in its formative history, rejected a hierarchical model of ministry in defining what ministry was, has now reclaimed that paradigm to say who ministers must be, and thereby to preclude the service of women. Does the synod's resistance to gender equality reflect its attitude toward women, or toward a far larger issue — its resistance to the modernist agenda gender equality represents? Preservation of a rigid gender role structure is a recognized mark of a religious fundamentalism that legitimates its claims on women and the family through an appeal to verbally inspired scriptural texts.[5]

Additionally, women themselves have deferred to the theologians for determination of their status within the synod. The absence of women in the debate over women's service has been striking. No organization of either professional women or lay women has asked that women's voices be represented on the CTCR; no coalitions have been formed to encourage dialogue or to lobby the synod on women's issues. Rather, the ad hoc President's Commission on Women continues to address only the tasks and questions assigned to it by the synodical presi-

4. Alvin John Schmidt, *Veiled and Silenced: How Culture Shaped Sexist Theology* (Macon, Ga.: Mercer University Press, 1989), p. 198.
5. See Helen Hardacre, "The Impact of Fundamentalisms on Women, the Family, and Interpersonal Relations," in *Fundamentalisms and Society: Reclaiming the Sciences, the Family, and Education.* ed. Martin E. Marty and R. Scott Appleby (Chicago: The University of Chicago Press, 1993), pp. 129-50.

dent. Perhaps most significantly, any informal or unofficial groups wishing to raise questions regarding women's status in the church are generally dismissed as troublesome feminists whose questions are interpreted as challenges to Missouri's every authority — scripture, men, and the synod itself.

The question of the ordination of women has as yet been officially addressed only tangentially by the synod. Aside from the participation of a group of four theologians at an inter-Lutheran meeting in 1969, the subject of women in ordained ministry has been neither studied nor debated by the church body. Lack of thorough or informed discussion, however, has not produced a lack of opinion. Positions both pro and con have been stated in letters, articles, and convention resolutions. The events of the 1970s which led to schism in the church left the conservative remnant of the synod — those who were most opposed to the action taken by other Lutherans to ordain women in 1970 — intact and in charge. The synod's firm prohibition of women in public ministry, the symbolic signifier of its position on biblical inerrancy, has been accompanied by the presupposition that there is no need to study a position that will never change. To that end, Missouri has been exempt both from any organized internal pressure and from external or cultural pressure to ordain women. How has the virtual silence on the issue of ordination been interpreted by those in authority? Have presuppositions on the part of the CTCR — the official synodical agency tasked to discuss the service, and thereby the ordination, of women — precluded the possibility that there might be women in the synod who struggle with a sense of calling to the public ministry in a church body that will not affirm that call?

In its 1985 report, *Women in the Church: Scriptural Principles and Ecclesial Practice,* the CTCR addressed this question in one sentence, declaring simply that "such a call is denied to women by 'a command of the Lord,'" though they do not cite where that command might be found.[6] Distinct but not entirely removed from the Lutheran concept of calling, perhaps nothing is more intensely personal than a divine call to the public or pastoral ministry. Since synodical understanding of

6. Commission on Theology and Church Relations, *Women in the Church: Scriptural Principles and Ecclesial Practice* (St. Louis: Concordia Publishing House, 1985), p. 42. No footnote or citation is included to indicate the pertinent scriptural reference.

the ministry ties the office to the external call of a congregation,[7] and does not directly address, but seems to imply, an interior call *(vocatio interna)* from God,[8] there remains a question as to the validity of a woman's perception of a personal call in light of the church's definition of public call. May women be called by God in the same manner as men when they may not be called by the church in the same manner? Is it, then, even appropriate to suggest that women are "called" to ministry when they are members of a church body that denies the office of public ministry to women? Nevertheless, there are women in the Missouri Synod who believe they are called to public ministry, the same conviction with which many men have entered the synod's seminaries.[9]

Since its notorious schism in the 1970s, the church body that retained the banner of the Missouri Synod is at once more conservative and more dogmatic than it had been prior to the troubles. In a church that continues to have no recognized female theological voice, a frequent observation suggests that the church is losing its best and brightest young women due to the synod's strident resistance to reconsider the woman question. For it is not only women who wish to be pastors who are leaving the church, but women who find their church's ban on the ordination of women to be contrary to their own position on women in church and society.[10] To those on the CTCR in particular, the prohibition of women from ordained ministry is a vital issue, one that must be consistently reaffirmed even as the synod tries to accommodate increasingly disparate congregational praxis. John Reumann,

7. C. F. W. Walther, *Church and Ministry: Witnesses of the Evangelical Lutheran Church on the Question of the Church and the Ministry,* trans. J. T. Mueller (St. Louis: Concordia Publishing House, 1987), Concerning the Holy Ministry or the Pastoral Office, Thesis VI.

8. William Arndt, "The Doctrine of the Call into the Holy Ministry," *Concordia Theological Monthly* 25 (1954): 337-52. Arndt considered the inner call a conviction that God wants an individual to be a minister of the Gospel. Because this is a subjective assessment, in and of itself such a call is insufficient without the valid and objective element, the call of a congregation.

9. See Mary Todd, "Unopened Gifts: Women and the Call to Public Ministry in the Lutheran Church–Missouri Synod," *The Cresset* 56 (1993): 4-9.

10. Additionally, the "enduring conservatism" of the synod has led to a "brain drain," as Frederick Luebke notes in the Epilogue to his essay, "The Immigrant Condition as a Factor Contributing to the Conservatism of the Lutheran Church–Missouri Synod," in Luebke, *Germans in the New World: Essays in the History of Immigration* (Urbana: University of Illinois Press, 1990), p. 12.

chairman of the LCUSA joint study on the ordination of women, does not think the church will be able to have it both ways indefinitely:

> Admission of women to ordination cannot help but reshape the ministry itself and ultimately theology. . . . These things have long been undergoing change, and our only alternative is to disfranchise women, bar all recent cultural, social change, canonize the patriarchal society of ages past, and let the "orders of the fall" ride sovereign over God's original will at creation and redemptive impulses in the earliest church.[11]

Hope anticipates a church transformed by actualization of the Gospel message, a church that practices what it preaches.[12] Women who want the church of their heritage to do just that feel a dissonance with their church. Rosemary Radford Ruether describes their dilemma:

> Women seeking ministerial roles are caught between two equally daunting possibilities. Either this tradition is true precisely because it has been continuously taught, enforced, and re-enforced, and therefore aspiration to ministry and existence in the ministry is contrary to God's will and Christ's intention for the church. Or the church has been deeply apostate, denying to women — who have probably been in every age more than the majority of faithful Christians — full membership in the body of Christ and thus full recognition of that equal redemption won them by Christ.[13]

Women who believe they are called to ministry — who Beverly Wildung Harrison calls "uncompromising agents of transformation of the church, in the church"[14] — also believe that they are speaking with a prophetic voice, calling the church to be faithful to the vision of its mission. The presence of such women in the Missouri Synod raises far-

---

11. John H. P. Reumann, *Ministries Examined: Laity, Clergy, Women, and Bishops in a Time of Change* (Minneapolis: Augsburg Publishing House, 1987), p. 124.

12. On hope, see Marie Schroeder, "Issues: Trouble Enough? Women's Ordination," *Missouri in Perspective* 3 (2 August 1976): 5, and Letty Russell, *Household of Freedom: Authority in Feminist Theology* (Philadelphia: The Westminster Press, 1987), pp. 17-28.

13. Rosemary Radford Ruether, "Why I Stay in the Church: Grace in the Midst of Failings," *Sojourners* 23 (1994): 15-16.

14. Beverly Wildung Harrison, "Keeping Faith in a Sexist Church: Not for Women Only," in *Making the Connections: Essays in Feminist Social Ethics,* ed. Carol S. Robb (Boston: Beacon Press, 1985), p. 231.

reaching questions. What does the synod teach its children and youth about its doctrine of ministry? Does the synodical stance on a verbally inerrant scripture not translate to the use and teaching of scripture in the local congregation? What degree of loyalty, if any, do pastors and their congregations hold to the synod's identity as defined by its positions on scripture and women? At what level of the church is the resistance to female clergy really rooted, synodical commission or local parish? Does the congregational polity of the synod — in which varying degrees of women's service are permitted depending on local practice — contribute to a woman's perception that her church does not mean what it officially says? If the inconsistency of congregational practice means that the synod is composed of six thousand individual enclaves, each following its own understanding of adherence to synodical policy, what, then, is the church, and what good an advisory-only synod?

Women are neither seeking to exercise authority over men nor willing to deny what they believe is a calling from God to serve in public pastoral ministry. Authority, however, remains central in the synod's perception of the problem, because a woman in the pastoral office would have to exercise authority, and the synod says women may not exercise authority over men. By what authority do women claim a call to ministry, a call they consider authoritative in itself, when the synod, according to its doctrine of ministry, denies them recognition of the call as transmitted from God through a congregation? The challenge a woman faces is therefore in the choice she makes in response to her sense of call and to the dissonance in her church body between the gender inclusivity of the Gospel and the reality of synodical praxis.

Unfortunately, the silence of women's voices on the subject of women in ordained ministry until now has been misunderstood as absence of women's voices on that subject, in which case it must be asked whether authority is conceptualized in the synod so that female voices are excluded from it.[15] The inclusion of women's voices introduces a genuine challenge to the church. Feminist theory would argue that women's stories, because women are "authors of their own lives," are authoritative in and of themselves, and are to be taken seriously.[16] Authority so under-

15. Kathleen B. Jones, "On Authority: Or, Why Women Are Not Entitled to Speak," in *Feminism and Foucault: Reflections on Resistance,* ed. Irene Diamond and Lee Quinby (Boston: Northeastern University Press, 1988), p. 120.

16. See, e.g., Personal Narratives Group, ed., *Interpreting Women's Lives: Feminist Theory and Personal Narratives* (Bloomington, Ind.: Indiana University Press, 1989).

stood provides a foundation for women's agency in making decisions and taking initiative.[17] Indeed, the validity of women's experience is foundational to feminist theology,[18] which describes authority in terms of partnership, relationship, and mutuality in contrast to the usual hierarchical or vertical sense of authority.[19] Given all this, how, then, are we to understand the authority and the reality of women's lives?

Is any reconciliation or common ground possible or even likely in what appears to be a hopeless standoff between two polarized notions of authority and their very different meanings for this church body? While agreeing on the authority of scripture, women called to ministry and the theologians of the church disagree on where that authority is vested, in the literal reading of proscriptive Pauline passages or in a holistic reading of the Gospel. While agreeing on the divinity of the call, they disagree as to whether woman by her ontological nature is capable of receiving a call from God. While agreeing that the office of public ministry is an office of service, they disagree on the meaning of authority in servanthood, and the locus of that authority. Women's desire to serve reflects an understanding of the place of the ordained minister as one "set in the midst of the faithful community," a model that differs from the usual reference to clergy as "set apart."[20]

Until and unless the Missouri Synod reverses its prohibition on women in public ministry, the presence of women who believe they are called to such ministry raises a challenge not only to the church's theo-

17. Ann Kirkus Wetherilt, *That They May Be Many: Voices of Women, Echoes of God* (New York: Continuum, 1994), pp. 56-58.

18. Rosemary Radford Ruether, *Sexism and God-Talk: Toward a Feminist Theology* (Boston: Beacon Press, 1983, 1993), pp. 12-16; Pamela Dickey Young, *Feminist Theology/Christian Theology: In Search of Method* (Minneapolis: Fortress Press, 1990), ch. 3; Russell, *Household of Freedom,* pp. 29-36. For the classic critique of the use of masculine experience as normative in theology, see Valerie Saiving, "The Human Situation: A Feminine View," in *Womanspirit Rising: A Feminist Reader in Religion,* ed. Carol Christ and Judith Plaskow (San Francisco: HarperCollins, 1979, 1992), pp. 25-42.

19. Karen L. Bloomquist, "We as Ministers, Amen!" in *Women in a Strange Land: Search for a New Image,* ed. Clare Benedicks Fischer, Betsy Brenneman, and Anne McGrew Bennett (Philadelphia: Fortress Press, 1975), p. 72; Fran Ferder and John Heagle, *Partnership: Women and Men in Ministry* (Notre Dame: Ave Maria Press, 1989); and Russell, *Household of Freedom.*

20. Barbara Brown Zikmund, "Ordination from the Woman's Perspective," in *We Belong Together: Churches in Solidarity with Women,* ed. Sarah Cunningham (New York: Friendship Press, 1992), p. 88.

logians but also to the church's understanding of public ministry itself. The words of the indomitable M. Carey Thomas in 1901 depict that challenge:

> You may say you do not think that God intended a woman to be a bridge-builder. You have, of course, a right to this prejudice; but as you live in America, . . . you will probably not be able to impose it on women who wish to build bridges.[21]

The Problem of Scripture

The Missouri Synod is a biblical church (though some today would instead say biblicist). Synodical theologians' reliance on the order of creation depends on a particular interpretation of scripture, and it is in this regard that the synod has in the late twentieth century frequently been accused of having adopted common cause with fundamentalism. Sometimes the charge comes from its own clergy, as in the case of one pastor who suggested that his synod was "becoming a Protestant fundamentalist church with a Lutheran face."[22] The literature on fundamentalism, however, tends to see the Missouri Synod as an anomaly because of its confessional stance, its ethnicity, its sacramentalism, and its high regard for the ministry. The issue on which Missouri and fundamentalists converge is their agreement on a verbally inspired and inerrant scripture.

Lutherans have historically argued over interpretation of the Lutheran confessions far more than they have over the authority of scripture. Unlike the running battle in the Southern Baptist Convention since the mid-twentieth century, conflict in Missouri over the proper way to interpret scripture led in the 1970s to synodical schism.[23] There would be — indeed, because those in power determined there could be

21. M. Carey Thomas, "Should the Higher Education of Women Differ from that of Men?" *Educational Review* 21 (1901): 1-10. Quoted in Barbara M. Cross, ed., *The Educated Woman in America: Selected Writings of Catharine Beecher, Margaret Fuller, and M. Carey Thomas* (New York: Teachers College Press, 1965), p. 148.

22. Martin R. Noland, "Comprehending Missouri's Dissent: Holding Fast to Grace," *Lutheran Forum* 23 (1989): 18.

23. For Missouri's experience in a comparative context, see Edwin S. Gaustad, "The Bible and American Protestantism," in *Altered Landscapes: Christianity in America, 1938-1985,* ed. David W. Lotz (Grand Rapids: Wm. B. Eerdmans Publishing Co., 1989), pp. 209-25.

— no coexistence between Missourians who insisted on a verbally inerrant Bible, and Missourians, also theologically conservative, who worried about requiring and binding adherence to verbal inerrancy. An observer of the Baptist struggle notes that "the affirmation of the inerrancy of any body of literature generates pressure to generate a *second* source of inerrancy, namely, the interpreter of the first source."[24] In Missouri's case, the synod had ascribed that role to itself, thereby narrowing not only its doctrine of scripture but the confessional subscription on which it was founded.

In its dependence on the repetition of selective ("proof") texts to support its proscriptions on women's service, Missouri further aligns itself to a fundamentalist use of scripture.[25] Such citation of authoritative texts thereby becomes a means of ending discussion, because of the authority inherent in the phrase, "Thus says the Lord . . . ," which inhibits alternative viewpoints. When the literal reading of scripture becomes a doctrine, those who refuse to accept the literal text verge on unbelief if not heresy. The Lutheran confessions, on the other hand, call for "an interpretation which rests on the total testimony rather than on isolated texts."[26] Not only, then, is proof-texting opposed to a confessional stance, but appeal to a biblical literalism relieves the laity of its responsibility for biblical literacy through an ongoing, reflective study of scripture and the perspective offered in the confessional writings. Coupled with an ahistorical sense of the synod's past, the identity of the church is then shaped by those theologians who require uncritical obedience to orthodoxy as they speak it, and a laity that prefers to defer to clerical authority so long as that authority does not challenge an Americanized, populist, and naive view of "the Bible." Additionally, the synod's insular identity amid a pluralistic religious landscape further isolates the church.

24. Joe E. Barnhart, "What's All the Fighting About? Southern Baptists and the Bible," in *Southern Baptists Observed: Multiple Perspectives on a Changing Denomination,* ed. Nancy Tatom Ammerman (Knoxville: The University of Tennessee Press, 1993), p. 134.

25. On patterns of fundamentalist use of scripture, see Kathleen C. Boone, *The Bible Tells Them So: The Discourse of Protestant Fundamentalism* (Albany: State University of New York Press, 1989), especially her discussion of fundamentalist preference for Pauline rather than Gospel texts, chapter 4.

26. Theodore G. Tappert, "The Word of God According to the Lutheran Confessions," in *The Maturing of American Lutheranism,* ed. Herbert T. Neve and Benjamin A. Johnson (Minneapolis: Augsburg Publishing House, 1968), p. 67.

Is the synod's Stephan-era legacy of pietism, with its accompanying separatist and biblicist tendencies, a contributor to its fundamentalist leanings? What role does the heritage of theological intolerance begun with the seventeenth-century dogmaticians and carried on by Walther and Pieper contribute to a church body whose theology is expressed in absolute terms? In the early twentieth-century controversy between modernists and fundamentalists, the synod chose not to take sides, though leaning toward the fundamentalist position. Does Missouri still reject the fundamentalist label, and if it were to claim it, at what risk?

The Problem of Polity

The Missouri Synod is a congregational church. But what does that mean to the current observer of the state of the church? Russell Richey has identified two competing forces in the denominations of American Protestantism at the end of the twentieth century, forces more fundamental even than Robert Wuthnow's classic liberal-conservative demarcation. Richey locates the more basic fissure between the denominational structure and its congregations, especially in the case of larger parishes:

> Congregations increasingly chart their own courses. Less preoccupied with denominational identity and less impressed with denominational delivery systems, congregations, particularly those with sufficient resources to function independently . . . behave like consumers. . . .
>
> At the other extreme, and partly in response to denominational consumerism or indifference, can be found an exaggerated denominationalism. . . . Adherence to denominational practice and structure attests or tests denominational integrity.[27]

In the Missouri Synod, Richey's "hyperdenominationalism" is evidenced formally by repeated convention resolutions in which the syn-

27. Russell E. Richey, "Denominations and Denominationalism: An American Morphology," in *Reimagining Denominationalism: Interpretive Essays,* ed. Robert Bruce Mullin and Russell E. Richey (New York: Oxford University Press, 1994), pp. 89-90.

odical position on various doctrines and practices is reaffirmed, coupled with informal demands that erring congregations cease and desist in practices that are at variance from declared policy. Yet inconsistency in local practice is inherent in the synod's polity that guarantees independent and autonomous locally sovereign congregations. A congregation may resist synodical pressure to conform by simply ignoring it. The result of this paradox is a sadly schizophrenic character that has really never been examined since the synod adopted this governance model. Like father, like son — as the synod eschewed the larger religious vista, some of its congregations have behaved in similar fashion. Whether choosing to reject synodical demands for conformity or simply distancing themselves from the synod's endemic theological conflict, these congregations function largely as private enclaves only loosely affiliated with the church body, practicing what sociologist R. Stephen Warner calls "de facto congregationalism."[28]

Evidence of Warner's "de facto congregationalism" in the Missouri Synod is found in the vastly disparate levels of activity in which women are involved — from not being allowed in the chancel except to prepare the altar for worship, to serving as worship assistants, communion servers, and lectors; from being elected congregational officers and board chairs to not being allowed voting privilege in congregational meetings.[29] This disparity is no more than the logical result of the synod's polity, which is based on congregational autonomy except in matters of doctrine and conscience. Where the synod and some of its congregations obviously disagree is whether the question of women's service, like the question of admission to the eucharist (known in Missouri as open vs. close/d communion), is a matter of doctrine or *adiaphoron*.

Additionally, variance in congregational practice may go virtually unnoticed as most parishioners have little community with other Mis-

---

28. R. Stephen Warner, "The Place of the Congregation in the Contemporary American Religious Configuration," in *American Congregations,* vol. 2: *New Perspectives in the Study of Congregations,* ed. James P. Wind and James W. Lewis (Chicago: The University of Chicago Press, 1994), pp. 73-78.

29. See Randall Balmer, *Grant Us Courage: Travels Along the Mainline of American Protestantism* (New York: Oxford University Press, 1996), ch. 6. Balmer's interesting account of his visit to a Missouri Synod congregation relates the perspectives of several members on the character of one congregation where women may not vote in parish meetings.

souri Synod Lutherans beyond their own church buildings, and so remain unaware of discrepancy in practice, as well as disconnected from any knowledge or concern over a debate that looms far larger at the synodical level than at the local. Sovereignty of the local congregation has long been the hallmark of Missouri Lutheranism, but has it now been sacrificed to the authority of synod? Particularly worrisome to those who see a move toward centralization in the office of synodical president were resolutions passed on the last day of the 1998 convention — an event the *Christian News* heralded as "the best convention ever"[30] — directing district presidents to "carry out the resolutions of the synod pertaining to public doctrine and practice" and affirming the synodical president's ecclesiastical supervision of those district presidents.[31] In this troubling ecclesiology, what mission holds the church together?

The Problem of Authority

Is the answer to any or all of these issues perhaps in the problematic definition of authority?[32] There are countless questions that must be asked of the concept. What does authority require — obedience? obligation? respect? loyalty? submission? sacrifice? surrender? reverence? consent? hierarchy? accountability? John Diggins argues, based on the etymology of the word, that authority "implies, among other things, the capacity of a power to enlarge itself, grow, expand, initiate action, inspire belief, command allegiance, and authorize the rightness of things."[33] Diggins's positive sense of authority contrasts sharply with an authority defined by conservative theologians as that which, for example, women may not "usurp."

30. Walter Otten, "The Best Convention Ever," *Christian News* 36 (July 27, 1998): 1. In an accompanying caption under a picture of synodical president A. L. Barry, the paper claimed, "The Synodical President is now the most powerful executive officer in Lutheranism. No Lutheran President of any larger Lutheran Church has similar authority."

31. Missouri Synod, *Proceedings,* 1998, 149.

32. See, e.g., Robert McAfee Brown's chapter on "Authority: The Achilles' Heel of Protestantism," in his *The Spirit of Protestantism* (New York: Oxford University Press, 1965), pp. 171-85.

33. John P. Diggins, "The Three Faces of Authority in American History," in *The Problem of Authority in America,* ed. John P. Diggins and Mark E. Kann (Philadelphia: Temple University Press, 1981), p. 22.

Ethicist Philip Turner struggled with the notion of authority in the church in his 1990 Arthur Carl Piepkorn lecture at Gettysburg Theological Seminary, and came to the conclusion that

> what our churches are arguing over . . . is not the authority of Scripture or confessions but over those things to which reference *must* be made when authority is exercised, over their correct interpretation, and over their relative weight in settling disputes.[34]

Turner gets to the core of it. The Missouri Synod's struggle over the locus of authority on theological disputes finds delegate conventions at odds with the Commission on Theology and Church Relations, Commission members at odds with one another over the use of scripture, and congregations looking for definitive guidance from an advisory synod whose preferred approach is to refer questions back to committees and commissions for further study. Amid this confusing structure, more moderate voices challenge what they believe is the synod's heteronomy (defined by Paul Tillich as arbitrariness[35]) — the authority it claims for itself — by claiming an alternative authority, one based on the Gospel.

Even a church whose tradition has been one of difference and isolation from other Christians, as the Missouri Synod has regularly claimed about itself, cannot escape the stresses that impact society at large. So theologian Douglas John Hall does not think churches should be surprised by the crisis of authority in the church today. What has been claimed as authoritative — whether the Bible, tradition, or some sort of church structure — Hall considers to be no more than provisional authorities, authoritative for a limited time only. However, not wishing to deny these authorities, Hall cautions against the church's tendency toward authoritarianism regarding them, at which point "authority becomes an end in itself."[36] Ultimate authority, Hall and Turner agree, belongs only to God. That may seem all too obvious, yet those who act in the name of God, as the institutional church claims, do not always recognize clearly the distinction.

---

34. Philip Turner, "Authority in the Church: Excavations Among the Ruins," *First Things* 8 (December 1990): 29.

35. Paul Tillich, *A History of Christian Thought: From Its Judaic and Hellenistic Origins to Existentialism,* ed. Carl E. Braaten (New York: Simon & Schuster, 1968), p. 289.

36. Douglas John Hall, *Thinking the Faith: Christian Theology in a North American Context* (Minneapolis: Fortress Press, 1989), pp. 427-49.

In 1995, in a national study of the Missouri Synod, the Search Institute reported an underlying theme in the results of their study of 2,300 adults and youth: *"The LCMS's traditional strength in doctrine and beliefs is not being experienced and lived out in the lives of most members in congregations."*[37] Suggesting the need for a "major culture change" within the congregations of the synod, the authors found "an over-emphasis on teaching the core theological beliefs of the church at the expense of effectively challenging people to live their lives as expressions of their faith and beliefs." In imagining a culture shift in which the individual is more actively and less passively involved in his or her faith journey, the report notes that "the concept of authority takes on an added meaning."

Identity and Mission

Much of the problem the Missouri Synod has in defining its identity is the result of a distorted use of its past, reflected in selective recollection and an eclectic use of history.[38] The commonly heard reference in speeches and prayers to "our beloved Synod" is meant to serve as a code by which church members are to remember fondly a seamless and pristine past. But what vision of mission is articulated by this posture?

In the end, a church body begun in withdrawal through emigration remains a Lockean aggregate of individual congregations, each guarding its own boundaries. Calls for conformity in practice rather than for cohesion or coherence in doctrine mark the synod's late twentieth-century identity.

One can also hear frequent description of the synod's posture by outsiders as Missouri's "siege mentality." What is it these conservative Lutherans are so desperate to conserve? Having chosen to limit theological discussion by its stance on verbal scriptural inerrancy, the synod in-

37. Peter L. Benson, Eugene Roehlkepartain, and I. Shelby Andress, *Congregations at Crossroads: A National Study of Adults and Youth in The Lutheran Church–Missouri Synod* (Minneapolis: Search Institute, 1995), p. 31. Emphasis in the original.

38. See the compelling essay by David C. Steinmetz, "The Necessity of the Past," in *Memory and Mission: Theological Reflections on the Christian Past* (Nashville: Abingdon Press, 1988), pp. 17-34. See also Mary Todd, "Hostage to History: The Use and Abuse of History and Memory in The Lutheran Church–Missouri Synod," in *Essays and Reports* 17: 1996 (St. Louis: Lutheran Historical Conference, 1999).

sists it accepts proudly the charge that it is a church of repristination theology, declaring itself "heir to the Reformation principle of *sola Scriptura* and the Reformation's confessional legacy."[39] However, critics who consider repristination theology to be little more than endless restatement of theological proof-texts suggest that the synod has misinterpreted Luther's emphasis on *sola Scriptura* to the exclusion of his parallel focus on faith, *sola fide*. Kent Knutson offered a word of precaution to Missouri ten years before he became president of the American Lutheran Church:

> In repristination theology the . . . substance of theology is centered about the Word, the absolute revelation. Faith is reinterpreted into categories which are completely subservient to this Word principle. Faith is a gift of the Word. It is controlled by the Word from eternity and throughout its perseverance to the end. It is determined by the Word in its entirety. Faith is an entity which exists wholly within the shadow of the absolute. The Word which is at the center and completely in control is the kind of Word that can assume such responsibility. It is a completely divine Word and as such must assume the character of inerrancy and infallibility and in this way elevated to the realm of absolute supernaturalness. Truth is conceived as a golden ring. It cannot be broken at any point or the whole system collapses.
>
> The kind of church concept that arises from this is simple enough. There is no community here, for the Word is in such control that it needs no community for its life. It can exist completely and independently in a book. The relationship of men to truth can and indeed must exist in a one-to-one relationship. Any community that assumes any importance is a threat to this absolute Word, for it would vie with its supremacy and find satisfaction in its own existence, which would lead to a sense of independence. Under these circumstances the pattern of isolation and exclusiveness and possessiveness is understandable. The banner of pure doctrine is hoisted. Biblical criticism, or the idea of change, or suggestions of mutuality in theological interchange and growth would, of course, be enemies of the whole concept. No change in this concept of the church can be expected without a change in the whole approach to the theological enterprise.[40]

39. Quentin F. Wesselschmidt, "Repristination Theology and the Doctrinal Position of The Lutheran Church–Missouri Synod," in *Light for Our World: Essays Commemorating the 150th Anniversary of Concordia Seminary, St. Louis, Missouri,* ed. John W. Klotz (St. Louis: Concordia Seminary, 1989), p. 97.

40. Kent S. Knutson, "The Community of Faith and the Word: An Inquiry

Missouri's "pattern of isolation," to which Knutson refers, earns the synod frequent charges of sectarianism as it engages cautiously in ecumenical activities if not refraining from them completely, justifying its behavior in its historic fear of theological pollution.

Additionally, the "siege mentality" can be observed not only vis-à-vis other Lutherans and other denominations, but within the synod itself. The ultraconservatives who gained the synodical presidency in 1992 have since solidified their control of the so-called praesidium (the president and five vice presidents of synod) in the 1995 and 1998 elections. Hard-line conservatives believe they have by this action restored to the synod its historic theological identity. Others in Missouri disagree, suggesting instead that all they have succeeded in restoring is the legalism of earlier eras. What few would doubt is the return of the polemical rhetoric so characteristic of the synod over much of its history. Ralph Bohlmann lamented this development:

> [C]haracter attacks abound within Missouri . . . mean-spirited propaganda and raw ward politics have become the stock-in-trade of a political network that seeks nothing less than the control of the synod and its structure, or that ends justify means, while lives and ministries are weakened if not destroyed. We seem to be so powerless, perhaps even unwilling, to stop it.[41]

Conclusion

The history of the Missouri Synod records a pattern in which separate entities and ideas have been conflated, resulting in a series of confusions that have not served the church well:

- At first it was Stephan and the church, which left the emigrants wondering whether they even were still a church in the wake of Stephan's exile.
- Through Walther and Pieper's repristinating reliance on the words of earlier theologians, the synod collapsed scripture and

---

into the Concept of the Church in Contemporary Lutheranism" (Ph.D. diss., Columbia University, 1961), pp. 341-42.

41. Ralph A. Bohlmann, "Missouri Lutheranism, 1945 and 1995," *Lutheran Forum* 30 (February 1996): 17.

the Lutheran confessions into one source, rather than under-standing the confessions as the proper explication of scripture.

- When the recitation of Missouri's own church fathers' words was added to those of Luther and the dogmaticians, Theodore Graebner observed that the synod was found to be suffering under the burden of its own infallibility.[42]

- Another of its theologians, Arthur Carl Piepkorn, cautioned Missouri against a dangerous trend in convincing itself that upholding a doctrine of the verbal inerrancy of scripture would "guarantee the orthodoxy of the church."[43]

- Persistent use of the term "Word of God" to refer only to scripture instead of the broader tripartite usage referring to the incarnate Christ, the proclaimed word, and the written word has confounded the synod's confession of *sola scriptura*.

- For half of its history Missouri thought the orthodox Lutheran faith could be preserved only through the German language, thereby deferring both the assimilation of its people and the extension of its mission into the surrounding American culture.

- For all of its history the synod has held that fellowship with other Lutherans requires absolute agreement in doctrine, thereby obviating the possibility of compromises, such as the one over polity in which the synod itself was born.

- Finally, the theologians of the church have collapsed the principle of "order of creation" into its doctrine of ministry, a means by which they have reintroduced the notion of hierarchy that was supposedly sent into exile with Stephan.

To borrow a favorite question of Martin Luther's, *what does this mean?* Where, as the twentieth century turns, does Missouri stand in light of and in relation to its historic claim to be the voice of confessional Lutheranism in America? Are both internal and external observers' charges of sectarianism grounded in anything other than accusation? Are the issues to which Missouri clings in order to define its place on the pluralist spectrum of American religion — the verbal inerrancy

---

42. Theodore Graebner, "The Burden of Infallibility: A Study in the History of Dogma," *Concordia Historical Institute Quarterly* 38 (1965): 88-94.
43. Arthur Carl Piepkorn, "What Does 'Inerrancy' Mean?" *Concordia Theological Monthly* 36 (1965): 591.

of scripture and the prohibition of women from the pastoral office — really matters of Lutheran identity? Is adherence to the fusion of these two principles necessary to this church body's self-definition? And why is the issue of authority so very central to synodical identity and discourse?

Nothing in Missouri's history as an emigrant community that sustained its cultural isolation and delayed assimilation into American society through language retention makes this church body especially unique, for its story is common to many pilgrims who hoped for the unimpeded pursuit of their particular religious goals in the United States. The paradox of Missouri is how its separatist escape from the demands of doctrinal and cultural conformity in Germany has led to the imposition of just such conformity in America, a conformity to the fundamentalist Americanizing of Christianity. Defining itself more often by what it is not than in a positive statement of what the church is, the question remains: Must Missouri always incline to the extreme or is another option possible — a return to a genuine catholic and confessional posture? And how inclusive will its mission and vision be?

APPENDIX

Brief Outline of the Emigration Code[1]

Par. 1. *Confession of Faith*

All the undersigned accept with upright hearts the tenets of the Lutheran faith, as contained in God's Word of the Old and New Testaments, and set forth and confessed in the Symbolical Writings of the Lutheran Church. They therefore accept these writings in their entirety and without any addition. They accept these writings according to the simple sense of their wording, as they have, since their origin, been unanimously and uniformly understood and applied — during the 16th, 17th, and first part of the 18th century by the entire Lutheran Church, and from that time on by all who have not departed from the old, pure, Lutheran faith.

Par. 2. *Emigration — its cause, purpose, and goal*

After the calmest and most mature reflection they find themselves confronted with the impossibility, humanly speaking, of retaining this faith pure and unadulterated in their present homeland, of confessing it, and of transmitting it to their descendants. They are, therefore, constrained by their conscience to emigrate and to seek a land where this faith is not endangered, and where they consequently can serve God

---

1. As translated by Walter O. Forster in *Zion on the Mississippi: The Settlement of the Saxon Lutherans in Missouri 1839-1841* (St. Louis: Concordia Publishing House, 1953), pp. 566-68. The original is in the Saxon Immigration Collection, Concordia Historical Institute, St. Louis, Missouri.

281

undisturbed, in the manner which he has graciously revealed and established, and enjoy undisturbed the unabridged and pure means of grace (which God has instituted for the salvation of all men), and preserve them this unabridged and pure for themselves and their descendants.

> To these means of grace belong primarily: the office of reconciliation in its entire scope and with unrestricted freedom, pure and free divine worship, unabridged and pure preaching of God's Word, unabridged and pure Sacraments, pastoral ministration and the care of souls without let or hindrance.

A land such as they seek is the United States of North America, where complete religious and civil liberty prevails and energetic and effective protection is given against foreign countries as nowhere else in the world. These States they therefore have chosen as the goal, and, indeed, the only goal of their emigration, and consequently as their new home.

Par. 3. *Ecclesiastical and Civil Code*
On the basis of the confession of faith made in Par. 1, and of the purpose of the emigration stated in Par. 2, the undersigned solemnly promise to subject themselves with Christian sincerity and willingness to the ecclesiastical and civil codes which are to be established, as well as to the school code and especially to the system of church discipline to be introduced.

Par. 4. *Place of Settlement*
The place of settlement in the United States of America shall be chosen in one of the Western states: in Missouri or Illinois, or perhaps in Indiana.

Par. 5. *Itinerary*
The city of St. Louis in the State of Missouri, centrally located in all these states and also their commercial center, shall be the immediate goal of the journey. From this city a survey can be made for the site to be selected for the settlement in the afore-mentioned states.
    The port of embarkation in Europe shall be Hamburg, the port of debarkation in the United States of North America, New Orleans, and from there the journey shall continue by river steamer on the Mississippi to the afore-mentioned immediate goal of the journey, St. Louis.

Par. 6. *Purchase of land*

With St. Louis as headquarters, a tract of contiguous land shall be purchased by a committee of the entire body of emigrants, and, after deduction of what must be reserved for church, school, and community, separate plots of this land shall be sold to each individual according to his needs. These lands collectively shall form the township, or area of the city. Each one is at liberty to purchase as much land as he pleases outside the township.

Par. 7. *Assumption of all church and community expenditures for five years*

The undersigned bind themselves for five years jointly to raise all church and community expenditures, as these will be fixed from year to year by a committee to be established by church and community. Each one shall contribute in proportion to his means. These contributions shall be apportioned with Christian fairness and care, partly according to value of the real estate (tax on immovable property), partly according to the amount of the other property and income (tax on movable property). Land which members of the community own outside of the township shall likewise be liable for these expenditures according to a fair proportion.

Par. 8. *Mutual Support*

The undersigned, who solemnly promise to conduct themselves in a Christian manner toward each other at all times, do indeed obligate themselves to mutual assistance and support by word and deed, as is proper among Christians. But in order to avoid misunderstandings, let it be noted that no kind of joint ownership of property shall ever take place or be permitted; rather, each one is and shall remain empowered to make disposition of his private property as he sees fit.

Par. 9. *The Credit Fund*

For temporarily defraying the expenditures necessary for the needs of church, school, and community, to support indigent emigrants through cash advances, and to purchase the afore-mentioned contiguous tract of land, a Fund for Cash Advances, or a Credit Fund, shall be established. Accordingly, the expenses noted will be met with cash advances from this Fund, and for each disbursement which this fund makes, especially also for loans to indigent emigrants, the whole community, as well as the land to be purchased, is surety, however, with the exception of that portion of land which is to be transferred to church and school.

Whatever is left over, after the deduction of all expenses and losses and of that portion of the land to be bought which is to be transferred to church and school (cf. Par. 6), will in due time be distributed among those who deposit money in this Fund, in proportion to the amount of the deposit.

The amount of these deposits, of which the capital of the Fund consists, depends upon the free will of each individual.

Par. 10. *Christian simplicity in all transactions*
In all dealings, in all promises and assurances, Christian simplicity, integrity, and truthfulness must obtain, and therefore all formalities and red tape which are not indispensable shall be avoided.

Par. 11. *Freedom of participation*
The undersigned herewith declare, affirm, and testify before everyone that complete freedom of choice was allowed each one of them either to go along or to stay at home; that no one urged another to haste, but that they rather made it the duty of one another, frequently and thoroughly to consider the matter, and by all means most carefully to weigh all difficulties which might arise; and that, accordingly, each one made his decision with complete freedom and calm consideration, without haste and deliberately.

Stephan's Investiture[1]

Right Reverend Sir,
Beloved Father in Christ,

Your Reverence has, according to the gracious council of God, remained standing as the last, unshakable pillar on the ruins of the now devastated Lutheran Church in Germany, to which all those have clung in the name of the Lord who have still earnestly cared for the right way to salvation, the true Church, and its holy Confessions. Among these there were also 5 servants of God's Word, by whom you were loved and honored as spiritual father, and approached for counsel and judgment in all important matters which pertained to their own welfare or that of their congregations. Accordingly, you have already for a long time occupied the position of a bishop and performed episcopal functions among us. However, this has become even more apparent since the plan, considered according to God's Word, of transplanting the Lutheran Church from Germany to the United States has been put into execution. You have been recognized by all individual congregations and congregation members as the father of all, as highest shepherd of souls, and as leader; without the name of a bishop you have exercised the office of bishop with paternal kindness,

1. As translated by Walter O. Forster in *Zion on the Mississippi: The Settlement of the Saxon Lutherans in Missouri 1839-1841* (St. Louis: Concordia Publishing House, 1953), pp. 288-90. Original is in the Saxon Immigration Collection, Concordia Historical Institute, St. Louis, Missouri.

firmness, justice, care, and wisdom. Now that you are about to step on the soil of America, it becomes urgently necessary that this inner, tacit choice receive external and public expression. We have been instructed by you in many things, and from this instruction an abiding conviction has resulted in us that an episcopal form of polity, in accord with the Word of God, with the Old Apostolic Church, and with our Symbolical Writings, is indispensable. Such a form of polity, in which a greater or smaller number of clergymen are subordinated to a bishop in the government of the Church and form a council with him and under his leadership, is therefore our joint, fervent, and earnest desire. It is also our abiding conviction that the real purpose of our emigration, as it is expressed in Par. 2 of our Emigration Code, can be attained only under a free episcopal form of polity.

In consequence of all this, therefore, we approach you with the reverent, urgent plea: Accept, Reverend Father, also for the future the office of bishop among us, bestowed upon you by God, and grant that we may now already express with this name our unqualified confidence in your fatherly love and pastoral faithfulness toward us, and the assurance of our sincere, complete, and childlike obedience toward you.

We are doing this at the same time in the name of the 4 clergymen who, together with their congregations, have preceded us, in the firm confidence that they fully agree with us in this matter and that we are only expressing what we already heard from them and what you, Right Reverend Sir, if it pleases God, will shortly hear from them personally.

May Jesus Christ, the chief Bishop of all our souls, who has bought His Church with His own blood, hear our prayer for you and permit you, as our leader on the way to eternity, to hold the bishop's staff among us until the most distant limit of your — God grant it — very high old age, for our spiritual and temporal welfare, for the building of the ruined Lutheran Zion, for the blessing of all Christendom, and to the glory of the Triune God, to whom alone be praise and honor in the Church which is in Jesus Christ.

On board the *Olbers,* January 14, in the year of grace 1839.

Otto Herman Walther . . .
Gotthold Heinrich Loeber . . .
Ernst Gerhard Wilhelm Keyl . . .
Carl Ferdinand Wilhelm Walther . . .

Walther's Theses on Church and Ministry[1]

Part One: Concerning the Church

THESIS I

The church in the proper sense of the term is the congregation [*Gemeinde*] of saints, that is, the aggregate of all those who, called out of the lost and condemned human race by the Holy Spirit through the Word, truly believe in Christ and by faith are sanctified and incorporated in Christ.

THESIS II

To the church in the proper sense of the term belongs no wicked person, no hypocrite, no unregenerate, no heretic.

THESIS III

The church in the proper sense of the word is invisible.

---

1. C. F. W. Walther, *Church and Ministry (Kirche und Amt): Witnesses of the Evangelical Lutheran Church on the Question of the Church and the Ministry,* trans. J. T. Mueller (St. Louis: Concordia Publishing House, 1987). Originally published as *Die Stimme unserer Kirche in der Frage von Kirche und Amt,* 3rd ed., 1875.

THESIS IV
It is to this true church of believers and saints that Christ gave the keys of the kingdom of heaven, and it is the proper and only possessor and bearer of the spiritual, divine, and heavenly gifts, rights, powers, offices, and the like that Christ has procured and are found in His church.

THESIS V
Though the true church in the proper sense of the term is essentially [according to its true nature] invisible, its existence can nevertheless be definitely recognized, namely, by the marks of the pure preaching of God's Word and the administration of the sacraments according to Christ's institution.

THESIS VI
In an improper sense Scripture also calls the visible aggregate of all the called, that is, of all who confess and adhere to the proclaimed Word and use the holy sacraments, which consists of good and evil [persons], "church" (the universal [catholic] church); so also it calls its several divisions, that is, the congregations that are found here and there, in which the Word of God is preached and the holy sacraments are administered, "churches" (*Partikularkirchen* [particular or individual churches]). This it does especially because in this visible assembly the invisible, true, and properly so-called church of believers, saints, and children of God is hidden; outside this assembly of the called no elect are to be looked for [anywhere].

THESIS VII
As visible congregations that still have the Word and the sacraments essentially according to God's Word bear the name "church" because of the true invisible church of sincere believers that is found in them, so also they possess the power [authority] that Christ has given to His whole church, on account of the true invisible church hidden in them, even if there were only two or three [believers].

THESIS VIII
Although God gathers for Himself a holy church of elect also where His Word is not taught in its perfect purity and the sacraments are not administered altogether according to the institution of Jesus Christ, if only God's Word and the sacraments are not denied entirely but both

remain in their essential parts, nevertheless, every believer must, at the peril of losing his salvation, flee all false teachers, avoid all heterodox congregations or sects, and acknowledge and adhere to orthodox congregations and their orthodox pastors wherever such may be found.

A. Also in heterodox and heretical churches there are children of God, and also there the true church is made manifest by the pure Word and the sacraments that still remain.

B. Every believer for the sake of his salvation must flee all false teachers and avoid all heterodox congregations and sects.

C. Every Christian for the sake of his salvation is in duty bound to acknowledge and adhere to orthodox congregations and orthodox pastors, wherever he can find such.

THESIS IX

To obtain salvation, only fellowship in the invisible church, to which alone all the glorious promises regarding the church were originally given, is absolutely necessary.

Part Two: Concerning the Holy Ministry or the Pastoral Office

THESIS I

The holy ministry or pastoral office is an office distinct from the priesthood of all believers.

THESIS II

The ministry of the Word or the pastoral office is not a human institution but an office that God Himself has established.

THESIS III

The ministry is not an arbitrary office but one whose establishment has been commanded to the church and to which the church is ordinarily bound till the end of time.

THESIS IV

The ministry is not a special or, in opposition to that of ordinary Christians, a more holy state, as was the Levitical priesthood, but it is a ministry of service.

THESIS V

The public ministry [*Predigtamt*] has the power to preach the Gospel and administer the holy sacraments as well as the power of spiritual judgment.

THESIS VI

   A. The ministry of the Word [*Predigtamt*] is conferred by God through the congregation as the possessor of all ecclesiastical power, or the power of the keys, by means of its call, which God Himself has prescribed.

   B. The ordination of the called [persons] with the laying on of hands is not a divine institution but merely an ecclesiastical rite [*Ordnung*] established by the apostles; it is no more than a solemn public confirmation of the call.

THESIS VII

The holy ministry [*Predigtamt*] is the power, conferred by God through the congregation as the possessor of the priesthood and all church power, to exercise the rights of the spiritual priesthood in public office in the name of the congregation.

THESIS VIII

The pastoral ministry [*Predigtamt*] is the highest office in the church, and from it stem all other offices in the church.

THESIS IX

   A. To the ministry there is due respect as well as unconditional obedience when the pastor uses God's Word.

   B. The minister must not tyrannize the church. He has no authority to introduce new laws or arbitrarily to establish adiaphora or ceremonies.

   C. The minister has no right to inflict and carry out excommunication without his having first informed the whole congregation.

THESIS X

To the ministry of the Word, according to divine right, belongs also the duty [*Amt*] to judge doctrine, but laymen also possess this right. Therefore, in the ecclesiastical courts (consistories) and councils they are accorded both a seat and vote together with the clergy.

A Statement[1]

We, the undersigned, as individuals, members of Synod, conscious of our responsibilities and duties before the Lord of the Church, herewith subscribe to the following statement:

ONE
We affirm our unswerving loyalty to the great evangelical heritage of historic Lutheranism. We believe in its message and mission for this crucial hour in the time of man.
> We therefore deplore any and every tendency which would limit the power of our heritage, reduce it to narrow legalism, and confine it by manmade traditions.

TWO
We affirm our faith in the great Lutheran principle of the inerrancy, certainty, and all-sufficiency of Holy Writ.
> We therefore deplore a tendency in our Synod to substitute human judgments, synodical resolutions, or other sources of authority for the supreme authority of Scripture.

---

1. *Speaking the Truth in Love — Essays related to A Statement. Chicago, Nineteen Forty-Five* (Chicago: Willow Press, n.d.), pp. 7-9. Emphasis in original. Signed and dated September 7, 1945, at Chicago, Illinois.

THREE

We affirm our conviction that the Gospel must be given free course so that it may be preached in all its truth and power to all the nations of the earth.

> We therefore deplore all man-made walls and barriers and all ecclesiastical traditions which would hinder the free course of the Gospel in the world.

FOUR

We believe that the ultimate and basic motive for all our life and work must be love — love of God, love of the Word, love of the brethren, love of souls.
We affirm our conviction that the law of love must also find application to our relationship to other Lutheran bodies.

> We therefore deplore a loveless attitude which is manifesting itself within Synod. This unscriptural attitude has been expressed in suspicions of brethren, in the impugning of motives, and in the condemnation of all who have expressed differing opinions concerning some of the problems confronting our Church today.

FIVE

We affirm our conviction that sound exegetical procedure is the basis for sound Lutheran theology.

> We therefore deplore the fact that Romans 16:17, 18 has been applied to all Christians who differ from us in certain points of doctrine. It is our conviction, based on sound exegetical and hermeneutical principles, that this text does not apply to the present situation in the Lutheran Church of America.
> We furthermore deplore the misuse of First Thessalonians 5:22 in the translation "avoid every appearance of evil." This text should be used only in its true meaning, "avoid evil in every form."

SIX

We affirm the historic Lutheran position concerning the central importance of the una sancta *and the local congregation. We believe that there should be a re-emphasis of the privileges and responsibilities of the local congregation also in the matter of determining questions of fellowship.*

> We therefore deplore the new and improper emphasis on the synodical organization as basic in our consideration of the problems of the Church. We believe that no organizational loyalty can take the place of loyalty to Christ and His Church.

SEVEN

We affirm our abiding faith in the historic Lutheran position concerning the centrality of the Atonement and the Gospel as the revelation of God's redeeming love in Christ.

We therefore deplore any tendency which reduces the warmth and power of the Gospel to a set of intellectual propositions which are to be grasped solely by the mind of man.

EIGHT

We affirm our conviction that any two or more Christians may pray together to the Triune God in the name of Jesus Christ if the purpose for which they meet and pray is right according to the Word of God. This obviously includes meetings of groups called for the purpose of discussing doctrinal differences.

We therefore deplore the tendency to decide the question of prayer fellowship on any other basis beyond the clear words of Scripture.

NINE

We believe that the tern "unionism" should be applied only to acts in which a clear and unmistakable denial of Scriptural truth or approval of error is involved.

We therefore deplore the tendency to apply this non-Biblical term to any and every contact between Christians of different denominations.

TEN

We affirm the historic Lutheran position that no Christian has a right to take offense at anything which God has commanded in His Holy Word. The plea of offense must not be made a cover for the irresponsible expression of prejudices, traditions, customs, and usages.

ELEVEN

We affirm our conviction that in keeping with the historic Lutheran tradition and in harmony with the Synodical resolution adopted in 1938 regarding Church fellowship, such fellowship is possible without complete agreement in details of doctrine and practice which have never been considered divisive in the Lutheran Church.

TWELVE

We affirm our conviction that the Lord has richly, singularly, and undeservedly blessed our beloved Synod during the first century of its existence in America. We pledge the efforts of our hearts and hands to go to the building of Synod as the second century opens and new opportunities are given us by the Lord of the Church.

Bibliography

Concordia Historical Institute (Archives of the LCMS), St. Louis, Missouri

William Frederick Arndt Papers
John W. Behnken Papers
Ralph A. Bohlmann Papers
Theodore Graebner Papers
William Koepchen Papers
Walter A. Maier Papers
Lawrence B. Meyer Papers
J. T. Mueller Papers
J. A. O. Preus Papers
Martin Scharlemann Papers
A. C. Stellhorn Papers
Executive Office Files
Commission on Constitutional Matters Files
Commission on Theology and Church Relations Files
Saxon Emigration Collection
Statement of the Forty-Four Collection

Archives of the Evangelical Lutheran Church in America, Chicago, Illinois

Arthur Carl Piepkorn Papers
Lutheran Council in the USA Collection

BIBLIOGRAPHY

Private Collections

Walter Stuenkel Papers, Committee on Woman Suffrage files
Russell Prohl Papers

Interviews

Robert W. Bertram
Ralph A. Bohlmann
Jean Garton
Richard P. Jungkuntz
David C. Leege
Marie Meyer
Florence Montz
Louise Mueller
Nancy Nicol Nemoyer
Leon G. Rosenthal
Alvin J. Schmidt
Edward H. Schroeder
Olive Wise Spannaus

Archives of Cooperative Lutheranism, Chicago — Oral History Collection

Conrad Bergendoff
Ralph A. Bohlmann
Herbert J. A. Bouman
Richard R. Caemmerer
James R. Crumley
E[dward]. J[ulius]. Friedrich
Alfred G. Fuerbringer
George Harkins
Oliver R. Harms
Harold L. Hecht
William H. Kohn
Fred Kramer
A[dalbert]. R. Kretzmann
Robert E. A. Lee
Selma Mayer
Frederick W. Meuser
Arnold Mickelson
Samuel H. Nafzger
Paul D. Opsahl
Jacob A. O. Preus

Bibliography

Arthur C. Repp
John H. P. Reumann
Martin H. Scharlemann
John H. Tietjen
Roland P. Wiederaenders
Walter F. Wolbrecht

Publications

Der Lutheraner
Lutheran Witness
Lutheran Education
Lutheran School Journal
Lutheran Women's Quarterly
Reporter
Evangelisches-Schulblatt

Reports

LCMS, Committee on Woman Suffrage
LCMS, Commission on Theology and Church Relations
    Woman Suffrage in the Church
    Report on Equal Rights Amendment
    Human Sexuality: A Theological Perspective
    Women in the Church: Scriptural Principles and Ecclesial Practice
    The Ministry: Offices, Procedures, and Nomenclature
    The Service of Women in the Church
    Biblical Revelation and Inclusive Language
LCMS, President's Commission on Women
    God's Woman for All Generations
ELCA, Commission for Women
    Twenty Years after the Ordination of Women: Reports on the Participation of Ordained Women

Minutes

LCMS, Commission on Theology and Church Relations, 1962-1970
LCMS, Task Force on Women, 1974-1977
LCMS, President's Commission on Women, 1983-1986
LCMS, International Lutheran Women's Missionary League, 1986-1991
LCMS, *Proceedings* [convention action and minutes], 1847-1998
LCMS, *Workbook* [reports and memorials to conventions], 1962-1998

Primary Sources: Books and Essays

Baepler, Walter A. *A Century of Grace: A History of the Missouri Synod, 1847-1947*. St. Louis: Concordia Publishing House, 1947.

Baier, Johann Wilhelm. *Compendium Positivae Theologiae, Adjectis Notis Amplioribus*, edited by C. F. W. Walther. St. Louis: Concordia Publishing House, 1879.

Baumgaertner, John, ed. *A Tree Grows in Missouri*. Milwaukee: Agape Publishers, 1975.

Benson, Peter L., Eugene Roehlkepartain, and I. Shelby Andress. *Congregations at Crossroads: A National Study of Adults and Youth in The Lutheran Church–Missouri Synod*. Minneapolis: Search Institute, 1995.

Bente, F. *Historical Introductions to the Book of Concord*. St. Louis: Concordia Publishing House, 1965.

Birkner, H. "Der Lutheraner from 1844 to 1847." In *Ebenezer: Reviews of the Missouri Synod During Three Quarters of a Century*, edited by W. H. T. Dau. St. Louis: Concordia Publishing House, 1922.

Bohlmann, Ralph A. *Principles of Biblical Interpretation in the Lutheran Confessions*. Revised edition. St. Louis: Concordia Publishing House, 1983.

Both, Arthur. "The Missouri Synod and the Buffalo Synod." In *Ebenezer: Reviews of the Missouri Synod During Three Quarters of a Century*, edited by W. H. T. Dau. St. Louis: Concordia Publishing House, 1922.

Bouman, Herbert J. A. "The Ordination of Women and Its Implications for Church Fellowship." LCMS, English District *Proceedings*, 1972.

Brief Statement of the Doctrinal Position of the Missouri Synod. St. Louis: Concordia Publishing House, 1932.

Brunner, Peter. *The Ministry and the Ministry of Women*. St. Louis: Concordia Publishing House, 1971.

Buenger, Theodore. "The Saxon Immigrants of 1839." In *Ebenezer: Reviews of the Work of the Missouri Synod During Three Quarters of a Century*, edited by W. H. T. Dau. St. Louis: Concordia Publishing House, 1922.

Caemmerer, Richard R. *The Church in the World*. St. Louis: Concordia Publishing House, 1949.

Caemmerer, Richard R., and Erwin L. Lueker. *Church and Ministry in Transition*. St. Louis: Concordia Publishing House, 1964.

Concordia Theological Seminary. *A Century of Blessing, 1846-1946*. Springfield, Ill.: Concordia Seminary, 1946.

Danker, Frederick W. *No Room in the Brotherhood: The Preus-Otten Purge of Missouri*. St. Louis: Clayton Publishing House, Inc., 1977.

Dau, W. H. T. *Woman Suffrage in the Church*. St. Louis: Concordia Publishing House, 1923.

Dau, W. H. T., ed. *Ebenezer: Reviews of the Work of the Missouri Synod During Three Quarters of a Century*. Augmented edition. St. Louis: Concordia Publishing House, 1922.

Engelder, Th. "Why Missouri Stood Alone." In *Ebenezer: Reviews of the Missouri Synod During Three Quarters of a Century,* edited by W. H. T. Dau. St. Louis: Concordia Publishing House, 1922.

Engelder, Th., W. Arndt, Th. Graebner, and F. E. Mayer. *Popular Symbolics: The Doctrines of the Churches of Christendom and of Other Religious Bodies Examined in the Light of Scripture.* St. Louis: Concordia Publishing House, 1934.

Evangelical Lutheran Synod of Missouri, Ohio, and Other States. *Synodical Handbook.* St. Louis: Concordia Publishing House, 1924.

Fischer, Ludwig. *Das falsche Märtyrerthum oder die Wahrheit in der Sache der Stephanier. Nebst etlichen authentischen Beilagen [The False Martyrdom or the Truth in the Matter of the "Stephanier" in addition to a Number of Authentic Appendices].* Translated by Fred Kramer (1985). Leipzig: Wilh. Alex. Kuenzel, 1839.

Flacius, Matthias. *Liber de veris et falsis Adiaphoris.* Magdeburg, 1549.

Freitag, Alfred J. *College with a Cause: A History of Concordia Teachers College.* St. Louis: Concordia Publishing House, 1964.

Friedrich, Julius A. "Dr. C. F. W. Walther." In *Ebenezer: Reviews of the Missouri Synod During Three Quarters of a Century,* edited by W. H. T. Dau. St. Louis: Concordia Publishing House, 1922.

Graebner, Theodore. *The Borderland of Right and Wrong.* St. Louis: Concordia Publishing House, 1938.

Graebner, Theodore. *Our Pilgrim Fathers: The Story of the Saxon Emigration of 1838: Retold Mainly in the Words of the Emigrants.* St. Louis: Concordia Publishing House, 1919.

Graebner, Theodore. *Pastor and People: Letters to a Young Preacher.* St. Louis: Concordia Publishing House, 1932.

Graebner, Theodore. *The Problem of Lutheran Union and Other Essays.* St. Louis: Concordia Publishing House, 1935.

Guenther, Gotthold. *Die Schicksale und Abentueur der aus Sachsen ausgewanderten Stephanier. Ihre Reise nach St. Louis, ihr Aufenthalt daselbst und Zustand ihrer Colonie in Perry-County.* Dresden: Verlag von C. Heinrich, 1839.

Hanssen, Theodor. *The Historical Open Questions among American Lutherans.* Burlington, Ia.: The Lutheran Literary Board, 1936.

Hennig, Karl. "Die Auswanderung Martin Stephans." *Zeitschrift für Kirchengeschichte,* LVIII. Stuggart, 1939.

Hochstetter, Christian. *Die Geschichte der Evangelisch-lutheranischen Missouri-Synode in Nord-Amerika, und ihrer Lehrkampfe von der sachsichen Auswanderung im Jahre 1838 an bis zum Jahre 1884.* Dresden: Heinrich J. Naumann, 1885.

Joerz, Jerald C., and Paul McCain, eds. *Church and Ministry: The Collected Papers of the 150th Anniversary Theological Convocation of The Lutheran Church–Missouri Synod.* St. Louis: The Lutheran Church–Missouri Synod, 1998.

Kowert, H. "The Organization of the Missouri Synod in 1847." In *Ebenezer: Reviews of the Missouri Synod During Three Quarters of a Century,* edited by W. H. T. Dau. St. Louis: Concordia Publishing House, 1922.

Loeber, G. H. *Der Hirtenbrief des Herrn Pastor Grabaus zu Buffalo vom Jahre 1840.* New York: H. Ludwig & Co., 1849.

Loeber, G. H. *History of the Saxon Lutheran Immigration to East Perry County, Missouri in 1839.* Translated by Vernon Meyr. Cape Girardeau, Mo.: Center for Regional and Cultural Heritage, 1983.

Luther, Martin. *Luther's Works.* American edition, edited by Jaroslav Pelikan and Helmut T. Lehman. St. Louis and Philadelphia: Concordia Publishing House and Fortress Press, 1955-86.

Luther, Martin. *Martin Luther's Basic Theological Writings,* edited by Timothy F. Lull. Minneapolis: Fortress Press, 1989.

The Lutheran Annual 1996 of The Lutheran Church–Missouri Synod. St. Louis: Concordia Publishing House, 1995.

Lutheran Church–Missouri Synod. *Handbook.* St. Louis: Concordia Publishing House, 1995.

Lutheran Church–Missouri Synod. *Statistical Yearbook.* St. Louis: Concordia Publishing House, 1995.

Meyer, Carl S. *Log Cabin to Luther Tower: Concordia Seminary During One Hundred and Twenty-five Years Toward a More Excellent Ministry, 1839-1964.* St. Louis: Concordia Publishing House, 1965.

Meyer, Carl S. "Ohio's Accord with Missouri, 1868-1880." In *The Maturing of American Lutheranism,* edited by Herbert T. Neve and Benjamin A. Johnson. Minneapolis: Augsburg Publishing House, 1968.

Meyer, Carl S., ed. *Moving Frontiers: Readings in the History of the Lutheran Church–Missouri Synod.* St. Louis: Concordia Publishing House, 1964, 1986.

Meyer, Lawrence B. *Missouri in Motion.* St. Louis: Concordia Publishing House, 1969.

Meyer, Marie, Marva Dawn, Dot Nuechterlein, Elizabeth Yates, and Richard Hinz. *Different Voices/Shared Vision: Male and Female in the Trinitarian Community.* Delhi, N.Y.: ALPB Books, 1992.

Mueller, Arnold C. *The Ministry of the Lutheran Teacher: A Study to Determine the Position of the Lutheran Parish School Teacher Within the Public Ministry of the Church.* St. Louis: Concordia Publishing House, 1964.

Mueller, John Theodore. *Christian Dogmatics: A Handbook of Doctrinal Theology for Pastors, Teachers, and Laymen.* St. Louis: Concordia Publishing House, 1934, 1955.

Pieper, Franz. *Christian Dogmatics.* 3 vols. St. Louis: Concordia Publishing House, 1950.

Pieper, Franz. *What Is Christianity? and Other Essays.* Translated by J. T. Mueller. St. Louis: Concordia Publishing House, 1933.

Piepkorn, Arthur Carl. "*Ius Divinum* and *Adiaphoron* in Relation to Structural Problems in the Church: The Position of the Lutheran Symbolical Books." In *Lutherans and Catholics in Dialogue V: Papal Primacy and the Universal Church,* edited by Paul C. Empie and T. Austin Murphy. Minneapolis: Augsburg Publishing House, 1974.

Piepkorn, Arthur Carl. "What the Symbols Have to Say about the Church." In *The Church: Selected Writings of Arthur Carl Piepkorn,* edited by Michael P. Plekon and William S. Wiecher. Delhi, N.Y.: ALPB Books, 1993.

Polack, W. G. *The Building of a Great Church: A Brief History of the Lutheran Church in America With Special Reference to the Evangelical Lutheran Synod of Missouri, Ohio, and Other States.* Second edition. St. Louis: Concordia Publishing House, 1941.

Polack, W. G. *The Life of C. F. W. Walther.* St. Louis: Concordia Publishing House, 1935, 1947.

Prohl, Russell C. *Woman in the Church: A Restudy of Woman's Place in Building the Kingdom.* Grand Rapids: Wm. B. Eerdmans Publishing Company, 1957.

Scharlemann, Martin H. *The Making of a Theologian: Selected Works of Martin H. Scharlemann,* edited by Richard P. Lieske. St. Louis: Concordia Seminary, 1984.

Schwermann, Albert H. "The Doctrine of the Call." In *The Pastor at Work,* edited by Richard R. Caemmerer et al. St. Louis: Concordia Publishing House, 1960.

Speaking the Truth in Love — Essays Related to "A Statement." Chicago, 1945. Chicago: Willow Press, n.d.

Spitz, Lewis W., Sr. *The Life of C. F. W. Walther.* St. Louis: Concordia Publishing House, 1961.

Steffens, D. H. "The Doctrine of the Church and the Ministry." In *Ebenezer: Reviews of the Missouri Synod During Three Quarters of a Century,* edited by W. H. T. Dau. St. Louis: Concordia Publishing House, 1922.

Stellhorn, A. C. *Schools of The Lutheran Church–Missouri Synod.* St. Louis: Concordia Publishing House, 1963.

Suelflow, August R., ed. *Heritage in Motion: Readings in the History of The Lutheran Church–Missouri Synod, 1962-1995.* St. Louis: Concordia Publishing House, 1998.

Tappert, Theodore G., ed. and trans. *The Book of Concord: The Confessions of the Evangelical Lutheran Church.* Philadelphia: Fortress Press, 1959.

Tiemeyer, Raymond. *The Ordination of Women: A Report Distributed by Authorization of the Church Body Presidents as a Contribution to Further Study, Based on the Materials Produced through the Division of Theological Studies of the Lutheran Council in the U.S.A.* Minneapolis: Augsburg Publishing House, 1970.

Tietjen, John H. *Memoirs in Exile: Confessional Hope and Institutional Conflict.* Minneapolis: Fortress Press, 1990.

Tietjen, John H. *Which Way to Lutheran Unity? A History of Efforts to Unite the Lutherans of America.* St. Louis: Concordia Publishing House, 1966.

Vehse, Carl Eduard. *Die Stephan'sche Auswanderung nach Amerika* [*The Stephanite Emigration to America*] (1840). Translated by Rudolph Fiehler. Tucson, Ariz.: Marion R. Winkler, 1975.

von Polenz, Gottlob. *Die öffentliche Meinung und der Pastor Stephan. Ein Fragment.* Dresden and Leipzig: Commission der Urnoldischen Buchhandlung, 1840.

Walther, C. F. W. *Amerikanisch-Lutherische Pastoraltheologie.* St. Louis: Druckerei der Synode von Missouri, Ohio, u.a. Staaten, 1872.

Walther, C. F. W. *Church and Ministry (Kirche und Amt): Witnesses of the Evangelical Lutheran Church on the Question of the Church and the Ministry.* Translated from the third edition (1875) by J. T. Mueller. St. Louis: Concordia Publishing House, 1987.

Walther, C. F. W. *Editorials from "Lehre und Wehre."* Translated by Herbert J. A. Bouman. St. Louis: Concordia Publishing House, 1981.

Walther, C. F. W. *Die rechte Gestalt einer vom Staate unabhängigen Evangelisch Lutherischen Ortsgemeinde.* Second edition. St. Louis: Aug. Wiebusch & Son, 1864.

Walther, C. F. W. *Walther Speaks to the Church: Selected Letters by C. F. W. Walther,* edited by Carl S. Meyer. St. Louis: Concordia Publishing House, 1973.

Weisheit, Eldon. *The Zeal of His House: Five Generations of Lutheran Church–Missouri Synod History (1847-1972).* St. Louis: Concordia Publishing House, 1973.

Wesselschmidt, Quentin F. "Repristination Theology and the Doctrinal Position of The Lutheran Church–Missouri Synod." In *Light for Our World: Essays Commemorating the 150th Anniversary of Concordia Seminary, St. Louis, Missouri,* edited by John W. Klotz. St. Louis: Concordia Seminary, 1989.

Zerbst, Fritz. *The Office of Woman in the Church.* Translated by Albert G. Merkens. St. Louis: Concordia Publishing House, 1955.

Primary Sources: Articles

Arndt, William. "The Chief Principles of New Testament Textual Criticism." *Concordia Theological Monthly* 5 (1934): 577-84.

Arndt, William. "The Doctrine of the Call into the Holy Ministry." *Concordia Theological Monthly* 25 (1954): 337-52.

Bauer, Walter E. "To Recall As Well As I Can." *Concordia Historical Institute Quarterly* 43 (1970): 171-73.

Bickel, L. G. "Woman Teachers." *Lutheran School Journal* 66 (1931): 406-9.

Bohlmann, Ralph A. "Missouri Lutheranism, 1945 and 1995." *Lutheran Forum* 30 (1996): 12-17.

Buenger, Emilie. "Letters of Emilie Buenger to C. F. W. Walther." *Concordia Historical Institute Quarterly* 17 (January 1945): 106-10.

Burgdorf, Paul H. "Pastor Martin Stephan's Published Sermons on the Christian Faith." *Concordia Historical Institute Quarterly* 63 (1990): 91-96.

Coates, Thomas. "'A Statement' — Some Reminiscences." *Concordia Historical Institute Quarterly* 43 (1970): 159-64.

Constable, John. "Synod: More than Advisory?" Evangelical Lutherans in Mission, n.d.

Dau, W. H. T. "Scripture Proof in the View of the Modernists." *Theological Quarterly* 19 (1915): 65-71.

"Do Modernists Play Fair?" *Theological Monthly* 7 (1927): 65-73.

Bibliography

Eiselmeier, John. "The Feminization of the Teaching Profession." *Lutheran School Journal* 60 (1925): 17-20.

Engelbrecht, Harold H. "Concerning 'A Statement.'" *Concordia Historical Institute Quarterly* 43 (1970): 167-70.

Fritz, John H. C. "Will the Fundamentalists Win Out in Their Fight Against the Modern Liberalists?" *Theological Monthly* 4 (1924): 234-42.

Garton, Jean. "Women's Service to the Church: What Are the Questions?" *Issues in Christian Education* 26 (1992): 5-7.

Graebner, Theodore. "The Burden of Infallibility: A Study in the History of Dogma." *Concordia Historical Institute Quarterly* 38 (1965): 88-94.

Graebner, Theodore. "'The Cloak of the Cleric.'" *Concordia Historical Institute Quarterly* 44 (1971): 3-12.

Graebner, Theodore. "For a Penitent Jubilee." *Concordia Historical Institute Quarterly* 45 (1972): 3-28.

Graebner, Theodore. "Synod and Congregation." *The Lutheran Witness* (August 28, 1945): 277-78.

Hemmeter, Bernard H. "Reflections on the Missouri Synod." *Concordia Historical Institute Quarterly* 43 (1970): 174-77.

Judisch, Douglas. "Theses on Woman Suffrage in the Church." *Concordia Theological Monthly* 41 (1977): 36-45.

Jungkuntz, Richard. "The Problem of Authority in the Lutheran Church–Missouri Synod." *Review and Expositor* 75 (1978): 235-48.

Kretzmann, A. T. "The Statement of the 44, 1945-1979." *Concordia Historical Institute Quarterly* 55 (1982): 69-81.

Kretzmann, P. E. "The Position of the Christian Woman, Especially as Worker in the Church." *Concordia Theological Monthly* 1 (1930): 351-60.

Lindemann, Herbert. "Personal Reflections on the Twenty-Fifth Anniversary of the Publication of 'A Statement.'" *Concordia Historical Institute Quarterly* 43 (1970): 164-66.

Lindemann, Paul. "The Woman in the Church." *Theological Quarterly* 24 (1920): 30-48, 103-21.

Maurer, Albert V. "Women Teachers in the Church." *Lutheran Education* 93 (1958): 214-21.

Meyer, Carl S. "The Historical Background of 'A Brief Statement.'" *Concordia Theological Monthly* 32 (1961): 403-28, 466-82, 526-42.

Meyer, Carl S. "The Role of 'A Brief Statement' Since 1932." *Concordia Theological Monthly* 33 (1962): 199-209.

Meyer, Carl S. "Walther's Theology of the Word." *Concordia Theological Monthly* 43 (1972): 262-83.

Mueller, Arnold C. "Women Teachers." *Lutheran Education* 89 (1953): 65-68.

Nafzger, Samuel F. "The CTCR Report on 'The Ministry.'" *Concordia Theological Quarterly* 47 (1983): 97-129.

Nafzger, Samuel F. "The Doctrinal Position of the LCMS on the Service of Women in the Church." *Concordia Journal* 18 (1992): 112-31.

Pieper, August. "Are There Legal Restrictions in the New Testament?" *Theologische Quartalschrift* 13 (July 1916): 157-82.

Pieper, Walter C. "C. F. W. Walther Revealed in His Letters." *Concordia Historical Institute Quarterly* 34 (1961): 17-22.

Piepkorn, Arthur Carl. "The Sacred Ministry and Holy Ordination in the Symbolical Books of the Lutheran Church." *Concordia Theological Monthly* 40 (1969): 552-73.

Piepkorn, Arthur Carl. "Walther and the Lutheran Symbols." *Concordia Theological Monthly* 32 (1961): 606-20.

Piepkorn, Arthur Carl. "What Does 'Inerrancy' Mean?" *Concordia Theological Monthly* 36 (1965): 577-93.

Polack, W. G. "An Interesting Contemporary Clipping on the Saxon Immigration." *Concordia Historical Institute Quarterly* 12 (1939): 21-24.

Preus, J. A. O. "Lutheran Identity Is Insistence on Truth." Dialog 16 (1977): 292-95.

Schöne, Jobst. "Pastoral Letter on the Ordination of Women to the Pastoral Office of the Church." *Concordia Theological Quarterly* 59 (1995): 301-16.

Schroeder, Edward H. "Law-Gospel Reductionism in the History of The Lutheran Church–Missouri Synod." *Concordia Theological Monthly* 43 (1972): 232-47.

Schroeder, Edward H. "The Orders of Creation — Some Reflections on the History and Place of the Term in Systematic Theology." *Concordia Theological Monthly* 43 (1972): 165-78.

Schroeder, Edward H. "The Role of Women in the Church of Jesus Christ." *Advance* (October 1970): 10-12.

Selle, C. A. T. "The Office of Pastor as School Overseer." *Evangelisches-Schulblatt* 4 (1869). Translated by Mark Nispel. Tms (photocopy).

Walther, C. F. W. "Authority in the Church." *Concordia Theological Monthly* 44 (1973): 375-78.

Walther, C. F. W. "Bringing Souls to Christ: Every Christian's Desire and Duty." *Gnadenjahr: Predigten über die Evangelien des Kirchenjahrs* (St. Louis: Concordia Publishing House, 1891). Translated by Bruce Cameron in *Missio Apostolica: Journal of the Lutheran Society for Missiology* 6 (1998): 6-16.

Walther, C. F. W. "Fidelity to the Written Word: The Burden of the Missouri Synod, C. F. W. Walther's Foreword to *Lehre und Wehre*, 1860." *Concordia Journal* 1 (1975): 69-85.

Walther, C. F. W. "Why Should Our Pastors, Teachers and Professors Subscribe Unconditionally to the Symbolical Writings of Our Church." *Concordia Theological Monthly* 18 (1947): 241-53.

Winter, J. Frederick Ferdinand. "Mr. J. Frederick Ferdinand Winter's Account of the Stephanite Emigration." *Concordia Historical Institute Quarterly* 12/13 (1939/1940): 48-57, 83-88, 122-28, 158-61.

Zaunick, Rudolph. "Der Dresdner Stadtphysikus Friedrich August Röber (1765-1827) ein sächsischer Gesundheitswissenschaftler in der Nachfolge Johann Peter Franks." *Acta Historica Leopoldina* 4 (1966): 5-75.

Bibliography

Secondary Sources: Books and Essays

Abrams, Ray H. *Preachers Present Arms: The Role of the American Churches and Clergy in World Wars I and II, with Some Observations on the War in Vietnam.* Revised edition. Scottsdale, Penn.: Herald Press, 1933, 1969.

Adams, James. *Preus of Missouri and the Great Lutheran Civil War.* New York: Harper & Row, 1977.

Albers, James W. "Perspectives on the History of Women in the Lutheran Church–Missouri Synod during the Nineteenth Century." In *Essays and Reports* 9 (1980). St. Louis: The Lutheran Historical Conference, 1982.

Althaus, Paul. *The Theology of Martin Luther.* Translated by Robert C. Schultz. Philadelphia: Fortress Press, 1966.

Ammerman, Nancy Tatom. *Baptist Battles: Social Change and Religious Conflict in the Southern Baptist Convention.* New Brunswick, N.J.: Rutgers University Press, 1990.

Ammerman, Nancy Tatom. "North American Protestant Fundamentalism." In *Fundamentalisms Observed,* edited by Martin E. Marty and R. Scott Appleby. Chicago: University of Chicago Press, 1991.

Ammerman, Nancy Tatom, ed. *Southern Baptists Observed: Multiple Perspectives on a Changing Denomination.* Knoxville: University of Tennessee Press, 1993.

Anders, Sarah Frances, and Marilyn Metcalf-Whittaker. "Women as Lay Leaders and Clergy: A Critical Issue." In *Southern Baptists Observed: Multiple Perspectives on a Changing Denomination,* edited by Nancy Tatom Ammerman. Knoxville: University of Tennessee Press, 1993.

Arand, Charles P. *Testing the Boundaries: Windows to Lutheran Identity.* St. Louis: Concordia Publishing House, 1995.

Asheim, Ivar, and Victor R. Gold, eds. *Episcopacy in the Lutheran Church? Studies in the Development and Definition of the Office of Church Leadership.* Philadelphia: Fortress Press, 1970.

Astin, Helen S., and Carole Leland. *Women of Influence, Women of Vision: A Cross-Generational Study of Leaders and Social Change.* San Francisco: Jossey-Bass Publishers, 1991.

Baber, Harriet E. "The Ordination of Women, Natural Symbols, and What Even God Cannot Do." In *Women in the World's Religions: Past and Present,* edited by Ursula King. New York: Paragon House, 1987.

Balmer, Randall. "American Fundamentalism: The Ideal of Femininity." In *Fundamentalism and Gender,* edited by John Stratton Hawley. New York: Oxford University Press, 1994.

Balmer, Randall. *Grant Us Courage: Travels Along the Mainline of American Protestantism.* New York: Oxford University Press, 1996.

Barnhart, Joe E. "What's All the Fighting About? Southern Baptists and the Bible." In *Southern Baptists Observed: Multiple Perspectives on a Changing Denomination,* edited by Nancy Tatom Ammerman. Knoxville: University of Tennessee Press, 1993.

Barr, James. *Holy Scripture: Canon, Authority, Criticism*. Philadelphia: Westminster Press, 1983.

Barr, James. *The Scope and Authority of the Bible*. Philadelphia: Westminster Press, 1980.

Barth, Karl. *Christian Dogmatics,* volume III: *The Doctrine of Creation*. Edinburgh: T. & T. Clark, 1958.

Barton, John. *People of the Book? The Authority of the Bible in Christianity*. Louisville: Westminster/John Knox Press, 1988.

Bawer, Bruce. *Stealing Jesus: How Fundamentalism Betrays Christianity*. New York: Crown Publishers, 1997.

Bedell, Kenneth B., and Alice M. Jones. *Yearbook of American and Canadian Churches 1994*. Nashville: Abingdon Press, 1994.

Bellinger, Libby. "More Hidden than Revealed: The History of Southern Baptist Women in Ministry." In *The Struggle for the Soul of the SBC: Moderate Responses to the Fundamentalist Movement,* edited by Walter B. Shurden. Macon, Ga.: Mercer University Press, 1993.

Bendroth, Margaret Lamberts. *Fundamentalism and Gender, 1875 to the Present*. New Haven: Yale University Press, 1993.

Bendroth, Margaret Lamberts. "The Search for 'Women's Role' in American Evangelicalism, 1930-1980." In *Evangelicalism and Modern America,* edited by George Marsden. Grand Rapids: Wm. B. Eerdmans Publishing Company, 1984.

Bengston, Gloria E., ed. *Lutheran Women in Ordained Ministry 1970-1995: Reflections and Perspectives*. Minneapolis: Augsburg Fortress, 1995.

Benne, Robert. *The Paradoxical Vision: A Public Theology for the Twenty-first Century*. Minneapolis: Fortress Press, 1995.

Bergendoff, Conrad. *The Doctrine of the Church in American Lutheranism*. Philadelphia: Board of Publication of the United Lutheran Church in America, 1956.

Berger, Peter. *The Heretical Imperative: Contemporary Possibilities of Religious Affirmation*. Garden City, N.Y.: Anchor Press/Doubleday, 1979.

Bird, Phyllis A. "The Authority of the Bible." In *The New Interpreter's Bible,* vol. 1, edited by Leander Keck. Nashville: Abingdon Press, 1994.

Bird, Phyllis A. "Biblical Authority in the Light of Feminist Critique." In Bird, *Missing Persons and Mistaken Identities: Women and Gender in Ancient Israel*. Minneapolis: Fortress Press, 1997.

Blaisdell, Charles R., ed. *Conservative, Moderate, Liberal: The Biblical Authority Debate*. St. Louis: CBP Press, 1990.

Bledstein, Burton J. *The Culture of Professionalism: The Middle Class and the Development of Higher Education in America*. New York: W. W. Norton & Company, 1978.

Bloomquist, Karen L. "Traditioning, Truth-Telling, Transforming." In *Lutheran Women in Ordained Ministry, 1970-1995: Reflections and Perspectives,* edited by Gloria E. Bengston. Minneapolis: Augsburg Fortress, 1995.

Bibliography

Bloomquist, Karen L. "We as Ministers, Amen!" In *Women in a Strange Land: Search for a New Image,* edited by Clare Benedicks Fischer, Betsy Brenneman, and Anne McGrew Bennett. Philadelphia: Fortress Press, 1975.

Boone, Kathleen C. *The Bible Tells Them So: The Discourse of Protestant Fundamentalism.* Albany: State University of New York Press, 1989.

Bouman, Walter R., and Sue M. Setzer. *What Shall I Say? Discerning God's Call to Ministry.* Chicago: Evangelical Lutheran Church in America, 1995.

Braaten, Carl E. *Principles of Lutheran Theology.* Philadelphia: Fortress Press, 1983.

Braaten, Carl E., and Robert Jensen. *Christian Dogmatics.* 2 vols. Philadelphia: Fortress Press, 1984.

Braaten, Carl E., and Robert Jensen, eds. *Reclaiming the Bible for the Church.* Grand Rapids: Wm. B. Eerdmans Publishing Company, 1995.

Bradley, James E., and Richard A. Muller. *Church History: An Introduction to Research, Reference Works, and Methods.* Grand Rapids: Wm. B. Eerdmans Publishing Company, 1995.

Brasher, Brenda E. *Godly Women: Fundamentalism and Female Power.* New Brunswick: Rutgers University Press, 1998.

Bratt, James D. "Protestant Immigrants and the Protestant Mainstream." In *Minority Faiths and the American Protestant Mainstream,* edited by Jonathan D. Sarna. Urbana: University of Illinois Press, 1998.

Brauer, Jerald C. *Protestantism in America: A Narrative History.* Revised edition. Philadelphia: Westminster Press, 1965.

Brekus, Catherine A. *Strangers and Pilgrims: Female Preaching in America, 1740-1845.* Chapel Hill: University of North Carolina Press, 1998.

Brereton, Virginia Lieson, and Christa Ressmeyer Klein. "American Women in Ministry: A History of Protestant Starting Points." In *Women of Spirit: Female Leadership in the Jewish and Christian Traditions,* edited by Rosemary Radford Ruether and Eleanor McLaughlin. New York: Simon and Schuster, 1979.

Bringas, Ernie. *Going by the Book: Past and Present Tragedies of Biblical Authority.* Charlottesville, Va.: Hampton Roads Publishing Company, 1996.

Brown, Dale W. *Understanding Pietism.* Grand Rapids: Wm. B. Eerdmans Publishing Company, 1978.

Brown, Robert McAfee. *The Spirit of Protestantism.* New York: Oxford University Press, 1965.

Brunner, Emil. *The Divine Imperative.* Translated by Olive Wyon. Philadelphia: Westminster Press, 1947.

Butler, Jonathan M. "Introduction: The Historian as Heretic," to *Prophetess of Health: Ellen G. White and the Origins of Seventh-day Adventist Health Reform* by Ronald L. Numbers. Knoxville: University of Tennessee Press, 1992.

Campbell, Dennis M. *Who Will Go for Us? An Invitation to Ordained Ministry.* Nashville: Abingdon Press, 1994.

Carr, Anne E. *Transforming Grace: Christian Tradition and Women's Experience.* San Francisco: Harper & Row, 1988.

Carroll, Jackson W. *As One with Authority: Reflective Leadership in Ministry.* Louisville: Westminster/John Knox Press, 1991.

Carroll, Jackson W., and Wade Clark Roof, eds. *Beyond Establishment: Protestant Identity in a Post-Protestant Age.* Louisville: Westminster/John Knox Press, 1993.

Carroll, Jackson W., Barbara Hargrove, and Adair T. Lummis. *Women of the Cloth: A New Opportunity for the Churches.* San Francisco: Harper & Row, 1983.

Chafe, William. *The Paradox of Change: American Women in the Twentieth Century.* New York: Oxford University Press, 1991.

Chaves, Mark. *Ordaining Women: Culture and Conflict in Religious Organizations.* Cambridge: Harvard University Press, 1997.

Chittister, Joan. *Job's Daughters: Women and Power.* New York: Paulist Press, 1990.

Clanton, Jann Aldredge. *In Whose Image? God and Gender.* New York: Crossroad Publishing Company, 1990.

Cloke, Gillian. *'This Female Man of God': Women and Spiritual Power in the Patristic Age, 350-450.* New York: Routledge, 1995.

Clouse, Bonnidell, and Robert G. Clouse. *Women in Ministry: Four Views.* Downers Grove, Ill.: InterVarsity Press, 1989.

Cobb, John B., Jr. *Becoming a Thinking Christian.* Nashville: Abingdon Press, 1993.

Coburn, Carol K. *Life at Four Corners: Religion, Gender, and Education in a German-Lutheran Community, 1868-1945.* Lawrence, Kans.: University Press of Kansas, 1992.

Conser, Walter H., Jr. *Church and Confession: Conservative Theologians in Germany, England, and America, 1815-1866.* Macon, Ga.: Mercer University Press, 1984.

Conzen, Kathleen Neils. "The Germans." In *Harvard Encyclopedia of American Ethnic Groups,* edited by Stephen Thernstrom et al. Cambridge: Harvard University Press, 1980.

Cothen, Grady C. *The New SBC: Fundamentalism's Impact on the Southern Baptist Convention.* Macon, Ga.: Smyth & Helwys Publishing, Inc., 1995.

Countryman, L. William. *Biblical Authority or Biblical Tyranny? Scripture and the Christian Pilgrimage.* Valley Forge: Trinity Press International, 1994.

Crawford, Janet, and Michael Kinnamon. *In God's Image: Reflections on Identity, Human Wholeness and the Authority of Scripture.* Geneva: World Council of Churches, 1983.

Cressey, David. *Coming Over: Migration and Communication between England and New England in the Seventeenth Century.* New York: Cambridge University Press, 1987.

Cross, Barbara M., ed. *The Educated Woman in America: Selected Writings of Catharine Beecher, Margaret Fuller, and M. Carey Thomas.* New York: Teachers College Press, 1965.

Cunningham, Sarah, ed. *We Belong Together: Churches in Solidarity with Women.* New York: Friendship Press, 1992.

Darling, Pamela W. *New Wine: The Story of Women Transforming Leadership and Power in the Episcopal Church.* Cambridge, Mass.: Cowley Publications, 1994.

Bibliography

Davis, Stephen T. *The Debate About the Bible: Inerrancy versus Infallibility.* Philadelphia: Westminster Press, 1977.

DeBerg, Betty A. *Ungodly Women: Gender and the First Wave of American Fundamentalism.* Minneapolis: Fortress Press, 1990.

DeBerg, Betty A. *Women and Women's Issues in North American Lutheranism: A Bibliography.* Minneapolis: Augsburg Fortress Publishing House, 1992.

Diehl, Judith Ruhe. *A Woman's Place: Equal Partnership in Daily Ministry.* Philadelphia: Fortress Press, 1985.

Diggins, John P. "The Three Faces of Authority in American History." In *The Problem of Authority in America,* edited by John P. Diggins and Mark E. Kann. Philadelphia: Temple University Press, 1981.

Diggins, John P., and Mark E. Kann. *The Problem of Authority in America.* Philadelphia: Temple University Press, 1981.

Dolan, Jay. *The American Catholic Experience: A History from the Colonial Times to the Present.* Garden City, N.Y.: Image Books, 1985.

Doniger, Wendy. "The Authority of the Parental Metaphor." In *Religion and the Authority of the Past,* edited by Tobin Siebers. Ann Arbor: The University of Michigan Press, 1993.

Douglass, Jane Dempsey. *Women, Freedom and Calvin.* Philadelphia: Westminster Press, 1985.

Dozier, Verna J. *The Authority of the Laity.* Bethesda, Md.: Alban Institute, Inc., 1982, 1992.

Drevlow, Arthur H., John M. Drickamer, and Glenn E. Reichwald. *C. F. W. Walther, the American Luther: Essays in Commemoration of the 100th Anniversary of Carl Walther's Death.* Mankato, Minn.: Walther Press, 1987.

Drickamer, John M. "The Election Controversy." In *C. F. W. Walther, the American Luther: Essays in Commemoration of the 100th Anniversary of Carl Walther's Death,* edited by Arthur H. Drevlow, John M. Drickamer, and Glenn E. Reichwald. Mankato, Minn.: Walther Press, 1987.

Dunfee, Susan Nelson. *Beyond Servanthood: Christianity and the Liberation of Women.* Lanham, Md.: University Press of America, 1989.

Elert, Werner. *Morphologie des Luthertums.* Second edition. Munich: C. H. Beck'sche Verlagbuchhandlung, 1952.

Elert, Werner. *The Structure of Lutheranism,* volume 1: *The Theology and Philosophy of Life of Lutheranism Especially in the Sixteenth and Seventeenth Centuries.* Translated by Walter A. Hansen. St. Louis: Concordia Publishing House, 1962.

Ermarth, Margaret Sittler. *Adam's Fractured Rib: Observations on Women in the Church.* Philadelphia: Fortress Press, 1970.

Everist, Norma Cook. "Sisters Together in Ministry." In *Lutheran Women in Ordained Ministry, 1970-1995: Reflections and Perspectives,* edited by Gloria E. Bengston. Minneapolis: Augsburg Fortress, 1995.

Ewald, Alfred H. "From a German Jail: Who Has Authority in the Church?" In *Church Roots: Stories of Nine Immigrant Groups That Became the American Lutheran*

Church, edited by Charles W. Lutz. Minneapolis: Augsburg Publishing House, 1985.

Ferder, Fran, and John Heagle. *Partnership: Women and Men in Ministry.* Notre Dame: Ave Maria Press, 1989.

Ferguson, Robert U., Jr., ed. *Amidst Babel, Speak the Truth: Reflections on the Southern Baptist Convention Struggle.* Macon, Ga.: Smyth & Helwys Publishing, Inc., 1993.

Ferm, Robert L. *Piety, Purity, Plenty: Images of Protestantism in America.* Minneapolis: Fortress Press, 1991.

Ferm, Virgilius. *The Crisis in American Lutheran Theology: A Study of the Issue between American Lutheranism and Old Lutheranism.* New York: The Century Co., 1927.

Fischer, Clare Benedicks, Betsy Brenneman, and Anne McGrew Bennett. *Women in a Strange Land: Search for a New Image.* Philadelphia: Fortress Press, 1975.

Fishburn, Janet. *Confronting the Idolatry of Family: A New Vision for the Household of God.* Nashville: Abingdon Press, 1991.

Flowers, Ronald B. *Religion in Strange Times: The 1960s and 1970s.* Macon, Ga.: Mercer University Press, 1984.

Forster, Walter O. *Zion on the Mississippi: The Settlement of the Saxon Lutherans in Missouri 1839-1841.* St. Louis: Concordia Publishing House, 1953.

Fowler, Robert Booth. *Unconventional Partners: Religion and Liberal Culture in the United States.* Grand Rapids: Wm. B. Eerdmans Publishing Company, 1989.

Frey, Stephanie. "In a Different Voice." In *Serving the Word: Lutheran Women Consider Their Calling,* edited by Marilyn Preus. Minneapolis: Augsburg Publishing House, 1988.

Fulbrook, Mary. *A Concise History of Germany.* Cambridge: Cambridge University Press, 1993.

Fulbrook, Mary. *Piety and Politics: Religion and the Rise of Absolutism in England, Württemberg and Prussia.* Cambridge: Cambridge University Press, 1983.

Gaustad, Edwin S. "The Bible and American Protestantism." In *Altered Landscapes: Christianity in America, 1938-1985,* edited by David W. Lotz. Grand Rapids: Wm. B. Eerdmans Publishing Company, 1989.

Gerlach, Russel L. *Immigrants in the Ozarks: A Study in Ethnic Geography.* Columbia, Mo.: University of Missouri Press, 1976.

Gilkey, Langdon. "The Christian Congregation as a Religious Community." In *American Congregations,* volume 2: *New Perspectives in the Study of Congregations,* edited by James P. Wind and James W. Lewis. Chicago: University of Chicago Press, 1994.

Gillespie, Joanna Bowen. *Women Speak: Of God, Congregations, Change.* Valley Forge: Trinity Press International, 1995.

Gillespie, Patricia, and Mary Mathews. *Voices from Within: Faith-Life Stories of Women in the Church.* Pasadena: Hope Publishing House, 1994.

Gnuse, Robert. *The Authority of the Bible: Theories of Inspiration, Revelation and the Canon of Scripture.* Mahweh, N.J.: Paulist Press, 1985.

Gomes, Peter J. *The Good Book: Reading the Bible with Mind and Heart.* New York: William Morrow, 1996.

Graebner, Alan. "Birth Control and the Lutherans: The Missouri Synod as a Case Study." In *Women in American Religion,* edited by Janet Wilson James. Philadelphia: University of Pennsylvania Press, 1978.

Graebner, Alan. *Uncertain Saints: The Laity in the Lutheran Church–Missouri Synod 1900-1970.* Westport, Conn.: Greenwood Press, 1975.

Grane, Leif. *The Augsburg Confession: A Commentary.* Translated by John Rasmussen. Minneapolis: Augsburg Publishing House, 1987.

Granquist, Mark. "Lutherans in the United States, 1930-1960: Searching for the 'Center.'" In *Re-Forming the Center: American Protestantism, 1900 to the Present,* edited by Douglas Jacobsen and William Vance Trollinger, Jr. Grand Rapids: Wm. B. Eerdmans Publishing Company, 1998.

Greenleaf, Robert K. *Servant Leadership: A Journey into the Nature of Legitimate Power and Greatness.* New York: Paulist Press, 1977.

Grenz, Stanley J., and Denise Muir Kjesbo. *Women in the Church: A Biblical Theology of Women in Ministry.* Downers Grove, Ill.: InterVarsity Press, 1995.

Grindal, Gracia. "Getting Women Ordained." In *Called and Ordained: Lutheran Perspectives on the Office of the Ministry,* edited by Todd Nichol and Marc Kolden. Minneapolis: Fortress Press, 1990.

Grindal, Gracia. "How Lutheran Women Came to Be Ordained." In *Lutheran Women in Ordained Ministry, 1970-1995: Reflections and Perspectives,* edited by Gloria E. Bengston. Minneapolis: Augsburg Fortress, 1995.

Grindal, Gracia. "Women in Lutheran Tradition." In *Serving the Word: Lutheran Women Consider Their Calling,* edited by Marilyn Preus. Minneapolis: Augsburg Publishing House, 1988.

Gritsch, Eric W., and Robert W. Jenson. *Fortress Introduction to Lutheranism.* Minneapolis: Fortress Press, 1994.

Gritsch, Eric W., and Robert W. Jenson. *Lutheranism: The Theological Movement and Its Confessional Writings.* Philadelphia: Fortress Press, 1976.

Gundry, Patricia. *Neither Slave Nor Free: Helping Women Answer the Call to Church Leadership.* San Francisco: Harper & Row, 1987.

Gustafson, David A. *Lutherans in Crisis: The Question of Identity in the American Republic.* Minneapolis: Fortress Press, 1993.

Hadden, Jeffrey K. *The Gathering Storm in the Churches: The Widening Gap Between Clergy and Laymen.* Garden City, N.Y.: Doubleday & Company, 1969.

Hahn, Celia Allison. *Growing in Authority, Relinquishing Control: A New Approach to Faithful Leadership.* Bethesda, Md.: Alban Institute, 1994.

Hall, Douglas John. *The Future of the Church: Where Are We Headed?* United Church of Canada, The United Church Publishing House, 1989.

Hall, Douglas John. *Thinking the Faith: Christian Theology in a North American Context.* Minneapolis: Fortress Press, 1991.

Hamann, Henry P. *The Bible Between Fundamentalism and Philosophy.* Minneapolis: Augsburg Publishing House, 1980.

Hansen, Marcus Lee. *The Atlantic Migration, 1607-1860: A History of the Continuing Settlement of the United States.* Cambridge: Harvard University Press, 1940.

Hardacre, Helen. "The Impact of Fundamentalisms on Women, the Family, and Interpersonal Relations." In *Fundamentalisms and Society: Reclaiming the Sciences, the Family, and Education,* edited by Martin E. Marty and R. Scott Appleby. Chicago: University of Chicago Press, 1993.

Harrison, Beverly Wildung. "Keeping Faith in a Sexist Church: Not for Women Only." In *Making the Connections: Essays in Feminist Social Ethics,* edited by Carol S. Robb. Boston: Beacon Press, 1985.

Harrisville, Roy A. *Ministry in Crisis: Changing Perspectives on Ordination and the Priesthood of All Believers.* Minneapolis: Augsburg Publishing House, 1987.

Hassey, Janette. *No Time for Silence: Evangelical Women in Public Ministry Around the Turn of the Century.* Grand Rapids: Academie Books, 1986.

Hatch, Nathan O. *The Democratization of American Christianity.* New Haven: Yale University Press, 1989.

Hatch, Nathan O., and Mark A. Noll. *The Bible in America: Essays in Cultural History.* New York: Oxford University Press, 1982.

Hayter, Mary. *The New Eve in Christ: The Use and Abuse of the Bible in the Debate About Women in the Church.* Grand Rapids: Wm. B. Eerdmans Publishing Company, 1987.

Heintzen, Erich H. *Love Leaves Home: Wilhelm Loehe and the Missouri Synod.* St. Louis: Concordia Publishing House, 1973.

Hill, Jim, and Rand Cheadle. *The Bible Tells Me So: Uses and Abuses of Holy Scripture.* New York: Anchor Doubleday, 1996.

Hillis, Bryan V. *Can Two Walk Together Unless They Be Agreed? American Religious Schisms in the 1970s.* Brooklyn: Carlson Publishing Inc., 1991.

Hinlicky, Paul R. "Afterword: Why Women May Be Ordained." In *Different Voices/ Shared Vision: Male and Female in the Trinitarian Community,* by Marie Meyer, Marva J. Dawn, Dot Nuechterlein, Elizabeth A. Yates, and Richard T. Hinz. Delhi, N.Y.: ALPB Books, 1992.

Huber, Elaine C. *Women and the Authority of Inspiration: A Reexamination of Two Prophetic Movements from a Contemporary Feminist Perspective.* Lanham, Md.: University Press of America, 1985.

Huffines, Marion L. "Language-Maintenance Efforts Among German Immigrants and Their Descendants in the United States." In *America and the Germans: An Assessment of a Three-Hundred-Year History,* edited by Frank Trommler and Joseph McVeigh. 2 volumes. Philadelphia: University of Pennsylvania Press, 1985.

Hull, Gretchen Gaebelein. *Equal to Serve: Women and Men in the Church and Home.* Old Tappan, N.J.: Fleming H. Revell Company, 1987.

Hutchinson, William R. *The Modernist Impulse in American Protestantism.* Durham, N.C.: Duke University Press, 1992.

Hutchinson, William R., ed. *Between the Times: The Travail of the Protestant Establishment in America, 1900-1960.* Cambridge: Cambridge University Press, 1989.

Bibliography

Jacobsen, Douglas, and William Vance Trollinger, Jr., eds. *Re-Forming the Center: American Protestantism, 1900 to the Present.* Grand Rapids: Wm. B. Eerdmans Publishing Company, 1998.

James, Robison B., ed. *The Unfettered Word: Confronting the Authority-Inerrancy Question.* Macon, Ga.: Smyth & Helwys Publishing, Inc., 1994.

Jewett, Paul. *The Ordination of Women: An Essay on the Office of Christian Ministry.* Grand Rapids: Wm. B. Eerdmans Publishing Company, 1980.

Jodock, Darrell. *The Church's Bible: Its Contemporary Authority.* Minneapolis: Fortress Press, 1989.

Johnson, Paul, and Sean Wilentz. *The Kingdom of Matthias: A Story of Sex and Salvation in Nineteenth-Century America.* New York: Oxford University Press, 1994.

Jones, Kathleen B. *Compassionate Authority: Democracy and the Representation of Women.* New York: Routledge, 1993.

Jones, Kathleen B. "On Authority: Or, Why Women Are Not Entitled to Speak." In *Feminism and Foucault: Reflections on Resistance,* edited by Irene Diamond and Lee Quinby. Boston: Northeastern University Press, 1988.

Jordahl, Leigh D. "Schmucker and Walther: A Study of Christian Response to American Culture." In *The Future of the American Church,* edited by Philip J. Hefner. Philadelphia: Fortress Press, 1968.

Kann, Mark E. "Consent and Authority in America." In *The Problem of Authority in America,* edited by John P. Diggins and Mark E. Kann. Philadelphia: Temple University Press, 1981.

Katzenstein, Mary Fainsod. *Faithful and Fearless: Moving Feminist Protest Inside the Church and Military.* Princeton: Princeton University Press, 1998.

Keller, Rosemary Skinner. "Patterns of Laywomen's Leadership in Twentieth-Century Protestantism." In *Women and Religion in America,* volume 3: *1900-1968,* edited by Rosemary Radford Ruether and Rosemary Skinner Keller. San Francisco: Harper & Row, 1986.

Kennedy, Eugene, and Sara C. Charles. *Authority: The Most Misunderstood Idea in America.* New York: The Free Press, 1997.

Kienzle, Beverly Mayne, and Pamela J. Walker. *Women Preachers and Prophets Through Two Millennia of Christianity.* Berkeley: University of California Press, 1998.

Klein, Christa R. "Denominational History as Public History: The Lutheran Case." In *Reimagining Denominationalism: Interpretive Essays,* edited by Robert Bruce Mullin and Russell E. Richey. New York: Oxford University Press, 1994.

Kloha, Betty. *Women, Prodigal Equals: Can We Be Equal and Submissive?* Milwaukee: Northwestern Publishing House, 1989.

Klug, Eugene F. A. *Church and Ministry: The Role of Church, Pastor, and People from Luther to Walther.* St. Louis: Concordia Publishing House, 1993.

Kohlhoff, Dean. "Lutherans and the New Deal: The Missouri Synod as a Case Study." In *Essays and Reports 9* (1980). St. Louis: The Lutheran Historical Conference, 1982.

Kolb, Robert. *Confessing the Faith: Reformers Define the Church, 1530-1580.* St. Louis: Concordia Publishing House, 1991.

Kraemer, Hendrik. *A Theology of the Laity*. Philadelphia: Westminster Press, 1958.

Kraemer, Ross Shepard. *Her Share of the Blessings: Women's Religions Among Pagans, Jews, and Christians in the Greco-Roman World*. New York: Oxford University Press, 1992.

Kuenning, Paul P. *The Rise and Fall of American Pietism: The Rejection of an Activist Heritage*. Macon, Ga.: Mercer University Press, 1988.

Lagerquist, L. DeAne. *From Our Mothers' Arms: A History of Women in the American Lutheran Church*. Minneapolis: Augsburg Publishing House, 1987.

Lagerquist, L. DeAne. "There Are Many Workers in God's Household." In *Serving the Word: Lutheran Women Consider Their Calling*, edited by Marilyn Preus. Minneapolis: Augsburg Publishing House, 1988.

Lakoff, George. *Moral Politics: What Conservatives Know That Liberals Don't*. Chicago: University of Chicago Press, 1996.

Landwehr, Janet. "Whether Women, Too, Can Be Pastors." In *Serving the Word: Lutheran Women Consider Their Calling*, edited by Marilyn Preus. Minneapolis: Augsburg Publishing House, 1988.

Larson, Edward J. *Trial and Error: The American Controversy Over Creation and Evolution*. New York: Oxford University Press, 1985.

Larson, Janet Karsten. "Missouri's 'Daughters in the Re-formation.'" In *In God's Image: Towards Wholeness for Women and Men*, edited by Lavonne Althouse and Lois K. Snode. New York: Division for Mission in North America, Lutheran Church in America, 1976.

Latourette, Kenneth Scott. *The Nineteenth Century in Europe: The Protestant and Eastern Churches*, volume 2, *Christianity in a Revolutionary Age*. New York: Harper and Brothers, 1959.

Lawless, Elaine J. *Holy Women, Wholly Women: Sharing Ministries of Wholeness Through Life Stories and Reciprocal Ethnography*. Philadelphia: University of Pennsylvania Press, 1993.

Lawless, Elaine J. "Not So Different a Story After All: Pentecostal Women in the Pulpit." In *Women's Leadership in Marginal Religions: Explorations Outside the Mainstream*, edited by Catherine Wessinger. Urbana: University of Illinois Press, 1993.

Lazareth, William H. *Two Forms of Ordained Ministry: A Proposal for Mission in Light of the Augsburg Confession*. Minneapolis: Augsburg, 1991.

Lazareth, William H., and Peri Rasolondraibe. *Lutheran Identity and Mission: Evangelical and Evangelistic?* Minneapolis: Fortress Press, 1994.

Leonard, Bill J. *God's Last and Only Hope: The Fragmentation of the Southern Baptist Convention*. Grand Rapids: Wm. B. Eerdmans Publishing Company, 1990.

LeSueur, Stephen C. *The 1838 Mormon War in Missouri*. Columbia, Mo.: University of Missouri Press, 1987.

Levan, Christopher. *Living in the Maybe: A Steward Confronts the Spirit of Fundamentalism*. Grand Rapids: Wm. B. Eerdmans Publishing Company, 1998.

Lienhard, Joseph T. *The Bible, the Church, and Authority: The Canon of the Christian Bible in History and Theology*. Collegeville, Minn.: The Liturgical Press, 1995.

Bibliography

Lincoln, Bruce. *Authority: Construction and Corrosion.* Chicago: University of Chicago Press, 1994.

Lindner, Eileen W., ed. *Yearbook of American and Canadian Churches 1998.* Nashville: Abingdon Press, 1998.

Lohse, Bernhard. "The Development of the Office of Leadership in the German Lutheran Churches: 1517-1918." In *Episcopacy in the Lutheran Church? Studies in the Development and Definition of the Office of Church Leadership,* edited by Ivar Asheim and Victor R. Gold. Philadelphia: Fortress Press, 1970.

Lotz, David W., ed. *Altered Landscapes: Christianity in America, 1935-1985.* Grand Rapids: Wm. B. Eerdmans Publishing Company, 1989.

Luebke, Frederick C. *Bonds of Loyalty: German-Americans and World War I.* DeKalb, Ill.: Northern Illinois University Press, 1974.

Luebke, Frederick C. *Germans in the New World: Essays in the History of Immigration.* Urbana: University of Illinois Press, 1990.

Luebke, Frederick C. "The Immigrant Condition as a Factor Contributing to the Conservatism of the Lutheran Church–Missouri Synod." Chapter in *Germans in the New World: Essays in the History of Immigration.* Urbana: University of Illinois Press, 1990.

Lueker, Erwin L., ed. *Lutheran Cyclopedia.* St. Louis: Concordia Publishing House, 1954, 1975.

Lueking, F. Dean. *A Century of Caring: The Welfare Ministry Among Missouri Synod Lutherans, 1868-1968.* St. Louis: LCMS Board for Social Ministry, 1968.

Lueking, F. Dean. *Mission in the Making: The Missionary Enterprise Among Missouri Synod Lutherans, 1846-1963.* St. Louis: Concordia Publishing House, 1964.

Marquart, Kurt E. *Anatomy of an Explosion: Missouri in Lutheran Perspective.* Fort Wayne: Concordia Theological Seminary Press, 1977.

Marquart, Kurt E. *The Church and Her Fellowship, Ministry and Governance,* volume 9, *Confessional Lutheran Dogmatics,* edited by Robert Preus. Fort Wayne: The International Foundation for Lutheran Confessional Research, 1990.

Marsden, George. *Fundamentalism and American Culture: The Shaping of Twentieth-Century Evangelicalism, 1870-1925.* New York: Oxford University Press, 1980.

Marsden, George. *Understanding Fundamentalism and Evangelicalism.* Grand Rapids: Wm. B. Eerdmans Publishing Company, 1991.

Marsden, George, ed. *Evangelicalism and Modern America.* Grand Rapids: Wm. B. Eerdmans Publishing Company, 1984.

Marty, Martin E. "Fundamentals of Fundamentalism." In *Fundamentalism in Comparative Perspective,* edited by Lawrence Kaplan. Amherst: The University of Massachusetts Press, 1992.

Marty, Martin E. *Health and Medicine in the Lutheran Tradition: Being Well.* New York: Crossroad, 1986.

Marty, Martin E. *Modern American Religion,* volume 1: *The Irony of It All, 1893-1919.* Chicago: University of Chicago Press, 1986.

Marty, Martin E. *Modern American Religion,* volume 2: *The Noise of Conflict, 1919-1941.* Chicago: University of Chicago Press, 1991.

Marty, Martin E. *Modern American Religion,* volume 3: *Under God, Indivisible, 1941-1960.* Chicago: University of Chicago Press, 1996.

Marty, Martin E. "Public and Private: Congregation as Meeting Place." In *American Congregations,* volume 2: *New Perspectives in the Study of Congregations,* edited by James P. Wind and James W. Lewis. Chicago: University of Chicago Press, 1994.

Marty, Martin E. *Religious Crises in Modern America.* Waco, Tex.: Baylor University Press, 1980.

Marty, Martin E. *A Short History of Christianity.* Second edition. Philadelphia: Fortress Press, 1987.

Marty, Martin E., and R. Scott Appleby. *The Glory and the Power: The Fundamentalist Challenge to the Modern World.* Boston: Beacon Press, 1992.

Marty, Myron A. *Lutherans and Roman Catholicism: The Changing Conflict, 1917-1963.* Notre Dame: University of Notre Dame Press, 1968.

May, Melanie, ed. *Women and Church: The Challenge of Ecumenical Solidarity in an Age of Alienation.* Grand Rapids: Wm. B. Eerdmans Publishing Company, for the Commission on Faith and Order, National Council of the Churches of Christ in the USA, 1991.

Mayer, F. E. *The Religious Bodies of America.* Fourth edition. St. Louis: Concordia Publishing House, 1961.

McCloy, Wilfred M. *The Masterless: Self and Society in Modern America.* Chapel Hill: University of North Carolina Press, 1994.

Mead, Sidney. *The Lively Experiment: The Shaping of Christianity in America.* New York: Harper & Row, 1963.

Melton, J. Gordon. *The Churches Speak On: Women's Ordination: Official Statements from Religious Bodies and Ecumenical Organizations.* Detroit: Gale Research Inc., 1991.

Meyer, Ruth Fritz. *Women on a Mission: The Role of Women in the Church from Bible Times up to and including a History of the Lutheran Women's Missionary League during Its First Twenty-Five Years.* St. Louis: Concordia Publishing House, 1967.

Mickelsen, Alvera. *Women, Authority and the Bible.* Downers Grove, Ill.: InterVarsity Press, 1986.

Mohr, Mary Hull. "Being at Home in the Church." In *Serving the Word: Lutheran Women Consider Their Calling,* edited by Marilyn Preus. Minneapolis: Augsburg Publishing House, 1988.

Morgan, David T. *The New Crusades, the New Holy Land: Conflict in the Southern Baptist Convention, 1969-1991.* Tuscaloosa: University of Alabama Press, 1996.

Mullin, Robert Bruce. "Denominations as Bilingual Communities." In *Reimagining Denominationalism: Interpretive Essays,* edited by Robert Bruce Mullin and Russell E. Richey. New York: Oxford University Press, 1994.

Mullin, Robert Bruce, and Russell Richey, eds. *Reimagining Denominationalism: Interpretive Essays.* New York: Oxford University Press, 1994.

Mundinger, Carl S. *Government in the Missouri Synod: The Genesis of Decentralized Government in the Missouri Synod.* St. Louis: Concordia Publishing House, 1947.

Bibliography

Nelson, E. Clifford, ed. *The Lutherans in North America.* Revised edition. Philadelphia: Fortress Press, 1975, 1980.

Nesbitt, Paula D. *Feminization of the Clergy in America: Occupational and Organizational Perspectives.* New York: Oxford University Press, 1997.

Neuhaus, Richard John, ed. *The Bible, Politics, and Democracy.* Grand Rapids: Wm. B. Eerdmans Publishing Company, 1987.

Neve, Herbert T., and Benjamin A. Johnson, eds. *The Maturing of American Lutheranism.* Minneapolis: Augsburg Publishing House, 1968.

Newbigin, Lesslie. *Truth and Authority in Modernity.* Valley Forge: Trinity Press International, 1996.

Nichol, Todd, and Marc Kolden, eds. *Called and Ordained: Lutheran Perspectives on the Office of the Ministry.* Minneapolis: Fortress Press, 1990.

Noll, Mark A. *Between Faith and Criticism: Evangelicals, Scholarship, and the Bible in America.* Second edition. Grand Rapids: Baker Book House, 1991.

Noll, Mark A. *The Scandal of the Evangelical Mind.* Grand Rapids: Wm. B. Eerdmans Publishing Company, 1994.

Norén, Carol M. *The Woman in the Pulpit.* Nashville: Abingdon Press, 1991.

O'Connor, Richard. *The German-Americans: An Informal History.* Boston: Little, Brown and Company, 1968.

O'Gara, Margaret. "Ecumenism and Feminism in Dialogue on Authority." In *Women and Church: The Challenge of Ecumenical Solidarity in an Age of Alienation,* edited by Melanie A. May. Grand Rapids: Wm. B. Eerdmans Publishing Company, 1991.

Ohanneson, Joan. *Woman: Survivor in the Church.* New York: Harper & Row, 1980.

Olson, James Stuart. *The Ethnic Dimension in American History.* Second edition. New York: St. Martin's Press, 1994.

Olson, Jeannine E. *One Ministry, Many Roles: Deacons and Deaconesses Through the Centuries.* St. Louis: Concordia Publishing House, 1992.

Osiek, Carolyn. *Beyond Anger: On Being a Feminist in the Church.* New York: Paulist Press, 1986.

Osmer, Richard Robert. *A Teachable Spirit: Recovering the Teaching Office in the Church.* Louisville: Westminster/John Knox Press, 1990.

Pahl, Jon. *Hopes and Dreams of All: The International Walther League and Lutheran Youth in American Culture, 1893-1993.* Chicago: Wheat Ridge Ministries, 1993.

Parvey, Constance. "A Christian Feminist's Struggle with the Bible as Authority." In *Women's and Men's Liberation: Testimonies of Spirit,* edited by Leonard Grob, Riffat Hassan, and Haim Gordon. Westport, Conn.: Greenwood Press, 1991.

Pauck, Wilhelm. *From Luther to Tillich: The Reformers and Their Heirs,* edited by Marion Pauck. San Francisco: Harper & Row, 1984.

Pelikan, Jaroslav. *From Luther to Kierkegaard: A Study in the History of Theology.* St. Louis: Concordia Publishing House, 1950.

Pelikan, Jaroslav. *The Vindication of Tradition.* New Haven: Yale University Press, 1984.

Personal Narratives Group. *Interpreting Women's Lives: Feminist Theory and Personal Narratives.* Bloomington: Indiana University Press, 1989.

Phillips, J. B. *Your God Is Too Small.* New York: Macmillan Publishing Company, 1961.

Pickle, Linda Schelbitzki. *Contented Among Strangers: Rural German-Speaking Women and Their Families in the Nineteenth-Century Midwest.* Urbana: University of Illinois Press, 1996.

Pragman, James H. *Traditions of Ministry: A History of the Doctrine of Ministry in Lutheran Theology.* St. Louis: Concordia Publishing House, 1983.

Prelinger, Catherine M., ed. *Episcopal Women: Gender, Spirituality and Commitment in an American Mainline Denomination.* New York: Oxford University Press, 1992.

Preus, Marilyn, ed. *Serving the Word: Lutheran Women Consider Their Calling.* Minneapolis: Augsburg Publishing House, 1988.

Preus, Robert D. *The Theology of Post-Reformation Lutheranism,* volume 1: *A Study of Theological Prolegomena.* St. Louis: Concordia Publishing House, 1970.

Preus, Robert D. *The Theology of Post-Reformation Lutheranism,* volume 2: *God and His Creation.* St. Louis: Concordia Publishing House, 1972.

Ramshaw, Gail. *Under the Tree of Life: The Religion of a Feminist Christian.* New York: Continuum, 1998.

Ressmeyer, Ruth Bretscher. *Neither Male nor Female: Wholeness for Women and Men in Christ.* East Northport, N.Y.: St. Paul's Commission on Women, 1977.

Reumann, John H. P. *Ministries Examined: Laity, Clergy, Women, and Bishops in a Time of Change.* Minneapolis: Augsburg Publishing House, 1987.

Rhodes, Lynn N. *Co-Creating: A Feminist Vision of Ministry.* Philadelphia: Westminster Press, 1987.

Rice, John R. *Bobbed Hair, Bossy Wives and Women Preachers: Significant Questions for Christian Women Settled by the Word of God.* Wheaton, Ill.: Sword of the Lord Publishers, 1941.

Richey, Russell E. "Denominations and Denominationalism: An American Morphology." In *Reimagining Denominationalism: Interpretive Essays,* edited by Robert Bruce Mullin and Russell E. Richey. New York: Oxford University Press, 1994.

Rippley, La Vern J. "Ameliorated Americanization: The Effect of World War I on German-Americans in the 1920s." In *America and the Germans: An Assessment of a Three-Hundred-Year History,* edited by Frank Trommler and Joseph McVeigh, 2 volumes. Philadelphia: University of Pennsylvania Press, 1985.

Rippley, La Vern J. *The German-Americans.* Lanham, Md.: University Press of America, 1984.

Robbins, Jerry K., ed. *The Essential Luther: A Reader on Scripture, Redemption, and Society.* Grand Rapids: Baker Book House, 1991.

Roeber, A. G. *Good and Faithful Servants: The Centennial History of the Lutheran Home and Services to the Aged Ministry in Arlington Heights, Illinois, 1892-1992.* Arlington Heights, Ill.: Lutheran Home for the Aged, 1991.

Roeber, A. G. *Palatines, Liberty, and Property: German Lutherans in Colonial British America.* Baltimore: Johns Hopkins University Press, 1993.

Romero, Joan Arnold. "The Protestant Principle: A Woman's-Eye View of Barth and Tillich." In *Religion and Sexism: Images of Women in the Jewish and Christian Traditions,* edited by Rosemary Radford Ruether. New York: Simon and Schuster, 1974.

Roof, Wade Clark, and William McKinney. *American Mainline Religion: Its Changing Shape and Future.* New Brunswick, N.J.: Rutgers University Press, 1987.

Rudnick, Milton. *Fundamentalism and the Missouri Synod: A Historical Study of Their Interaction and Mutual Influence.* St. Louis: Concordia Publishing House, 1966.

Ruether, Rosemary Radford. *Sexism and God-Talk: Toward a Feminist Theology.* Boston: Beacon Press, 1983, 1993.

Ruether, Rosemary Radford, and Rosemary Skinner Keller, eds. *In Our Own Voices: Four Centuries of American Women's Religious Writing.* San Francisco: HarperCollins, 1995.

Russell, Letty M. "Authority and the Challenge of Feminist Interpretation." In *Feminist Interpretation of the Bible,* edited by Letty M. Russell. Philadelphia: Westminster Press, 1985.

Russell, Letty M. *Household of Freedom: Authority in Feminist Theology.* Philadelphia: Westminster Press, 1987.

Russell, Letty M. "Women and Ministry: Problem or Possibility?" In *Christian Feminism: Visions of a New Humanity,* edited by Judith L. Weidman. San Francisco: Harper & Row, 1984.

Saiving, Valerie. "The Human Situation: A Feminine View." In *Womanspirit Rising: A Feminist Reader in Religion,* edited by Carol Christ and Judith Plaskow. San Francisco: HarperCollins, 1979, 1992.

Schaff, Philip. *America: A Sketch of Its Political, Social, and Religious Character,* edited by Perry Miller. Cambridge, Mass.: The Belknap Press of Harvard University Press, 1961.

Schlink, Edmund. *Theology of the Lutheran Confessions.* Translated by Paul F. Koehneke and Herbert J. A. Bouman. Philadelphia: Muhlenberg Press, 1961.

Schmidt, Alvin John. *Veiled and Silenced: How Culture Shaped Sexist Theology.* Macon, Ga.: Mercer University Press, 1989.

Schmidt, Frederick W., Jr. *A Still Small Voice: Women, Ordination, and the Church.* Syracuse: Syracuse University Press, 1996.

Schmidt, Stephen A. *Powerless Pedagogues: An Interpretive Essay on the History of the Lutheran Teacher in the Missouri Synod.* River Forest, Ill.: Lutheran Education Association, 1972.

Schneider, Carl E. *The German Church on the American Frontier: A Study in the Rise of Religion among the Germans of the West.* St. Louis: Eden Publishing House, 1939.

Schultz, Rima Lunin. "Women's Work and Women's Calling in the Episcopal Church: Chicago, 1880-1989." In *Episcopal Women: Gender, Spirituality, and Commitment in an American Mainline Denomination,* edited by Catherine M. Prelinger. New York: Oxford University Press, 1992.

Sennett, Richard. *Authority.* New York: W. W. Norton, 1980.

Shipps, Jan. *Mormonism: The Story of a New Religious Tradition*. Urbana: University of Illinois Press, 1985.

Shipps, Jan. "Remembering, Recovering, and Inventing What Being the People of God Means: Reflections on Method in the Scholarly Writing of Denominational History." In *Reimagining Denominationalism: Interpretive Essays,* edited by Robert Bruce Mullin and Russell E. Richey. New York: Oxford University Press, 1994.

Shurden, Walter B., ed. *The Struggle for the Soul of the SBC: Moderate Responses to the Fundamentalist Movement*. Macon, Ga.: Mercer University Press, 1993.

Skillrud, Harold C., J. Francis Stafford, and Daniel F. Martensen, eds. *Scripture and Tradition: Lutherans and Catholics in Dialogue IX*. Minneapolis: Augsburg, 1995.

Sklar, Kathryn Kish. *Catharine Beecher: A Study in American Domesticity*. New York: W. W. Norton, 1973.

Solberg, Richard. "Foundations of the Missouri System of Higher Education." In *Essays and Reports* 11 (1984). St. Louis: Lutheran Historical Conference, 1986.

Spaude, Paul. *The Lutheran Church Under American Influence: A Historico-philosophical Interpretation of the Church and Its Relation to Various Modifying Forces in the United States*. Burlington, Ia.: The Lutheran Literary Board, 1943.

Spencer, Aida Besançon. *Beyond the Curse: Women Called to Ministry*. Nashville: Thomas Nelson Publishers, 1985.

Steinmetz, David C. *Memory and Mission: Theological Reflections on the Christian Past*. Nashville: Abingdon Press, 1988.

Stendahl, Krister. *The Bible and the Role of Women: A Case Study in Hermeneutics*. Translated by Emilie T. Sander. Philadelphia: Fortress Press, 1966.

Stendahl, Krister. "There Was More to It than I Thought and There Is Even More to Come: Retrospective Prospects." In *Lutheran Women in Ordained Ministry, 1970-1995: Reflections and Perspectives,* edited by Gloria E. Bengston. Minneapolis: Augsburg Fortress, 1995.

Stevens, Leland. *A History of the Missouri Synod as Told by the Lutheran Witness*. Alamagordo, N.M.: Leland Stevens, 1997.

Stimpson, Catherine. "'Thy Neighbor's Wife, Thy Neighbor's Servants': Women's Liberation and Black Civil Rights." In *Women in Sexist Society: Studies in Power and Powerlessness,* edited by Vivian Gornick and Barbara K. Moran. New York: New American Library, 1971.

Stoeffler, F. Ernest. *German Pietism During the Eighteenth Century*. Leiden: E. J. Brill, 1973.

Stoeffler, F. Ernest. *The Rise of Evangelical Pietism*. Leiden: E. J. Brill, 1965.

Suelflow, Roy A. "Franz August Otto Pieper: Orthodoxist or Confessionalist?" In *Essays and Reports* 8 (1978). St. Louis: The Lutheran Historical Conference, 1980.

Swartley, Willard M. *Slavery, Sabbath, War, and Women: Case Studies in Biblical Interpretation*. Scottsdale, Penn.: Herald Press, 1983.

Swierenga, Robert P. "Religion and Immigrant Behavior: The Dutch Experience." In *Belief and Behavior: Essays in the New Religious History,* edited by Philip R.

Vandermeer and Robert P. Swierenga. New Brunswick, N.J.: Rutgers University Press, 1991.

Taege, Marlys. *WINGS: Women in God's Service: The Fiftieth Anniversary History of the Lutheran Women's Missionary League of the Lutheran Church–Missouri Synod*. St. Louis: Lutheran Women's Missionary League, 1991.

Tanner, Kathryn. *The Politics of God: Christian Theologies and Social Justice*. Minneapolis: Fortress Press, 1992.

Tappert, Theodore G. "Lutheran Ecclesiastical Government in the United States of America." In *Episcopacy in the Lutheran Church? Studies in the Development and Definition of the Office of Church Leadership,* edited by Ivar Asheim and Victor R. Gold. Philadelphia: Fortress Press, 1970.

Tappert, Theodore G. "The Word of God According to the Lutheran Confessions." In *The Maturing of American Lutheranism,* edited by Herbert T. Neve and Benjamin A. Johnson. Minneapolis: Augsburg Publishing House, 1968.

Tappert, Theodore G., ed. *Lutheran Confessional Theology in America, 1840-1880*. New York: Oxford University Press, 1972.

Tavard, George H. *Woman in Christian Tradition*. Notre Dame: University of Notre Dame Press, 1973.

Thurston, Anne. *Because of Her Testimony: The Word in Female Experience*. New York: Crossroad, 1995.

Tillich, Paul. *A History of Christian Thought: From Its Judaic and Hellenistic Origins to Existentialism,* edited by Carl E. Braaten. New York: Simon & Schuster, 1968.

Todd, Mary. "Hostage to History: The Use and Abuse of Memory and History in The Lutheran Church–Missouri Synod." *Essays and Reports* 17 (1996). St. Louis: The Lutheran Historical Conference, 1999.

Todd, Mary. "Now Is the Kairos — The Right Time." In *Lutheran Women in Ordained Ministry, 1970-1995: Reflections and Perspectives,* edited by Gloria E. Bengston. Minneapolis: Augsburg Fortress, 1995.

Trexler, Edgar. *Anatomy of a Merger: People, Dynamics, and Decisions That Shaped the ELCA*. Minneapolis: Augsburg, 1991.

Tucker, Ruth A., and Walter Liefeld. *Daughters of the Church: Women and Ministry from New Testament Times to the Present*. Grand Rapids: Academie Books, 1987.

Vandermeer, Philip, and Robert P. Swierenga. *Belief and Behavior: Essays in the New Religious History*. New Brunswick, N.J.: Rutgers University Press, 1991.

Wacker, Grant. "The Demise of Biblical Civilization." In *The Bible in America: Essays in Cultural History,* edited by Nathan O. Hatch and Mark A. Noll. New York: Oxford University Press, 1982.

Wangerin, Walter, Jr. *Ragman and Other Cries of Faith*. San Francisco: Harper Collins, 1984.

Warner, R. Stephen. "The Place of the Congregation in the Contemporary American Religious Configuration." In *American Congregations,* volume 2: *New Perspectives in the Study of Congregations,* edited by James P. Wind and James W. Lewis. Chicago: University of Chicago Press, 1994.

BIBLIOGRAPHY

Watson, JoAnn Ford. *A Study of Karl Barth's Doctrine of Man and Woman.* New York: Vantage Press, 1995.

Weber, Timothy P. "The Two-Edged Sword: The Fundamentalist Use of the Bible." In *The Bible in America: Essays in Cultural History,* edited by Nathan O. Hatch and Mark A. Noll. New York: Oxford University Press, 1982.

Weidman, Judith L., ed. *Women Ministers: How Women Are Redefining Traditional Roles.* San Francisco: Harper & Row, 1985.

Weiser, Frederick S. *Love's Response: A Story of Lutheran Deaconesses in America.* Philadelphia: The Board of Publication of the United Lutheran Church in America, 1962.

Wentz, Abdel Ross. *A Basic History of Lutheranism in America.* Philadelphia: Muhlenberg Press, 1955.

Wentz, Richard E. *Why People Do Bad Things in the Name of Religion.* Macon, Ga.: Mercer University Press, 1993.

Wetherilt, Ann Kirkus. *That They May Be Many: Voices of Women, Echoes of God.* New York: Continuum, 1994.

Wiederaenders, Robert C., ed. *Historical Guide to Lutheran Church Bodies of North America.* Second edition. Lutheran Historical Conference, 1998.

Wiesner, Merry. "Luther and Women: The Death of Two Marys." In *Feminist Theology: A Reader,* edited by Ann Loades. Louisville: Westminster/John Knox Press, 1990.

Williams, E. Louise. "A Heart for Service: The Lutheran Deaconess." In *Serving the Word: Lutheran Women Consider Their Calling,* edited by Marilyn Preus. Minneapolis: Augsburg Publishing House, 1988.

Wind, James P., and James W. Lewis. *American Congregations,* volume 2: *New Perspectives in the Study of Congregations.* Chicago: University of Chicago Press, 1994.

Winter, Miriam Therese, Adair Lummis, and Allison Stokes. *Defecting in Place: Women Claiming Responsibility for Their Own Spiritual Lives.* New York: Crossroad, 1994.

Wire, Antoinette Clark. *The Corinthian Women Prophets: A Reconstruction through Paul's Rhetoric.* Minneapolis: Fortress Press, 1990.

Wohlrabe, John C., Jr. *Ministry in Missouri Until 1962: An Historical Analysis of the Doctrine of the Ministry in the Lutheran Church–Missouri Synod.* St. Louis: Concordia Seminary, 1992.

Wold, Margaret Barth. "We Seized the Spirit's Moment." In *Lutheran Women in Ordained Ministry, 1970-1995: Reflections and Perspectives,* edited by Gloria E. Bengston. Minneapolis: Augsburg Fortress, 1995.

Wolf, Richard C., ed. *Documents of Lutheran Unity in America.* Philadelphia: Fortress Press, 1966.

Wuthnow, Robert. *The Restructuring of American Religion: Society and Faith Since World War II.* Princeton: Princeton University Press, 1988.

Wuthnow, Robert. *The Struggle for America's Soul: Evangelicals, Liberals, and Secularism.* Grand Rapids: Wm. B. Eerdmans Publishing Company, 1989.

Young, Pamela Dickey. *Feminist Theology/Christian Theology: In Search of Method*. Minneapolis: Fortress Press, 1990.

Zikmund, Barbara Brown. "Ordination from the Woman's Perspective." In *We Belong Together: Churches in Solidarity with Women*, edited by Sarah Cunningham. New York: Friendship Press, 1992.

Zikmund, Barbara Brown. "Winning Ordination for Women in Mainstream Protestant Churches." In *Women and Religion in America*, volume 3: *1900-1968*, edited by Rosemary Radford Ruether and Rosemary Skinner Keller. New York: Harper & Row, 1986.

Zikmund, Barbara Brown. "Women's Organizations: Centers of Denominational Loyalty and Expressions of Christian Unity." In *Beyond Establishment: Protestant Identity in a Post-Protestant Age*, edited by Jackson W. Carroll and Wade Clark Roof. Louisville: Westminster/John Knox Press, 1993.

Zikmund, Barbara Brown, Adair T. Lummis, and Patricia Mei Yin Chang. *Clergy Women: An Uphill Calling*. Louisville: Westminster John Knox Press, 1998.

Secondary Sources: Articles

Arand, Charles P. "The Confessionalism of Missouri in the Early Twentieth Century." *Concordia Historical Institute Quarterly* 70 (1997): 194-203.

Badham, Linda. "The Irrationality of the Case Against Ordaining Women." *The Modern Churchman*, new series 27 (1984): 13-22.

Barciauskas, Rosemary Curran, and Debra B. Hull. "Other Women's Daughters: Integrative Feminism, Public Spirituality." *Cross Currents* 38 (1988): 32-52.

Braaten, Carl E. "God in Public Life: Rehabilitating the 'Orders of Creation.'" *First Things* 8 (1990): 32-38.

Brauer, Ruth. "Tracing Women's Service in the Missouri Synod." *Concordia Historical Institute Quarterly* 36 (1963): 5-13.

Brighton, Louis A. "The Ordination of Women: A Twentieth-Century Gnostic Heresy?" *Concordia Journal* 8 (1982): 12-18.

Brueggemann, Eugene V. "A Question of Faithfulness." *Lutheran Forum* 26 (May 1992): 14-19.

Busch, Edward E. "Another Turning Point." *Currents in Theology and Mission* 2 (1975): 75-81.

Chaves, Mark. "Ordaining Women: The Diffusion of an Organizational Innovation." *American Journal of Sociology* 101 (January 1996): 840-73.

Christopherson, K. E. "Fundamentalism: What Led Up to It, How It Got among Us, and What We in Academe Do about It." *Dialog* 19 (1980): 209-14.

Coiner, Harry G. "A Study of the 'Ordination of Women' Issue." *Currents in Theology and Mission* 2 (1975): 221-27.

Coleman, Richard J. "Biblical Inerrancy: Are We Going Anywhere?" *Theology Today* 31 (1975): 295-303.

Constable, John. "Of Congregational and Synodical Authority." *Concordia Theological Monthly* 43 (April 1972): 212-31.

BIBLIOGRAPHY

"The Conundrum of Authority." Editorial, *Lutheran Forum* 30 (1996): 4.

Cwirla, William M. "Grabau and the Saxon Pastors: The Doctrine of the Holy Ministry, 1840-1845." *Concordia Historical Institute Quarterly* 68 (1995): 84-99.

Dietz, Paul T. "The Transition from German to English in the Missouri Synod from 1910 to 1947." *Concordia Historical Institute Quarterly* 22 (1949): 97-127.

"For the Ordination of Women: A Study Document Prepared by the Faculty of Christ Seminary-Seminex." *Currents in Theology and Mission* 6 (1979): 132-43.

Franzmann, Martin H. "On Change in Theology." *Concordia Theological Monthly* 38 (1967): 5-9.

Green, Lowell C. "Grabau and Walther: Theocentric versus Anthropocentric Understanding of Church and Ministry." *Logia* 5 (1996): 25-40.

Grindal, Gracia. "Luther's Theology as a Resource for Feminists." *Dialog* 24 (1985): 32-36.

Gritsch, Eric W. "Convergence and Conflict in Feminist and Lutheran Theologies." *Dialog* 24 (1985): 11-18.

Gude, George J. "A Reflective Look at the Structure of The Lutheran Church–Missouri Synod." *Concordia Historical Institute Quarterly* 69 (1996): 21-40.

Gude, George J. "Women Teachers in the Missouri Synod." *Concordia Historical Institute Quarterly* 44 (1971): 163-70.

Hannah, John. "The Ordination of Women and Lutheran Destiny." *Lutheran Forum* 31 (1997): 39-42.

Harris, Paul R. "Angels Unaware." *Logia* 3 (January 1994): 35-42.

Hein, Steven. "The Crisis of Biblical Authority: A Historical Analysis." *Concordia Theological Quarterly* 41 (1977): 61-77.

Heinecken, Martin J. "Luther and the 'Orders of Creation' in Relation to a Doctrine of Work and Vocation." *Lutheran Quarterly* 4 (November 1952): 393-414.

Heintze, R. W. "Editorial." *Concordia Historical Institute Quarterly* 4 (1932): 1-5.

Heintze, R. W. "Religious Organization in Missouri Before 1839." *Concordia Historical Institute Quarterly* 1 (1929): 91-94.

Hemmeter, H. B. "Early English Mission Efforts in the Missouri Synod." *Concordia Historical Institute Quarterly* 11 (1938): 67-74.

Hinlicky, Paul R. "Evangelical Authority." *Lutheran Forum* 27 (1993): 58-62.

Huggins, Marvin A. "Martin Stephan: First Lutheran Bishop in America." *Concordia Historical Institute Quarterly* 44 (1971): 141-42.

Hummel, Horace D. "Lutheranism and the Inerrancy of Scripture." *Concordia Journal* 14 (April 1988): 102-14.

Jelen, Ted G. "Weaker Vessels and Helpmeets: Gender Role Stereotypes and Attitudes toward Female Ordination." *Social Science Quarterly* 70 (1989): 579-85.

Jenson, Robert. "Missouri and the Existential Fear of Change." *Dialog* 14 (1975): 247-50.

Ji, Won Yong. "Where Are the Lutherans Going?" *Concordia Journal* 24 (1998): 3-4.

Joerz, Jerald C. "Walther and the Ministry." *Concordia Historical Institute Quarterly* 63 (1990): 123-31.

Bibliography

Johnson, Daniel S. "The Ministry and the Schoolmaster: The Relation and Distinction between the Offices of Pastor and Teacher in the Missouri Synod." *Logia* 6 (1997): 13-22.

Johnson, Neil M. "The Patriotism and Anti-Prussianism of the Lutheran Church–Missouri Synod 1914-1918." *Concordia Historical Institute Quarterly* 39 (1966): 99-118.

Jordahl, Leigh D. "The Theology of Franz Pieper: A Resource for Fundamentalistic Thought Modes Among American Lutherans." *Lutheran Quarterly* 23 (1971): 118-37.

Jordan, Horst W. "Some Concerns About Current Confessional Statements." *Concordia Theological Monthly* 45 (1974): 27-34.

Jungkuntz, Theodore. "Authority — A Charismatic Perspective." *Currents in Theology and Mission* 3 (1976): 171-77.

Jungkuntz, Theodore, and Walter E. Keller. "The Question of the Ordination of Women." *The Cresset* 42 (1978), reprint, 1-8.

Keller, Rosemary Skinner, Ann Braude, Maureen Ursenbach Beecher, and Elizabeth Fox-Genovese. "Forum: Female Experience in American Religion." *Religion and American Culture* 5 (Winter 1995): 1-21.

Klug, Eugene. "Luther on the Ministry." *Concordia Theological Quarterly* 47 (1983): 293-303.

Koenig, Richard E. "What's Behind the Showdown in the LCMS? Church and Tradition in Collision." *Lutheran Forum* 6 (1972): 17-20.

Koenig, Richard E. "What's Behind the Showdown in the LCMS? Conservative Reaction: 1965-69." *Lutheran Forum* 7 (1973): 18-21.

Koenig, Richard E. "What's Behind the Showdown in the LCMS? Missouri Turns Moderate, 1938-65." *Lutheran Forum* 7 (1973): 19-29.

Koenig, Robert J., and Greg Koenig. "The Saxon Immigration of 1839: Why They Came; Why They Succeeded." *Concordia Historical Institute Quarterly* 69 (1996): 41-47.

Koerner, Gustav. "The Old Lutherans and Bishop Stephan." *Concordia Historical Institute Quarterly* 33 (1960): 81-84.

Kramer, William A. "The Saxons in Missouri." *Concordia Historical Institute Quarterly* 60 (1987): 2-18.

Kretzmann, Karl. "That Log Cabin in Perry County." *Concordia Historical Institute Quarterly* 19 (1947): 152-60.

Kretzmann, P. E. "The Beginnings of Permanent English Language Work in Missouri." *Concordia Historical Institute Quarterly* 3 (1931): 100-105.

Lagerquist, L. DeAne. "Who I Am and What I Do." *The Cresset* 56 (March 1993): 10-13.

Lawless, Elaine J. "Rescripting Their Lives and Narratives: Spiritual Life Stories of Pentecostal Women Preachers." *Journal of Feminist Studies in Religion* 7 (1991): 53-71.

BIBLIOGRAPHY

Liebman, Robert C., John R. Sutton, and Robert Wuthnow. "Exploring the Social Sources of Denominationalism: Schisms in American Protestant Denominations, 1890-1980." *American Sociological Review* 53 (1988): 343-52.

Lindberg, Carter. "Pietism and the Church Growth Movement in a Confessional Lutheran Perspective." *Concordia Theological Quarterly* 52 (1988): 129-47.

Lotz, David W. "The Sense of Church History in Representative Missouri Synod Theology." *Concordia Theological Monthly* 42 (1971): 597-619.

Lueker, Erwin L. "Doctrinal Emphases in the Missouri Synod." *Concordia Theological Monthly* 43 (1972): 198-211.

Lueker, Erwin L. "Function of Symbols and of Doctrinal Statements." *Concordia Theological Monthly* 32 (1961): 274-85.

Lynch, John E. "The Ordination of Women: Protestant Experience in Ecumenical Perspective." *Journal of Ecumenical Studies* 12 (1975): 173-97.

Maier, Paul L. "Bohlmann and the 44: A Response." *Lutheran Forum* 30 (1996): 20-21.

Manley, Robert N. "Language, Loyalty and Liberty: The Nebraska State Council of Defense and the Lutheran Churches, 1917-1918." *Concordia Historical Institute Quarterly* 37 (1964): 1-15.

Marsden, George. "Forum." *Religion and American Culture* 3 (1993): 9-15.

Maurer, Heinrich H. "Studies in the Sociology of Religion: IV. The Problem of Group Consensus; Founding the Missouri Synod." *American Journal of Sociology* 30 (1924-25): 665-82.

Maxwell, Lee A. "Women in Church and Ministry." *Journal of English District Pastors* 5 (1993): 3-16.

Meilaender, Gilbert. "How Churches Crack Up: The Case of the Lutheran Church–Missouri Synod." *First Things* 14 (1991): 38-42.

Moellering, Ralph. "Lutherans on Social Problems, 1917-1940." *Concordia Historical Institute Quarterly* 42 (1969): 27-40.

Mueller, Charles S., Sr. "History, Mystery and Gift." Lutheran Church Extension Fund and the LCMS Foundation, 1997.

Mueller-Roebke, Jenny. "Why These Questions Deserve a Response." *Issues of Christian Education* 26 (1992): 8-13.

Mundinger, Gerhard H. "Wilhelm Löhe." *Concordia Historical Institute Quarterly* 70 (1997): 2-19.

Murphy, George L. "An Appeal to Missouri for the Ordination of Women." *Lutheran Forum* 24 (1990): 6-8.

Nispel, Mark. "Office and Offices: Some Basic Lutheran Philology." *Logia* 6 (1997): 5-11.

Nohl, Frederick. "The Lutheran Church–Missouri Synod Reacts to United States Anti-Germanism During World War I." *Concordia Historical Institute Quarterly* 35 (1962): 49-66.

Noland, Martin R. "Comprehending Missouri's Dissent: Holding Fast to Grace." *Lutheran Forum* 23 (1989): 18-21.

Noll, Mark. "The Lutheran Difference." *First Things* 20 (1992): 31-40.

Owen, Ralph Dornfield. "The Old Lutherans Come." *Concordia Historical Institute Quarterly* 20 (1947): 3-56.

Parvey, Connie. "Ordain Her, Ordain Her Not." *Dialog* 8 (1969): 203-8.

Peters, Larry A. "A Church Held Captive by a Loss of Authority." *Lutheran Forum* 32 (1998): 23-27.

Pfabe, Jerrald K. "Conflict in Missouri's Past — The Analysis of Theodore Graebner." *Issues in Christian Education* 8 (1974): 12-17.

Pickle, Linda Schelbitzki. "Women of the Saxon Immigration and Their Church." *Concordia Historical Institute Quarterly* 57 (1984): 146-61.

Piehl, Charles K. "Ethnicity, the Missouri Synod, and the Mission of the Church." *Currents in Theology and Mission* 2 (1975): 239-44.

Pittelko, Roger D. "The Office of the Holy Ministry in the Life of the Church: A View from the Parish." *Logia* 2 (January 1993): 33-40.

Preus, J. A. O., III. "The Holy Ministry and the Holy Priesthood: The Gospel Office and the Office from the Gospel." *Concordia Journal* 24 (1998): 36-42.

Preus, Robert D. "Confessional Lutheranism in Today's World." *Concordia Theological Quarterly* 54 (1990): 99-116.

Robbert, Louise Buenger. "Lutheran Families in St. Louis and Perry County, Missouri, 1839-1870." *Missouri Historical Review* 82 (1988): 424-38.

Robinson, Jack T. "The Spirit of Triumphalism in The Lutheran Church–Missouri Synod." *Currents in Theology and Mission* 1 (1974): 13-20.

Roeber, A. G. "Almost Persuaded? The Anguish of Lutheran Identity and America's Culture Wars." *Lutheran Forum* 30 (1996): 22-27.

Ruether, Rosemary Radford. "Why I Stay in the Church: Grace in the Midst of Failings." *Sojourners* 23 (July 1994): 14-17.

Rupprecht, Roland O. "Gotthold Heinrich Loeber." *Concordia Historical Institute Quarterly* 11 (1938): 48-54.

Scaer, David P. "Lutheran Viewpoints on the Challenge of Fundamentalism: Eschatology." *Concordia Journal* 10 (1984): 4-11.

Scaer, David P. "Missouri at the End of the Century: A Time for Reevaluation." *Logia* 7 (1998): 39-52.

Scaer, David P. "The Validity of the Churchly Acts of Ordained Women." *Concordia Theological Quarterly* 53 (1989): 3-20.

Schaaf, James L. "Wilhelm Loehe and the Missouri Synod." *Concordia Historical Institute Quarterly* 45 (1972): 53-67.

Schaibley, Robert W. "Gender Considerations on the Pastoral Office in Light of I Corinthians 14:33-36 and I Timothy 2:8-14." *Logia* 3 (April 1994): 45-51.

Schroeder, Marie. "Issues: Trouble Enough? Women's Ordination." *Missouri in Perspective* 3 (August 2, 1976): 5.

Sommer, Martin S. "The English Language in the Missouri Synod." *Concordia Historical Institute Quarterly* 10 (1937): 65-68.

Stellhorn, A. C. "The Saxon Centennial and the Schools, III. Settlement in Missouri." *Lutheran School Journal* 74 (April 1939): 342-48.

BIBLIOGRAPHY

Stellhorn, A. C. "The Saxon Centennial and the Schools, IV. Rescue from Doctrinal Uncertainty." *Lutheran School Journal* 74 (May 1939): 390-95.

Streufert, Waldemar B. "Clementine Buenger Neumueller, Saxon Immigrant." *Concordia Historical Institute Quarterly* 26 (1953): 132-35.

Suelflow, August R. "Nietzsche and Schaff on American Lutheranism." *Concordia Historical Institute Quarterly* 23 (1951): 145-58.

Suelflow, August R. "Walther and Church Polity." *Concordia Theological Monthly* 32 (1961): 632-41.

Teigen, Erling. "The Universal Priesthood in the Lutheran Confessions." *Logia* 1 (October 1992): 9-15.

Todd, Mary. "Musings on the Ministry/s of Women." *Lutheran Education* 134 (1998): 4-8.

Todd, Mary. "Thinking about History: The Missouri Compromise." *Lutheran Forum* 31 (1997): 43-46.

Todd, Mary. "Unopened Gifts: Women and the Call to Public Ministry in The Lutheran Church–Missouri Synod." *The Cresset* 56 (1993): 4-9.

Toepper, Robert M. "Rationale for the Preservation of the German Language in the Missouri Synod of the Nineteenth Century." *Concordia Historical Institute Quarterly* 41 (1968): 156-67.

Turner, Philip. "Authority in the Church: Excavations Among the Ruins." *First Things* 8 (1990): 25-31.

Wehmeier, Waldemar W. "Calling a Pastor: How It Evolved in the Missouri Synod." *Currents in Theology and Mission* 4 (1977): 269-75.

Wehmeier, Waldemar W. "Missouri and Public Doctrine." *Currents in Theology and Mission* 2 (1975): 23-31.

Weiser, Frederick S. "The Lutheran Deaconess Movement." *Lutheran Forum* 28 (1994): 20-24.

Wohlrabe, John C., Jr. "The Americanization of Walther's Doctrine of the Church." *Concordia Theological Quarterly* 52 (1988): 1-27.

Wuerffel, Stella. "Women of the Saxon Immigration." *Concordia Historical Institute Quarterly* 35 (1962): 14-17, 81-95.

Zersen, David John. "C. F. W. Walther and the Heritage of Pietist Conventicles." *Concordia Historical Institute Quarterly* 62 (1989): 10-25.

Unpublished Sources

Bachmann, Ernest Theodore. "The Rise of Missouri Lutheranism." Ph.D. diss., University of Chicago, 1946.

Bouman, Walter R. "The Unity of the Church in 19th c. Confessional Lutheranism." Ph.D. diss., Heidelberg University, 1962.

Chaves, Mark. "The Symbolic Significance of Women's Ordination." Unpublished manuscript, July 1995.

Bibliography

Graebner, Alan N. "The Acculturation of an Immigrant Lutheran Church: The Lutheran Church–Missouri Synod, 1917-1929." Ph.D. diss., Columbia University, 1965.

Greising, Jack Howard. "The Status of Confessional Conservatism: Background and Issues in the Lutheran Church-Missouri Synod." Ph.D. diss., St. Louis University, 1972.

Hayes, Laurie Ann Schultz. "The Rhetoric of Controversy in the Lutheran Church–Missouri Synod with Particular Emphasis on the Years 1969-1976." Ph.D. diss., University of Wisconsin–Madison, 1980.

Knutson, Kent S. "The Community of Faith and the Word: An Inquiry into the Concept of the Church in Contemporary Lutheranism." Ph.D. diss., Columbia University, 1961.

Koepchen, William. "Pastor Martin Stephan and the Saxon Emigration of 1838." Unpublished manuscript, 1935.

Labore, Richard Donald. "Traditions and Transitions: A Study of the Leadership of the Lutheran Church–Missouri Synod During a Decade of Theological Change, 1960-1969." Ph.D. diss., St. Louis University, 1980.

Lipscomb, Steven. *Battle for the Minds*, videotape, 1997.

Mauelshagen, Carl. "American Lutheranism Surrenders to Forces of Conservatism." Ph.D. diss., University of Minnesota, 1936.

Neeb, Larry W. "Historical and Theological Dimension of a Confessing Movement within the Lutheran Church–Missouri Synod." D.Min. thesis, Eden Theological Seminary, 1975.

Rudisill, Alvin Stewart. "The Doctrine of the Church in American Lutheranism with a View to Future Ecumenicity." Ph.D. diss., Drew University, 1967.

Stevens, Leland Robert. "The Americanization of the Missouri Synod as Reflected within the *Lutheran Witness*." Ph.D. diss., St. Louis University, 1986.

Warner, R. Stephen. "Women's Place, Women's Space." In "Communities of Faith." Unpublished manuscript, July 1989.

Weinrich, William. "'It Is not Given to Women to Teach': A *Lex* in Search of a *Ratio*." Unpublished manuscript, 1991.

White, Laurence L. "The Role of Women in The Lutheran Church–Missouri Synod: A Study in Historical Development and Theological Change." Unpublished manuscript, 1991.

White, Laurence L. "The Transformation of Missouri." Keynote address, Lutheran Concerns Association, 1996.

Wohlrabe, John C., Jr. "An Historical Analysis of the Doctrine of the Ministry in the Lutheran Church–Missouri Synod until 1962." Th.D. diss., Concordia Seminary, St. Louis, 1987.

Wollenburg, George F. "The Office of the Holy Ministry and the Ordination of Women." Unpublished manuscript, 1990.

Zetto, J. Jeffrey. "Aspects of Theology in the Liturgical Movement in the Lutheran Church–Missouri Synod, 1930-1960." Th.D. diss., Christ Seminary–Seminex, 1982.

Index

Adiaphora, 12, 74, 189, 192, 195, 219, 252-53, 254, 273

Adiaphoristic Controversy, 12, 194, 252

AELC. *See* Association of Evangelical Lutheran Churches

ALC. *See* American Lutheran Church

Altenburg Debates, 59-60, 62-63, 65, 67, 75, 82, 94, 142

American Lutheran Church (ALC), 130, 132, 133, 141, 176, 191, 204, 206, 207, 209-10, 217, 218-21, 277

Antirationalists, 21-22

Association of Evangelical Lutheran Churches (AELC), 228-29, 248

Augsburg Confession, 7-8, 9, 12, 73, 87-88, 150, 244

Baptists, 44, 102n.17, 270-71

Barry, Alvin, 243, 244, 245, 247

Bartling, Victor, 159, 190

Bartling, Walter, 190

Behnken, John W., 126, 134-38, 142, 153-54, 159, 163, 167-68, 171-72, 175, 183

Bente, Friedrich, 100

Bertram, Robert, 212-15, 219

Bohlmann, Ralph, 207, 218, 230, 236-37, 239, 240, 242-46, 250

Book of Concord, 6, 7, 12, 18, 128

Bouman, Herbert J. A., 103

Brief Statement, 2-3, 127-31, 132, 140, 179, 181-82, 188, 223

Brohm, Theodor Julius, 26

Brunner, Peter, 217-18, 254-55

Buenger, Johann Friedrich, 26, 36-37, 48, 66

Buerger, Ernst Moritz, 26, 46-47, 52, 56-57, 58, 59

Buffalo Synod, 18, 75, 84, 128, 130, 132

Caemmerer, Richard, 133

Call, divine, 78, 79, 82, 113, 268, 269, 290

"Call to Openness and Trust," 226

Calvin, John, 156n.41, 198-99

Calvinists, 19, 90-91

CCM. *See* Commission on Constitutional Matters

Chicago Study Club, 132

Christian News, 222-23, 223n.66, 249, 250, 274

College of Presidents, 124, 134, 174, 178, 184, 204

Commission on Constitutional Matters (CCM), 183, 186, 227

Commission on Theology and Church Relations (CTCR), 184-97, 199, 212, 219, 227, 230, 232-36, 237, 239-40, 243, 244-47, 248, 255, 256, 264, 265, 266, 275

Committee on Woman Suffrage (1953), 152-53, 159, (1956), 163-78, 184, 198

Concordia College (Milwaukee), 163

Concordia College (Seward), 111, 112

Concordia Publishing House, 13-14, 149, 154, 159, 164, 167, 217, 217n.49

Concordia Seminary (St. Louis), 90, 95, 121, 136, 145, 149, 154, 159, 178, 180, 181, 188, 204, 206, 212, 213, 215, 221-27, 236

Concordia Seminary (Springfield), 188, 205, 212

Concordia Senior College (Fort Wayne), 72, 163, 173, 216n.46

Concordia Teachers College (River Forest), 112, 237

Concordia Theological Seminary (Fort Wayne), 242n.153

Confessional Lutheran, 132

Confessionalism, 3, 8, 20-21, 70, 79, 80, 85, 88, 127

Conventicles, 25, 27, 32

Credit Fund, 34-35, 44, 46, 50, 51-53, 57, 59, 283

CTCR. *See* Commission on Theology and Church Relations

Dau, W. H. T., 100, 149-51, 199

Deaconesses, 116-20, 142, 232, 232n.111, 237

Definite Platform, 87-88

Der Anzeiger des Westens, 43, 45, 48

Der Lutheraner, 68-71, 75, 76, 95, 144, 149, 254

Division of Theological Studies (DTS), 195, 207, 210, 212-13, 216-17, 252, 253, 255

Doctrinal review, 14, 14n.45, 167-68

Dogmaticians, 11, 19, 95, 128, 140, 272, 279

Dresden, 22-23, 27-32

DTS. *See* Division of Theological Studies

Dubuque consultation, 212-16, 253

Duden, Gottfried, 31

Ecumenism, 1, 98

Eerdmans, Wm. B., 164, 167

ELCA. *See* Evangelical Lutheran Church in America

ELiM. *See* Evangelical Lutherans in Mission

Emigration Code, 35, 281

English District/Synod, 93, 166, 166n.72, 215

Episcopal polity, 33, 39-42, 46, 55, 60-63, 261

Episcopalians, 4, 44

Equal Rights Amendment, 234-35

Evangelical Lutheran Church in America (ELCA), 1-2

Evangelical Lutherans in Mission (ELiM), 226-28

Evangelical Lutheran Synod, 179n.121, 205, 206

Faithful to Our Calling, Faithful to Our Lord, 226

Fellowship, 127-35, 140-41, 147, 203-6, 211, 218-22, 223, 236, 253, 279, 292

Feminism, 107, 146, 209, 230, 247, 249, 250, 265

Finnish Lutherans, 149, 163

Fischer, H. F., 33-34, 41-42, 53

Flacius, Matthias, 12, 194-95, 252

Formula of Concord, 8, 10, 12
"Forty-Four," The, 131-38, 182, 200, 222
Free conferences, 87-88, 89, 92
Friedrich, E. J., 131
Fritschel, Gottfried, 90
Fuerbringer, Alfred, 181
Fuerbringer, Ottomar, 26
Fundamentalism, 4, 5, 12, 99, 100-103, 132, 139, 146, 181, 190, 225, 264, 270-72, 280
Fundamentalist/modernist controversy, 98, 99-104, 130, 139-40, 146, 272

Garton, Jean, 230, 232, 237-38, 242
General Council, 88
General Synod, 24, 70, 87-88, 117
Grabau, J. A. A., 73-75, 79-82, 84, 89
Graebner, Theodore, 100, 106, 136-37, 146-47, 229, 253, 279
Guenther, Louise, 40, 50

Haas, Harold, 231
Harms, Oliver, 183, 187, 190, 203-5, 212, 253
Headship, 5, 161, 165, 213, 235, 264
Herzberger, Friedrich, 116-19
Hirtenbrief, 73
Hoffmann, Oswald, 170
Homrighausen, Edgar, 167-68, 172, 174, 176

Intersynodical (Chicago) Theses, 128-29, 132, 141
Iowa Synod, 84, 90, 128, 130, 132
Itinerants, 82-83

Jaeckel, Gustav, 33-34, 47, 53
Jungkuntz, Richard, 188-92, 194-96

Keyl, Ernst Gerhard Wilhelm, 26, 47-48, 52
Knutson, Kent, 220-21, 277-78

Kramer, Fred, 159, 212
Krauth, Charles Porterfield, 95
Kretzmann, A. T., 135
Kretzmann, Martin L., 188
Kretzmann, O. P., 133, 138
Kretzmann, P. E., 124
Kurtz, Benjamin, 24, 29, 87, 95

Language, 79, 89, 92-94, 97, 104-7, 139, 260, 279
Lay associations, 120-27
LCA. *See* Lutheran Church in America
LCUSA. *See* Lutheran Council in the USA
Leege, David, 191-94, 193n.171, 219
Leipzig, 22, 26, 32, 91
Lindemann, J. C. W., 109
LLL. *See* Lutheran Laymen's League
Loeber, G. H., 47-48, 52, 58, 62, 74
Loehe, Wilhelm, 72, 75-76, 79-81, 83-86, 89, 117
Loy, Matthias, 89, 91
Luther, Martin, 8-12, 18, 19, 21, 31, 54, 59, 66, 68, 69, 70, 95, 140, 148, 170, 198-99, 210, 277, 279
Lutheran Church in America (LCA), 206-7, 216, 217, 221
Lutheran Church–Missouri Synod, The: constitution, 6, 183, 200, 226; conventions (1850), 80, (1851), 84, (1897), 110, (1917), 105, (1920), 111, (1923), 111, (1926), 112, (1929), 112, 128, (1932), 129, (1938), 122, 125, 130, 132, 152, (1941), 113, 125, (1944), 126, 132, (1947), 130, (1953), 114, 152, 159, (1956), 130, 153, 159, 187, (1959), 171, 182, 187, (1962), 178, 183-84, (1965), 187-88, 190, 196, (1967), 190, (1969), 190, 196, 203-6, 212, 221, 223, (1971), 220, 224, (1973), 226, 230, 235, (1975), 228, 232, (1977), 233, (1981), 236, (1989), 243, (1992), 243, (1995), 259,

(1998), 260, 274; name changes, 77, 105, 141, 259-60

Lutheran confessions, 9, 11, 19, 22, 55, 63, 67, 75, 81, 83, 95, 97, 130, 131, 155, 165, 210, 252, 270, 271, 275, 279

Lutheran Council in the USA (LCUSA), 188, 195, 203, 206-18, 219, 220, 221, 222, 231, 252, 266

Lutheran Deaconess Association, 117-18, 123

Lutheran Laymen's League (LLL), 121-23

Lutheran Witness, 93-94, 100, 102, 104, 118, 136, 144-46, 151, 153, 164, 167, 169, 171, 177, 186, 250, 253

Lutheran Women's Missionary League (LWML), 126-27, 164, 231, 233-34, 241-42, 251

Lutheran Woman's Quarterly, 126

Lutheran World Federation, 208

Lutherans for Openness and Trust, 223

LWML. *See* Lutheran Women's Missionary League

Marbach, Franz Adolph, 33, 34, 59

Mayer, Herbert, 212

Meuser, Fred, 217

Melanchthon, Philipp, 12, 194-95

Merkens, Albert, 154, 159, 254

Methodists, 4, 44

Meyer, Marie, 237, 241, 250

Michigan Synod, 77

Ministry, doctrine of, 3, 5, 10, 80, 113, 116, 130, 184, 268, 279

Minnesota Synod, 89

Mission Affirmations, 188

Missouri in Perspective, 227

Moderate Lutherans, 17, 51

Modernism, 99-100, 103

Moellering, Armin, 190

Montz, Florence, 231, 232, 242

Mormons, 25n.27, 43, 43n.78

Morris, Helen, 232, 233

Mueller, Bernhard G., 163-64, 166-67, 170, 172, 175

Mueller, J. T., 152

Mueller, Louise, 239-41

National Lutheran Council, 127

Nemoyer, Nancy, 237, 239-41

Neology, 22, 29

New Lutherans, 17-18, 51

Nineteenth Amendment, 143, 146

Norwegian Synod, 89, 91

Office of Woman in the Church, 154

Ohio Synod, 76-77, 89, 91, 92, 128, 130, 132

Old Lutherans, 17-18, 41, 50, 69, 73, 75, 84

Open questions, 83-84, 88, 128, 253

Order of creation, 5, 155, 156n.41, 157-61, 165, 167, 177, 187, 189, 193, 196, 198-99, 213, 215, 216, 218, 235, 239, 243, 246, 254-56, 264, 270, 279

Order of redemption, 160, 165, 167, 177, 189

Ordination, 74, 82, 115n.71, 116n.76, 184, 290

Ordination of women, 2, 4, 5, 7, 15, 115n.71, 155, 158-59, 162, 187, 189, 192, 193, 195, 198, 208-22, 229, 230-31, 234, 237-38, 240, 243, 247-57, 263, 265-70

Otte, Jan, 229

Otten, Herman, 222-23

Parochial schools, 66, 83, 106, 107, 110, 283

Pastoral office, 2, 8-9, 18, 28, 54-55, 73-74, 78-79, 108-9, 155, 196, 236, 238, 245, 246, 260-63, 289

PCW. *See* President's Commission on Women

Perry County, 45, 47-51, 56-57, 61n.127, 62, 65, 67, 68, 76, 78, 82, 86, 107, 261

Pieper, Francis (Franz), 90, 94, 98-99, 101, 127-29, 140, 143, 148-49, 152, 156n.41, 204, 225, 272, 278

Piepkorn, Arthur Carl, 225, 252, 275, 279

Pietism, 19-20, 22, 25, 28, 54, 63, 272

Polity, 3, 6, 78, 272-74

Predestination Controversy, 89-92, 127-28

Premillennialism ("chiliasm"), 102

Presbyterians, 4, 44, 102n.17, 165

President's Commission on Women (PCW), 236-47, 248, 249, 250, 264

Preus, J. A. O., 179n.121, 205-6, 212, 216-20, 222, 223, 225-26, 228, 233-34, 236, 253

Preus, Robert, 179n.121, 242n.153

Priesthood of all believers, 8-10, 20, 54-55, 62, 67-68, 74, 82, 133, 261, 263, 289

Prohl, Russell, 163-78, 181, 190, 198, 235; *Woman in the Church,* 164, 168, 177

Protest, 53-58, 61-63, 65, 67

Prussian Union, 21, 73, 203n.2

Rationalism, 19-21, 26, 100

Reformation, 8-9, 11, 83, 155

Repristination, 15, 95, 140, 277-78

Resolution Nine, 182-83, 183n.133, 184

Reumann, John, 215

Roman Catholics, 4-5, 6, 8-9, 10, 12, 19, 43-44, 90, 104, 110, 130, 194, 207, 232n.111, 252, 255n.185

St. John's Church (Dresden), 22-23, 29-30, 37

Saxon Emigration, 18, 22, 29, 31-42, 54, 56-58, 61

Saxony, 3, 17, 21, 26, 28-29, 32, 33, 36, 61, 96, 100

Scharlemann, Martin, 178-83, 185, 188-89, 193-94, 212-15

Schiotz, Frederik, 210, 216, 220

Schmidt, Alvin, 231, 233

Schmidt, Friedrich, 90-91

Schmucker, Samuel, 87, 95

Schroeder, Edward, 159, 198-99, 212-14

Scripture: authority of, 2, 10, 11, 19, 22, 99, 100, 130, 138, 140, 200, 206, 208, 215, 217, 218-19, 227, 231, 269, 270-72, 275; historical-critical method and, 100, 204; verbal inerrancy of, 2, 3, 5, 7, 11, 99-100, 140, 146, 179-82, 204, 222, 276, 279

Seminex, 227-29

Sieck, Louis, 145-46

Sihler, Wilhelm, 72, 75-76, 89, 94

Sola scriptura, 10, 135, 183, 200, 253, 277, 279

Spannaus, Olive, 242, 255

Sprecher, Samuel, 87

A Statement, 131-38, 141-42, 147, 182-83, 222, 291-94

"A Statement of Scriptural and Confessional Principles," 224, 226

Stephan, Martin, 22-63, 65, 73, 81, 222, 261-62, 272, 278, 279; deposition, 48-49, 53-54, 56, 61-62, 137; investiture, 38-42, 285-86

Stephanism, 26-32, 36-38, 43-44, 60

Stoeckhardt, George, 110, 114

Stuenkel, Walter, 163, 166-78

Synodical Conference, 88-92, 95, 116, 118-19, 120, 128, 204, 206

Task Force on Women, 230-34, 236, 237, 242, 248-49, 255

Teachers: female, 109-16, 178, 232n.111; male, 112-15, 119; parochial school, 5, 108-16, 119-20, 142, 200, 232, 262

Tennessee Synod, 92
Tiemeyer, Raymond, 216
Tietjen, John, 215, 226, 227
Trinity (St. Louis): congregation, 66, 68, 75-77, 95; constitution, 66-67, 93, 120, 150

ULCA. *See* United Lutheran Church in America
Unionism, 21-22, 79, 87, 102, 103, 138, 203, 207, 293
United Lutheran Church in America (ULCA), 176

Valparaiso University, 118, 133, 212
Vatican II, 207
Vehse, Carl Eduard, 34, 36, 39-40, 46-50, 52-59, 67, 86, 261
Voices/Vision, 250
von Einsiedel, Count Detlev, 28-29

Walther, C. F. W., 26-27, 37, 47, 52, 58, 59-61, 61n.127, 62-63, 65-71, 75-77, 79-84, 86, 89-96, 98, 107, 109, 137, 140, 148, 198, 200, 225, 228, 254, 255, 261, 262, 272, 278; doctrine of ministry, 67, 83, 262;

Theses on Ministry, 80-81, 235-36, 287-90
Walther League, 120-23
Walther, O. H., 26, 38, 41, 58, 59, 65
Wambsganss, Philip, 118, 123
Weis, Adelia, 170
Wente, Walter, 163, 166, 167, 173-75, 198
Wiederaenders, Roland, 166-67, 204-5
Wisconsin Synod, 1n.1, 89, 128, 206
"Woman question," 6, 142, 143, 190, 201, 208, 230, 241, 243, 246, 266
Woman suffrage: church, 107, 111, 121, 142, 148-78, 185-201, 206, 222, 249, 263; civil, 98, 143-47
Women in the Church: Scriptural Principles and Ecclesial Practice, 240, 265
Women's service in the church, 3, 4, 6, 15, 142, 200
World Council of Churches, 155
World War I, 98, 104-6, 144
World War II, 15, 114, 154, 204
Wyneken, Friedrich Conrad Dietrich, 71-72, 75, 84, 86, 94

Zerbst, Fritz, 154-55, 157-59, 165, 169, 191, 198-99, 217-18, 235, 254-55